THE READER'S
COMPANION TO
SOUTH
AFRICA

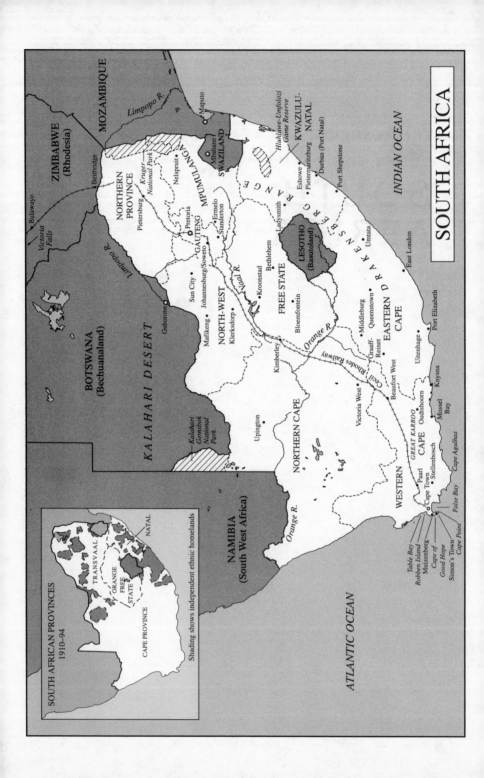

SOUTH AFRICA

SOUTH AFRICAN PROVINCES 1910–94

Shading shows independent ethnic homelands

TRANSVAAL

ORANGE FREE STATE

NATAL

CAPE PROVINCE

ZIMBABWE (Rhodesia)

MOZAMBIQUE

BOTSWANA (Bechuanaland)

NAMIBIA (South West Africa)

KALAHARI DESERT

Kalahari Gemsbok National Park

NORTHERN PROVINCE

GAUTENG

MPUMALANGA

SWAZILAND

KWAZULU-NATAL

NORTH-WEST

FREE STATE

LESOTHO (Basutoland)

DRAKENSBERG RANGE

NORTHERN CAPE

EASTERN CAPE

WESTERN CAPE

GREAT KARROO

INDIAN OCEAN

ATLANTIC OCEAN

Limpopo R.

Maputo

Mbabane

Hluhluwe-Umfolozi Game Reserve

Beitbridge

Bulawayo

Victoria Falls

Limpopo R.

Gaborone

Sun City

Mafikeng

Klerksdorp

Kimberley

Upington

Orange R.

Orange R.

Vaal R.

Pietersburg

Nelspruit

Pretoria

Johannesburg/Soweto

Kroonstad

Bethlehem

Bloemfontein

Ermelo

Standerton

Ladysmith

Eshowe

Pietermaritzburg

Durban (Port Natal)

Port Shepstone

Umtata

East London

Middleburg

Queenstown

Graaff-Reinet

Beaufort West

Port Elizabeth

Uitenhage

Knysna

Mossel Bay

Oudtshoorn

Victoria West

Cecil Rhodes Railway

Kruger National Park

Paarl

Stellenbosch

Cape Town

False Bay

Cape Agulhas

Table Bay
Robben Island
Muizenberg
Cape of Good Hope
Simon's Town
Cape Point

THE READER'S
COMPANION TO
SOUTH
AFRICA

EDITED BY **ALAN RYAN**

A Harvest Original

Harcourt Brace & Company

SAN DIEGO   NEW YORK   LONDON

Library of Congress Cataloging-in-Publication Data
The reader's companion to South Africa/edited by Alan Ryan.—1. ed.
p.   cm.
ISBN 0-15-600558-1
1. South Africa—Description and travel. I. Ryan, Alan, 1943–
DT1732.R43   1999
916.804—dc21   98-19327

Text set in Fairfield Light
Designed by Camilla Filancia, based on a design by Trina Stahl

Printed in the United States of America
First edition
E D C B A

This book is dedicated to
CHRISTA MALONE
for knowing all the right words

Nkosi sikelel' i Afrika
Maluphakanisw' upondo lwayo
Yizwa imitandazo yetu
Usi sikelele

Sikelel' amadol' asizwe
Sikelela kwa nomlisela
Ulitwal' ilizwe ngomonde
Uwu sikelele

God bless Africa
Raise up her spirit
Hear our prayers
And bless us

Bless the leaders
Bless also the young
That they may carry the land with patience
Bless them

CONTENTS

INTRODUCTION

I FIRST CAME TO UNDERSTAND THE ESSENTIAL TRUTH about South Africa nearly twenty years ago, standing in a record shop in London.

My longtime interest in South Africa had resurfaced and combined with my interest in Jamaican reggae and Brazilian music, and I wanted to go back to the roots of both of them. At that time, you couldn't just run over to Tower Records or HMV and load up on *soukous* from Zaire or palm-wine music from Ghana or Nigeria. The records just were not readily available in the United States. If you were lucky, you might turn up something by King Sunny Adé or Chief Ebenezer Obey; if you were luckier still, you might find an album by Franco or Tabu Ley Rochereau. And there were a few collections of "township jive" from South Africa, but not many. So I thought I'd look in London.

I was having dinner one night at the Calabash, a wonderful African restaurant near Covent Garden, and I went early to visit the African Cultural Centre there. The shop had no records, but a nice man told me that I wanted to visit Stern's African Record Centre in Soho. I agreed, and I was there the next morning.

For the next month or so, I found time almost every day to stroll up Charlotte and Whitfield Streets, up past Fitzroy Square of literary fame, to Stern's. The tiny shop was on a residential street that was something rather less than palatial. I became friends with Charles Easmon, a member of the Ga tribe of the coastal region of Ghana and one of the three owners of Stern's. For hours at a time, I listened to the records Charles played for me. I met and talked with some of the African musicians who came through London while I was there. I talked with visitors from around the world and with nonmusical Africans from all over the continent—students and businessmen and young hopefuls dreaming of success. And all the while, I was listening to music from Angola, Zaire, Cameroon, Gabon, Côte d'Ivoire, Senegal, Ghana, Nigeria, Mali.

But I heard almost nothing from South Africa. I think I first heard in Stern's an album by Thomas Mapfumo of Zimbabwe, something by the Bhundu Boys, something else by Mahlathini and the Mahotella Queens. But nothing else. No *kwela*. No *mbaqanga*. No township jive.

I mentioned my interest again to Charles for the first time in several weeks.

"Oh," he said, "yes, you are interested in South African music." He looked regretful. "I don't really know South African music very well."

Then he put down the beer he was drinking on this warm afternoon, wrote a telephone number and address on a pad, tore off the sheet, and handed it to me.

"Here," he said. "Ring up Jumbo Van Renen and his wife, Mary, and talk to them. Jumbo is a South African living here in exile. He knows more about South African music than anyone else."

In the next few years, the world changed for Charles and Stern's and Jumbo. The world discovered African pop music, and Stern's rapidly grew into the largest importer of African recordings, then launched a successful record label of its own. And Jumbo Van Renen became a successful and respected producer of African recordings in London.

My world had changed that afternoon as well.

I never got over the words "in exile," or the matter-of-fact way Charles said them.

I knew the headlines from South Africa, of course, and the stories, and the television images. They were violent, horrifying, so extreme and outrageous, in fact, that they seemed almost unbelievable. What was wrong with South Africa? What was wrong with its paranoid paramilitary groups? What was wrong with its leaders? Their entrenched positions, their stubborn refusal to see the light—indeed, their refusal to foresee the future that would inevitably overwhelm them—seemed too much to believe.

But there, on a piece of paper in my hand, while Charles's words hung in the air, was the name of a man—a talented man, a *special* man, at that—whose country had driven him into exile.

I never thought of South Africa the same way again.

———

These *Reader's Companion* volumes—now covering Mexico, Cuba, Alaska, and Ireland, in addition to South Africa—are meant to provide a widescreen, time-lapse portrait of the places they focus on.

"The whole point of a travel book," Alec Waugh wrote in 1958, "is that it should be dated." The real value of old travel books, he continued, is the way they preserve for us "how certain places struck certain people twenty, fifty, eighty years ago."

I like reliving other people's travels, seeing through their eyes, and then measuring their responses against my own. Perhaps a traveler ten years ago, or a hundred or more, saw something I missed or something that would have meant nothing to me or something that isn't there anymore.

And, although many of the selections in each of the *Reader's Companion* books describe the very same scenes, the writers do not always agree on what they see. A good example is in *The Reader's Companion to Cuba*. When Richard Henry Dana Jr. visited Havana in 1859, he raved about its beauty. "Have I ever seen a city view so grand?" he exclaimed. Anthony Trollope visited Havana, too, but his reaction was very different. "There is nothing attractive about the town of Havana," he growled. Trollope also visited in 1859. In fact, the visits of the two writers appear to have overlapped. They might have passed each other in the street, but they came away with very different impressions.

And here's another instance of the same thing in the present volume on South Africa. Many of the selections that follow describe visits to Cape Town, and all of them rave. Even those who are appalled at the country's political life and at the daily lives of the majority of its people lament the fact that apartheid took root on such beautiful ground. Everybody loves Cape Town, with its picturesque architecture, sparkling Table Bay before it, and Table Mountain looming above. Almost everybody, that is.

Evelyn Waugh spent less than a day there in March 1931, took a quick look around, then bought a ticket and sailed away that very afternoon. In *Remote People,* he dismisses Cape Town in a single, nasty paragraph: "At last we arrived in Cape Town; a hideous city that reminded me of Glasgow; trams running between great stone offices built in Victorian Gothic; one or two gracious relics of the eighteenth century; down-at-heel Negroes and half-castes working in the streets; dapper Jews in the shops."

All of the selections in the *Reader's Companion* books are by visitors to the places they write about. They bring a stranger's questions and curiosity, not a native's assumptions, to their observations. And in that, they are just like you and me when we travel.

An interesting question arose as I was making selections for this book. As I read countless records of travel in South Africa, several themes and topics emerged as dominant: the beauty of Cape Town; the pleasures of Durban; the wealth of Johannesburg; the drama of the country's topography; the variety of its animal life; . . . and, always, over and over again, the misery and hopelessness of the country's black population. Every visitor, no matter what interest or business has brought him or her to the country, is moved to comment on it. Sometimes the comments are couched in terms of simple decency, sometimes in political language. So universal is this that, when I gathered my final selections together and put them in chronological order, I found that—aside from the scenic views—they formed a virtual history of oppression and, after 1948, apartheid. In fact, they form a kind of suspense story, as writer after writer, visitor after visitor, foresees what South Africa itself cannot see: impending disaster. In the end, as we know, that disaster was averted and decency prevailed. But it was a close call.

As I saw this scenario developing, I had in mind that conversation in the London record shop. And then I reread an essay by Angus Wilson about his 1961 visit to the land where his mother was born. Near the end of that essay, Wilson writes, "I can imagine now that the reader will be asking, is all South African life made up of racial politics? Broadly speaking, I think, the answer is yes."

I agree. I think that the history of this country's problems and struggles is one of the most interesting things about it. And I'm glad that those dark stories and dour predictions are here, together with all the descriptions of the beautiful seaside Cape Drive, the green hills of KwaZulu, the depths of a gold mine, the luxuries of the Blue Train, and on and on.

A few comments are necessary,

All of these selections are presented exactly as they first appeared. Only obvious typographical errors have been corrected. For one thing, this means that many place names appear in now discarded forms and spellings. Cape Town, for example, used to be Capetown.

More important, many names have changed significantly. Here are a few. Port Natal became Durban. Bechuanaland became Botswana. Rhodesia became Zimbabwe. Basutoland became Lesotho. Zululand became KwaZulu, and the province of Natal became KwaZulu-Natal.

It should also be noted that writers use the language of their times, and some words and names did not always, in some contexts, have the same implications they have today to our ears and eyes. Such words appearing in these selections include *Kaffir, native,* and perhaps even *Negro. Coloured,* on the other hand, has been used in a technical way in South Africa, a country that long felt a need to distinguish races with excruciating precision. The country's coloured population are those neither black nor white; they are those of mixed race, Indian, or Asian.

There's a new South Africa now, one that initially stirred to life when F. W. de Klerk became president and took its first breath the day Nelson Mandela walked out of prison. And, as it happens, the civic motto of one South African city, Durban, has proved prophetic. *"Debile principium melior fortuna sequetur,"* it reads in Latin. In English: "Better fortune will follow a weak beginning."

South Africa, once reviled and ostracized by most of the civilized world, is well on its way to becoming one of history's great success stories.

Some of the people and things that first fired my interest in South Africa forty years ago and kept that interest alive are as varied as the novels of Olive Schreiner and Alan Paton; the plays of Athol Fugard; the music of Joseph Shabalala and Ladysmith Black Mambazo, Johnny Clegg and Sipho Mchunu, Abdullah Ibrahim, Bob Marley, and Burning Spear; the music and the autobiography of Miriam Makeba, a true *sangoma;* the good work and passionate musical knowledge of CC Smith and Roger Steffens of *The Beat* magazine; Gloria Keverne, who invited me to Pietermaritzberg; and the young lady who sat beside me at Yankee Stadium for Nelson Mandela's visit and asked me the meaning of the words when we sang *Nkosi Sikelele Afrika.*

I owe warm thanks to Jill Bauman, John Coyne, Linda Funk, Eleanor Garner, Ellen Levine, Dawn Mulvihill, and all my pals at the Chariot.

I owe very special thanks to my editor, Christa Malone, whose version of editorial tough love has enhanced all five books on which we've worked together. She has cared about these books as much as I do—

especially about this one on South Africa—and her good taste and judgment have improved every page. For that reason, this book is dedicated to her.

—ALAN RYAN
New York City
September 1998

THE READER'S COMPANION TO
SOUTH AFRICA

G. H. MASON

Port Natal and Pietermaritzburg: 1850

"AS WE APPROACHED THE NARROW ENTRANCE OF THE INNER BAY, A PICTURE
PRESENTED ITSELF THAT APPEARED MORE LIKE THE VISION OF SOME 'FAIRY
DREAM' THAN A DELIGHTFUL REALITY."

On the first of March in 1850, a young man of twenty-one named George
Holditch Mason sat in his room at Sidney-Sussex College, Cambridge,
trying to settle on the future course of his life. He had completed his first
year at the university, but the mathematical formulas, the Greek choruses,
and the Latin prose that filled his mind had done nothing to clarify his
thoughts. He stared out the window, he tried to work, he took a walk,
he returned and took a nap. Nothing helped. In the evening, his younger
brother visited and confessed that he had been struggling with the same
thoughts of a vague future. They sat before the fire, talking, and it wasn't
long before "the thought presented itself of seeking our fortunes in foreign
lands." Before they went to bed that night, the brothers had pledged themselves "to take passages by the first ship, and set sail for Port Natal, South
Africa, at that time only just become a portion of the Queen's dominions,
and scarcely known, except as a land where half-crowns would buy broad
acres, and 'where a perpetual summer reigned throughout the entire
year.'"

In the next month, they raised capital of £300. After paying for their
passage, buying and shipping stores and gear, and paying an agent who
would secure land for them in Natal under a popular emigration scheme,
they reached the Liverpool docks during the first week of April with £40.
Through a mix-up, there were no berths on the Indiaman transporting
their gear. They had to follow on a later ship, but, with misgivings and

dreadful seasickness, they and one hundred and fifty other passengers were soon on their way.

Eventually, after affording them glimpses of Portugal and Africa, and making a stop for fresh water at Rio de Janeiro, the ship ran five hundred miles to the south of the Cape of Good Hope, in order to avoid the much-feared Cape storms, before turning east to round the Cape and then running due north toward Port Natal, the modern city of Durban. But a storm did pursue them, snapping the mizzen topmast and sending heavy seas sweeping across the decks. When the storm receded, they continued northward and finally approached within a mile of the coast near Port Natal, where they found two large East Indiamen riding at their moorings. One of them was the ship that carried all of the Mason brothers' possessions. It was evening by then and the captain anchored the ship near the two others, ready to enter the sheltered harbor behind a high wooded bluff at dawn.

During the night, a storm sprang up, and by dawn the Indiaman carrying their baggage had slipped its anchor and was driven against the rocks at the foot of the bluff. As it turned out, all the crew and passengers on board were saved but all the big ship's cargo was destroyed. The Mason brothers had six more days to contemplate the loss of all their gear before the storm finally abated and boats came out to carry passengers ashore.

In later years, George Mason returned to Cambridge to complete his education, but he had a terrific story to tell. He told it in Life with the Zulus of Natal, South Africa, published in London in 1855. Written in a plain and lively style, completely free of the pomposity so common in Victorian travel writing, it is a young man's book of adventure and ought to be considered a classic of its kind, worthy to stand on the same shelf as Richard Henry Dana Jr.'s Two Years Before the Mast. The excerpt that follows begins as George and his brother, with other passengers from their ship, are being rowed toward the sandy beach in the harbor of Port Natal.

Natal was named by the Portuguese explorer Vasco da Gama, who sailed into the excellent harbor on Christmas Day of 1497. Englishmen made the first permanent settlement at Port Natal in 1823. In 1835, the name was changed to Durban in honor of Sir Benjamin D'Urban, governor of the Cape Colony. The city and the region flourished, aided by sunny subtropical weather and further warmed by the Mozambique current. By the 1860s, much of the region was given over to sugar plantations worked by Indian workers brought in from Calcutta; after their five years of indentured labor, many opted to remain, and modern Durban has a very large Indian population. The region prospered even more after gold was discovered in the Witwatersrand in 1886 and after a seawall was built and the channel entrance to the harbor at Durban was dredged to a depth of forty feet, thus admitting larger vessels, at the end of the nineteenth century. The University of Natal was founded in 1910. Today, Durban is a city of one million and South Africa's vacation capital, offering guaranteed sunshine and long golden beaches.

The Mason brothers first set foot ashore where the city's Victoria Embankment now borders the harbor.

Fifty miles inland from Durban is the small city of Pietermaritzburg, founded in 1838, well preserved in its Victorian state, and now the capital of KwaZulu-Natal. The fifty miles that George Mason walked over trackless grassland and wooded hills is now traversed by the N3 highway. (Past Pietermaritzburg, the N3 continues northwest to Johannesburg, which didn't exist in Mason's time.) The white-gabled Church of the Vow in the center of town, now the home of the Voortrekker Museum, was built in 1841, so it was already standing when Mason first arrived. At that time, Pietermaritzburg had five hundred houses, fifteen hundred people, and thirty-six thousand acres of common pasturage in its fertile valley. For another description of Pietermaritzberg, see the selection by H. V. Morton.

In modern times, Durban, Pietermaritzburg, and the pastoral landscape of Natal have seen some of the fiercest fighting among the Zulu-based Inkatha Freedom Party and the Xhosa and African National Congress factions. Among the many victims was Headman Shabalala, brother of Joseph Shabalala and member of the singing group Ladysmith Black Mambazo.

In 1994—the year the African National Congress won a free election, three hundred and fifty years of white rule ended, and Nelson Mandela became president—the name of Natal province was officially changed to KwaZulu-Natal.

AS WE APPROACHED THE NARROW ENTRANCE OF THE Inner Bay, a picture presented itself that appeared more like the vision of some "fairy dream" than a delightful reality. Behind, lay the Outer Bay, a beautiful but dangerous roadstead, formed by a deep indentation in the well-wooded coast and the projecting bluff promontory. Floating on its heaving bosom lay the second Indiaman and the vessel we had just quitted—quite motionless—with their snow-white canvass spread in the bright sunshine, to get dry, and backed by the endless Indian ocean. On our right, the stately bluff, clothed with magnificent timber and dense evergreen bush down to the very water's edge, rose almost perpendicularly from its bed of billows. While to the left lay a vast forest—many thousand acres in extent—running from the tongue of land at the entrance of the inner harbour, called "The Point," along its whole northern (or left hand) side, till it meets a wood-crowned range of heights called the "Berea Hills," which sweep round two-thirds of this vast wood-skirted basin.

A minute more, and we are passing—almost within arm's length of the few projecting timbers, that still pointed out the grave of all our earthly goods, sunk fathoms deep in the briny element. Now we are on the bar! Another moment, and we are running up the narrow channel that lies between the lofty bluff and woody point. Only a few seconds, and our sluggish craft, tugged by a row-boat, chanting a lively air—has fairly entered the unrivalled "Harbour Bay"—a sheet of water, of at least ten thousand acres, completely land-locked by the Bluff and Berea ranges, except at the narrow inlet, which too, by a sudden bend, is lost to view, when once you enter. Fancy yourself thus floating on a vast lake of deep, transparent water, eight or ten miles in length, walled in right and left by masses of unbroken forest (evergreen*), stretching up mountain sides almost to the bright blue sky; then carry your powers of imagination still further, and picture this vast lake growing wider and wider as it stretches inland, till it terminates in a succession of slopes, extending from the water's edge to a distant chain of mountains, connecting the bluff with the Berea hills. Fancy, moreover, these slopes dotted over with thriving homesteads, with cultivated fields, with thousands of acres of wild, waving, deep green grass, with droves of depasturing cattle and herds of noble deer. Add to the picture also a thriving seaport town (Durban), reposing at the foot of this slope, under the shade of the dense bush; and fancy a cloud of pleasure boats, with their tiny sails, skimming the polished surface of this vast mirror, hiding themselves amongst floating islands and romantic creeks. Yes! Fancy this lovely picture lying in silent grandeur beneath a spotless canopy, and the brilliant sun of Southern Africa, and

*On the coast of Natal, trees are green through the entire year.

yet the conception, however vivid, will far—very far—fall short of the surpassing reality of that enchanting spot.

Our boats now approached the custom-house, before which lay, anchored in deep water, several colonial coasting vessels, of from fifty to a hundred tons (larger vessels being unable to cross the bar at that time). Passing through these, we grounded in about three feet of water, directly opposite the custom-house, where we found a crowd of colonists, emigrants, and natives, assembled to welcome our safe arrival.

Now, at that early stage of the colony, no quay had been formed for unlading boats, so that passengers were obliged to get from the boat to the shore as they best could. This, however, was nothing for gentlemen, but extremely inconvenient for ladies, who were obliged either to walk through some yards of water, or else to submit to be carried on shore by gentlemen, a process which produced considerable amusement amongst the lookers-on.

I was agreeably surprised at the appearance of the natives, although they did not seem at all overdone with clothing. Instead of the dull negro race I had expected to see, I found a most intelligent race of really handsome men—strong, active, and high-spirited. Indeed, so great was their gallantry, that when some of the blushing ladies (younger ones, of course) demurred at being carried ashore in gentlemen's arms, a score or more of these strapping fellows rushed to the rescue, and volunteered, in terms quite unintelligible, their gratuitous assistance in carrying them ashore; services which, I need hardly say, were declined by the now thoroughly shocked ladies, who forthwith resigned themselves to the care of their fellow-countrymen, and so at last set foot on the soil of Southern Africa.

ONCE SAFELY ON SHORE, WE BEGAN TO LOOK ABOUT FOR A suitable place of accommodation wherein to pass the night—now fast drawing on—the sun being already about to finish his daily journey. But the only buildings at this *Point* consisted of a custom-house, a small eating-house, a guard-room for a detachment of military, and the before-named blockhouse. Now, as there was no probability of finding lodgings at any of these, it was necessary to repair at once to Durban—distant a couple of miles—or else pitch our tent in the Bush, near the landing-place, where we stood.

I should have remarked that some little uneasiness was felt by most of the new-comers at the loose character of the soil, which, in fact, was nothing more or less than common sea-sand; although there was some satisfaction in seeing that—with such a salubrious climate—even barren sea-sand would produce masses of splendid evergreens, such as I never witnessed before nor since; amongst which were growing, in wild profusion, the huge cactus, deep crimson martingola, starch and castor-oil plants, Cape gooseberries, and endless sweet-scented creepers, forming altogether an unbroken and almost impenetrable mass of bush.

But, to proceed. Having at length decided that it would be unadvisable to set out for the town at that late hour—since we should be obliged to leave at the landing-place a number of loose articles that we had brought on shore—we determined on pitching our tent at the nearest convenient spot; a plan that was immediately adopted by our two Scotch friends, and a respectable married Yorkshire man. Moreover, as they each possessed tents, it was agreed that we should all encamp together, the more readily to assist and protect each other, if necessary.

Fortunately a magistrate happened to come up at this moment, who not only gave us permission to carry out our plan, but kindly directed us to an opening in the surrounding thicket, that quickly brought us to a picturesque little glen—scarcely an acre in extent—partially cleared, and quite shut in by sand-hills, clothed with the prevailing bush.

We immediately selected a most romantic spot for our encampment, just under a thick clump of martingola trees, in the centre of the glen, and commenced operations by pitching a large bell tent—belonging to one of the Scotchmen—into which we at once conveyed the luggage of the whole party, to preserve it from the dampness of the night, as well as from the fingers of certain of our *worthy* fellow-passengers, who were loitering about in a very unaccountable manner.

Night had by this time overtaken us, and, as it was extremely dark, we abandoned the idea of pitching all the tents; but, appropriating the one already completed to the three ladies and the luggage, we rigged up a temporary shelter for the five gentlemen close by.

While thus busily engaged, we had lost sight of the good housewives. They, however, had not been idle; one having procured water from a well in the neighbouring thicket, and prepared coffee; another had purchased beef-steaks, bread, sugar, &c., at the eating-house (before-named); while the third—with the assistance of some Caffres—had kindled a blazing fire before the tent-door, spread a table-cloth in the centre of the tent, procured cups, saucers, plates, dishes, and indeed every thing that the time and situation enabled her to do, preparatory to our assembling together to partake of supper.

Having at length constructed a sort of *gipsy-tent* for the accommodation of the gentlemen, we all adjourned to the *ladies'* tent; where, using boxes for chairs, and forming a family circle round the interior, we proceeded to do ample justice to the fare. Now, whether it was owing to the long interval since breakfast, to the goodness of the colonial provisions, or the cookery, I cannot say; but, certainly, we all enjoyed our first meal on shore most thoroughly.

The day's cares being now over, and the cravings of hunger appeased, we began to contemplate the peculiarly romantic situation of our snug little evening party. Indeed, it seemed hardly possible to believe that we were *really* ten thousand miles from our old homes, sitting at the remotest part of Africa, on the confines of the Indian ocean, with nothing but a fluttering sheet of canvass between us and the howling wind, that swept through the surrounding bush; with only a flickering rush-light, stuck in the soft sea-sand at our feet, to save us from sharing the pitch-dark night with the prowling beasts of prey that roamed through the adjacent jungle. Yet we had only to look around, and be at once convinced that such was the case; though, for all this, we were as merry and contented as though feasting in a college-hall, or the canvass of the dimly lighted tent had been the tapestry of a brilliant drawing-room.

Without—every thing was still, excepting the occasional rustle of the night wind in the foliage of the trees, the distant roar of the surf, as it dashed itself upon the rocky bluff, and the laughing jabber of a dozen Caffres sitting close-huddled in a ring, about the still blazing fire at the tent door, wrapped up in cotton blankets, devouring the remnants of our late meal, and sipping a basin of coffee, bestowed on them by one of the kind ladies.

It was a pretty sight to watch the expression of countenance displayed by the different heads that formed the sable ring, as the sparkling flame shot up on high, throwing a momentary glare on all around, revealing their jet-black visages, their snow-white teeth, and sparkling eyes, together with the keen-edged "assegais" (Caffre spears) with which each one was armed.

Having at length finished their supper, they suddenly dived into the surrounding bush, and as suddenly emerged, each bearing a bundle of wood upon his shoulder. Then, heaping fresh fuel on the fire, they approached the open door of the tent, and thrusting in their woolly heads, saluted us with "Slalla gooshley," literally (Rest in peace), after which, displaying two rows of pearls, set in polished frames of ebony, they vanished once more like supernatural beings, amongst the dense jungle encircling our little encampment.

I will now make a slight diversion from my subject, in order to relate a few incidents connected with the first acquisition of Natal by the British government. At the same time, I must observe once for all, that these, together with similar reports that I may have occasion to notice hereafter, are given by me *only as I received them* from persons *professing* to have been eyewitnesses, without the slightest intention on my part of vouching for their veracity; although I think it highly probable that the main points may be substantially correct, while the detail has been coloured, or perhaps altogether added, by tradition and party feeling.

Eight years previous to my visit, Natal was an independent state, containing upwards of twenty thousand white inhabitants, emigrants from the eastern province of the Cape colony. These people were for the most part farmers, or as they are called "Boers," who had migrated in consequence of the dangerous policy pursued by the *then* colonial government, with respect to the treatment of the Caffre tribes.

Natal had long been known to be the most salubrious, as well as the most fertile portion of Southern Africa, and, at the time of the Boers' migration, had just been depopulated by Chaka, king of the Zulus; who, however, had retired from his conquest into his native fastnesses in the Zulu-land, Natal being too free from bush for Caffre retention.

This territory, in extent about equal to Ireland, with its capacious harbour, its rich soil, and great abundance of minerals, naturally attracted the attention of the Boers, who forthwith established themselves in it as an independent people. Scarcely, however, had they taken possession of the country, before the Zulus recrossed the frontier river (Tugella), and slaughtered every man, woman, and child they came across; sweeping off the sheep, horses, cattle, and every thing else, into their own country.

This atrocity, of course, was resented by the Boers, who quickly placed their wives and children in "Laagers" (stockades), while they themselves took the field against the invaders.

At length, after several years of incessant fighting, the Boers had succeeded, not only in clearing Natal of the enemy, but in penetrating into the heart of Zulu-land; destroying their chief city (Goonloove), expelling Dingaan (the successor of Chaka), and placing Panda, a friendly chief, on the Zulu throne.

This done, they returned to Natal, and made an equitable distribution of the land amongst those who had taken part in the war; in six, four, two, and one thousand acre grants, according to the services rendered by the different individuals.

They now enjoyed a few months of peace, and employed their time in laying out towns, building houses, planting orchards and vineyards, enclosing as well as cultivating corn-fields; and, indeed, so great was their industry, that, besides producing enough for their own consumption, they actually exported fourteen thousand pounds' worth of produce to "the Cape" and Mauritius.

About this time, the importance of securing Natal as a British colony induced the government to send a body of troops, to occupy the new district in the name of the Queen.

Now, the Boers had not quitted the "old colony" from any want of loyalty; but simply that they might remove their families and property from the disastrous wars, which their intimate acquaintance with the character of the natives told them must result from the British policy towards the Caffres. When, therefore, the troops landed at Durban, the seaport of Natal, they were received with the greatest courtesy and attention by the majority of the Boers, who were very glad to have a body of well-armed men always at hand, ready to resist any future invasion of the Zulus.

A proclamation quickly made its appearance, calling upon the Boers to deliver up their arms and ammunition, and forbade their interfering with the settlement of Zulus within the district. This led to an altercation with the British commander, who at once saw the reasonableness of the Boers' complaint, and desisted from putting the terms of the proclamation into force. Being recalled, however, a Major Smith was sent to replace him, who at once came to blows with the Boers, and got so severely handled that he lost part of his artillery, the regimental colours, and a great many men. At this unexpected reverse, he made a truce with the Boers for a fortnight's cessation of hostilities, ostensibly for the purpose of burying the dead; but no sooner had the Dutch returned to their farms, than the English commenced building a stockade, and by the expiration of the fortnight had constructed a "log fort" of prodigious strength, so that the unsuspecting Boers, on returning from their farms, found the position quite unassailable, and had, moreover, the *satisfaction* of knowing, that any of them who might be taken would be treated as rebels and hanged forthwith.

This exasperated the Boers, who, taking advantage of the fact of the supplies of ammunition and provisions being stored at the Point (two miles from the stockade), and guarded by only thirty or forty men, rushed down unexpectedly upon the little detachment, ripped up the artillerymen at their guns, stormed a small guard-house, massacred all within it, and took the entire magazine, with guns, powder, shot, provisions, and a number of prisoners.

They now returned to the principal stockade, and opened trenches (which still exist) so as to get within range; then lining these ditches with "crack shots," they bored a hole in every hat or head that made its appearance above the parapet. Besides this, they brought the captured guns to bear on the English works, and also cut off their supply of water; so that the hundred and fifty men (composing the garrison) were reduced to the greatest extremity. Still the besieged managed to get a scanty supply of water by sending out children, under cover of the guns, to a neighbouring spring (knowing that the Boers would not shoot children). And, as they also possessed a number of horses, they refused to listen to any terms of surrender until the last one was eaten.

At this critical moment, a man named King undertook to break through the Dutch lines during the night, swim his horse over the bay, and ride for Graham's-town, a distance of six hundred miles, to obtain reinforcements.

In this extraordinary feat he was quite successful; and on the very day that the last horse was eaten in the stockade, the Fawn (a sloop of war) appeared in the offing, and anchored ready for crossing the bar at high tide. Soon afterwards, the fifty-gun frigate, Southampton, also made its appearance, and poured such a shower of shot and shell into the Bluff forest, that the Boers, who had lined it with riflemen, in anticipation of the sloop running over the bar, were obliged to beat a speedy retreat.

At the rise of the tide, the troops, two hundred in number, were mustered on the deck of the sloop; and, though the depth of water at the bar was very small, less than the draught of the vessel, still they determined on crossing it, if possible; so, clapping on all sail, they stood for the inner harbour, grounded on the bar, floundered over it at the cost of breaking the ship's back, and ran ashore high and dry near the present landing-place, where the wreck still remains.

Of course, the Boers were waiting to receive them, but the troops charging furiously with the bayonet, they broke and fled before suffering any severe loss, and never ceased their flight till they arrived at Cowie's Hill, some twelve miles from the port.

On reaching the stockade, the sight that presented itself was heart-rending, the men being reduced to mere skeletons, and scarcely able to lift a gun, having been living on scanty supplies of horse flesh and biscuit for nearly six weeks.

The following day a body of troops set out in pursuit of the Boers, who, in turn, fell back upon Maritzberg, the capital of the colony, distant fifty miles in the interior, where they continued for some months un-molested.

At length, however, a formidable division of cavalry, infantry, and artillery, was despatched to Maritzberg, where several thousand Boers had formed a "waggon camp," and were waiting an attack of the royal forces; but instead of marching the soldiers to attack their position, as at the *first disastrous engagement* near the port, the English commander opened fire with round shot on the waggons, which had the desired effect; for in less than ten minutes the whole body of Boers were in full retreat for the interior.

Leaving Maritzberg, they gave up all thoughts of further opposition, and determined on abandoning Natal. For this purpose they assembled the remaining farmers from all parts of the district; and on a stated day crossed the Drackensberg mountains, and established themselves in an open district, lying on the banks of the Orange River.

From this they have since been expelled by their implacable enemies (at least they think them such), the English; and at the present moment these twenty thousand of our best colonists are settled five hundred miles inland from Natal, over the Vaal River, where they have become rich and prosperous; more so, indeed, than the colonists in any part of "the Cape," and under the present enlightened colonial policy have been recognised as an independent people.

But to return to my subject. We were about breaking up the snug little party in the tent, when one of the ladies related a tale she had heard from a woman at the coffee-shop—namely, that "the surrounding bush was full of tiger-cats, and sundry beasts of prey"; and, moreover, "that a man had been lately attacked, and seriously hurt by them." Now, situated as we were in a lonely wood, it was impossible not to be startled at such an announcement; each bush, we fancied, concealed a lurking tiger, ready to pounce out and carry off his prey.

Under these circumstances, it was agreed that a watchfire should be kept up near the tents throughout the night. Accordingly, having divided the remaining hours of darkness into five equal parts, and drawn lots for the turns at the watchfire, we took leave of the ladies, and left them in possession of their tent.

It happened that my turn of keeping watch commenced at two o'clock in the morning, and lasted till three; after which my brother's turn commenced. So, making up a blazing fire, and giving the first sentinel a great-coat, a glass of grog, and brace of loaded pistols, we adjourned to the gentlemen's tent, where, wrapping ourselves in blankets, we made the damp sea-sand our bed, and fell asleep.

Precisely at two I was roused by the last watchman, who, having delivered up the coat and pistols, took his place in the tent, and dozed off to sleep. Seating myself on a stool by the fire, under the shelter of a martingola bush, I proceeded to heap fresh fuel on the dying embers; then, hanging the great-coat loosely over my shoulders, I took the pistols, and watched the curling flame skipping from thorn to thorn, and crackling as it shot forth its bright train of sparks high into the pitch-dark canopy by which it was enshrouded.

Now, I certainly did not sleep at my post; but, somehow or other, the hour slipped away before I thought it half ended. It was still pitch-dark; a gentle breeze was making a rustling in the leaves; a few night-birds—disturbed by the unwonted glare—came flitting overhead to learn its meaning, and quickly disappeared in the deep recesses of the wood. While, ever and anon, my timid imagination would try to persuade me that some wild beast was causing the rustling of the boughs; till—fearing lest I really should become afraid—I grasped my pistols and a blazing brand, and cautiously approached the spot from whence the noise proceeded; but all *there* I found silent and motionless; while *now* the rustling issued from yonder corner of the secluded glen.

It was indeed a dreary spot; but for all that there was something in the wild solitude that took my fancy; so much so, indeed, that I could not persuade myself to rouse my brother to his watch, and therefore proceeded to keep both my own and his.

At length the stars began to lose their recent brightness; traces of the approaching daylight appeared in the eastern horizon, and slowly spread till a red tinge came over that quarter of the skies: the air became piercing cold; the tall gaunt forms of noble timber-trees emerging from the black night kept coming into view; while thousands of little songsters welcomed the break of day with their sweet warbling melody.

All danger being now over, I took a ramble about the surrounding bush; passing through clumps of martingolas and narrow Caffre footpaths till I suddenly came upon the well (before named). Thence I found my way to the beach, and secured a bundle of splinters from the wreck for our fire. Next I reached the custom-house, before which a drowsy sentinel was pacing up and down—hugging his awkward musket. Scrambling over some heaps of merchandise and boxes—strewed along the beach above high-water mark—and again entering the recesses of the bush, I suddenly found myself standing at the open door of a guard-room, within which some half dozen sleepy soldiers were sitting doubled up, over the embers of a wood fire, with their loaded muskets piled in a stack, close at hand, ready for service at a moment's notice.

IT WAS GETTING QUITE LIGHT ERE I REGAINED THE SE-cluded spot occupied by our tents, where I found everything silent and undisturbed, just as when I left an hour previously. And as we had agreed amongst ourselves, the night before, to have breakfast over by times—so as to complete our proposed encampment early in the morning, before the heat of the day set in—I commenced making up the fire; after which I formed a triangle, and suspended a kettle of water from it over the flame. This done, I took the emptied pail, and started for the well to obtain a fresh supply, having first provided myself with a hooked stick, for lowering the bucket. On reaching the well, I let down my bucket, whirled it round a time or two to get it filled, and was in the act of drawing it up, when an unexpected calamity befell me.

To make myself understood, however, I should observe, that my own watch had got out of order on the voyage, and that I had borrowed my brother's—an old ancestral one of vast dimensions—for the night, which ill-fated watch I had safely deposited in my waistcoat pocket.

Now, while thus drawing the water, I heard a heavy splash below; but the faint light and deep shade of the overhanging bush prevented my seeing the cause. I therefore hauled up my bucket, and set off for the tents, without a single thought of the "big watch."

Having at length boiled the kettle, I roused my companions, whose first question of course was, "What's the time?" But on feeling for the watch, I discovered that it had vanished! In an instant, the late *splash* recurred to my mind; and, starting off at full speed, I quickly reached the woody recess in which the well was situated. But what was my chagrin at finding a crowd of Caffres busily employed in drawing water to cook their breakfast!

Of course, I gave up all hopes of ever seeing the watch again; but at the same time, pushing my way through the swarthy group, I gained the brink of the well; when stooping down, and carefully surveying the surface of the silt at the bottom, I discovered the missing watch lying face upwards in about four feet of water.

The joy of beholding my old friend once more can be better imagined than described; and as the whole depth of the well was scarcely nine feet, my first impulse was to jump down and grasp it in my hand; but this the Caffres would not allow, either from fear of thickening the water, or from a slight misgiving that my intentions were suicidal. However, on my making gestures and pointing out the watch to them, they discovered the cause of my anxiety; and, laughing heartily at the mishap, procured a barbed assegai, with which they quickly fished it up and restored it to me, when, to my surprise, I found that the water had not injured it in the least.

By this time the occupants of the tents were all up, and had set out a breakfast table on a plot of grass, in a cool shady spot, under a large clump of evergreen. They had also procured planks from the wreck to serve as benches, and obtained a fresh supply of provisions from Caffres despatched from the town with things for sale.

Scarcely were we seated before our party was augmented by the arrival of the captain and several of our shipmates—including the stout gentleman and Manxman—who were all on their way to the Point to look after the luggage, which, as I before remarked, they had been obliged to leave on the beach all night; and, as a matter of course, they were all invited to share our breakfast, to which they readily assented; and, seating themselves on the boxes and bundles lying about our tents, they related their adventures of the night.

The majority of our guests were any thing but satisfied with the little they had seen of the town—Durban, which they described as being "knee-deep in sand." While with regard to Byrne, the projector of the emigration scheme under which we had all come out, it was asserted, "that he was wholly unknown in the colony"; and moreover, "that his agent, Moreland, had already refused to accept some heavy bills drawn on him by Byrne, in favour of several individual passengers."

This was sad news for us! For, after our ruinous loss by the wreck, we had nothing to fall back upon but the fifty pounds transmitted by means of Byrne: and, if that too was lost, we should then be altogether undone! Indeed, as it was, our condition was any thing but enviable. Ten thousand miles from home, with only five-and-thirty pounds wherewith to board and keep ourselves, until such time as we could get our land, bring it under cultivation, and produce a crop for the market!

Nor were *we* the *only* ones likely to suffer by this Byrne; for our Scotch friends also had been induced to part with a hundred pounds, in exchange for his (Byrne's) worthless bills on Moreland; so that by the time breakfast was over, and our guests had departed to see after their baggage—we, the Scotchmen, and their two wives, were nearly at our wit's end.

In the midst of our calamities, it was some consolation to know that, at least, we should get our grants of land; since we possessed guarantees from the emigration commissioners—securing us our farms under all circumstances. Alas! how little did we understand colonial business. But of that I shall have occasion to speak hereafter.

At length we called a council of the five gentlemen and three ladies, to deliberate on the course to be adopted; which resulted in its being unanimously agreed to complete our encampment, and live at common charges for the ensuing week; by which time it was thought we should know more about the colony, and the best plans to be pursued; besides, that it would enable us to get our remaining baggage landed, without the trouble of running from the town to the Point each time the surf-boat came from the ship.

This part of the business being settled, we fell to work at our tents; and having learnt of a soldier that the precise site of the ladies' tent was the spot on which the massacre had taken place a few years before, we thought it as well to move our encampment a little further into the glen; so, striking the said tent, we removed more into the bush, and by noon had quite a little canvass town of our own.

The remainder of the day was occupied in conveying boxes from the beach to the tents, as the boats happened to bring ashore any belonging to us or the rest of our party. In this work we all helped each other; and when, occasionally, a very heavy case turned up, we formed slings, and carried it on poles between several of us; while the indefatigable ladies worked right manfully in conveying the lighter articles, arranging them in the different tents, and preparing savoury dishes for meal-times; in which latter operation they were materially assisted by the common soldiers of the 45th, who kindly lent us camp kettles and sundry other cooking utensils, besides supplying us gratuitously with greens and herbs from their garden, and the services of several Caffres for washing up plates, &c.

In this manner we spent our first week on shore; during which period the greater portion of ours and friends' baggage had been landed. We had also ascertained that no cash would be forthcoming from Byrne's agent; that our hundred acre grant of land was to be made at the Illovo, fifty miles inland, and thirty west of the capital; also, that six weeks would elapse before the locality would be fixed upon, and two months more before the land could be legally transferred to us, by which time the much dreaded wet season would be at its height. We were therefore obliged to abandon all thoughts of settling on our farms, and began to look about us for some way of profitably employing our time and reduced capital.

The few days thus pleasantly spent in our encampment at the Point had enabled us to gain a considerable insight into our future colonial prospects, simply by conversing with old settlers, as well as by observing the character and appearance of the various classes that frequented the landing-place, or lounged about the custom-house. First of all appeared thriving merchants, whose bronzed faces and familiarity with the Dutch and Caffre language, bespoke a long residence in that sunny clime. These carried prosperity on their countenances; and as they came cantering over the sands, mounted on strong cobs, attended by ladies on light graceful palfreys, with long riding habits, and broad-brimmed straw hats flapping in the refreshing breeze, one could scarcely keep from envying the happy lot of South African merchants.

Next, there were not a few gentlemanly persons, of good address, whose time was wholly spent in loitering about the beach, basking in the bright sunshine, or lounging on heaps of luggage, ever watching for an opportunity of entering into conversation with *newly arrived* emigrants. These *disinterested* people would congratulate us on selecting Natal as our future country, and begin telling marvellous tales of fortunes realized by cotton-growers; then going on to say, "How many thousand acres of land they owned"—"How many acres of cotton they should have in bearing *next* year"—"How many hundred cattle they possessed"—"How many waggons they had *on the road*"—"How many Caffres they employed." In a word, "That they were the leading men in the colony."

Now, a person's garb and gait will often belie his tongue; and so I rather wondered at not seeing more yeomanlike costumes than tight white ducks! dress coats! fancy waistcoats! pumps on their feet, and plumes of ostrich feathers in their caps! and, moreover, how men, with so much business always on hand, could thus sit wasting their time and spending day after day in idleness! Politely inviting you to "take a *weed*" from their cigar case; and then extolling the coast lands, remarking, at the same time, "how admirably tobacco grew on their estates!" and in conclusion, leaking out, that "they had a farm for sale, the finest in the colony"—and "at the lowest figure." Of course, it is needless to say that their estates existed only in their own imaginations; although, in the event of finding a dupe, they would no doubt have sold him somebody's farm in the neighbourhood, and bolted with the first instalment of the purchase-money.

Another class consisted of Boers, who had not joined in the general migration at the capture of the colony by the English. These men were exactly what you would expect to find: tall, athletic, freckled with sun-beams, attired in snow-white canvass trousers, bright blue cloth jackets with brass buttons, and broad brimmed, sugar-loaf, felt hats. Here and there you might find one on horseback; but the majority of them preferred the driving box of the ponderous waggon, where, seated behind a straggling train of fourteen draught oxen, yoked two and two, they made the very woods echo again with their "yeck"—"yeck!" and the loud crack of the prodigious whip.

The description of the colony at large given by these two last-named classes (viz. the beach loungers, and the Boers) widely differed; for, while the former declaimed against all parts, except the coast districts, the latter had only to point to their waggon load of wool, butter, corn, or their well-conditioned spans of oxen; and ask the other to produce the like from any part of the coast division.

Still, however, the accounts of "dust storms," "tempests," "locusts," and "rocky wildernesses," which all classes at the seaport gave of the inland districts, were so alarming that *our party*, together with several fellow-passengers, expressed a strong wish for one or two to proceed inland some fifty or sixty miles, and make a report upon the true character of the colony.

Now, in our reduced circumstances, we could very ill afford the time or expense of such a journey; but as it was a general wish, amongst a number of our friends, that *we* should undertake it, we consented; although it is only honest to say, that in so doing we had a secondary object in view, namely, of purchasing land for ourselves, in the capital, intending to lay out our thirty-five pounds in buying a "town allotment"; we having determined to work as labourers, until our savings, and the proceeds of a crop or two enabled us to commence business for ourselves. In this decision some, doubtless, will condemn us; but when they consider that town lands were advancing every day—almost every hour—in value, and that provisions were rising still more rapidly,—I think they will then agree, that our decision was really the best, and the speculation the safest we could adopt.

About this time, we received advices from England that a few bags of seed wheat, and two ploughs—a present from a friend—would come out in a small brig, so as to arrive soon after us: and thus another obstacle presented itself to prevent our proposed journey. However, this was got over, by the party at the tents undertaking to see after its landing for us, and also to take charge of our tent and luggage during our absence.

Every thing being thus arranged, we started upon our tour, at noon— on the sixth day after our arrival: having first provided ourselves with a bag of provisions for the way, a tin kettle, two thick blankets, a fowling-piece, and brace of pistols. Our road lay through the dense forest that extends from the Point to Durban; and though the boughs of overhanging timber trees nearly shut out the brilliant sky, and fiery sunbeams, still the two miles of sand, wellnigh "knee-deep," and our heavy loads, made us very slow travellers.

At length we emerged from the thicket, and discovered an extensive plain covered with stunted grass and straggling bush, bounded on one side by the forest we had just left, on the second by the Berea hills and woods, and on the third by the town of Durban. The nearest portion of this plain had been assigned to the emigrants for an encamping ground, and was dotted over with canvass tents, covered carts, gipsy-tents, hovels, cooking utensils, washed linen, men and women in groups of ten and twelve, squatting round fires, devouring half-cooked beef-steaks, and roaring out over the brandy bottle. While the farther corner was occupied by the camp, or rather stockade, before alluded to—where two hundred troops are stationed.

Our direct course lay through the *emigrants'* camp; but as we intended to buy a few necessaries for our journey, we turned aside, and passed up the principal street of Durban. At that time, no attention had been paid to enclosing the property on either side of the streets; so that the town—though really possessing many good houses, and numbers of large mercantile establishments—appeared like a confused mass of dwellings, pitched about indiscriminately,—here an extensive store, brick and slated, with plate glass front, and costly stock of goods; and close by a miserable thatched cottage, built of the abominable "wattle and dab." There, too, would be pretty villas, standing in well cultivated gardens, abounding with oranges and lemons, pine apples, bananas, coffee, cotton, and indeed every known production from the English water-cress to the rare exotic; and all round these lovely gardens, would be public houses, retail shops, Caffre huts, inhabited by filthy Hottentots, pigsties, and what else I know not; while to complete the picture of misery, the sand was allowed to drift at pleasure over the whole town, so that in many cases the streets were next to impassable. In fact, it is impossible to imagine a place more admirably adapted for a handsome and thriving seaport town; but at the same time so wretchedly mismanaged. So much for the Durban of *those days*.

As we quitted the town, and drew near the Berea hills—over which the waggon road lay—we fell in with two fellow shipmates, attired in Turkish costume, with daggers, and loaded pistols slung at their belts, who also were journeying towards Maritzberg, the capital. We did not, however, think it desirable to travel in such queer company, so, quickening our pace, we bade them "good bye," and began the long tedious ascent of the hills before us.

It was nearly four o'clock before we gained the summit of this woody range; which, though scarcely six miles from our tents, had taken us three hours to accomplish, on account of the endless sand. Here the road improved and became comparatively hard; we therefore sat down on a fallen tree, and rested while we emptied the sand from our shoes.

The view from this eminence was strikingly grand: far away lay the vast Indian ocean, sparkling in the sunshine as it heaved and throbbed; next came the bay of Natal, with its ships at anchor, tossing amidst the foaming billows, apparently intent on committing suicide, at the foot of the bluff promontory.

Then comes the glassy "Inner bay," as it is called, reposing beneath the sombre shade of the deep-tinted forests by which it is engulfed, with countless pleasure boats skimming its polished surface; and here and there along its margin a fishing party, or a picnic turn out. Next, the town of Durban discovers itself, in the shape of straggling snow-white buildings, dotted about, and almost lost in "bush," looking far more like a large English country village than a rising seaport town. And lastly you arrive at the magnificent forest—miles in extent all ways—that clothes the vast range of heights on which you stand; through which the sandy waggon track has broken a way below, leaving the spreading boughs to meet again above, and thus to form a most magnificent arcade, festooned with thousands of flowering plants and sweet-scented creepers.

But as the *would-be-Turks* were now overtaking us, we resumed our march, and soon came up with a party of Durban gentlemen, who gave us some useful information relative to our journey, and also informed us that the adjacent wood abounded with elephants, leopards, wild boars, deer, &c. &c., at the same time pointing out thick timber trees, that had recently been broken down by the first-named monsters.

On emerging from the Berea woods, the country presents an un-dulating surface for several miles, consisting of gentle hills and lonely dales, waving in tall rank grass, broken at intervals by masses of dark bush, and dotted over with "Caffre craals" (or native huts), with their patches of Indian corn, and herds of goats, or cows.

Traversing this delightful tract of country, in the cool of the day, with the full splendour of the setting sun throwing a lustre on the already enchanting scenery—and the excitement at seeing a noble deer, now and then, go skipping playfully along the shady vales, almost within range, or a brace of "pows" (wild turkeys) crossing our path a few hundred yards ahead, and the unexpected change from the loose sandy soil of Durban— altogether so enlivened our drooping spirits, that, by the time we had travelled ten miles from Durban, our estimation of Natal had risen at least fifty per cent, even on what we had read of its charms, and the advantages it offered to colonists.

By sunset we reached an extensive cotton farm, where many hundred acres of cotton of the finest quality was growing wild, and blowing about in the wind, with nobody to gather it, or turn it to account; although there were good farm buildings, and a substantial house on the estate. Passing on, we travelled the next two miles in the dark, and having de-viated from the path, lost our way; but at length found ourselves before a roadside house, called "The German Hotel," where we determined on taking up our abode for the night.

This hotel consisted of a long row of thatched buildings, surrounded by a verandah; opening on to which were several doors, and numerous little casements, all bespeaking the ingenuity and mechanical skill of the industrious Germans, who built and inhabited it. The whole place wore an aspect of simplicity and homely comfort, with its poultryyard, its "craal" for the cattle, a stack of firewood, a coffee-mill fixed to a stump under the verandah; while beams of light from a blazing fire issued through the open doors and casements, throwing a flickering glare on the overhanging bush, beneath which it was wellnigh buried. Within, the appearance exactly corresponded with the exterior: the several rooms, into which it was divided, being all open to the thatch, and only separated from each other by partitions running even with the house-walls; while the entire furniture—consisting of tables, stools, a sofa, and a few bedsteads, bore unmistakeable proofs of being "home made."

The principal room was occupied by a few old German settlers from the neighbourhood and á large party of newly arrived English emigrants, all eating, drinking, smoking, and singing promiscuously, waited on by half a dozen grown up sons and daughters of the host and hostess, who themselves were too busily engaged cooking in the adjoining kitchen to attend to any thing besides. Having obtained a private room, and secured two beds for the night, we ordered supper, and, while it was preparing, made a survey of our rude apartment.

THE ONLY FURNITURE POSSESSED BY OUR ROOM CONSISTED of two rough wooden bedsteads, a few chairs, and a three-legged table, on which was placed a long dip candle in a brass stick. The whitewashed walls were gaily decorated with coloured prints of fox hounds and English steeple chasers, together with engravings cut from the sheets of *The Illustrated London News;* while from the dark smoke-stained roof hung sundry flitches of bacon, pumpkins, choice ears of seed corn, and long waving cobwebs.

After a few minutes the room door flew open and a bouncing German lassie, all smiles and roses, made her appearance with a tray and clean white cloth, on which were arranged cups and saucers, bread, butter, fried eggs, bacon, tea, and coffee. Having deposited the tray on the table, and busied herself in putting the room a little to rights—taking care meanwhile to show her great agility—she gave us a hand-bell and withdrew, leaving us to enjoy the substantial meal before us.

The mirth of the party in the adjoining room was quite sufficient to have kept us awake had we retired to our beds at the conclusion of supper. We therefore rang for the table to be cleared, and sat till near midnight, reading some colonial papers, which the said bouncing lassie had considerately brought us. By this time the sounds in the adjacent compartment had gradually died off to the low-toned conversation of a few inveterate smokers, and the heavy snoring of a drunken emigrant lying under the tap-room table. Now, as we intended to start before daybreak next morning, we rang, and asked for our bill, including the two beds; and, to our agreeable surprise, found that the entire charge for the two was but three shillings.

It was still dark, next morning, when we arose and set out for Maritzberg; the air was fresh, and loaded with fragrant odours from a neighbouring garden; a heavy dew hung upon the drooping boughs, and swayed the blades of tender grass almost to the ground; while, miles away, the breakers on the bluff kept up a ceaseless roar, like that of water rushing down a cataract.

A young German lad kindly accompanied us at first starting, to point out a turn of the road; who also informed us that the distance to Maritzberg was about forty miles. We therefore determined on making it a *two days'* journey, that we might the better observe the country as we passed along; besides that, my brother was far from well: he having shown symptoms of colonial fever during the preceding day and night.

Passing through several cotton plantations, all so completely clothed with white wool (hanging in large pods, the size of hen's eggs) that, in the dim twilight, you might almost have mistaken them for snow-clad fields, but for the bright yellow flowers of the unripe pods, and the deep green foliage of the graceful shrubs on which they grew, our road now brought us to one of the thousand brooks which run amongst the hills, throughout the length and breadth of this well-watered land; then, traversing a couple of miles of park-like country, it led us to the foot of "Cowie's Hill," where the old road was blocked up with bushes, and a new cutting had been made, so as to avoid the formidable ascent—nay, mountain peak—over which the old waggon track lay.

Of course we followed the level road, which enabled us to get an insight to the formation of these vast hills. The sun had by this time risen, scattering his brilliant beams over the beauteous scenery around, and causing the foliage of the different shrubs to sparkle and glitter with pendant dewdrops; on our right, stretching up to the clouds, lay the celebrated "Cowie's Hill," while to our left, far down in a secluded valley, lay a neat farm, with an English-built house, and about fifty acres of well-cultivated land.

This cutting is about two miles long, and just in the middle it is crossed, at right angles, by the old Dutch waggon road, which crowns the highest peak of the neighbouring range, and runs down a fearful incline, to the depths of the ravine below. How ever any man or beast, much more a loaded waggon, could get up and down such a sickening precipice, was and is still a mystery to me!

We next passed over an extensive plain, of some four thousand acres, nearly circular in form, and completely shut in by lofty hills. A lovely spot! but wholly lying waste; presenting a surface of long waving grass, broken only by here and there a rivulet, a clump of bush, or solitary lone tree. And though it has *since* become the site of a thriving town (Pine-town), at *that* time it bore no traces of human habitation, beyond the framework of a *wattle and dab* hut, which Murray, the proprietor of the whole flat, was that day commencing.

Hitherto, the soil over which we had travelled was of a light friable nature, containing a good deal of fine sand; and, though the entire face of the country was clothed with the richest vegetation, and studded thickly with timber, yet it was manifest that, for the successful cultivation of cereals, it would require claying continually, or else an immense amount of manure; which latter article it was difficult to obtain, as "the Ticks"* (which abound in the coast district) make cattle keeping a very doubtful speculation.

On leaving "Pine-town Flat," we ascended Murray's Hill, scarcely inferior to the great Cowie, and spent a couple of hours in passing over a broad open table land, some miles in extent. Here the character of the country completely changed, the soil became good and almost free from bush; the grass was shorter and less rank than near the coast, and thickly interspersed with brilliant flowers of scarlet, blue, white, and purple. By this time, however, the day had well commenced; we therefore gathered a few sticks as we passed along, and on arriving at a sparkling stream that issued from the hill-side, near a deserted homestead (Pearson's farm), we unpacked our provisions, made some coffee, and rested till near noontide.

Resuming our journey, we at length reached Botha's "half-way house," where we intended to get dinner, and to wait until the heat of the day was over. This house was beautifully situated immediately under an almost impassable ridge of hills, packed one upon another, and rising still higher and higher, till they ended in distant conical peaks, or abrupt surfaces of perpendicular rock. The host was proprietor of a six thousand acre farm, stretching along the valley beneath these mountains, and had enclosed several acres, on which were growing excellent crops of oats, barley, peas, and potatoes.

*The "Tick" is really a "land leech," only of a spherical instead of an elongated form.

Having conducted us to the travellers' room—a comfortable apartment with folding glass doors, a chintz sofa, and neat furniture—our host brought us the remnants of a cold suckling pig for dinner, and left us in company with a most entertaining young Dutchman, who gave us a brief outline of his own adventures during the late war with the English.

It appeared that this Boer had command of a detachment of boats, whilst the English were besieged in their stockade at Durban. To use his own words, "One day a sloop cast anchor off the bluff, and I was ordered to take my boats and capture her, on behalf of the republic. So, manning a couple of boats, I rowed alongside, hailed the captain, and bade him throw a rope's-end. I and a half dozen men then hauled ourselves on deck, where no body was to be seen except the captain; who, on hearing my errand, and finding himself taken prisoner, became very friendly, laughed heartily, and bade me open the hatchways and see what a splendid cargo he had on board. But what was my horror on removing *the hatches*, at finding some hundred troops with loaded carbines and set bayonets, waiting to rush on deck! In this predicament I endeavoured to jump over board, but the captain prevented me, saying, 'No, sir! We shall swing you to the *yard-arm* first, as a traitor and a rebel.' However, I remarked that the Boers would at once serve all their captives in the same way, amounting in all to nearly a hundred, which produced a change in the captain's intentions, and saved my neck."

Leaving Botha's, our first business was to climb the formidable barrier before us; but that accomplished, one still more formidable presented itself. Happily the *late* Dr. Stanger had cut round it for about a mile, chiefly through red sandstone. From this cutting, which is very narrow, indeed only just a ledge on the mountain side—you get a "bird's-eye view" of Potgeiter's farm, down in a well-watered valley to the left, with a snug Dutch homestead, a large orchard, some fields of ripening corn, and droves of cattle, forming a pretty picture when contrasted with the barren steeps, and wild craggy peaks, by which it is walled in all round.

As we proceeded the country became still more rugged, the hills assumed a conical shape, the road became one unbroken sheet of greenish marble; right and left lay huge blocks of magnificent granite—red and blue—perched upon hill tops, or lodging on the brink of some yawning chasm, ready to rush headlong down to the unfathomable ravines below. At length we reached Cheeseborough's accommodation house, lying on the banks of a mountain torrent, in the very centre of this rocky wilderness. Passing on, we began the wearisome ascent of the "Big Hill"; and after an hour's hard work, exclusive of stoppages, we gained its summit, from whence the surrounding country for miles was visible.

The sun was now setting, we were still twenty miles from Maritzberg, and ten from the next road-side house; but, what was worse, my brother was again becoming ill. However, we had no choice but to push on and reach the road-side house as quickly as possible. At length we got clear away from the "Big Hill"; and, for the next few miles, passed over an undulating country of rich black soil, equal to the finest English loam. Following a well-beaten track, we rounded a low flat hill; on the farther side of which a couple of waggons were drawn up for the night. A large fire—midway between the two—surrounded by Caffres, was burning brightly; the owner, Mariamne, a Frenchman, lay reading by fire-light under the hinder part of one, having made his position snug by hanging blankets round. A bright brass coffee kettle, a canister of sugar, and a large breakfast cup, lay in the grass close by, just as they had been thrown aside, and left for a future occasion. The Caffres were eating rice from a large iron pot, digging it out with wooden spoons; the cattle too were feasting themselves on the rich grass, that covered the whole surface of country, and every thing betokened perfect contentment.

On our approach, a shaggy dog saluted us with a snarling half-uttered bark, and looked to his master as though to gain his approbation; who, however, visited him with a kick for his pains, and begged that we would not be afraid, as the dog meant no mischief, but acted more from custom than from thinking us suspicious characters. At the same time insisting on our taking a seat, and drinking a cup of strong hot coffee.

From this good-hearted man we learned, that the distance to Luscomb's road-side house was still eight miles; but that there was an "American mission station" close by (that is, within a mile), over the adjoining little hill. Now, we had plenty of provisions, blankets, and every thing needful for encamping in the open air, if necessary; but as we were both very much heated with our long walk, besides that my brother was far from being well, we determined either to push on to Luscomb's, or else seek shelter for the night at the mission station.

Having fixed on the latter course, we crossed the hill in the direction pointed out by our informant, and in ten minutes reached the station; where we found the venerable missionary "Shrœder," I believe; who not only gave us shelter and a night's lodging, but also prepared for us a substantial supper and breakfast, to help us on our way next morning. It was impossible not to be struck with the great but unostentatious kindness of the venerable gentleman and his good lady, which, indeed, is one of those bright memoirs of past times and foreign lands, that frequently recur to my mind as it ponders over the past, the present, and the future, and asks "What have I been?"—"What am I now?"—"What shall I be?"

Starting at daybreak, we commenced the remaining eighteen miles of our journey. The first few led us through a rich open district, quite free from bush, but ill supplied with water, there being no *constant* stream for several miles; and at that time no wells. We now entered "Thorny Bush," or "Uys Doorn's," a long narrow belt of forest land, one mile in breadth, and twenty in length, possessing very little good timber, the trees being chiefly of the mimosa or acacia species, but affording an inexhaustible supply of fire-wood for the capital, besides producing considerable quantities of gum and tanning bark.

On the borders of this forest, nearest the capital, stood Luscomb's house of entertainment, where we procured some coffee and cold roast beef. At noon we took our departure, and once more set out for Maritzberg, distant about ten miles. The waggon track here plunged down the precipitous bank of a small rivulet, and ascended the opposite one still more abruptly; the stream itself being only a few inches deep, and very narrow, but fifteen or twenty feet below the rocky banks that contained it. Another mile of picturesque scenery brought us to a deeply wooded valley, at the bottom of which a little brook of sparkling water rippled amongst the smooth stones, and buried itself in the adjoining thicket. Immediately beyond this lay a vast hill, possessing scarcely sufficient soil to hide its *iron stone* ribs, that protruded at several places, in the form of immense "boulders." From the crown of this hill we obtained our first glimpse of the *now* city of Maritzberg, appearing in the distance to be nothing more than a few straggling snow-white buildings, with a red brick fort at one end, and an even plain of some thousand acres at the other, interspersed with a few hedgerows and ornamental shrubs, lying in the hollow of a semicircle, formed by a long range of wood-crowned heights, reaching nearly to the clouds.

Descending a succession of slopes, through a track of fine grazing land, we at length reached the bridge over the Little Bushman's river, a deep and rapid stream running along the whole length of the town, at an average distance of five hundred yards from the outside tier of gardens. The place now wore a very different aspect to what it did from Uys

Doorn's hill. The streets were wide, the houses large and commodious, while the plan in which the town was laid out gave it a very prepossessing appearance, it being nearly two miles long by one in breadth, with ten principal streets running from end to end, crossed at right angles by six others of equal width, but less thickly occupied. Moreover, the frowning hills, which in the distance seemed as though overhanging the town, now showed themselves to be five miles away, presenting a splendid slope of many thousand acres, clothed with luxuriant grass, and scattered over with droves of cows and oxen, with *here* a woody kloof, and *there* a little fountain breaking out of the bare rock, and sparkling in the bright sunshine. The town too presented an animating scene; scores of Caffres were going in and out with things for sale, heavily laden waggons were jolting through the streets, parties of "red coats" were strolling about, merchants were trotting briskly from store to store, while fashionable ladies and dandified young gentlemen were promenading or cantering over the adjacent hills on their fleet steeds.

Now, what with the dust and heat, we were in any thing but in a desirable condition for entering the busy capital; so, taking advantage of the shelter afforded by the bridge, we unpacked our travelling bag, enjoyed a good wash at the river side, shaved, brushed, and polished up a little, preparatory to making our entry into the town.

While thus engaged, a lad of sixteen passed under the bridge, on the opposite side of the river, wild-duck shooting, and stopped to have a little conversation. Now, as he appeared extremely intelligent, we took the opportunity of making a few inquiries relative to the town and adjacent country, to all of which he gave ready answers; and, bidding us "good-day," pursued the course of the river; but, suddenly turning again, he exclaimed, "if you call on Mr. Archbell, Long Market-street, he will give you better information than I can; besides that, he has a deal of land on sale just now. Mind you call, good-day."

At first we were inclined to suspect it a hoax; but as the latter part of the speech enabled us to inquire about the purchase of some land— a very important part of our errand—we determined on directing our steps as recommended. Accordingly, crossing the bridge, we passed between two neat cemeteries—Dutch and English—and entered the capital by the middle *Cross-street* (Commercial-road). A hundred and fifty yards brought us to Burgher-street; crossing it, another hundred and fifty brought us to Loop-street; another interval as before, and then came Long Market-street—by which time we began to form some idea of the extent and beauty of this extraordinary place; since there yet remained Church—Pieter Maritzberg—Boom—and Greyling-streets untraversed, each separated by an interval of one hundred and fifty yards, and still we were only crossing the town in its narrowest direction.

Lengthways, the above-named streets ran in parallel straight lines from the "Camp Hills," at the extreme left of the town, down an uniform declivity of nearly two miles in length, and terminated in a vast plain covered with rich herbage. Constant streams of limpid water from the neighbouring hills flowed in open channels at the sides of these streets, between the foot-paths and the horse-road. While long hedgerows of figs, roses, quinces, almonds, peaches, and pomegranates, together with weeping willows, seringaboom, oak, Australian gum, lemon, and various fruit trees, gave the whole place the appearance of a vast panorama. Here would be the well-appointed residence of some *old Cape colonist*; close by, perhaps, the dilapidated house and overgrown orchard of an expatriated Boer; near it, again, a newly opened store, crammed with articles for sale, from a rusty ploughshare to a flitch of American bacon, or a fancy stock of haberdashery; while, ever and anon, the fashionable European structure of some *new emigrant* would rise through the tall rank grass and thrifty fruit trees of an old deserted garden.

On reaching Long Market-street, we turned down by the Market-square, an area of from twenty to thirty acres, surrounded by public buildings and old-established mercantile firms (comparatively speaking), until we arrived at the house described by the lad; which, indeed, could scarcely be mistaken, from the fact of its being built with blocks of blue ironstone, very high, and standing in a large garden, with a row of seringas before it.

On rapping at the old-fashioned front door, what was our surprise at its being opened by *the identical lad!* who forthwith conducted us into a comfortable parlour, with old Spanish mahogany furniture, and a good library of valuable books, where we found a short active gentleman of about sixty, very polite, but straightforward. This was his father, Mr. Archbell; who, besides discharging the important functions of editor of the *Natal Independent* and mayor (styled "chairman") of the municipality, was, moreover, one of the earliest missionaries of the Wesleyan body to the heathen natives of this part of South Africa.

MARK TWAIN

Durban, Johannesburg, Kimberley: 1896

"EVERYTHING NEAT AND TRIM AND CLEAN LIKE THE TOWN. THE LOVELIEST
TREES AND THE GREATEST VARIETY I HAVE EVER SEEN ANYWHERE, EXCEPT
APPROACHING DARJEELING. HAVE NOT HEARD ANY ONE CALL NATAL THE
GARDEN OF SOUTH AFRICA, BUT THAT IS WHAT IT PROBABLY IS."

Mark Twain, with his wife and daughter, landed at Durban on May 6,
1896. South Africa was the last country Twain was visiting on a round-the-
world tour, and he spent ten weeks there in all, giving lectures in fifteen
cities and towns. Exhausted from his travels and only partly refreshed by
two weeks of rest on Mauritius, Twain still took the opportunity to explore
widely in the time available between his public appearances. He did succeed in having a private meeting with Paul Kruger, then president of the
Transvaal, but he failed to meet the legendary Cecil Rhodes. Since Twain
allows that Rhodes is either a "lofty and worshipful patriot and statesman,"
or, just possibly, "Satan come again," it is questionable whether Rhodes
would have enjoyed a visit from this outspoken and acerbic American
celebrity. In any case, Twain penned one of history's most vivid comments
on Rhodes: "When he stands on the Cape of Good Hope, his shadow falls
to the Zambesi."

The rickshas, drawn by Zulu men, that Twain sees in the streets of
Durban were still very new in 1896. A wealthy local merchant, Sir Mar-
shall Campbell, imported the idea in 1893 and they immediately caught
on as urban taxis. Sources differ on the numbers, but fifteen years or so
after Twain's visit, there were as many as two thousand rickshas plying the
streets of this small but busy city. In time, competition led the Zulu run-
ners to decorate their rickshas—and, later, themselves—with bright colors

and tribal designs, and they remained a major local attraction in Durban into the 1970s.

Today, fewer than two dozen of the colorful rickshas remain, and there are fewer all the time. They are usually clustered in front of the Tropicana Hotel on Marine Parade, giving rides to tourists on Durban's Miracle Mile along the beautiful beachfront. Americans of a certain age will be reminded of the popular rolling chairs on the boardwalk in the earlier heyday of Atlantic City.

FROM DIARY:

ROYAL HOTEL. COMFORTABLE, GOOD TABLE, GOOD SER-vice of natives and Madrasis. Curious jumble of modern and ancient city and village, primitiveness and the other thing. Electric bells, but they don't ring. Asked why they didn't, the watchman in the office said he thought they must be out of order; he thought so because some of them rang, but most of them didn't. Wouldn't it be a good idea to put them in order? He hesitated—like one who isn't quite sure—then conceded the point.

May 7. A bang on the door at 6. Did I want my boots cleaned? Fifteen minutes later another bang. Did we want coffee? Fifteen later, bang again, my wife's bath ready; 15 later, my bath ready. Two other bangs; I forget what they were about. Then lots of shouting back and forth, among the servants, just as in an Indian hotel.

Evening. At 4 P.M. it was unpleasantly warm. Half-hour after sunset one needed a spring overcoat; by 8 a winter one.

Durban is a neat and clean town. One notices that without having his attention called to it.

'Rickshas drawn by splendidly built black Zulus, so overflowing with strength, seemingly, that it is a pleasure, not a pain, to see them snatch a 'ricksha along. They smile and laugh and show their teeth—a good-natured lot. Not allowed to drink; 2s per hour for one person; 3s for two; 3d for a course—one person.

The chameleon in the hotel court. He is fat and indolent and contemplative; but is business-like and capable when a fly comes about—reaches out a tongue like a teaspoon and takes him in. He gums his tongue first. He is always pious, in his looks. And pious and thankful both, when Providence or one of us sends him a fly. He has a froggy head, and a back like a new grave—for shape; and hands like a bird's toes that have been frost-bitten. But his eyes are his exhibition feature. A couple of skinny cones project from the sides of his head, with a wee shiny bead of an eye set in the apex of each; and these cones turn bodily like pivot-guns and point every-which-way, and they are independent of each other; each has its own exclusive machinery. When I am behind him and C. in front of him, he whirls one eye rearwards and the other forwards—which gives him a most Congressional expression (one eye on the constituency and one on the swag); and then if something happens above and below him he shoots out one eye upward like a telescope and the other downward—and this changes his expression, but does not improve it.

Natives must not be out after the curfew bell without a pass. In Natal there are ten blacks to one white.

Sturdy plump creatures are the women. They comb their wool up to a peak and keep it in position by stiffening it with brown-red clay—half of this tower colored, denotes engagement; the whole of it colored, denotes marriage.

None but heathen Zulus on the police; Christian ones not allowed.

May 9. A drive yesterday with friends over the Berea. Very fine roads and lofty, overlooking the whole town, the harbor, and the sea—beautiful views. Residences all along, set in the midst of green lawns with shrubs and generally one or two intensely red outbursts of poinsettia—the flaming splotch of blinding red a stunning contrast with the world of surrounding green. The cactus tree—candelabrum-like; and one twisted like gray writhing serpents. The "flat-crown" (should be flat-roof)—half a dozen naked branches full of elbows, slant upward like artificial supports, and fling a roof of delicate foliage out in a horizontal platform as flat as a floor; and you look up through this thin floor as through a green cobweb or veil. The branches are japanesic. All about you is a bewildering variety of unfamiliar and beautiful trees; one sort wonderfully dense foliage and very dark green—so dark that you notice it at once, notwithstanding there are so many orange trees. The "flamboyant"—not in flower, now, but when in flower lives up to its name, we are told. Another tree with a lovely upright tassel scattered among its rich greenery, red and glowing as a fire-coal. Here and there a gumtree; half a dozen lofty Norfolk Island pines lifting their fronded arms skyward. Groups of tall bamboo.

Saw one bird. Not many birds here, and *they* have no music—and the flowers not much smell, they grow so fast.

Everything neat and trim and clean like the town. The loveliest trees and the greatest variety I have ever seen anywhere, except approaching Darjeeling. Have not heard any one call Natal the garden of South Africa, but that is what it probably is.

It was when Bishop of Natal that Colenso raised such a storm in the religious world. The concerns of religion are a vital matter here yet. A vigilant eye is kept upon Sunday. Museums and other dangerous resorts are not allowed to be open. You may sail on the Bay, but it is wicked to play cricket. For a while a Sunday concert was tolerated, upon condition that it must be admission free and the money taken by collection. But the collection was alarmingly large and that stopped the matter. They are particular about babies. A clergyman would not bury a child according to the sacred rites because it had not been baptized. The Hindoo is more liberal. He burns no child under three, holding that it does not need purifying.

The King of the Zulus, a fine fellow of 30, was banished six years ago for a term of seven years. He is occupying Napoleon's old stand—St. Helena. The people are a little nervous about having him come back, and they may well be, for Zulu kings have been terrible people sometimes—like Tchaka, Dingaan, and Cetewayo.

There is a large Trappist monastery two hours from Durban, over the country roads, and in company with Mr. Milligan and Mr. Hunter, general manager of the Natal Government railways, who knew the heads of it, we went out to see it.

There it all was, just as one reads about it in books and cannot believe that it is so—I mean the rough, hard work, the impossible hours, the scanty food, the coarse raiment, the Maryborough beds, the *tabu* of human speech, of social intercourse, of relaxation, of amusement, of entertainment, of the presence of women in the men's establishment. There it all was. It was not a dream, it was not a lie. And yet with the fact before one's face it was still incredible. It is such a sweeping suppression of human instincts, such an extinction of the man as an individual.

La Trappe must have known the human race well. The scheme which he invented hunts out everything that a man wants and values—and withholds it from him. Apparently there is no detail that can help make life worth living that has not been carefully ascertained and placed out of the Trappist's reach. La Trappe must have known that there were men who would enjoy this kind of misery, but how did he find it out?

If he had consulted you or me he would have been told that his scheme lacked too many attractions; that it was impossible; that it could never be floated. But there in the monastery was proof that he knew the human race better than it knew itself. He set his foot upon every desire that a man has—yet he floated his project, and it has prospered for two hundred years, and will go on prospering forever, no doubt.

Man likes personal distinction—there in the monastery it is obliterated. He likes delicious food—there he gets beans and bread and tea, and not enough of it. He likes to lie softly—there he lies on a sand mattress, and has a pillow and a blanket, but no sheet. When he is dining, in a great company of friends, he likes to laugh and chat—there a monk reads a holy book aloud during meals, and nobody speaks or laughs. When a man has a hundred friends about him, evenings, he likes to have a good time and run late—there he and the rest go silently to bed at 8; and in the dark, too; there is but a loose brown robe to discard, there are no night clothes to put on, a light is not needed. Man likes to lie abed late—there he gets up once or twice in the night to perform some religious office, and gets up finally for the day at two in the morning. Man likes light work or none at all—there he labors all day in the field, or in the blacksmith shop or the other shops devoted to the mechanical trades, such as shoemaking, saddlery, carpentry, and so on. Man likes the society of girls and women—there he never has it. He likes to have his children about him, and pet them and play with them—there he has none. He likes billiards—there is no table there. He likes outdoor sports and indoor dramatic and musical and social entertainments—there are none there. He likes to bet on things—I was told that betting is forbidden there. When a man's temper is up he likes to pour it out upon somebody—there this is not allowed. A man likes animals—pets; there are none there. He likes to smoke—there he cannot do it. He likes to read the news—no papers or magazines come there. A man likes to know how his parents and brothers and sisters are getting along when he is away, and if they miss him—there he cannot know. A man likes a pretty house, and pretty furniture, and pretty things, and pretty colors—there he has nothing but naked aridity and somber colors. A man likes—name it yourself: whatever it is, it is absent from that place.

From what I could learn, all that a man gets for this is merely the saving of his soul.

It all seems strange, incredible, impossible. But La Trappe knew the race. He knew the powerful attraction of unattractiveness: he knew that no life could be imagined, howsoever comfortless and forbidding, but somebody would want to try it.

This parent establishment of Germans began its work fifteen years ago, strangers, poor, and unencouraged; it owns 15,000 acres of land now, and raises grain and fruit, and makes wines, and manufactures all manner of things, and has native apprentices in its shops, and sends them forth able to read and write, and also well equipped to earn their living by their trades. And this young establishment has set up eleven branches in South Africa, and in them they are Christianizing and educating and teaching wage-yielding mechanical trades to 1,200 boys and girls. Protestant Missionary work is coldly regarded by the commercial white colonists all over the heathen world, as a rule, and its product is nicknamed "rice-Christians" (occupationless incapables who join the church for revenue only), but I think it would be difficult to pick a flaw in the work of these Catholic monks, and I believe that the disposition to attempt it has not shown itself.

Tuesday, May 12. Transvaal politics in a confused condition. First the sentencing of the Johannesburg Reformers startled England by its severity; on the top of this came Kruger's exposure of the cipher correspondence, which showed that the invasion of the Transvaal, with the design of seizing that country and adding it to the British Empire, was planned by Cecil Rhodes and Beit—which made a revulsion in English feeling, and brought out a storm against Rhodes and the Chartered Company for degrading British honor. For a good while I couldn't seem to get at a clear comprehension of it, it was so tangled. But at last by patient study I have managed it, I believe. As I understand it, the Uitlanders and other Dutchmen were dissatisfied because the English would not allow them to take any part in the government except to pay taxes. Next, as I understand it, Dr. Kruger and Dr. Jameson, not having been able to make the medical business pay, made a raid into Matabeleland with the intention of capturing the capital, Johannesburg, and holding the women and children to ransom until the Uitlanders and the other Boers should grant to them and the Chartered Company the political rights which had been withheld from them. They would have succeeded in this great scheme, as I understand it, but for the interference of Cecil Rhodes and Mr. Beit, and other Chiefs of the Matabele, who persuaded their countrymen to revolt and throw off their allegiance to Germany. This, in turn, as I understand it, provoked the King of Abyssinia to destroy the Italian army and fall back upon Johannesburg; this at the instigation of Rhodes, to bull the stock market.

❦

THE DUKE OF FIFE HAS BORNE TESTIMONY THAT MR. RHODES deceived him. That is also what Mr. Rhodes did with the Reformers. He got them into trouble, and then stayed out himself. A judicious man. He has always been that. As to this there was a moment of doubt, once. It was when he was out on his last pirating expedition in the Matabele country. The cable shouted out that he had gone unarmed, to visit a party of hostile chiefs. It was true, too; and this daredevil thing came near fetching another indiscretion out of the poet laureate. It would have been too bad, for when the facts were all in, it turned out that there was a lady along, too, and she also was unarmed.

In the opinion of many people Mr. Rhodes is South Africa; others think he is only a large part of it. These latter consider that South Africa consists of Table Mountain, the diamond mines, the Johannesburg gold fields, and Cecil Rhodes. The gold fields are wonderful in every way. In seven or eight years they build up, in a desert, a city of a hundred thousand inhabitants, counting white and black together; and not the ordinary mining city of wooden shanties, but a city made out of lasting material. Nowhere in the world is there such a concentration of rich mines as at Johannesburg, Mr. Bonamici, my manager there, gave me a small gold brick with some statistics engraved upon it which record the output of gold from the early days to July, 1895, and exhibit the strides which have been made in the development of the industry: in 1888 the output was $4,162,440; the output of the next five and a half years was (total) $17,585,894; for the single year ending with June, 1895, it was $45,553,700.

The capital which has developed the mines came from England, the mining engineers from America. This is the case with the diamond mines also. South Africa seems to be the heaven of the American scientific mining engineer. He gets the choicest places, and keeps them. His salary is not based upon what he would get in America, but apparently upon what a whole family of him would get there.

The successful mines pay great dividends, yet the rock is not rich, from a Californian point of view. Rock which yields ten or twelve dollars a ton is considered plenty rich enough. It is troubled with base metals to such a degree that twenty years ago it would have been only about half as valuable as it is now; for at that time there was no paying way of getting anything out of such rock but the coarser-grained "free" gold; but the new cyanide process has changed all that, and the gold fields of the world now deliver up fifty million dollars' worth of gold per year which would have gone into the tailing-pile under the former conditions.

The cyanide process was new to me, and full of interest; and among the costly and elaborate mining machinery there were fine things which were new to me, but I was already familiar with the rest of the details of the gold-mining industry. I had been a gold miner myself, in my day, and knew substantially everything that those people knew about it, except how to make money at it. But I learned a good deal about the Boers there, and that was a fresh subject. What I heard there was afterwards repeated to me in other parts of South Africa. Summed up—according to the information thus gained—this is the Boer:

He is deeply religious, profoundly ignorant, dull, obstinate, bigoted, uncleanly in his habits, hospitable, honest in his dealings with the whites, a hard master to his black servant, lazy, a good shot, good horseman, addicted to the chase, a lover of political independence, a good husband and father, not fond of herding together in towns, but liking the seclusion and remoteness and solitude and empty vastness and silence of the veldt; a man of a mighty appetite, and not delicate about what he appeases it with—well satisfied with pork and Indian corn and biltong, requiring only that the quantity shall not be stinted; willing to ride a long journey to take a hand in a rude all-night dance interspersed with vigorous feeding and boisterous jollity, but ready to ride twice as far for a prayer-meeting; proud of his Dutch and Huguenot origin and its religious and military history; proud of his race's achievements in South Africa, its bold plunges into hostile and uncharted deserts in search of free solitudes unvexed by the pestering and detested English, also its victories over the natives and the British; proudest of all, of the direct and effusive personal interest which the Deity has always taken in its affairs. He cannot read, he cannot write; he has one or two newspapers, but he is apparently not aware of it; until latterly he had no schools, and taught his children nothing; news is a term which has no meaning to him, and the thing itself he cares nothing about. He hates to be taxed and resents it. He has stood stock still in South Africa for two centuries and a half, and would like to stand still till the end of time, for he has no sympathy with Uitlander notions of progress. He is hungry to be rich, for he is human; but his preference has been for riches in cattle, not in fine clothes and fine houses and gold and diamonds. The gold and the diamonds have brought the godless stranger within his gates, also contamination and broken repose, and he wishes that they had never been discovered.

I think that the bulk of those details can be found in Olive Schreiner's books, and she would not be accused of sketching the Boer's portrait with an unfair hand.

Now what would you expect from that unpromising material? What ought you to expect from it? Laws inimical to religious liberty? Yes. Laws denying representation and suffrage to the intruder? Yes. Laws unfriendly to educational institutions? Yes. Laws obstructive of gold production? Yes. Discouragement of railway expansion? Yes. Laws heavily taxing the intruder and overlooking the Boer? Yes.

The Uitlander seems to have expected something very different from all that. I do not know why. Nothing different from it was rationally to be expected. A round man cannot be expected to fit a square hole right away. He must have time to modify his shape. The modification had begun in a detail or two, before the Raid, and was making some progress. It has made further progress since. There are wise men in the Boer government, and that accounts for the modification; the modification of the Boer mass has probably not begun yet. If the heads of the Boer government had not been wise men they would have hanged Jameson, and thus turned a very commonplace pirate into a holy martyr. But even their wisdom has its limits, and they will hang Mr. Rhodes if they ever catch him. That will round him and complete him and make him a saint. He has already been called by all other titles that symbolize human grandeur, and he ought to rise to this one, the grandest of all. It will be a dizzy jump from where he is now, but that is nothing, it will land him in good company and be a pleasant change for him.

Some of the things demanded by the Johannesburgers' Manifesto have been conceded since the days of the Raid, and the others will follow in time, no doubt. It was most fortunate for the miners of Johannesburg that the taxes which distressed them so much were levied by the Boer government, instead of by their friend Rhodes and his Chartered Company of highwaymen, for these latter take *half* of whatever their mining victims find, they do not stop at a mere percentage. If the Johannesburg miners were under their jurisdiction they would be in the poor-house in twelve months.

I have been under the impression all along that I had an unpleasant paragraph about the Boers somewhere in my note-book, and also a pleasant one. I have found them now. The unpleasant one is dated at an interior village, and says:

Mr. Z. called. He is an English Afrikander; is an old resident, and has a Boer wife. He speaks the language, and his professional business is with the Boers exclusively. He told me that the ancient Boer families in the great region of which this village is the commercial center are falling victims to their inherited indolence and dullness in the materialistic latter-day race and struggle, and are dropping one by one into the grip of the usurer—getting hopelessly in debt—and are losing their high place and retiring to second and lower. The Boer's farm does not go to another Boer when he loses it, but to a foreigner. Some have fallen so low that they sell their daughters to the blacks.

Under date of another South African town I find the note which is creditable to the Boers:

Dr. X. told me that in the Kafir war 1,500 Kafirs took refuge in a great cave in the mountains about 90 miles north of Johannesburg, and the Boers blocked up the entrance and smoked them to death. Dr. X. has been in there and seen the great array of bleached skeletons—one a woman with the skeleton of a child hugged to her breast.

The great bulk of the savages must go. The white man wants their lands, and all must go excepting such percentage of them as he will need to do his work for him upon terms to be determined by himself. Since history has removed the element of guesswork from this matter and made it certainty, the humanest way of diminishing the black population should be adopted, not the old cruel ways of the past. Mr. Rhodes and his gang have been following the old ways. They are chartered to rob and slay, and they lawfully do it, but not in a compassionate and Christian spirit. They rob the Mashonas and the Matabeles of a portion of their territories in the hallowed old style of "purchase" for a song, and then they force a quarrel and take the rest by the strong hand. They rob the natives of their cattle under the pretext that all the cattle in the country belonged to the king whom they have tricked and assassinated. They issue "regulations" requiring the incensed and harassed natives to work for the white settlers, and neglect their own affairs to do it. This is slavery, and is several times worse than was the American slavery which used to pain England so much; for when this Rhodesian slave is sick, superannuated, or otherwise disabled, he must support himself or starve—his master is under no obligation to support him.

The reduction of the population by Rhodesian methods to the desired limit is a return to the old-time slow-misery and lingering-death system of a discredited time and a crude "civilization." We humanely reduce an overplus of dogs by swift chloroform; the Boer humanely reduced an overplus of blacks by swift suffocation; the nameless but right-hearted Australian pioneer humanely reduced his overplus of aboriginal neighbors by a sweetened swift death concealed in a poisoned pudding. All these are admirable, and worthy of praise; you and I would rather suffer either of these deaths thirty times over in thirty successive days than linger out one of the Rhodesian twenty-year deaths, with its daily burden of insult, humiliation, and forced labor for a man whose entire race the victim hates. Rhodesia is a happy name for that land of piracy and pillage, and puts the right stain upon it.

Several long journeys gave us experience of the Cape Colony railways; easy-riding, fine cars; all the conveniences; thorough cleanliness; comfortable beds furnished for the night trains. It was in the first days of June, and winter; the daytime was pleasant, the night-time nice and cold. Spinning along all day in the cars it was ecstasy to breathe the bracing air and gaze out over the vast brown solitudes of the velvet plains, soft and lovely near by, still softer and lovelier further away, softest and loveliest of all in the remote distances, where dim island-hills seemed afloat, as in a sea—a sea made of dream-stuff and flushed with colors faint and rich; and dear me, the depth of the sky, and the beauty of the strange new cloud-forms, and the glory of the sunshine, the lavishness, the wastefulness of it! The vigor and freshness and inspiration of the air and the sun—well, it was all just as Olive Schreiner had made it in her books.

To me the veldt, in its sober winter garb, was surpassingly beautiful. There were unlevel stretches where it was rolling and swelling, and rising and subsiding, and sweeping superbly on and on, and still on and on like an ocean, toward the far-away horizon, its pale brown deepening by delicately-graduated shades of rich orange, and finally to purple and crimson where it washed against the wooded hills and naked red crags at the base of the sky.

Everywhere, from Cape Town to Kimberley, and from Kimberley to Port Elizabeth and East London, the towns were well populated with tamed blacks; tamed and Christianized too, I suppose, for they wore the dowdy clothes of our Christian civilization. But for that, many of them would have been remarkably handsome. These fiendish clothes, together with the proper lounging gait, good-natured face, happy air, and easy laugh, made them precise counterparts of our American blacks; often where all the other aspects were strikingly and harmoniously and thrillingly African, a flock of these natives would intrude, looking wholly out of place, and spoil it all, making the thing a grating discord, half African and half American.

One Sunday in King William's Town a score of colored women came mincing across the great barren square dressed—oh, in the last perfection of fashion, and newness, and expensiveness, and showy mixture of unrelated colors,—all just as I had seen it so often at home; and in their faces and their gait was that languishing, aristocratic, divine delight in their finery which was so familiar to me, and had always been such a satisfaction to my eye and my heart. I seemed among old, old friends; friends of fifty years, and I stopped and cordially greeted them. They broke into a good-fellowship laugh, flashing their white teeth upon me, and all answered at once. I did not understand a word they said. I was astonished; I was not dreaming that they would answer in anything but American.

The voices, too, of the African women, were familiar to me—sweet and musical, just like those of the slave women of my early days. I followed a couple of them all over the Orange Free State—no, over its capital—Bloemfontein, to hear their liquid voices and the happy ripple of their laughter. Their language was a large improvement upon American. Also upon the Zulu. It had no Zulu click in it; and it seemed to have no angles or corners, no roughness, no vile s's or other hissing sounds, but was very, very mellow and rounded and flowing.

In moving about the country in the trains, I had opportunity to see a good many Boers of the veldt. One day at a village station a hundred of them got out of the third-class cars to feed. Their clothes were very interesting. For ugliness of shapes, and for miracles of ugly colors inharmoniously associated, they were a record.

The effect was nearly as exciting and interesting as that produced by the brilliant and beautiful clothes and perfect taste always on view at the Indian railway stations. One man had corduroy trousers of a faded chewing-gum tint. And they were new—showing that this tint did not come by calamity, but was intentional; the very ugliest color I have ever seen. A gaunt, shackly country lout six feet high, in battered gray slouched hat with wide brim, and old resin-colored breeches, had on a hideous brand-new woolen coat which was imitation tiger skin—wavy broad stripes of dazzling yellow and deep brown. I thought he ought to be hanged, and asked the stationmaster if it could be arranged. He said no; and not only that, but said it rudely; said it with a quite unnecessary show of feeling. Then he muttered something about my being a jackass, and walked away and pointed me out to people, and did everything he could to turn public sentiment against me. It is what one gets for trying to do good.

In the train that day a passenger told me some more about Boer life out in the lonely veldt. He said the Boer gets up early and sets his "niggers" at their tasks (pasturing the cattle, and watching them); eats, smokes, drowses, sleeps; toward evening superintends the milking, etc.; eats, smokes, drowses; goes to bed at early candlelight in the fragrant clothes he (and she) have worn all day and every week-day for years. I remember that last detail, in Olive Schreiner's "Story of an African Farm." And the passenger told me that the Boers were justly noted for their hospitality. He told me a story about it. He said that his grace the Bishop of a certain See was once making a business-progress through the tavernless veldt, and one night he stopped with a Boer; after supper was shown to bed; he undressed, weary and worn out, and was soon sound asleep; in the night he woke up feeling crowded and suffocated, and found the old Boer and his fat wife in bed with him, one on each side, with all their clothes on, and snoring. He had to stay there and stand it—awake and suffering—until toward dawn, when sleep again fell upon him for an hour. Then he woke again. The Boer was gone, but the wife was still at his side.

Those Reformers detested that Boer prison; they were not used to cramped quarters and tedious hours, and weary idleness, and early to bed, and limited movement, and arbitrary and irritating rules, and the absence of the luxuries which wealth comforts the day and night with. The confinement told upon their bodies and their spirits; still, they were superior men, and they made the best that was to be made of the circumstances. Their wives smuggled delicacies to them, which helped to smooth the way down for the prison fare.

In the train Mr. B. told me that the Boer jail-guards treated the black prisoners—even political ones—mercilessly. An African chief and his following had been kept there nine months without trial, and during all that time they had been without shelter from rain and sun. He said that one day the guards put a big black in the stocks for dashing his soup on the ground; they stretched his legs painfully wide apart, and set him with his back down hill; he could not endure it, and put back his hands upon the slope for a support. The guard ordered him to withdraw the support—and kicked him in the back. "Then," said Mr. B., "the powerful black wrenched the stocks asunder and went for the guard; a Reform prisoner pulled him off, and thrashed the guard himself."

NEXT TO MR. RHODES, TO ME THE MOST INTERESTING CON-vulsion of nature in South Africa was the diamond-crater. The Rand gold-fields are a stupendous marvel, and they make all other gold-fields small, but I was not a stranger to gold-mining; the veldt was a noble thing to see, but it was only another and lovelier variety of our Great Plains; the natives were very far from being uninteresting, but they were not new; and as for the towns, I could find my way without a guide through the most of them because I had learned the streets, under other names, in towns just like them in other lands; but the diamond mine was a wholly fresh thing, a splendid and absorbing novelty. Very few people in the world have seen the diamond in its home. It has but three or four homes in the world, whereas gold has a million. It is worth while to journey around the globe to see anything which can truthfully be called a novelty, and the diamond mine is the greatest and most select and restricted novelty which the globe has in stock.

The Kimberley diamond deposits were discovered about 1869, I think. When everything is taken into consideration, the wonder is that they were not discovered five thousand years ago and made familiar to the African world for the rest of time. For this reason the first diamonds were found on the surface of the ground. They were smooth and limpid, and in the sunlight they vomited fire. They were the very things which an African savage of any era would value above every other thing in the world excepting a glass bead. For two or three centuries we have been buying his lands, his cattle, his neighbor, and any other thing he had for sale, for glass beads: and so it is strange that he was indifferent to the diamonds—for he must have picked them up many and many a time. It would not occur to him to try to sell them to whites, of course, since the whites already had plenty of glass beads, and more fashionably shaped, too, than these; but one would think that the poorer sort of black, who could not afford real glass, would have been humbly content to decorate himself with the imitation, and that presently the white trader would notice the things, and dimly suspect, and carry some of them home, and find out what they were, and at once empty a multitude of fortune-hunters into Africa. There are many strange things in human history; one of the strangest is that the sparkling diamonds laid there so long without exciting any one's interest.

The revelation came at last by accident. In a Boer's hut out in the wide solitude of the plains, a traveling stranger noticed a child playing with a bright object, and was told it was a piece of glass which had been found in the veldt. The stranger bought it for a trifle and carried it away; and being without honor, made another stranger believe it was a diamond, and so got $125 out of him for it, and was as pleased with himself as if he had done a righteous thing. In Paris the wronged stranger sold it to a pawnshop for $10,000, who sold it to a countess for $90,000, who sold it to a brewer for $800,000, who traded it to a king for a dukedom and a pedigree, and the king "put it up the spout."* I know these particulars to be correct.

The news flew around, and the South African diamond-boom began. The original traveler—the dishonest one—now remembered that he had once seen a Boer teamster chocking his wagon-wheel on a steep grade with a diamond as large as a football, and he laid aside his occupations and started out to hunt for it, but not with the intention of cheating anybody out of $125 with it, for he had reformed.

We now come to matters more didactic. Diamonds are not imbedded in rock ledges fifty miles long, like the Johannesburg gold, but are distributed through the rubbish of a filled-up well, so to speak. The well is rich, its walls are sharply defined; outside of the walls are no diamonds. The well is a crater, and a large one. Before it had been meddled with, its surface was even with the level plain, and there was no sign to suggest that it was there. The pasturage covering the surface of the Kimberley crater was sufficient for the support of a cow, and the pasturage underneath was sufficient for the support of a kingdom; but the cow did not know it, and lost her chance.

The Kimberley crater is roomy enough to admit the Roman Coliseum; the bottom of the crater has not been reached, and no one can tell how far down in the bowels of the earth it goes. Originally, it was a

*From the Greek [word] meaning "pawned it."

perpendicular hole packed solidly full of blue rock or cement, and scattered through that blue mass, like raisins in a pudding, were the diamonds. As deep down in the earth as the blue stuff extends, so deep will the diamonds be found.

There are three or four other celebrated craters near by—a circle three miles in diameter would enclose them all. They are owned by the De Beers Company, a consolidation of diamond properties arranged by Mr. Rhodes twelve or fourteen years ago. The De Beers owns other craters; they are under the grass, but the De Beers knows where they are, and will open them some day, if the market should require it.

Originally, the diamond deposits were the property of the Orange Free State; but a judicious "rectification" of the boundary line shifted them over into the British territory of Cape Colony. A high official of the Free State told me that the sum of $400,000 was handed to his commonwealth as a compromise, or indemnity, or something of the sort, and that he thought his commonwealth did wisely to take the money and keep out of a dispute, since the power was all on the one side and the weakness all on the other. The De Beers Company digs out $400,000 worth of diamonds per week, now. The Cape got the territory, but no profit; for Mr. Rhodes and the Rothschilds and the other De Beers people own the mines, and they pay no taxes.

In our day the mines are worked upon scientific principles, under the guidance of the ablest mining-engineering talent procurable in America. There are elaborate works for reducing the blue rock and passing it through one process after another until every diamond it contains has been hunted down and secured. I watched the "concentrators" at work—big tanks containing mud and water and invisible diamonds—and was told that each could stir and churn and properly treat 300 carloads of mud per day—1,600 pounds to the carload—and reduce it to three carloads of slush. I saw the three carloads of slush taken to the "pulsators" and there reduced to a quarter of a load of nice clean dark-colored sand. Then I followed it to the sorting tables and saw the men deftly and swiftly spread it out and brush it about and seize the diamonds as they showed up. I assisted, and once I found a diamond half as large as an almond. It is an exciting kind of fishing, and you feel a fine thrill of pleasure every time you detect the glow of one of those limpid pebbles through the veil of dark sand. I would like to spend my Saturday holidays in that charming sport every now and then. Of course there are disappointments. Sometimes you find a diamond which is not a diamond; it is only a quartz crystal or some such worthless thing. The expert can generally distinguish it from the precious stone which it is counterfeiting; but if he is in doubt he lays it on a flatiron and hits it with a sledge-hammer. If it is a diamond it holds its own; if it is anything else, it is reduced to powder. I liked that experiment very much, and did not tire of repetitions of it. It was full of enjoyable apprehensions, unmarred by any personal sense of risk. The De Beers concern treats 8,000 carloads—about 6,000 tons—of blue rock per day, and the result is three pounds of diamonds. Value, uncut, $50,000 to $70,000. After cutting, they will weigh considerably less than a pound, but will be worth four or five times as much as they were before.

All the plain around that region is spread over, a foot deep, with blue rock, placed there by the company, and looks like a plowed field. Exposure for a length of time makes the rock easier to work than it is when it comes out of the mine. If mining should cease now, the supply of rock spread over those fields would furnish the usual 8,000 carloads per day to the separating works during three years. The fields are fenced and watched; and at night they are under the constant inspection of lofty electric searchlight. They contain fifty or sixty million dollars' worth of diamonds, and there is an abundance of enterprising thieves around.

In the dirt of the Kimberley streets there is much hidden wealth. Some time ago the people were granted the privilege of a free wash-up. There was a general rush, the work was done with thoroughness, and a good harvest of diamonds was gathered.

The deep mining is done by natives. There are many hundreds of them. They live in quarters built around the inside of a great compound. They are a jolly and good-natured lot, and accommodating. They performed a war-dance for us, which was the wildest exhibition I have ever seen. They are not allowed outside of the compound during their term of service—three months, I think it is, as a rule. They go down the shaft, stand their watch, come up again, are searched, and go to bed or to their amusements in the compound; and this routine they repeat, day in and day out.

It is thought that they do not now steal many diamonds—successfully. They used to swallow them, and find other ways of concealing them, but the white man found ways of beating their various games. One man cut his leg and shoved a diamond into the wound, but even that project did not succeed. When they find a fine large diamond they are more likely to report it than to steal it, for in the former case they get a reward, and in the latter they are quite apt to merely get into trouble. Some years ago, in a mine not owned by the De Beers, a black found what has been claimed to be the largest diamond known to the world's history; and as a reward he was released from service and given a blanket, a horse, and five hundred dollars. It made him a Vanderbilt. He could buy four wives, and have money left. Four wives are an ample support for a native. With four wives he is wholly independent, and need never do a stroke of work again.

That great diamond weighs 971 carats. Some say it is as big as a piece of alum, others say it is as large as a bite of rock candy, but the best authorities agree that it is almost exactly the size of a chunk of ice. But those details are not important; and in my opinion not trustworthy. It has a flaw in it, otherwise it would be of incredible value. As it is, it is held to be worth $2,000,000. After cutting it ought to be worth from $5,000,000 to $8,000,000, therefore persons desiring to save money should buy it now. It is owned by a syndicate, and apparently there is no satisfactory market for it. It is earning nothing; it is eating its head off. Up to this time it has made nobody rich but the native who found it.

He found it in a mine which was being worked by contract. That is to say, a company had bought the privilege of taking from the mine 5,000,000 carloads of blue rock, for a sum down and a royalty. Their speculation had not paid; but on the very day that their privilege ran out that native found the $2,000,000 diamond and handed it over to them. Even the diamond culture is not without its romantic episodes.

The Koh-i-Noor is a large diamond, and valuable; but it cannot compete in these matters with three which—according to legend—are among the crown trinkets of Portugal and Russia. One of these is held to be worth $20,000,000; another, $25,000,000, and the third something over $28,000,000.

Those are truly wonderful diamonds, whether they exist or not; and yet they are of but little importance by comparison with the one wherewith the Boer wagoner chocked his wheel on that steep grade as heretofore referred to. In Kimberley I had some conversation with the man who saw the Boer do that—an incident which had occurred twenty-seven or twenty-eight years before I had my talk with him. He assured me that that diamond's value could have been over a billion dollars, but not under it. I believed him, because he had devoted twenty-seven years to hunting for it, and was in a position to know.

A fitting and interesting finish to an examination of the tedious and laborious and costly processes whereby the diamonds are gotten out of the deeps of the earth and freed from the base stuffs which imprison them is the visit to the De Beers offices in the town of Kimberley, where the result of each day's mining is brought every day, and weighed, assorted, valued, and deposited in safes against shipping-day. An unknown and unaccredited person cannot get into that place; and it seemed apparent from the generous supply of warning and protective and prohibitory signs that were posted all about that not even the known and accredited can steal diamonds there without inconvenience.

We saw the day's output—shining little nests of diamonds, distributed a foot apart, along a counter, each nest reposing upon a sheet of white paper. That day's catch was about $70,000 worth. In the course of a year half a ton of diamonds pass under the scales there and sleep on that counter; the resulting money is $18,000,000 or $20,000,000. Profit, about $12,000,000.

Young girls were doing the sorting—a nice, clean, dainty, and probably distressing employment. Every day ducal incomes sift and sparkle through the fingers of those young girls; yet they go to bed at night as poor as they were when they got up in the morning. The same thing next day, and all the days.

They are beautiful things, those diamonds, in their native state. They are of various shapes; they have flat surfaces, rounded borders, and never a sharp edge. They are of all colors and shades of color, from dewdrop white to actual black; and their smooth and rounded surfaces and contours, variety of color, and transparent limpidity, make them look like piles of assorted candies. A very light straw color is their commonest tint. It seemed to me that these uncut gems must be more beautiful than any cut ones could be; but when a collection of cut ones was brought out, I saw my mistake. Nothing is so beautiful as a rose diamond with the light playing through it, except that uncostly thing which is just like it—wavy sea-water with the sunlight playing through it and striking a white-sand bottom.

Before the middle of July we reached Cape Town, and the end of our African journeyings. And well satisfied; for, towering above us was Table Mountain—a reminder that we had now seen each and all of the great features of South Africa except Mr. Cecil Rhodes. I realize that that is a large exception. I know quite well that whether Mr. Rhodes is the lofty and worshipful patriot and statesman that multitudes believe him to be, or Satan come again, as the rest of the world account him, he is still the most imposing figure in the British empire outside of England. When he stands on the Cape of Good Hope, his shadow falls to the Zambesi. He is the only colonial in the British dominions whose goings and comings are chronicled and discussed under all the globe's meridians, and whose speeches, unclipped, are cabled from the ends of the earth; and he is the only unroyal outsider whose arrival in London can compete for attention with an eclipse.

That he is an extraordinary man, and not an accident of fortune, not even his dearest South African enemies were willing to deny, so far as I heard them testify. The whole South African world seemed to stand in a kind of shuddering awe of him, friend and enemy alike. It was as if he were deputy-God on the one side, deputy-Satan on the other, proprietor of the people, able to make them or ruin them by his breath, worshiped by many, hated by many, but blasphemed by none among the judicious, and even by the indiscreet in guarded whispers only.

What is the secret of his formidable supremacy? One says it is his prodigious wealth—a wealth whose drippings in salaries and in other ways support multitudes and make them his interested and loyal vassals; another says it is his personal magnetism and his persuasive tongue, and that these hypnotize and make happy slaves of all that drift within the circle of their influence; another says it is his majestic ideas, his vast schemes for the territorial aggrandizement of England, his patriotic and unselfish ambition to spread her beneficent protection and her just rule over the pagan wastes of Africa and make luminous the African darkness with the glory of her name; and another says he wants the earth and wants it for his own, and that the belief that he will get it and let his friends in on the ground floor is *the* secret that rivets so many eyes upon him and keeps him in the zenith where the view is unobstructed.

One may take his choice. They are all the same price. One fact is sure: he keeps his prominence and a vast following, no matter what he does. He "deceives" the Duke of Fife—it is the Duke's word—but that does not destroy the Duke's loyalty to him. He tricks the Reformers into immense trouble with his Raid, but the most of them believe he meant well. He weeps over the harshly-taxed Johannesburgers and makes them his friends; at the same time he taxes his Charter-settlers 50 per cent, and so wins their affection and their confidence that they are squelched with despair at every rumor that the Charter is to be annulled. He raids and robs and slays and enslaves the Matabele and gets worlds of Charter-Christian applause for it. He has beguiled England into buying Charter waste paper for Bank of England notes, ton for ton, and the ravished still burn incense to him as the Eventual God of Plenty. He has done every-thing he could think of to pull himself down to the ground; he has done more than enough to pull sixteen common-run great men down; yet there he stands, to this day, upon his dizzy summit under the dome of the sky, an apparent permanency, the marvel of the time, the mystery of the age, an Archangel with wings to half the world, Satan with a tail to the other half.

I admire him, I frankly confess it; and when his time comes I shall buy a piece of the rope for a keepsake.

J. RAMSAY MacDONALD

The Orange Free State in ruins: 1902

"EVERY MILE OR SO WE CAME UPON THE TALL GUM TREES OR CACTUS HEDGE
OF A FARM, AND IN THE MIDST THE GAUNT BLACKENED GABLES STOOD LIKE
THE GHOSTS OF HAPPY HOMES."

*J. Ramsay MacDonald was a Scotsman who traveled widely in the early
years of the twentieth century. He wrote about his travels and his views for
the* Forward *and also for* Contemporary Review, *the* New Leader, *the*
Nation, *and other publications. Some of his essays "recalling wanderings
in the by-ways of interest and life" were gathered together as* Wanderings
and Excursions, *published in 1925.*

*MacDonald was quite a proper gentleman, but propriety never dulled
his sharp eyes and his equally sharp sense of humor. In one essay, he describes Honolulu as "the most absurd place in the world. It is a top-hat in
the tropics." And setting out on a journey was always exhilarating. "When
you go down to Clapham," he wrote elsewhere, "there is no romance about
Victoria Station. It is sordid and utilitarian. But when your journey is to
be beyond the rim of the world, romance meets you, even at Victoria, and
this noisy dull place becomes like the miserable doorkeeper of a palace."*

*In 1902 MacDonald traveled in South Africa, whose four disparate
parts—the Cape Colony, Natal, the Orange Free State, and the Transvaal—
would not be unified as a nation for another eight years. At the time of
his visit, the Second Boer War, pitting English colonists once more against
Afrikaner settlers, had recently ended with the defeat of the Afrikaners.
MacDonald saw nothing to smile about.*

*Antagonism between South Africa's two groups of settlers went back
a long way. In the early decades of the nineteenth century, Dutch settlers*

in the fertile lands of the Cape area grew increasingly resent
settlers. In the 1830s these Dutch farmers, the Boers, tried t
best of a bad situation. They packed up and moved, slowly
by oxcart to the interior, past the Vaal River. Their migrat
known as the Great Trek and the settlers themselves as the Voortrekke...
By the 1850s, having pushed the indigenous Zulus out of their way, the
Boers were established firmly enough to set up their own independent
republics, the Orange Free State and the Transvaal.

Then in 1867 diamonds were discovered in the interior and old ani-
mosities surfaced along with the precious stones. Each side felt all the
land, and all its vast wealth, should belong to them. Meanwhile, the Zu-
lus increasingly wanted both factions off their land. In 1879 the British
survived fierce battles with the Zulu forces of Cetshwayo at Isandhlwana
and Rorke's Drift, annexed Zululand (in Natal), and imprisoned Cetsh-
wayo. But in the following year they were defeated in the First Anglo-Boer
War.

A few years later, in 1886, gold was discovered at what would soon
become the city of Johannesburg. And by 1899, the Second Anglo-Boer
War had begun, lasting until 1902. By then, everyone had had enough,
and the Union of South Africa was finally established in 1910. Unfortu-
nately for the nation's future, the entire black population—the Zulu,
Xhosa, and other tribes—was excluded from all participation.

MacDonald provides a vivid picture of what was left when the fight-
ing was over and the smoke was only just beginning to clear.

WE TRIED TO GET ACROSS FROM MAFEKING TO JOHAN-
nesburg by cart, but there were no horses to be had. Then we tried
to cross in the same way from Kimberley to Bloemfontein, but so scarce
were horses and fodder that we were asked £30 for a Cape cart and two
horses, the usual price, we were told, being not more than £4 at the most.
But even then we were informed that we could have no guarantee that
we would be taken further than Boshof, not half-way to Bloemfontein,
as horse disease had broken out and communications might be cut off.
When at Pretoria we tried to arrange to drive from Barberton through
the Eastern Transvaal to Standerton, but reports came in from the districts we desired to pass through that everything was laid waste, that no

sport could be got, that there was not a scrap of food to be had. .aving had to abandon that route we were then anxious to leave the train at Standerton and drive thence and back to Ermelo. But we failed in making arrangements. Ermelo was completely destroyed. It had neither shelter nor food, and though we were prepared to take both with us, we again found it impossible to get horses.

Our next attempt at getting away from the railway was to drive westwards across the Orange River Colony from Harrismith to Kroonstad. This we accomplished. Our first stop was Bethlehem. Round the village so far as we could see not a farmhouse was standing, and on the way thither we passed the site of what were prosperous stores, but only a heap of stones marked where they had been. All had been burned. About one-fifth of the village itself had been destroyed, the houses on the outlying streets having been pulled to pieces to provide fuel for the troops; but when remarking upon the deplorable destruction, we were told that Bethlehem had suffered least of the villages in that part of the Colony. Starting from Bethlehem, we drove eastwards to Lindley. Our road lay through splendid grazing ground with frequent farms. Every one had been burned with the exception of Malan's farm by the False River, which had been used as a hospital up to the peace. The sad dreariness of that sunny Sunday drive will haunt me to my dying day. Every mile or so we came upon the tall gum trees or cactus hedge of a farm, and in the midst the gaunt blackened gables stood like the ghosts of happy homes. Sometimes the trees had been cut down, and the black ruins lay bare to the eye of anyone passing within half a dozen miles of the spot. A Kaffir kraal now and again, a stray white man wandering about amongst the ruins or over the empty fields, only added to the sense of desolation.

We outspanned for our morning meal in the garden of the General who had entertained us the previous evening in Bethlehem. His peach trees threw out scraggy blossoms from the thick, tall yellow reeds, the stumps of his gum trees stood rotting in the ground, his water dams were broken. His house, a substantial building of well-dressed stone, stood a grey ruin. When we walked up to what had been his front door, lizards scuttled away beneath the stones. Lying embedded in ashes was the iron framework of an upright grand piano, with its wires twisted over it in an entangling mass. The iron handles lay where they had fallen in the fire. Picture nails, brass studs, all the little metal knick-knacks of the best room of a well-to-do Boer, lay in the ashes just where they had fallen, and as though in grim irony, a copy of a Royal Reader, in English, fluttered only half-consumed in the kitchen doorway. The house had been burned in order to punish the General.

That evening we outspanned on the edge of the church square of Lindley. It was dark when we got there, but against the sky we could see roofless houses around us. Thanks to the genial hospitality of one of the heartiest and most typical Scotsmen it has ever been my good fortune to meet, we supped sumptuously from tins, in a room just reclaimed from ruins. It was roofed over with pieces of corrugated iron picked up on the streets; its window, from which the frames had been burnt out, was stuffed with sandbags. We made a strange company, and our host's tales of the war, and especially of the Highland Brigade, told in a Doric which had lost none of its richness by long contact with the veldt, mingled well with our strange surroundings. When I returned after midnight to my wagon to sleep, half a dozen Kaffirs squatted round a smoky fire in what used to be the yard of the hotel; my own men had covered themselves up under the wagon, and in the starlight I saw the heap of ruins which was all that remained of one of the prettiest villages of the Orange Free State.

When I woke next morning and looked out it was as though I had slept among some of the ancient ruins of the desert. Every house, without a single exception, was burnt; the church in the square was burnt. Had I been there a week before I should have had the place to myself. Before the war, Lindley was an Arcadia embowered in trees; now it lay shadeless on the yellow, parched veldt slope. A few faithful peach blossoms from blasted and broken branches struggled to respond to the warm touch of spring, and managed to throw a shimmer of pink amidst some of the ruins. The place had stood practically untouched, although taken and retaken many times, until February 1902, when a column entered it un-molested, found it absolutely deserted, and proceeded to burn it. The houses are so separated from each other by gardens that the greatest care must have been taken to set every one alight. From inquiries which I made from our officers and from our host, who was the chief intelligence officer for the district, there was no earthly reason why Lindley should have been touched. When burnt it was a more advantageous fighting ground for the Republicans than when intact, and the destruction done fell more heavily upon our friends than upon our enemies.

From Lindley we drove to Kroonstad. Once more the land was des-olate, and the farms invariably burned. A member of the South African Constabulary, a company of soldiers, a transport Repatriation Board wagon with a team of the most miserable and disease-eaten mules I ever saw, a family of Boers living in tents by a burnt farm near a drift, block-houses, trenches, barbed wire entanglements, were all we saw until the sun sank and left us in darkness, just within sight of the lights of Kroon-stad.

For three days—the 4th, 5th and 6th of October—we drove about 150 miles. The country was as waste as the edge of the Sahara; almost the only cattle we saw were carcasses rotting on the wayside; we passed only one farmhouse that was intact; we stopped at two villages, about one-fifth of one being destroyed, and of the other not a single roof re-mained. Some Kaffirs had broken up mealie patches in one or two places, but with that exception we could see nothing to show that a plough or a hoe had been put in the ground; and the sowing time was almost over.

E. ALEXANDER POWELL

Johannesburg, a laundry empire, and the Cullinan Diamond: ca. 1910

"STANDING BENEATH THE PORTE-COCHÈRE OF THE PALATIAL CARLTON HOTEL,
ONE COULD HEAR THE CLICK OF ROULETTE BALLS, THE RAUCOUS SCRAPE OF
FIDDLES, AND THE SHOUTS OF DRUNKEN MINERS ISSUING FROM A ROW OF
GAMBLING HELLS, DANCE HALLS, AND GIN PALACES."

*E. Alexander Powell was an American diplomat who traveled the world in
the consular service. Between travels he retreated to his home in Chevy
Chase, Maryland, where he found time to be a very prolific author.
Among his books were more than a dozen volumes on history and world
politics, including five on what was known in the twenties and thirties as
"the Great War." He also wrote more than a dozen volumes recounting his
travels and adventures around the world. As the following excerpt from his
1932* Yonder Lies Adventure! *shows, he had friends and contacts everywhere and an endless supply of stories to dine out on, including an in-
structive one about laundry.*

*At the time of which he writes, around 1910, Johannesburg was barely
a quarter of a century old. There was nothing there at all until gold was
discovered in 1886.*

*The Rand Club he mentions is still there, at the intersection of Love-
day, Commissioner, and Fox Streets. It began as little more than a shack
at this same location and Cecil Rhodes was one of the original directors.
The French Renaissance structure was built in 1904.*

THE LONG RAIL JOURNEY FROM THE ZAMBEZI TO Johannesburg was dusty, tedious, and uninteresting, but little we cared, for ahead of us lay "Joburg," the golden city, the metropolis of the Rand. I don't know what changes have taken place in Johannesburg in the twenty years since I was there, but in my time it was a city of contrasts, where European civilization met and mingled with the Last Frontier. Standing beneath the porte-cochère of the palatial Carlton Hotel, one could hear the click of roulette balls, the raucous scrape of fiddles, and the shouts of drunken miners issuing from a row of gambling hells, dance halls, and gin palaces still housed in one-story buildings of corrugated iron. A beplumed and bepainted Zulu would haul you in a rickshaw over asphalt pavements as clean as those of Fifth Avenue to a theater where you had the privilege of paying Metropolitan Opera House prices to witness much the same sort of performance you would see in a music hall on the Bowery. In the Rand Club, bronzed and booted prospectors, fresh from the mining districts of the Transvaal, Rhodesia, or the Congo, leaned upon the bar, said to be the longest in the world, rubbing shoulders with sleek, immaculately groomed financiers from Capel Court and Wall Street. In those unregenerate days Johannesburg was a spendthrift city, a place of easy-come and easy-go, for the mine workers were paid big wages, the mine managers received big salaries, the mine owners made big profits, and they all spent their money as readily as they made it.

Before leaving the United States a New York friend had given us a letter of introduction to one of the leading business men of Johannesburg, an American by the name of—well, suppose we call him Ryder. Upon calling at his office, however, I was informed that he was out of town.

The night of our departure for Cape Town, having packed our belongings, we had gone down to the restaurant for dinner when Ryder's card was brought in. I went out into the lobby to meet a slender, bearded man in the early forties, very brisk, very American.

"I only learned that you were in town an hour ago upon my return from Pretoria," he informed me. "Mrs. Ryder and I want you and your wife to come out to the house and make us a visit."

"I should like nothing better," I replied, "but, unfortunately, we are leaving by to-night's mail train for Cape Town."

"No, you're not," he assured me breezily. "I saw your luggage at the porter's desk when I came in, so I took the liberty of having it put in my car and of canceling your sleeping-car reservations. So stop making excuses and come along. My wife would never forgive me if I let you get away. I just won't take no for an answer."

Talk about your Southern hospitality! It has nothing on that of South Africa. We accepted the Ryders' invitation in the spirit in which it was given and spent a delightful week with them at their beautiful home in the outskirts of Johannesburg.

The story of Ryder's amazing rise to fortune is interesting, because it illustrates what could be accomplished by determination and energy in the South Africa of thirty-odd years ago.

In the late '90s Ryder was employed in a steam laundry in Chicago, operating a washing machine. One suffocatingly hot summer's day he and a fellow employee were lunching together in a cheap restaurant.

"Bill," said young Ryder, "I'm dead sick of Chicago and the laundry business. Hanged if I can see any future in it. Why don't we break away before we get into a rut? I have a few hundred dollars in the bank, and I guess you have a little saved up, so suppose we pool our resources and strike out for ourselves. How about it?"

"It's O.K. with me, Jim," replied the other. "The smell of hot steam and dirty clothing makes me sick at my stomach. But where shall we go? New York? San Francisco?"

"Hell, no!" said Ryder. "We wouldn't be any better off than we are here. There's been quite a lot in the papers lately about South Africa. They call it the 'Land of Opportunity' and I guess it is. From all I can gather, conditions out there are very much as they were in California in gold-rush days. Plenty of work at high wages for every one."

Unfortunately for the ambitious young Americans, however, they reached Cape Town at a singularly unpropitious moment. England had just declared war against the Boers; an army had set sail for Table Bay; the colony was in a turmoil; the British in the Rand had made a hasty exodus; the streets of the cities were filled with refugees vainly seeking employment. Try as they would, Ryder and his companion could not find work and their meager resources were rapidly dwindling. Soon they were on their uppers.

Meanwhile tens of thousands of British, Canadian, and Australian soldiers were disembarking from the transports. The streets of Cape Town were filled with men in sun helmets and khaki. Shortly arrived General Sir Redvers Buller to take command of the great offensive which was being prepared against the Boers.

"Bill," said Ryder, as they were dressing one morning in their frowzy boarding house to face another day of discouragement, "I have an idea. How much money have you left?"

"A couple of pounds and some odd silver."

"Hand it over, will you? That is, if you're willing to take a chance."

"Sure. I'll take a chance. We can't be much worse off than we are anyway."

Adding his own slender resources to those borrowed from his friend, Ryder bought himself a neat but inexpensive suit, a new pair of shoes, a hat, and fresh linen. Trim and prosperous looking, he made his way to British G.H.Q. and sent in his card to General Buller with a message that he had a matter of important business to discuss with him. After hours of waiting the American's patience was rewarded.

"Well, sir," snapped the famous soldier, when Ryder was ushered in, "I understand that you wish to see me on a matter of important business. You must be brief. I am a very busy man."

Ryder had rehearsed what he was going to say, and he wasted no time in coming to the point.

"General Buller," he began, "it is commonly reported that the British army in South Africa will soon number a quarter of a million men. What arrangements have you made for washing the clothing of those men?"

"Why," stammered the commander-in-chief, slightly taken aback, "I really haven't had time to give the matter consideration. I suppose they will wash their own clothes, or find natives to do their washing for them, as they did in India and the Sudan."

"Nonsense," the American said boldly. "Conditions are entirely different here in South Africa than they were in earlier campaigns. You are putting a huge army into the field. They will be fighting on the hot and dusty veldt. Unless they are provided with clean garments regularly they are bound to contract disease—their morale will go down."

"I hadn't thought of that," the general admitted. "I have had many other things on my mind."

"I have had a long experience in the laundry business," continued Ryder. (He saw no necessity of explaining that his experience had consisted in running a washing machine.) "I am familiar with every detail of it. I have worked out a scheme for field laundries which can move with the armies and keep your men supplied with clean clothing."

"God bless my soul!" exclaimed Buller. "Your suggestion is worth considering, young man. We'll have the quartermaster-general in and discuss it with him."

Incredible as it may sound, the youthful and unknown American succeeded in obtaining a contract to wash the clothing of the British Army in South Africa. When he presented this to the Cape Town representative of a great American bank, the latter was only too willing to finance the undertaking. Rush orders for machinery were cabled to manufacturers in the United States and within a few months the British soldiers fighting on the veldt and the sick and wounded in the hospitals were being regularly supplied with clean clothing, thanks to the resourcefulness and energy of an American.

After the war, Ryder remained on in South Africa, investing the money paid him by the British Government in a chain of steam laundries which stretched right across the country from Bulawayo to Bloemfontein. Later he established a number of dry-cleaning plants, for soap and water won't clean everything. The milliners of Paris decreed that the hats of smartly dressed women must be adorned with ostrich plumes, so, in order to meet the demand, Ryder bought a couple of ostrich farms. Within ten years after he had landed, unknown and almost penniless, at Cape Town, he had become one of the rich men of the Rand. He was offered the nomination for mayor of Johannesburg if he would become a British subject, in which case, it was hinted, a knighthood was in store for him.

"I am deeply honored by your offer, gentlemen," he is said to have replied to the delegation of citizens who waited on him, "but I shouldn't feel comfortable if I were to be addressed as 'Your Honor' or 'Sir James.' I prefer to remain a plain American laundryman."

In my time Pretoria was a capital in embryo, the imposing buildings which now house the government of the Union of South Africa then being in course of construction. Thirty miles northward across the veldt from Pretoria was the great hole in the ground known as the Premier Diamond Mine, then the newest and potentially the richest in South Africa. Here, in January, 1905, the surface manager, a Scotsman named McHardy, while strolling through the pit during the noon hour, saw the sparkle of what he at first thought to be a broken bottle. Prying it loose with his stick from the rubble in which it was embedded, he found it to be a diamond as large as a medium-sized grapefruit. Thrusting it into his pocket, he hastened to the offices of the mine. "Until I saw that bit o' carbon in the office safe," McHardy told me, "I was a vairy nairvous mon."

This remarkable stone, the largest diamond ever found, more than three times the size of any known stone, has since become known to the world as the Great Cullinan, being named after Sir Thomas Cullinan, one of the owners of the mine. Upon being cut it proved to be a pure white stone, 4 by 2¼ by 2 inches, weighing 3,025 carats, or 1.37 pounds. As the surface cleavage showed that it was undoubtedly a fragment of a much larger crystal, one cannot but wonder what the original stone was like.

The Great Cullinan was immediately purchased by the Transvaal Government—or, rather, the mine's share was purchased, for the government receives sixty per cent of the value of all diamonds found—and presented to King Edward. The question then arose of how a gem of such enormous value could be transported to England in safety, for no sooner was the news of its discovery made public than the master criminals of the world began laying plans to obtain possession of it. After many discussions and innumerable comments and an enormous amount of newspaper publicity, four men, armed to the teeth, left the Premier Mine, carrying with them a leather dispatch case. Crossing the thirty miles of open veldt to Pretoria under heavy escort, they boarded a special car attached to the mail train for Cape Town. In the liner by which they took passage to England a safe had been specially installed and in it was placed the dispatch case, two of the men remaining on duty beside the safe night and day. From Southampton a special train took them up to London and a strong guard of police and detectives escorted them to the bank at which the diamond was to be delivered. When the dispatch box was opened in the presence of a group of expectant officials it was found to contain nothing more valuable than a lump of coal! The stone itself had been wrapped in cotton wool and tissue paper, put in a cardboard box, and sent to England by parcels post, not even the postmaster-general being given an inkling that it was in the mails. I almost forgot to mention that McHardy, the discoverer of the great stone, was given a bonus of two thousand pounds, though it is a sad and peculiar commentary that within a year his wife died, the bank in which he put the money failed, and his house burned down.

FRANK G. CARPENTER

Victoria Falls: 1923

"AS WE STAND UPON THE BRIDGE, A TOWER OF GREEN ROCKS RISES BEFORE
US, BISECTING THE NARROW GORGE, AND THE WHOLE FLOOD OF THE
ZAMBESI BOILS AND SEETHES BELOW."

*Victoria Falls, named by the explorer and missionary David Livingstone in
1855, is not in South Africa. It is far to the north, on the Zambezi River,
which at that point forms the border between Zimbabwe (formerly Rhodesia) and Zambia (formerly Northern Rhodesia). But the famous sight, a
must for tourists to the region, is on the area's main railroad line, the old
Cape-to-Cairo route dreamed of by Cecil Rhodes, and is the northern ter-
minus of South Africa's luxury Blue Train.*

*In the first decades of the twentieth century, in a world without films
and television, readers treasured books like the fourteen volumes of Carpenter's World Travels. While there was certainly no lack of travel writing—indeed, travel literature is one of the nineteenth century's great gifts
to the twentieth—the publisher Doubleday, Page managed to present
Frank G. Carpenter as if he were one of the previous century's most popular lecturers on distant and exotic climes. His books were also endorsed
and distributed by the Chautauqua Home Reading Service as part of the
Chautauqua Institution's self-improvement program. They covered the
world and included such titles as* The Holy Land and Syria, Cairo to
Kisumu, Java and the East Indies, *and* Uganda to the Cape, *from which
the following selection is taken.*

*The Zambezi at this point is not as wide as Carpenter thought it, but
it is nearly a mile in width and the river drops four hundred feet. The
railroad bridge that Carpenter describes, completed in 1905, is still there.*

While he notes that Cecil Rhodes personally insisted on the exact location
of the bridge, he doesn't clearly explain why. Rhodes wanted it so close to
the thundering waters that spray from the falls would actually strike every
train that crossed.

ONE OF THE GRANDEST NATURAL WONDERS OF OLD
Mother Earth is out here in Africa. It is the falls of the mighty
Zambesi, one of the great rivers of the globe. It has been compared to
Niagara, though I find it almost impossible to liken one to the other.
Each is beautiful beyond description, but as a raging convulsion of Na-
ture, I should call Victoria Falls by far the more wonderful. The two may
be compared to a play. Niagara is a drama of but one act. Victoria has
many acts, each of which has several scenes.

The falls of Niagara surpass the Victoria Falls of the Zambesi in
volume, for over them pours the water-shed of half a continent. The great
basin of Lake Superior is six hundred feet above the Atlantic, and almost
one third of its drop is at Niagara. The Zambesi has its source in a swamp
a mile above the sea, and its waters have fallen two thousand feet in their
course of eight hundred miles before they make their mighty leap into
this basaltic gorge.

The Victoria Falls are twice as broad and more than twice as high
as Niagara. The river is two miles wide above the falls, and it narrows to
a mile where it plunges straight down over the cliffs into a gorge more
than four hundred feet deep. I could hear the thunder of its waters when
ten miles away, and the spray that rises up in five great columns known
as the "Five Fingers" can be seen fifty miles away. The natives call the
falls "Thundering Smoke," and from time immemorial the atmosphere of
mystery and superstition has hung over them. When Livingstone wanted
guides to help him explore them, he could hardly induce any of the blacks
to go along. The natives believed the region to be the home of terrible
demons and monsters of destruction. The Arab name for the place was
Musa-i-nunya, or "the end of the world."

Victoria Falls is in the heart of the wilderness. The only signs of
civilization in the vicinity are a hotel, the railroad station, a post office,

and a few bungalows. All the rest is forest filled with wild game. There are birds of strange plumage in the trees, and the great river itself is the home of many hippopotami. Standing upon the porch of the hotel near the falls, one looks for miles over land densely wooded. With a powerful glass he can see nothing but this vast expanse of green, broken only by the windings of the gorge at his feet and by the five pillars of mist that rise like the vapour from volcanoes until lost in the low-hanging clouds.

All the land within a radius of five miles of the falls has been set aside as a public park, which is to be left as Nature made it. Outside that radius is a reserve stretching for fifteen miles along one side of the river, and on the other side is a block of forest fifty miles square. No shooting is permitted in the woods, and no one is allowed to build so much as a farmhouse or any other structure that might detract from the natural beauty of the scene.

Notwithstanding all this, the Victoria Falls may be visited with almost as much comfort as Niagara. There are now trains de luxe, with dining cars, observation cars, and bathing accommodations, to bring one from Cape Town or Beira, while the hotel here would not be out of place in southern California. I have a suite of four rooms, including parlour, dressing room, bedroom, and bathroom. My apartment is lighted by electricity and cooled by an electric fan. The parlour has luxurious furniture and rugs, and even boasts a piano. The rate I pay for myself and my son is not extravagant, considering that we are off in the jungle. Besides our usual three meals every day, we have a cup of coffee on rising and afternoon tea. Our table waiters are natives in uniform, and our chambermen are black boys in white gowns.

But come with me and take a look at the falls. We shall first stroll down to the bridge that crosses the gorge through which the mighty river flows after it leaves the falls. You have probably heard of this bridge, which is one of the highest in the world. It was made in England and brought out here in sections. Although seven hundred white men and two thousand natives were employed in erecting it, so carefully was the work done that it cost the lives of only one European and one native. It is four hundred feet above the water and has a span of five hundred and fifty feet. It is so close to the falls that drops of spray fall upon the trains as they pass, and travellers have a glimpse of the cataract from the car windows. This is due entirely to Cecil Rhodes, who, in spite of his engineers' statement that the bridge could not be built so near the falls, insisted upon its being located where he wanted it.

As we stand upon the bridge, a tower of green rocks rises before us, bisecting the narrow gorge, and the whole flood of the Zambesi boils and seethes below. The yellow waters look like a vat of steaming molasses. Opposite the tower is another mass of green, far down in a second gorge. It contains palms, date trees, tree ferns, baobabs, and a jungle of smaller vegetation. It is known as the palm *kloof*, and is a great botanical garden kept only by Nature, and inhabited by monkeys and baboons.

Leaving the bridge, we take our first view of the cataract from its eastern end. The way is along green paths, under green trees, where the ground is so level that we cannot see the falls until we are close to them. The huge torrent bursts upon our vision all at once. It dashes over the rocks with a roar like a cannonade of artillery. The mist is so dense that we can see only a third of the distance across.

The sun is shining through the spray and there are rainbows above and below us, and in the great gorge itself. One a thousand feet long has stretched itself from wall to wall about three hundred feet under where we are standing. Its colours are more gorgeous than those of any rainbow I have ever seen. A child stood here the other day and asked her father why men did not lower themselves over the rocks by ropes and get the great bags of gold that the fairies say are always hidden at the ends of the rainbow.

Our next trip is to the Devil's Cascade, on the other end of the falls. To reach it, we must cross the bridge and walk through the park for about two miles. As we proceed, we frighten the monkeys, and strange birds fly about our heads. A thick mist is falling, and again we cannot see the cataract until we are right upon it. We sit down opposite the lip of the falls and watch the mighty waters pouring over the black rocks in volumes of yellow foam. The Zambesi is now muddy, because the river is in flood. In front of us is the great pit into which it falls, a vast cavern hundreds of feet deep. We cannot see its bottom, for out of it is rising such a volume of mist as exists nowhere else in the world. The western end of the falls is cut off from the main portion by Cataract Island, which lies several hundred feet out in the river. This western cataract alone is greater than any fall in Switzerland. It is only a little section of the Zambesi, but if it could be carried to the Alps it would be one of the wonders of Europe that tourists would travel thousands of miles to see.

The most remarkable view of Victoria Falls is from Livingstone Island, which divides the Zambesi in its centre. It is on the very edge of the falls, and when the river is high there is hardly a perceptible mark of division, the great cascade seemingly going down in one mighty sheet.

The island can be reached without danger only when the river is low. The water is now much too high for safety, but I was not aware of this at the time or I should not have thought of making the trip which I shall now describe.

Above the falls the Zambesi is two miles wide and full of green islands covered with a dense growth of papyrus and small trees. The banks are low, and as we made our way up the river we saw the spoor of many hippopotami. We did not attempt to embark in our canoe until we were perhaps a mile above the falls. Where we started, the water was quiet. For canoemen we had four half-naked blacks with bracelets on their arms and bands of wire tied around their legs between the knee and the calf. As we made our way out into the stream, we could see little droves of hippopotami swimming about. They looked so much like the rocks that only when they raised their black heads did we know what they were. Our boatmen were afraid of them, so we paddled off to one side. We went by one beast that threw its head high into the air and opened its mouth almost in our faces. It looked as though a side of beef had been split in half. The teeth were as big around as my wrist, and I could see the great white tusks embedded in the red jaws.

When we reached the middle of the river the canoemen stopped paddling. Our speed increased in the swift current and we had trouble making our way among the rocks. We soon came into the line of the spray, which fell like rain. The thunder of the waters was now so great that we had to yell to make ourselves heard. We seemed to be rushing right into the Devil's Cascade. After a number of narrow escapes, we fought our way out of the current and came to the black rocks of Livingstone Island. Here we fastened the boat and waded through the woods and across the pools to the knife edge of rock over which the Zambesi pours in its mighty plunge.

If you could double the height and width of Niagara, and then imagine yourself standing in its centre upon a space barely wide enough for your feet, with the raging cataract on each side, you might realize my position as I stood there. I was on a little section of bare black rock in the midst of the great torrent. All around, above and below me, was a fog so thick that I could see beyond it only when it was parted by the wind. There were times when I could not see ten feet in front of me. Then the mist would break, and I looked down into a bottomless pit filled with clouds that rose for a half mile up into the sky.

The mist dropped as a warm rain that, notwithstanding my rubber coat, drenched me to the skin. I tried to take notes, but the water obliterated the pencil marks as fast as I made them. I shut my memorandum book and put it into the pocket of my waterproof. When I took it out it was almost a pulp. The water had filled the pockets and I carried a quart or so with me back to the land.

Holding tight to the rocks, I picked my way along the edge of the falls as far as I could, looking down into the gorge now and then as the wind blew away the mist. I was peeping into an inferno, a roaring, foaming, raging hell that needed only brimstone and flame to fit it for the devil and the damned. I did not dare look long for fear a sudden desire might cause me to jump into the boiling mass—down, down, down, into that wide gorge up which the winds were hurling those clouds of spray.

It was from this island, which the natives called Kempongo, that David Livingstone had his first view of the cataract in 1855. He reached it in a canoe from the upper Zambesi. Noticing how many trees grew there in the rich soil kept continually moist by the spray from the falls, he christened it Garden Island and tried an orchard experiment. He planted, he says in his own account, "about a hundred peach and apricot stones and a quantity of coffee seeds. When the garden was prepared," he goes on, "I cut my initials on a tree, and the date 1855. That was the only instance in which I indulged in this piece of vanity."

To-day the Name Tree is still pointed out, although the initials and date are not really legible. There is little doubt as to the identity of the tree, however, as it was indicated years afterward by an old native who knew Livingstone and saw him cut the initials there. It has had to be surrounded by a guard to keep off tourists, by no means so modest as Livingstone, who not only wished to cut their initials in its trunk, but had begun to strip off and carry away pieces of its bark. There are no traces now of the garden, which Livingstone had hoped might prove the "parent of all the gardens that may yet be in this new country." Probably, as he feared, it was destroyed by the hippopotami.

While returning to the mainland, we several times narrowly escaped going over the falls. To keep us out of the current, the Negro boys who paddled us had to get out several times and lift the canoe through shallow places in the rapids. By wading and pushing, paddling and fighting the rocks, we at last got into smooth water, and, tired out, came back to the banks whence we had started. Although I consider the excursion one of the greatest experiences of my life, I feel much like the Texas father who, having just been blessed with his eleventh child, said:

"I would not take a million dollars for this one, but I would not give a nickel for another."

After exploring the great rocks lying in front of the falls, we walked through the Rain Forest, which the natives call "the place where the rain is born." It is a jungle of woods where day in and day out, for the greater part of the year, the leaves always drip. It is wet by the spray from the falls, and one cannot keep dry in it without rubber clothing. Whenever the wind blew, the drops became a shower. The vegetation was dense, but at the breaks in the woods the sun found its way in and turned the spray to a veil of fine lace. The raindrops on the leaves sparkled like jewels, and here and there were little rainbows extending from one tree to another.

In summer the forest is filled with flowers heavy with perfumes and rich in colour. There are yellow gladioli with blossoms so shaped that the spray cannot get inside them, tree orchids that seem almost to float from the branches, and great masses of pink and yellow and purple and crimson flowers that would make a botanist rave with delight. In this region, too, one may see the Musungula tree with its large brown and gold blooms. The bird that feeds on the insects in these flowers has wings that match the petals. In winter the great seed pods are sometimes four feet long. They are shaped like clubs and are so heavy that the natives are afraid to sleep under the tree for fear of being killed by falling pods.

Hundreds of thousands of horse-power are going to waste in the Victoria Falls every day, and the time is probably not far distant when this energy will be caught in hydro-electric plants and put to work. The flow of water over the falls is not the same the year round, and the available energy has been estimated at from three hundred thousand to six hundred thousand horse-power, depending upon the season. In addition to the four hundred-foot drop at the falls, there is another drop of seven hundred feet in the first fifteen miles of the gorges below. How soon this vast water-power will be developed depends largely upon the need for power in this region. The Victoria Falls and Transvaal Power Company, which is supplying the present demand for both electricity and the compressed air used in mining, will undoubtedly put to work the mighty power of the Zambesi as soon as conditions make it profitable.

A. W. WELLS

The Cape Peninsula and
Cape Town: late 1930s

"SEA POINT MIGHT BE CALIFORNIA, ST JAMES THE SOUTH OF FRANCE,
MUIZENBERG AUSTRALIA, KALK BAY AND SIMONSTOWN LITTLE FISHING PORTS
TUMBLED OUT OF CORNWALL OR DEVON."

*When the great travel writer H. V. Morton visited South Africa in 1948,
one of the books he carried with him was* South Africa *by A. W. Wells,
published in London by J. M. Dent in 1939. That should be recommenda-
tion enough for anyone else.*

*Wells's book is subtitled "A planned tour of the country to-day de-
scribing its towns, its scenic beauties, its wild and its historic places, and
telling of the men who made or discovered them." It also has "32 pages of
Coloured Maps," "30 Photogravure Illustrations," a reference section of
"Places and Things to See," a "Chronological Table of the Chief Events
in South Africa," an Afrikaans glossary, a bibliography, and an index. It's
still a handy book to have.*

In his preface, Wells describes South Africa *as "an attempt to combine the readability of a travel book and the usefulness of a guide-book: a
book which may be read in the home, the ship, or the train, completely
and without break, and yet be found valuable for reference in whatever
centre the South African may decide to holiday, or at whatever place the
ship or train of the overseas visitor may stop."*

*It is not, to be truthful, the sort of book that would normally find
a place in these Reader's Companion volumes, but its portrait of Cape
Town and the Cape Drive are so vivid and richly detailed, so thoroughly*

capturing a particular place at a particular time, that it absolutely belongs here.

The Cape Drive, which Wells so fully describes, has won a symphony of praise over the years. Mark Twain, like all visitors, admired "the beautiful sea-girt drives that wind about the mountains and through the paradise where the villas are."

Robben Island, however, is another story. The island, about seven miles off Cape Town, has been home to some of South Africa's least fortunate and happy people. It was first used as a penal colony for recalcitrant slaves in the seventeenth century, and since then has housed paupers, lepers, the insane, and criminals (black only), who were made to work in the island's limestone quarries. More recently, it was reserved as a place to isolate political prisoners, including Walter Sisulu and Nelson Mandela. Mandela spent nearly twenty years here, from 1963 to 1982, when, under the pressure of worldwide public sentiment, he was moved to another, somewhat less harsh, prison until his eventual release in 1990. During the years that Mandela spent on Robben Island, together with a large number of the country's political prisoners, the authorities found it necessary to rotate their guards more often than usual. The guards, it was discovered, could not help being influenced by the arguments of men they found so intelligent, reasonable, and decent.

Some of Cape Town's finest and oldest buildings are constructed of limestone blocks quarried from Robben Island.

THE CAPE POINT DRIVE

I

THE HOLIDAY SEASON IN CAPE TOWN IS FROM OCTOBER to March, exactly the reverse, of course, of what it is in the northern hemisphere, and during those months the average number of days on which rain falls is six.

Hotels and boarding-houses charge anything from 6s. 6d. to 27s. 6d. a day. Luxurious, first-class hotel accommodation can be had at from £7 7s. to £8 8s. a week, and good average boarding-house accommodation at from £3 3s. to £5 5s. a week, or £10 10s. to £12 12s. a month. If you are coming entirely new to the place, and are staying for some length of time, it might be quite a good idea to pick out a place, more or less at random, and suitable to your pocket, and stay there a day or two and look round before deciding on the place where you would like to spend the great proportion of your stay.

For this is where Cape Town differs from so many other cities: maybe altogether unlike any city you have known before. Because of that great, solid old mountain that can never be shifted (and no South African could be found to raise a pick on it if it could), Cape Town is not, and never can be, a compact, solid, square-like city on the European model. It is a long, straggling series of suburbs, stretching for nearly thirty miles, clinging mainly to the seashore and dipping inland a little only when the mountain will allow it. The actual city, which lies in the centre, is a busy cluster of streets where very few people live, but to which everybody comes to work: a sort of huge office and warehouse to which people stream in every morning by bus and tram and a very fine suburban electric railway (which many cities twice the size of Cape Town might envy), do their jobs, and stream out at night again to one of the score of little minor towns that make up the Cape Town whole.

It is because these little minor towns vary so decidedly and delightfully that you may care to hesitate a little before settling down too solidly. Even in the marine suburbs there is contrast. Sea Point might be California, St James the south of France, Muizenberg Australia, Kalk Bay and Simonstown little fishing ports tumbled out of Cornwall or Devon.

I I

Then there are the more inland suburbs (if you can count being inland half a dozen miles from the sea and the wind from the sea blowing right into them) like Rosebank and Rondebosch and Newlands and Kenilworth and Wynberg, shaded by fine oaks and pine and gum trees—the oaks so straight and tall and stately at Newlands as to turn the main road, at one point, almost into the long aisle of a cathedral.

Between these trees gleam the white walls, the red-tiled roofs of some of the finest modern houses in the Cape Peninsula, houses probably more diversified in style and origin than any other collection of houses to be found anywhere in the countries of the British Commonwealth. Many of these houses have fine, old Dutch gables, that are now generally accepted, in any sort of illustration of South Africa, as typifying the

Union's national domestic architecture, but there are also houses built on three or four old English models, houses in the Spanish mission style, houses so sleek and streamlined and modern that they might have been exported from Hollywood. South Africa has a very open and cosmopolitan mind about houses.

South Africa has always been cosmopolitan. The Portuguese, the English, the Dutch, the Germans, the French, all of them had landed in that same Table Bay in which your twenty-thousand-ton liner was so smoothly docked the other morning, and gone ashore before a single building stood there. The Portuguese, discoverers of two-thirds of the civilized world, were there first. The first known European to set foot in Table Bay was Antonio de Saldanha; and it is testimony to the effect which the great rock gateway, looming up three thousand feet high above him, had on a daring and roving navigator of that time, that he actually climbed to the top of it and named it Table Mountain one fine day in the year 1503.

Ninety years later three English ships, one of them commanded by Captain James Lancaster, on their way to India, put into Table Bay to revive their scurvy-stricken crews with fresh food and water. And when the English East India Company was formed and put under the command of Captain Lancaster, he at once directed, and for several years it so happened, that all ships of the fleet should call there for refreshment and barter cattle from the natives who, except for one rather sharp brush with the Portuguese, seem to have been a fairly reasonable and amenable lot.

Then the Dutch began to think of India, formed a company of their own that was very solidly and wisely directed, and were soon making huge profits.

There was some sort of proposal that the two companies, the English and the Dutch, should jointly build a proper sort of refreshment port, and have it fortified, at Table Bay, but somehow the idea fell through. The English ships called at Cape Town less frequently, and concentrated more on St Helena, while the Dutch became much more intimate with and enamoured of the place.

Indeed, one Dutch ship was wrecked there, and the crew actually stayed on the shores of Table Bay for six months. They made themselves huts, found a fine stream, sowed and gathered a huge crop of vegetables from seed which they happened to have with them, and came to the general conclusion that this was a very rich and pleasant land in which to live.

That wreck of the *Haarlem*, indeed, was almost like the spilling and sowing of a seed in itself, for no sooner had the wrecked officers returned to Amsterdam than they began to harass the directors of their company to establish the sort of refreshment station that the English and Dutch had failed to agree on establishing years before. And this time the directors agreed to establish such a station, and sent a ship's surgeon, Jan van Riebeek, in command of it. His chief job was to be the growing of vegetables for the company's vessels, lurching over the waters, and straining their canvas after the wealth and gold and precious stones of India.

Nobody ever guessed at that time that there might come a day when ships from the whole world—even from India itself—might come for the gold and precious stones that lay far beyond and behind the huge rock of Table Mountain that stood out at sea now merely as a hope and symbol for the keeping of scurvy out of sailors' blood.

That winter of van Riebeek's landing was a winter of exceptional rains, and he and his wife, Marie, must often have thought Cape Town a very different place to what the sailors of the *Haarlem* had painted it. Often the little party of settlers found themselves washed out of their homes, and forced to eat tough sea birds, hippopotami, and baboons to keep alive. But van Riebeek was a good, steady, God-fearing man—or perhaps God-trusting man might be a more accurate expression, for it is this trust in a sustenance from a Higher Power that stares out of almost every line of his faded old diary that has been preserved to this day, and may still be seen in the archives in Parliament Street. Not only did his vegetables grow apace, but he built a hospital, and established a general sort of health resort that gave relief and renewed health to hundreds of officials after their trying work in the Indies.

And yet that was always how van Riebeek himself seems to have regarded Cape Town: as a sort of rest camp behind the line. He appears to have been overjoyed when, after a stay of ten years and one month, he was promoted to sail to Batavia and later became the President of Malacca, now a little town of probably less than a thousand white people, a hundred and thirty miles to the north-west of Singapore, that nobody ever hears about unless, perchance, they stumble across it in a short story by Mr Somerset Maugham.

But that is the way with pioneers, as you will find, over and over again: they rarely gain a glimpse, not even so much as an intuitive gleam, of the fruits of their labours. Jan van Riebeek could never have imagined as he poured out to his wife his distresses that the company were doing nothing but making a silly little market gardener out of him, that there would one day be erected to him, and on the place where he first landed, a monument presented by an Englishman named Cecil Rhodes; that on every 6th April people would come to his monument and lay there wreaths of tribute; and that stretching about his feet there should be a single city containing half as many white people as can be found in the whole of the Dutch Indies.

III

Probably the best way to get to know Cape Town—to get to know any city—is to spend the first day quietly ambling about the streets with no great sense of direction and certainly in no great spirit of inquiry.

Most people praise the cafés as being particularly good. Café life, indeed, is a distinct feature of the South African social system, and nowhere more so than in Cape Town. The South African is a great drinker of tea. He has tea served to him every morning at six or seven o'clock before he gets up; he has tea served to him in his office, warehouse, or workshop at eleven o'clock in the middle of the morning; it is served to him again at four o'clock; and when he comes out of the bioscopes at night (he called cinemas "bioscopes" in the early silent days, and "bioscopes" they still largely remain to him), he feels he cannot go to bed without first of all going to some café and having a cup of tea or coffee. If he has any business deal to transact, or a housewife wants to meet another housewife from a distant part of the city, then they will arrange to have tea at Cartwright's, Cleghorn's, Markham's, Stuttaford's, or the Waldorf—to mention what are probably the five chief cafés and which have been stated in alphabetical order.

And these appointments are not only made by business men and housewives. They are made by the thousand every day by what are called young people of the opposite sexes. A young man in Cape Town invites a young woman to have morning or afternoon tea with him—and this applies right throughout South Africa, and to little towns of two or three thousand white population, as well as to the big cities—as he would to a theatre or a dance, and nearly always he will take her to a café for coffee and a long talk after the show at the picture theatre.

Perhaps after that first day or two's sauntering, it is better to do the bold, decisive thing and go to the great Marine Drive, or the Chapman's Peak Drive, as it is perhaps more familiarly called in Cape Town: the drive that has more than once been declared to be the finest marine drive in the world.

Many people are inclined to leave this whole day's tour until last, but that is a mistake. The visitor is likely to appreciate his stay in Cape Town far more if he quickly realizes the setting in which the city is enshrined.

Three hundred and fifty years ago, Sir Francis Drake declared: "This Cape is a most stately thing, and the fairest Cape we saw in the whole circumference of the earth"; while Froude wrote: "In all the world, there is perhaps no city so beautifully situated as Cape Town."

And the Duke of Windsor, when Prince of Wales, publicly stated: "It is indeed a happy circumstance that this city, so rich in historical associations, should be set in such beautiful surroundings, and the impression made on the traveller when the full majesty of Table Bay is revealed to him for the first time is one that must remain with him all his life."

The value of this marine drive to Cape Point (and of doing it early) is that it not only displays the beauty of the Cape, but introduces you to a score or more of places to which you may care to return and devote a whole day's picnic. Starting from Adderley Street, the main street of the city (and named after Mr Adderley, M.P., who raised such commotion against the proposal of England to land her convicts in South Africa that it was eventually agreed to carry them on), the touring buses strike out for Three Anchor Bay, and then on to Sea Point, Camp's Bay, Hout Bay, Kommetje, Cape Point, Simon's Town, Fish Hoek, Kalk Bay, Muizenberg, Retreat, Plumstead, Wynberg, Rondebosch . . . and so back to Cape Town. The names in themselves allure; and nowhere do you retrace your steps.

V

Sea Point, you will notice, has become so built up, right from the slopes of Signal Hill and Lion's Head to the very fringe of the sea, as to become almost part of Cape Town itself. And for that reason it is a very convenient suburb in which to stay—either permanently or while you are deciding which part of the peninsula most conforms with your individual taste. Not only is there an almost continuous service of trams and buses, taking little more than ten minutes to reach Adderley Street, but there is a fine promenade refreshingly laid out with huge patches of plain green lawn, and stretching in less ornate style past Three Anchor Bay and Green Point, once Cape Town's race course, but now given up to football and cricket pitches, almost right into the city. There are also at Sea Point hotels and boarding-houses of every possible type and range of tariff.

Yet Sea Point is no tame little seaside suburb of the bath-chair type. It has virility. It was called Sea Point because at this point the sea seemed to collect all its force and sweep down on the rocks. And on days of heavy seas, it does so still: the waves come rushing in, with great, long manes of spray flying, like chariots charging. You will see no other waves in the peninsula like the waves of Sea Point.

It is the common thing to say that bathing at Sea Point is cold, and this is quite true, but a lot of people will tell you they like it that way. One word of warning. Just because some day you pop your head over the wall of the Sea Point pavilion and see a lot of women bathing in the pool there, and a larger number of men basking on the walls outside, don't imagine that the pool is particularly warm that day. The very reverse. It means that on that day the current is particularly cold, and the women are bathing because even the slimmest of them are more bolstered up with fat than men are, and can stand the cold better.

Nearly half a dozen women must by now have swum the seven-mile distance between Cape Town pier and Robben Island—the Channel swim of South Africa—but no man has done it. It hasn't been the current that has beaten the men, for at least their physical strength has been equal to that of the women. They have had to be dragged out because of the cold—and the women have gone on.

But if its bathing is on the cool side, Sea Point has a compensating advantage. It has over twenty inches of rain a year less than the majority of other suburbs.

At night-time, and a mere stone's throw from the modern hotels and blocks of flats of Sea Point, the Green Point lighthouse sends one of the most powerful lights in Africa flashing over the water—over the old nearby wreck of the *Athens*, a victim of the great storm of May 1865, when sixteen vessels were thrown on to the shores of Table Bay. People rushing from their beds to the shores could hear the cries of drowning sailors in the darkness, but were powerless to help them. Only a pig escaped.

Out of the darkness flashes back the intermittent light of Robben Island.

And since, in Sea Point, either day or night it is impossible to become unconscious of Robben Island, perhaps it is better that what has to be said about it should be said now.

It has always been difficult to visit Robben Island, and probably not one per cent of people in Cape Town have been on it. It is more difficult than ever to visit to-day. Now and again bright people have come forward with the idea of what a wonderful pleasure island it might make (and as though the mainland hadn't enough pleasure to offer), but nothing has ever come of such proposals.

Far from being an island of pleasure, Robben Island has always been an island of sorrow, and the Island of Sorrow it has often been called.

Van Riebeek himself used it as a penal settlement—and incidentally found there hundreds of sheep which, it is thought, must have been left originally by some old British shipmaster. And then, as the years went on, it became an island for lepers, as well as for convicts. And after the lepers, the lunatics. The Island of Sorrow, you will see, was no misnomer.

Many years ago these lepers became half wild: so wild and so dissatisfied with their lot that one night they set fire to all their huts. On another night, and when a huge cask of rum somehow drifted ashore, they broke out of control, took their pannikins with them, and indulged in wild carousal on the beach. Some stark and bizarre pictures have been painted on this old island.

The lepers were removed from the island in 1931, and for long years before then their lot had been made as happy as lepers' lot can be. They were taken to Pretoria because chest complaints are often an accompaniment of leprosy, and it was thought that they would fare better in the clear, dry air of the north. The lunatics left, too, and with them the attendants of both.

Only the keepers of the light, that has burned since Van Riebeek ordered a fire to be lit on an iron grating whenever ships approached, remained behind. The homes of nearly two thousand people on this island—people who were there to look after the lepers and the lunatics—now lie deserted, their doors and windows swinging in the wind. A sports ground and golf course are in decay; the doors of the old church are locked; and swarming about the power station that once supplied light and life to the island are thousands of rabbits of the English variety—and that are nowhere found on the mainland—chased by hundreds of wild cats.

Now it has been decided to use the island for another sorrowful, though necessary, purpose. Guns are to be placed there to guard against the approach of enemy vessels, searchlights to probe the skies for enemy aircraft that may, in these days of war fever, dare to attack Cape Town.

V I

Beyond Sea Point are the pretty little bungalow village of Clifton and the white beaches of Camp's Bay, a corruption of "De Baai von Kamptz," von Kamptz being a sailor discharged from a Dutch vessel as being too sick to take home, but living long enough to have a place on the map, and now one of Cape Town's prettiest suburbs, latterly taking on a new lease of life, named after him.

Behind Camp's Bay stretch the twelve peaks of the Table Mountain range that are known as the Twelve Apostles, forming in their soft mauve shades, deepening to rich purple at sunset, a perfect background for the gleaming sands and blue waters that curve about their base. It has been said that no scene in the peninsula has been more frequently painted.

Steadily the road winds and climbs, and with a little dip inland comes Hout Bay, remarkable because not only is the bay, with its Sentinel Rock, just the idyllic sort of bay that might have fallen out of a pirate tale, but almost running down to the sands are grasslands, and in the ravines a quarter of a mile away oaks and pines so thick that only four or five years ago farmers hunted for the leopard that was thought to have strayed there, killing their poultry and scaring their dogs. The leopard was never found, but left definite traces of its presence.

Hout Bay is one of those rare places that seem to have every sort of attraction in a small space, and its sea- and mountain-girt golf course must be pretty well unique even in a country of unusually picturesque courses.

There comes the magnificent climb along Chapman's Peak—and you are a fortunate and much-travelled man if you know a more awesome stretch of marine road in any other country—and there is a point where the road is cut through sheer rock, and nearly every motorist feels himself compelled to get out and look at the sea dashing itself on the rocks at a distance of five hundred and forty feet below.

Almost with a sense of relief you find yourself winding down to the flatlands of Noordhoek and Kommetje, where not so very long ago a huge school of what are known as false killer whales threw themselves ashore, and so committed suicide.

Some of them remained alive for as much as a week—in one or two cases they actually gave birth to young—and efforts were even made to tow their huge carcasses into the water. The stronger the efforts to save them, the stronger their efforts to get back to land again and die there. Why? Photographs of the Kommetje beach, littered with these huge carcasses, were displayed in papers all over the world, but no scientist could be found anywhere who could give any sort of explanation.

All that the old fishermen in the neighbourhood could say was that probably a storm was brewing (there was one soon after the whales landed) and somehow they got panicky about it, and because one whale scooted in the direction of land, the rest made off after it. Whales are just like sheep, they say, the way they follow after one another—and so the matter dropped like some half-forgotten murder mystery.

And then, three or four years later, no fewer than two hundred and fifty of these creatures came ashore, thirty or forty miles away, at a point on the coast-line lying before the inland village of Mamre. A coloured fisherman who saw the amazing sight of them lashing themselves frenziedly out of the water declared that there was a strong wind blowing, and it seemed as though their blow-holes were choked with sand.

Yet when a similar occurrence took place in far-away Tasmania not long after, it was particularly noted that the night was calm and there was but a light wind. The whales showed not the slightest sign of sickness, yet thrashed the water into heavy foam in their efforts to leave it.

Why do whales, and not a casual, truant specimen, but hundreds of them at a time, sometimes flee in terror from their natural element and gasp themselves slowly to death on land, even preferring that death to being helped back into the water again?

That was the mystery which Kommetje first thrust upon the scientists of the world. The theory was even advanced that the whale was once a land animal, and perhaps these were strange, instinctive attempts to revert to its original element.

VII

Cape Point is not merely more or less the Land's End of Africa (the exact point is Cape Agulhas), but it is a cape which the Phoenicians are said to have circumnavigated six hundred years before Christ. It has two lighthouses—popularly called the old and the new. The old stands before you on the topmost cliffs; and although it is a pretty good climb, there is a good path all the way, and most people go there for the wonderful view that is to be seen—and far too many, perhaps, to inscribe their signatures on the lighthouse walls, until it seems that by now the signatures of the half the white people in the Union, and a very representative selection from most countries in Europe and the British Commonwealth, are written there.

The new lighthouse, which is built much lower down the cliff and is rarely visited by the tourist, was erected because the light of the old was often shrouded in the land mists; and a Portuguese ship, bearing the name of *Lusitania*, was wrecked more or less under the nose of the old lighthouse one particularly misty day not so many years ago, when the light was completely hidden. Fortunately her eight hundred souls were all rescued.

But other ships have not been so fortunate. Near here the ill-fated *Birkenhead* struck a sunken reef on the night of 25th February 1852—on board five hundred soldiers, with their wives and children, and a crew of one hundred and thirty-four.

The behaviour of the soldiers after the ship struck has become an immortal story. While the women and children were put into boats, bugles blared, the men fell into ranks, orderly as if they were on the parade ground, and remained so until the ship went down under them. Had they jumped and made for the boats, it is said, they would almost certainly have involved the women and children in disaster. Nearly four hundred soldiers perished.

This sea that stretches before you from the old lighthouse at Cape Point, most probably soft and gleaming and orange-tinted in the late afternoon sun, is also the home of the most famous legend of the sea—the legend of the *Flying Dutchman*.

There are variants of the legend—a German story and a story by Sir Walter Scott—but the most popular and generally accepted version is that the captain of the mysterious vessel was named Vanderdecken, and, for his blasphemies, was condemned to sail round the Cape for ever and for ever, unable to find his way to port. Disaster, swift and certain, is said to follow in his wake, and doom to him who sights his craft. The legend has been used in Wagner's opera *Der fliegende Holländer*; and to this day there are to be found sailormen willing enough to lend as respectful an ear to this ghost story of the sea, as millions of people are ready to express their whole-hearted belief in ghost stories of the land.

What few people are aware of (the disclosure was made by Mr Eric Rosenthal in a South African magazine) is that the late King George V, when sailing round South Africa as a midshipman, actually chronicled in his diary—afterwards published under the title of *The Cruise of H.M.S. Bacchante*, and copies of which are still in existence—that the *Flying Dutchman* had been seen by personnel of his squadron. Under the date of 11th July 1881, the late king, then aged sixteen, set down in his diary, short, straightforward, and sailorlike as you could wish:

> At four a.m. the *Flying Dutchman* crossed our bows. The look-out man on the forecastle reported her as close to the port bow, where also the officer of the watch clearly saw her. . . . A strange red light as of a phantom ship all aglow, in the midst of which light the mast, spars, and sails of a brig two hundred yards distant stood out in strong relief as she came up.

The remarkable thing was that, simultaneously with these happenings on the *Bacchante*, there came the flash of a Morse signal from H.M.S. *Cleopatra* and H.M.S. *Tourmaline* who were steaming by the *Bacchante's* starboard bow: "Have you seen the strange red light?" And yet when the ships sailed in the direction of the light (to quote the royal diary again) "no vestige whatever of any material ship was to be seen, either near or right away to the horizon, the night being clear and the sea calm."

But the strangest feature of the whole incident had still to be chronicled:

> At 10.45 a.m. the ordinary seaman who had this morning reported the *Flying Dutchman* fell from the foretopmast cross-trees and was smashed to atoms.

Which meant that twelve hours after the sailor had reported sighting the *Flying Dutchman*, the cruisers had hove to "with the headyards aback" and his body was committed to the waves.

> He was a smart royal yardman and one of the most promising young hands in the ship and every one feels sad at his loss.

So wrote the royal midshipman in a final note.

Simonstown is a place in which you might well linger a whole day. It is the Gibraltar, the Portsmouth of South Africa, and although the great majority of the shops and houses and churches and public buildings are of a South African design, the atmosphere of an English seaport—authentic as any port from which one of Marryat's heroes might have sailed—hangs curiously, persistently over the place.

Here, in Admiralty House, which lies at the foot of Red Hill, lives the admiral, who is commander-in-chief of the Africa Station, with a squadron carrying a floating population of 1,500 officers and men, and a dockyard employing about 540 men, 400 of whom may be counted South African. The admiral is responsible for the patrolling of the west and east coasts of Africa, and for guarding the Cape route of the British Commonwealth. The nearest naval yards to Simonstown—and it is really useless having modern warships unless you have naval yards, which are manufacturing towns in miniature, to repair them—are Gibraltar and Bombay, both five thousand miles away.

Probably you may get a glimpse of the admiral's flagship, the *Amphion*, the last word in modern cruiser construction, lying in the yard. You are certain to see the *General Botha*, for the simple reason that she never sails away from Simonstown. She is the ship that trains South African youths for a career on the sea.

You have only to drive through Simonstown, and note its churches and weather-beaten graveyards that stand oddly above the level of the road, to know that Simon's Town is old. Move among the old tombstones there, and you will find the graves of men who died fighting pirates.

The oldest house in Simonstown is near Admiralty House, and is used as part residency and part police court and magistrate's office. It is almost certain that Nelson visited it when eighteen years of age and returning to England as an invalid from Bombay on H.M.S. *Dolphin*, on 21st May 1776.

A famous figure of a different type—a man whose name, a few years ago, was on everybody's lips—lived here in this sun-splashed, rather somnolent-seeming old naval port for quite a considerable time. You would never guess his name. It was Edgar Wallace—one-time newsboy, milk deliverer, bricklayer's assistant, member of the Royal Army Medical Corps, reporter, editor, world-famous writer of thrillers and dramas, whose prodigious output of fiction became not only one of the marvels but one of the jokes of his day.

Edgar Wallace was a member of His Majesty's Forces in Simonstown. He called himself "a lousy linseed lancer," which meant that he was a hospital orderly.

Edgar Wallace married his first wife in Simonstown. She was a Miss Caldecott, daughter of the Wesleyan minister here, and those who remember him in those days say that her family were his mentors, and he went frequently with them to the services.

Mr James Tyrrell Wallace, now a well-known sporting journalist in South Africa, was then a member of the police force in Simonstown, and he can recall the many hours he and Edgar used to spend together discussing literature on quiet nights at the police station. He remembers Edgar diffidently showing him his first poem, which was later published in *The Owl*, a Cape Town magazine.

At Simonstown—or to be exact at Seaforth, which is a not too well-known but fine little bathing resort just before you arrive in Simonstown—you come to what may be called Cape Town's warm-water suburbs.

Seaforth, Simonstown, Glencairn, Fish Hoek, Kalk Bay, St James, Muizenberg, are all on the Indian Ocean, and the water is, therefore, warm. Cape Town itself, Sea Point, Clifton, Camp's Bay, Hout Bay, and Kommetje are all on the Atlantic Ocean, and the water is cold—or, at any rate, not so warm by ten to twelve degrees.

It is perhaps the fact that the majority of people prefer their bathing warm that has made Fish Hoek, for instance, spring into such great popularity these last few years, in spite of the fact that it is eighteen miles from Cape Town.

Fish Hoek wears the air of a holiday poster, frankly colourful and flamboyant, while Kalk Bay doesn't seem to worry much about holiday-makers (although it gets its share all right), but just goes on being a plain, simple little fishing town—many of whose fishermen, strangely enough, are descendants from Filipinos, wrecked there many years ago.

St James is a place of fine, solid hotels and boarding-houses that are every bit as solid as hotels. Skegness, St Ives, and Torquay, all in two or three miles, as it were.

But at the far end of St James—it is actually the place where St James and Muizenberg meet—this solidity of hotels and boarding-houses suddenly comes to an end, and gives place to a plain, thatched-roof cottage that is one of the most famous cottages in all Africa. It is the cottage in which Cecil John Rhodes died.

Near by is the lovely house owned by Sir Abe Bailey, who uses it, as he uses his house in London, as a place in which interesting and eminent people may meet one another—apologizing with a smile, these days, that he cannot rise to greet them, or for not taking too prominent a part in the discussion because he feels he hasn't a single leg to stand on! Or declaring that none of his political opponents can quarrel with him now that he has one leg in South Africa and one in England!

Rhodes would have liked Bailey as a neighbour. But Rhodes died—in his forties—nearly forty years ago; and all that last, strangely breathless summer, as Mrs Sarah Gertrude Millin, South Africa's foremost novelist and writer, has pointed out in her *Rhodes*, this man who had given his name to a whole country, pined and fought desperately for nothing more than a little air.

It was because he thought he might find more air in this cottage by the sea that he left his house at Groote Schuur; and in the cottage a hole was made in the wall, blocks of ice placed between the ceiling and the roof, and punkahs installed and waved—all to make a little air.

In the waiting mail boat that was to take him to an England where the air was cold and strong, a special cabin had been fitted with electric fans and oxygen tubes, but Rhodes died on the day he should have sailed.

Eight men and no women were with him when he died. They say his last words were: "So much to do, so little done"—and they have been accounted among the most tragic, pregnant words a great man ever uttered. Mrs Millin says that his last words were more simply human, more poignant than these. He said to one of his secretaries: "Turn me over, Jack."

The subject is still discussed. Even during this last year, long letters have been written in the South African press debating just what were those last words. Somebody has said that Jameson, seeing him going, and seeking to arouse him, ordered a general conversation in the room and Rhodes's last words were a rebuke: "Stop talking, you fellows!" to the eight men in the room, but that some little time before that, he did actually say those words: "So much to do, so little done." There has even been controversy as to where the words originated. It appeared to be settled when someone pointed out the verse in Tennyson's *In Memoriam*:

So many worlds, so much to do,
So little done, such things to be,
How know I what had need of thee,
For thou wert strong as thou wert true?

IX

Muizenberg! It is popular among a certain number of South Africans
to say the word a little disparagingly. They say it is "always so crowded,"
although there are never a fraction of the people—and ten times more
beach for them to sport on—that there are at any of the popular English
resorts on any English Bank Holiday.

They are mainly untravelled South Africans who talk this way about
Muizenberg. They do not appreciate that Muizenberg is undoubtedly one
of the finest beaches in the world (and you can include the famous
beaches of Sydney and Rio de Janeiro), a beach of which Kipling sang:

White as the sand of Muizenberg,
Spun before the gale.

And the setting of it! The high, green hill in the background; the
lovely curve of False Bay, studded, on one side, with white-gleaming, red-
roofed suburbs; and on the other, the faint, blue shapes of the Hottentot's
Hollands, "hills that in the noon of summer" (as a war poet once wrote
of hills far away from these) "seem a kind of blueness like the soul itself."

If you stay in Cape Town long you are likely to return again and
again to Muizenberg, not only to bathe, but to learn to surf, for which
the beach is famous. Go slowly with your surfing and get someone to
show you how to hold your board. Otherwise you may give yourself a
nasty knock.

A mile or so from Muizenberg is Lakeside, and at the moment a
plan is afoot to make this shallow, rush-bordered stretch of water the real
additional asset to Muizenberg which so many people have said it might
be with very little imagination and expense. What worries other people is
the disturbance and probably ejection of the birds there—for among bird-
lovers Lakeside has long been known as one of the most fascinating bird
haunts of the Cape.

And then the road turns suddenly from the sea, you begin to get
into what are called the southern suburbs of Cape Town, you see names

like Retreat, Heathfield, Diep River, and Plumstead slipping by, and quickly you are in Wynberg, which is probably a more self-contained town than any other suburb of Cape Town, has quite a fine park of its own (that does not err in being too park-like), and the largest Anglican church in the Western Province.

You are on the last stage of the Cape Point drive. The sun will most probably be near sinking, tingeing with redness the lovely avenues of old oaks as you make your way through Kenilworth, Newlands, and Rondebosch, silhouetting and throwing into trim, stately relief some of the loveliest houses to be found in all Cape Town.

Occasionally, and far below you, there gleams between the trees the broad sweep of the distant sea. There is thrill and inspiration and majesty in that view.

It was the view that Rhodes loved.

The spirit of the man broods along this whole avenue.

You see the house in which he lived, the university he dreamed of building and which is now built, the zoo he began, the Doric temple which is the Rhodes Memorial, and at the foot of which rears the bronze horseman of G. F. Watts, that is called "Physical Energy," and is a replica of the well-known work in Kensington Gardens.

Taken as a whole, and not without reason, universities throughout the world have probably the most favoured sites of any type of public building, but there can be few universities anywhere with a finer site than this. And that plain statement must suffice. You must see it and judge for yourself.

Groote Schuur is the name of Rhodes's old home, which he bequeathed to the successive Prime Ministers of South Africa, as Chequers in England was later bequeathed to British Premiers. South Africans picture it at its best when the great masses of the blue hydrangeas, or Christmas flowers as they are called at the Cape, swarm and flood about it almost as a sea (those same hydrangeas that Mrs Millin has described as "lying pallid in their tracks" during that summer of dreadful heat in which Rhodes died), but this big barn (*groote schuur*) of Jan van Riebeek, which Rhodes had restored and replanned as you see it to-day by a young architect known as Herbert Baker, has beauty at any time.

Only when the Prime Minister is not in residence, of course, and then only by the securing of a permit from the Public Works Department, are visitors allowed to go over it. Do not omit to note in the centre gable the bronze panel portraying the landing of van Riebeek, and inside the house the soap-stone birds from the Zimbabwe ruins and the silver elephant of Lobengula, and the staircase that reveals the strange passion—or would the psychologists call it an obsession?—that Rhodes had for collecting clocks. All the clocks he collected over twenty years are here.

All his life, and right up to that last hour in the little cottage at Muizenberg, Rhodes was concerned about time. He knew that his heart—his own mainspring—was faulty, had such a limited time to run.

Sometimes when Groote Schuur grew a little too crowded to be comfortable, Rhodes would steal away to his little rest house that he had Baker make for him near by: Baker, the rising young architect, who not only restored and replanned Groote Schuur and this rest house, but, with J. M. Swan, built the Rhodes Memorial; and then, as Sir Herbert Baker, became one of the leading figures of his profession.

Kipling stayed more than once in this rest house that was named later The Woolsack, and in Rhodes's will was a clause giving Kipling the tenancy of the house for his lifetime. The two men had a natural and instinctive appreciation of one another. They are Kipling's lines that you will read engraved on Swan's bust of Rhodes in the temple of the memorial:

> *His immense and brooding spirit still*
> *Shall quicken and control.*
> *Living he was the land, and dead*
> *His soul shall be her soul.*

All along this avenue, within a mile or two's range of Groote Schuur, there are places of interest: Westbrooke (named after Judge William Westbrooke Burton, one of the first judges of the Cape Supreme Court), the Wernher and Beit Medical School (Wernher and Beit were colleagues of Rhodes), and the great modern hospital opened only a year or two ago at Mowbray, that serves the whole of the Western Province and is said to be the largest hospital south of the equator.

And that industrial-looking area that stretches below you, brown and hazy, and stabbed here and there by the varied coloured funnels of ships in harbour, just before entering Cape Town, is Salt River and Woodstock; scene in the year 1773 of one of the most epic pages in South African history.

On this beach a Dutch farmer named Wolraad Woltemade, mounted on horseback, made no less than six journeys out to a wreck and brought back fourteen men from certain death. A seventh time he tried to reach the ship, and he himself was engulfed by the waters.

Apart from the fact that Woltemade is ever likely to remain one of the greatest heroes—if not the greatest—if South African boyhood, his name is kept intimately and rather grimly green among Cape Town's older people. Woltemade is the place where all Cape Town's cemeteries have been assembled.

GETTING TO KNOW CAPE TOWN

I

THE BEST WAY TO SEE CAPE TOWN ITSELF—AND THIS is a plan that can be commended to South Africans as well as to overseas visitors—is to make up your mind that on all those mornings or afternoons when you drift into town for tea or coffee you will see one place of interest.

Go first of all to the public gardens that lie at the head of Adderley Street, and in the very heart of the city (where all public gardens should be, but so often are not), and make these gardens, with their lovely trees gathered from all over the world, and under which scores of business girls and youths eat their lunch during the heat of summer, and the squirrels come out to pick up their scraps, your headquarters.

These are the gardens of long ago in which possibly van Riebeek, and certainly Adriaan van der Stel, a later governor, grew their vegetables for the scurvy-stricken sailors; and even before van Riebeek's time, John Davis, the Englishman who was chief pilot to the Dutch mariner Hout-man, wrote in his log in the year 1598: "This land is a good soile and an wholesome Aire full of good herbes as Mint, Catmint, Plantine, Ribwort, Trifolium, Scabious, and such like."

Here now are trees from Japan and Brazil and the Cocos Islands; statues of Rhodes and Sir George Grey, a former governor who did much for the furtherance of education in the country; the replica of an old bell tower that used to call the slaves to work; an old sundial and relic of the East India Company dating from 1781; the first blue gum that was ever planted in South Africa, and an old oak tree (it lies up the main path from the statue of Sir George Grey) that has lifted up into its trunk an old pump that once stood beside it.

Here, too, you may have tea in the open air, and all within a stone's throw stroll to the House of Assembly (the Union House of Parliament), the South African Museum, the Cape Archives, the South African Public Library, the Groote Kerk (which has been described as the Westminster Abbey of South Africa), the Cape Town Cathedral, and the Synagogue. These gardens are a remarkable focal point.

The House of Assembly sits normally from January to July, but the buildings may be inspected at any time if the necessary permission be obtained from the sergeant-at-arms.

The museum not only possesses a portion of a cross erected by Diaz in South Africa in the fifteenth century, and the old stones under which the earliest mariners to the Cape left their letters, but an unusually thrilling collection of stuffed animals (such as only Africa could produce), skeletons and the like, and the lifelike casts of Bushmen and Hottentots.

It is likely to surprise both South African and overseas visitors that in the South African Public Library, which stands at the bottom of the Avenue, there are not only the diaries of van Riebeek and Adam Tas (a famous leader of the dissatisfied burghers at the Cape), and manuscripts of Olive Schreiner, but copies of the first and second folios of Shakespeare; about a hundred fifteenth-century printed books, including one early German work of which no copy exists in Europe; about seventy-five volumes of illuminated manuscripts, some of them dating back to the tenth and eleventh centuries, and including a fine specimen on uterine vellum; a Greek psalter printed in Milan in 1481, which is said to be the third book ever printed in Greek; and a manuscript of Dante.

And in Victoria Street, immediately behind the gardens, are the Archives, where rare old documents establish, among other things, that, at one time and another, Clive of India, Captain Kidd, the pirate, and Alexander Selkirk, who is generally supposed to have been Robinson Crusoe, all visited Cape Town. You may also see here the passionate love letters of a young man of two hundred years ago—all complete with signature penned in his own blood.

I I

Five minutes' walk, or less, will bring you from books and documents to pictures.

In the South African Art Gallery are works by such famous overseas artists as: "After Fifty Years" by Frank Bramley, A.R.A., "Montreuil" by

P. Wilson Steer, O.M., "Miss Pettigrew" by Augustus John, and "The Countess of Lytton" by Ambrose McEvoy, R.A.

There is also a collection of works by South African artists that should be of particular value in helping the overseas visitor to attune his mind to the light and colour and general atmosphere of the country. "Kofman's Kloof" by Edward Rowarth, "The Lodge" by Pieter Wenning, "Near Koelenhof" by J. H. Pierneef, "The Hex River" by R. Gwelo Goodman, and "The Garden of Promise" by J. S. Morland are excellent examples of South African work.

This is not the only fine collection of paintings in Cape Town. Ten minutes' walk from the Gallery will bring you to the Michaelis Gallery in Greenmarket Square, and there you may see paintings by the great Flemish and Dutch masters.

See that you do not miss "A Taxidermist" by Rembrandt (attributed until a year ago to de Gelder), "Portrait of a Woman" by Frans Hals, "The Dancing Dog" by Jan Steen, "Mountainous Landscape" by Jacob van Ruisdael, and "A Breezy Day" by Jan van Goyen.

Almost alongside the Art Gallery in the Avenue is the Synagogue; at the foot, and behind the Library, is the Anglican Cathedral, to which extensive alterations have recently been made costing over £200,000; and a couple of hundred yards half-right down Adderley Street stands the Groote Kerk, mother church of the Dutch Reformed Church in South Africa, the foundation stone of which was laid in the year 1700 and under whose floors sleep eight of the old Dutch governors.

The clock in the Groote Kerk tower is the oldest in South Africa. A portion of this clock mysteriously disappeared in Cape Town one hundred and ten years ago, but there are still parts of the original mechanism which have functioned for two hundred and thirty years.

Here is a fact that scores of thousands of people passing the old Groote Kerk day after day do not know about it. Not only can it seat three thousand people, but there are only three—or maybe four—buildings in the world which have a bigger unsupported ceiling span.

III

Any day between 10 a.m. and 6 p.m., and at the mere cost of a sixpence, you may be escorted by a guide round the castle, which stands not far from the Cape Town railway station, and is the oldest building in South Africa—all the more interesting these days because a sum of

£20,000 is being spent on its restoration and so enabling it again to resume something of its old prestige and importance in the civic life of the country.

For that, it is pleasant to record, appears to have been the main mission of the castle since the earliest days of its existence. The guide will show you the moat, which was constructed by every one passing being compelled to carry away so many basketfuls of earth; the amazingly thick wall that took eight years to build; the well and grain chambers that were included in case of siege; the dividing wall which van der Stel had built through the centre of the place so that if one half of the castle were captured he might still hold out with the other. But he will also tell you that so far as can be traced, not a single hostile shot has ever been fired from it, or ever pierced its walls.

With its soft, green lawns, its old weather-scarred sundials, its simple, austere buildings—and the great walls of Table Mountain towering broodingly, comfortingly, above it—this earliest fort of White Africa might well seem a monastery, but for one or two disturbing and anomalous details.

There is, for instance, this constant mention of Lady Anne Barnard.

"And this beautiful old balcony, designed by a French architect, which you see here," the guide is saying, "was where Lady Anne Barnard received her guests. And this building was used as the governor's council chamber, as a church, and as a ballroom by Lady Anne Barnard."

Who was this Lady Anne Barnard?

The name of Lady Anne Barnard slips easily from the tongues of most people at the Cape, but it is not quite so simple to define her. In the later seventeen hundreds and early eighteen hundreds she was accounted one of the most brilliant women of her time, and even the Prince Regent wrote to her as "your ever and most affectionate friend, George P." Much to everybody's surprise, when she was forty-three, Lady Anne married Mr Barnard, the son of a bishop, who was twelve years her junior—not at all the sort of marriage everybody had expected her to make, either in social importance or as an alliance in intelligence, but there is every reason to believe that the union was quite successful.

One of Lady Anne's first jobs as a wife was to get her husband one, and through the influence of Henry Dundas, a minister of the Government of the time, she succeeded in getting him appointed as secretary to the Cape Colony. It is Lady Anne's letters, written from Cape Town home to Dundas, found at his death carefully tied and among his most cherished papers, and later published under the title of *South Africa a Century Ago* (Maskew Miller, Cape Town), that have added so richly and piquantly to the South African scene of this particular period.

The surprising thing about Lady Anne Barnard—as she reveals herself in these letters—is that she appears so much a woman of the twentieth century and of the atmosphere in which we now live. She has, indeed, all the supreme qualifications of the heroine of the modern novel and even of the talkie.

She was not only fond of pleasure but of doing unconventional things. Having heard that no woman had been to the top of Table Mountain, then she must go up with Mr Barrow (not with Mr Barnard, mark you) and found that "the best way to get down was to sit down and slip from rock to rock the best way one could." She liked or disliked people decisively, and not at all according to convention: she liked the Landdrost of Stellenbosch, but thought a certain new governor was a "very, very weak old soul." She uses slang (actually such modern-seeming expressions as "telling fibs," "poor me," and "a hop," meaning a dance), says airily in one passage that "things ran rather more than was agreeable in the flirting line at one time out here." Yet she is supremely practical: at one festivity she lights lamps "with the tails of sheep whose saddles we were eating," and she is glad that she carried to Africa "a map of an ox and a sheep, fearing that the Dutch butchers might cut up their meat awkwardly, nor was she mistaken."

Behind all her gaiety and balls and supper parties and receptions was the serious purpose. Not once through the whole book—not even in the passage that is about to be quoted—does she permit herself any prim, pre-Victorian, or Victorian moralizing, but there was just one day when, taking up her quill, she also took off her mask and wrote hot and burning passages which light up the character and whole fibre of the woman:

We had not long established ourselves before we found that great expectations had been formed of us. I was supposed to be a sort of binding cement, such, I presume, as the castles of antiquity were formerly made with, light, strong, and powerful, towards the associating together of the scattered atoms of society—and had they stopped there, they would have been right. But they hoped further— balls, card parties, races, a theatre, an opera, and the introduction of many London amusements such as they supposed I must be a promoter of, and must tire without having lived all my life in the midst of them. They "knew but little of Calista" if they supposed I reckon a small society improved by public amusements introduced that belong to a much farther advanced period. . . . No, what I wished chiefly to effect was, if possible, to bring the nations together on terms of good will, and, by having public days pretty often at the castle, to reconcile the Dutch by the attraction of fiddles and French horns.

Does Cape Town remember too much the daring Lady Anne Barnard of reception and the dance hall? Might not this woman who "so liked the Cape" and was always pouring scorn on those who sought to belittle it (sometimes tricking such people into proclaiming they were drinking the finest European wines when they were but drinking the very Cape wine that they were always declaring gave them the bowel-ache) be revered a little more as one of our first social ameliorators, if not our very first?

Dark, cruel things were done in this old castle, with its soft lawns and sundials, where Lady Anne Barnard held her balls—the dark, cruel things of the age, as this age has its darknesses and cruelties. No beast would be allowed to-day to live in the dark, ill-ventilated holes into which prisoners were cast then. Observe particularly the solitary confinement cells and the particularly diabolical arrangement of bars by which the prisoner was not even given the doubtful privilege of seeing his jailer. His food was put through the bar on a prong, and he was left to snatch it through a slit in the wall. Nor was there the slightest provision for any sort of sanitation.

You step still further down the passage. "Let us put out the light," says the guide, switching off the solitary electric bulb.

In the hot, heavy, pitch-black darkness, his voice rises: "And now we are in the dungeons where the rack and the thumbscrews and other tortures were used—some of them involving fire—and where the prisoners were often left to suffocate in the smoke and lack of air and the darkness."

The guide takes you to another balcony than the one on which Lady Anne received her guests—the balcony on which were read proclamations and sentences of death. Immediately somebody in the party wants to know whether this is where the men were sentenced to death by proclamation of Governor van Noot. The guide says it most probably is: although he is a little guarded as to whether the old dramatic story about van Noot, known to every South African school child, is true.

Van Noot, one of the most unjust and brutal of governors who ever came to the Cape, is said to have so starved his soldiers that a number attempted to desert. At first they were condemned to run the gauntlet ten times and then be sent as slaves to Batavia, but this was not strong enough for van Noot. He wanted them hanged.

It is said that everybody was in tears when they were led to the scaffold; and it was then that one of them turned towards the room in which he knew van Noot to be sitting, and declared: "I summon thee, Governor van Noot, before the judgment seat of the Omniscient God that thou may answer for my soul and the souls of my companions."

All the men having been executed, members of the council went to van Noot's house to report the fact. Van Noot was sitting at the far end of the audience chamber when they entered, but strangely did not respond in any way to their bowings. In horror they saw that he was dead. . . .

"That is the story that is told," says the guide, "and if you care to go along to Koopman de Wet's Museum in Strand Street, you will see there the chair in which van Noot is said to have been stricken. . . . But you should also go to Koopman de Wet's to see the lovely furniture there: old furniture such as probably existed in some of these rooms you have seen."

IV

The Koopman de Wet Museum in Strand Street is not so much a museum—in fact, in the accepted sense of the term it is not a museum at all—as an old Dutch house, dating from the eighteenth century, full of fine old Dutch furniture. It is a type of furniture which has become accepted, one might almost say beloved, by South Africans of all descent, as representing all that is best and finest in the household life and art of the country.

Here, in this house of Koopman de Wet, one may see some of the finest specimens to be found in the Union; and it is for the visitor, and particularly the travelled visitor, to judge whether (especially in this gaunt, steel era) it is not as fine furniture as can be found anywhere: really noble, sweeping, full-bellied stuff, that has in it not only the calm, the solidity, and serenity of old Europe, but, here and there, an odd twist and decorative effect from the east.

Skilled slaves from Batavia and Ceylon worked on some of these lovely, mellow stinkwood and satinwood pieces, as well as the early

European settlers. Why such an unlovely name as stinkwood for such a lovely wood is not quite clear. A closed drawer, opened after a long time, may smell a little, but it is quite a good wood smell and never offensive.

Trees of it still grow in the distant Knysna forests, and a limited amount of furniture from it is still being made. But every year there is keener and more excited competition to secure old stinkwood pieces at the sales in Long Street, which is the street where all Cape Town's antique and curio shops are clustered, and a fine place to browse about on one of the rare wet days of summer.

V

Long Street, and the streets that run parallel above it, are not the show streets of Cape Town, but they are the streets to which you will find both your feet and imagination turning the longer you stay here. They are, in a way, Cape Town as no other streets are—old Cape Town, cosmopolitan Cape Town.

In Long Street is the German Lutheran church and the Indian Mohammedan mosque; in Loop Street, immediately above, there is the Salvation Army citadel and the Malay mosque of the Strength of Islam. Here, on a certain morning each year, Malays may be seen gathered in their praying-gowns giving thanks, as Christians might be seen giving thanks on Easter morning, that the end has come to the thirty-day fast of Ramadán, during which they rise and eat their first meal of the day before dawn (before a white thread may be distinguished from a dark thread), and touch neither food nor drink, nor are they permitted the stimulant of perfume, until sunset.

There are many thousands of Malays living in Cape Town. They have been there ever since their ancestors were brought over as slaves by the East India Company, and Cape Town is as much home to them as London to a cockney.

Some of their women still wear the veil, dress in filmy, billowing gowns of what Cape Town people call Malay pink, or Malay blue, and the city will be a duller, drabber place—almost like a van Gogh painting with the colour drained out of it—when the last of them takes to a more European mode of dressing.

The men make a lot of furniture, do work as tailors, act as warehousemen, read the daily papers, and nearly all wear European clothes, except that they still keep to the fez as headgear. They are a very moral and orderly community, and what is particularly noticeable among them is their decided love of sport.

Not only is a special stand erected for them at the famous rugby ground at Newlands, where they will go into ecstasies over the sudden breaks and drop kickings of their favourite Springboks, but for long hours hundreds of them will stand in St George's Street, which is the Fleet Street of Cape Town, waiting anxiously for the fall of every wicket to be posted outside the newspaper offices of some test match in which South Africa is engaged six thousand miles away.

Yet they remain, in the bulk, strictly Mohammedan, keeping themselves to themselves, observing their customs and revering their saints.

Occasionally—and it is counted an honour and much besought by women—there may come an invitation to a European to attend a Malay wedding. Not that any women see much of the actual wedding ceremony, for not even the bride attends that. Only men go to the mosque, the father deputizing for the bride and coming home and telling her that she is now married.

But the bride certainly has her hour, or hours, of glory at home. There, on a sort of throne, she sits, attended by her three bridesmaids and surrounded by all her friends, eating sweetmeats and singing songs in her honour. And instead of having only one bridal dress, she has four— and her bridesmaids have four dresses as well. First, they may appear in gold, sit in majesty for half an hour, bow, and return in pale blue. Then another bow and a return in pink; still another bow and a final return in white.

VI

When you have a complete morning or afternoon to spare and want to see something interesting, go to one of these three places: Groot Constantia, Kirstenbosch, or the Round House at the Glen. You should go to all. Groot Constantia, which is easily reached from Wynberg, or via the De Waal Drive, was where Governor Simon van der Stel lived for twenty-six years, putting the final touch to the thatched roof and shapely gables of this best known and probably loveliest of all Dutch homesteads one fine day in 1685. In the large flagged rooms in which van der Stel lived may be seen some of the fine, massive furniture of his period, and in the cellars below (with air-holes smaller than the width of a man's body) he locked up at night the slaves who worked in his vineyards.

At Kirstenbosch, which may be reached by the same De Waal Drive, are the National Botanical Gardens, which are among the finest—and certainly as regards situation, or for what a royal visitor termed the garden wall—in the world.

The Round House lies in a pretty little valley known as the Glen between Camp's Bay and the Kloof Nek, and was once the shooting box of Lord Charles Somerset, an old Cape governor. And there was certainly good shooting to be had there. It is officially recorded that a lion killed eight sheep almost on the spot where you may now sip tea.

VII

Riding along the De Waal Drive above Rondebosch, or the Rhodes Road that joins the Drive from Constantia Nek, you will see down below you a long, wide, flat stretch of country that reaches lingeringly out to the sea. That is the Cape Flats.

There is probably no more unknown, less explored country on the fringe of any city than the Cape Flats of Cape Town. And it is difficult to say why it should be so. In any city less favoured by physical beauty than Cape Town, the Cape Flats might be its pride and playground. Apart from Zeekoe Vlei, which is the largest permanent stretch of water on the Flats, and has become so popular with yachting men that a handsome club house was recently opened, the place is unknown—and when people think of Zeekoe Vlei they are apt to think only of yachting. They know little of the wonderful bird life of the place: that not only are there nearly always wild duck, geese, plover, and a score or more of different species of waterfowl to be seen, but occasionally pelicans and flocks of flamingos.

Because for years they have only seen the Cape Flats from a blurred distance, most people are amazed, when they get down there, at the extent of the place. As a matter of fact, the area of the Cape Flats is, approximately, four hundred square miles: more than one-half of the Cape Division, which is about seven hundred and twenty-five square miles in extent.

Fifty years ago there was neither road nor track through the whole of this great tract, and neither tree nor shrub grew there; nothing but heath and bush. In the heat of summer the Flats were a wilderness of sand and dust; in winter they were either under water or in a state of morass. Hardly enough fuel could be found to boil water for coffee.

Then the Hon. J. X. Merriman, Prime Minister of the Cape, brought out batches of German peasant labourers. Some of them were so appalled by the land on which they were expected to settle that they forthwith sought employment elsewhere, but others stuck to their task and somehow houses were built of twigs and clay, a living was wrested from the ground by the men, while the women secured a few hens and themselves walked all the way to Cape Town to sell the eggs.

All during the week the men slaved from daylight to darkness, and on Sundays walked to church at Wynberg, slinging their black coats over their arms and carrying their boots and socks in their hands until the roads became passable enough to wear them.

To-day they have not only a church at Philippi—which is the central village of the colony—but a school and an orphanage; and when, four or five years ago, the settlers celebrated the fiftieth anniversary of their arrival, over one thousand people gathered in the orphanage grounds to pay tribute to their triumph over adversity. A choir of over a hundred voices sang a group of six songs tracing the history of their colony: their farewell to Germany, their homesickness, their thanksgiving for the school erected in 1884, and for their church erected in 1897.

VIII

One day you should either climb Table Mountain, or go up by the Table Aerial Railway, running since 1929, which transports the visitor from Adderley Street to the top in little over twenty minutes.

Table Mountain is 3,582 feet high (Devil's Peak, which is to the left, 3,300 feet, and Lion's Head to the right, about 1,800 feet), and there are half a dozen routes by which the mountain may be climbed by the ordinary, fairly athletic walker—chief among them being the Platteklip Gorge, which overlooks the centre of the town and may be approached through the gardens.

But Table Mountain is not a mountain with which liberties can be taken. Once the route has been decided on it should be stuck to rigidly and no attempt made at shortcutting or circumventing. And if mists come over the mountain (which may happen at any time) it is not merely wise but imperative that the party should stay where it is and wait until the mist rises.

No one should be deterred from climbing Table Mountain because of its rather tragic history, but it is no good ignoring that history—beginning, as it did, in the earliest days of settlement, when more than one party found itself attacked by wild beasts, or by escaped slaves, who used to inhabit the caves and roll down boulders at any person seen climbing towards their sanctuary.

The only wild animal seen there now—and he is hardly likely to cause any trouble—is the baboon, and an occasional poisonous snake may be seen.

A year or so ago, Mr Sidney Jarman, of Nigel, Johannesburg, celebrated his seventy-second birthday by riding his eight-year-old bicycle to Maclear's Beacon, the highest point on the mountain. Setting off by the footpath route from Constantia Nek, he rode quite a lot of the way and then wheeled and pushed and finally hauled his bicycle up the rest. Which seems to make the climbing of Table Mountain a very safe and simple business.

Yet hardly a year seems to pass but some fatality happens, and the mountain looms so closely over the town, becomes so much an intimate part of everybody's daily existence, that news of a mountain tragedy rings through the city like a funeral bell.

Even on the smaller, less precipitous, Lion's Head, disaster may happen. Years ago a fourteen-year-old Sea Point boy disappeared there, and hundreds of Sea Point residents and members of the Mountain Club went in search of him, and at length found him dead in a krantz. He had apparently left the usual route to pick flowers and fallen over a ledge.

Cape Town people still quote this tragedy as a remarkable case of premonition. The boy's mother declared that all the time she knew her son was dead. She told newspaper reporters that at half-past one that Sunday she was going into the dining-room when her son seemed to come to meet her, catch her by the arms, and draw her to him, as he often did playfully. Turning away shudderingly, she said to her daughter, the boy's sister: "Something has happened to Jimmy." The boy had gone out wearing a watch, and when the body was discovered it was found that the watch had stopped and been broken by the fall with the hands resting at half-past one.

Climbing the lower slopes of Table Mountain, one gets a fine bird's-eye view of this mother city of South Africa, second in age only to Quebec, and, outside Britain, among the cities of the Commonwealth that is now entering on one of the most dramatic and certainly changeful chapters of its career.

One result of the Abyssinian and Spanish wars, and their attendant unrest among shipping in Mediterranean, Suez, and Red Sea waters, was to bring back Cape Town's old prestige as the tavern of the seas as it existed in the days before the opening of the Suez and when Cape Town was the main port on the route to India, the East, Australia, and New Zealand. And a good deal of this enhancement has not only remained, but seems likely to be consolidated.

In the year of 1938, moreover, South Africa was one of the most prosperous countries in the world, bought thirty-seven million pounds' worth of goods from Britain alone, and, notwithstanding that she has a white population of only two million, against Australia's six and Canada's nine, was actually Britain's best customer.

If Cape Town is ever to leap ahead, it is obvious that she should leap ahead now. Within the next ten years she is to undergo such a facial transformation as few cities in the world have undergone, and probably only Rio de Janeiro and Buenos Aires can parallel in recent times.

You have learned how Cape Town's great enemy of expansion is Table Mountain. Streets of houses and shops have already crept up its sides at almost preposterous angles, but that fight is now to be declared at an end. The attack is to be concentrated at the opposite end of the city.

If Mahomet cannot move the mountain, then it is to be proved that at least Canute can sweep back the sea.

I X

What is now the foreshore and that portion of the bay extending for about two miles from the South Arm to Woodstock Baths is to be reclaimed from the sea that now covers it, and this will mean that an area as large as that of the present city will be available for the building of shops and offices and warehouses.

The new Adderley Street will extend twice its present length towards the sea. It will, moreover, be two hundred feet wide—twice the width of the existing thoroughfare—permitting of two forty-feet one-way thoroughfares on either side of a central garden and pedestrian way which will be sixty feet wide. Palms will line the pavements, which will be thirty feet wide on each side.

Not only will huge shops and offices, all carefully designed to preserve a harmonious whole, spring up all along this new and greater Adderley Street, but there will be new public buildings. The present railway station is to be replaced by a vast modern one with a courtyard in front of it, lower than the present building and on the site of the Cape Town Publicity Bureau. The present goods yard that exists at the foot of the present Adderley Street is to be set back almost to Woodstock.

An enormous city hall and civic centre is planned to occupy a site amid gardens on the new Adderley Street, roughly where the pier head now is.

There will be a much greater harbour, a vast graving dock, and a marine wall, enclosing the harbour on the sea side, which it is hoped will constitute one of the finest promenades in the world, enabling motorists to drive right out into the middle of the bay as it now exists.

It is anticipated that the reclaimed land will be available for building in two or three years' time after the sea has been swept from it. The harbour works and graving dock are likely to take nine years to finish, but the new quays for the mail ships should be ready long before that.

The cost of the whole scheme is to be £10,000,000.

It is to the credit of Cape Town that she is also to do something about her slums—and something quite as drastic and dramatic as about her foreshore. It is not without reason. Her District Six, and notorious Wells Square, had become a byword in the land. Hundreds of coloured families lived in single rooms and disease and crime grew apace. The death-rate in Cape Town among non-Europeans is 25.6 per 1,000, and among Europeans 10.5.

When Cape Town journalists wished to visit the worst parts of District Six to write of the things that existed there, they had to have a guide—so little did they know of this district, and such odd sequels might have attended their visit. Their guide was usually Bishop Lavis, Coadjutor Bishop of Cape Town, who has spent much of his life among the people living in these areas, and is revered by all of them.

But the practical man behind the scheme to wipe away this blot on the city has been Councillor M. J. Adams, Chairman of the Citizens' Housing League Utility Company, who, when the company's first houses were being built, spent his leave working on the job.

Now six million pounds are being spent in banishing the old and putting up twelve thousand new houses in twelve years—which means that a new city of fifty to sixty thousand people is to arise in Cape Town.

Add to this new city the reclaiming of another city from the sea, and you will realize that it is doubtful whether any other city in the world is likely to become more changed than Cape Town at the end of the next ten years.

NEGLEY FARSON

A meeting with D. F. Malan and
recruiting miners in Ovamboland: 1940

"WHEN THE DOCTOR HAD PASSED ONE, HE MARKED, WITH YELLOW CHALK,
THE LETTER A, B, OR C ON HIS NAKED CHEST. . . . THUS WAS THIS BLACK
HUMANITY GRADED."

In 1940, as war enveloped Europe and began to involve Africa as well,
journalist Negley Farson undertook a long and strenuous journey throughout the African continent. He visited southern Africa, then traveled up
the east coast to Tanganyika (now Tanzania) and Kenya, and on through
Uganda, heading west through the Congo region. He picked up malaria
on the way and was recovering in Accra in the Gold Coast (now Ghana)
when an earthquake struck the city.

There is no mistaking Farson's political views. "I believe that it is under the Englishman," he wrote in an author's note to his 1941 Behind
God's Back, "that the native will have the best chance of progress in Africa. . . . The British moral attitude towards their African holdings and
protectorates is above any except minor criticisms."

Farson's inquiries in South Africa, as elsewhere, focused on local sit-
uations and their political and possibly military implications for Europe in
the near and distant future.

In the second part of the selection that follows, Farson visits a recruiting center that supplies workers for the mines of South Africa. The
center is in Ovamboland, part of South-West Africa, which is now Namibia.

His meeting with Dr. D. F. Malan is a fascinating insight into one of

*South Africa's most influential politicians at the time. In 1934 Malan, a
right-wing extremist, had organized his Purified National Party, aiming to
implement by law the white supremacist policies inherent in the country's
long history of colonialism and in the attitudes of men like Cecil Rhodes
and the nation's founders.*

*Eight years after Farson's meeting with Malan, in 1948, the National
Party won a general (all-white) election and at once began instituting
apartheid ("apartness") as an official government policy. Repressive laws
followed quickly. The Suppression of Communism Act permitted the ban-
ning, without appeal, of anyone the government thought posed a threat.
The Group Areas Act restricted all nonwhites to townships. The Pass Laws
required all blacks to carry passbooks identifying them. The Immorality
Amendment Act made illegal any sexual contact between whites and non-
whites. The Reservation of Separate Amenities Act further formalized separation of the races. And on and on.*

*Through the fifties, sixties, and seventies, unrest in the nation inten-
sified, and a brief history of the period reads like a series of vivid headlines. In 1960 sixty-nine demonstrators against the Pass Laws were killed
in the Sharpeville Massacre, and the African National Congress was
banned. That same year, ANC leader Albert Luthuli won the Nobel
Peace Prize. In 1961 the Union of South Africa became the Republic of
South Africa. In 1964 Nelson Mandela and seven other ANC leaders were
tried, found guilty of treason, and sentenced to life imprisonment. In that
same year, South Africa was banned from the Olympic Games. In 1966
Dr. Hendrik Verwoerd, prime minister since 1958, was assassinated. In
1970 the Bantu Homelands Act officially made blacks aliens in their own
country. The 1970s were marked by widespread riots in Soweto and elsewhere. In 1977 political prisoner Steve Biko was murdered while in deten-
tion.*

*Reforms began slowly when P. W. Botha became president in 1980
and escalated when F. W. de Klerk succeeded him in 1989. In 1990 Nelson Mandela was released from prison. In 1993 de Klerk and Mandela
shared the Nobel Peace Prize. And in 1994 the world watched television
pictures of black South Africans peacefully lining up to vote for the first
time. The African National Congress won the majority and Mandela became president.*

PARTY POLITICS IN
SOUTH AFRICA

THE TROUBLE WITH SOUTH AFRICAN POLITICS (FROM England's point of view) is that there is not in them an Englishman of any consequence. And there are no young ones in sight. This gives rise to more trouble than the mere fact that some 60 per cent of the South Africans are of "Dutch" extraction (which might be anything, a Hollander, a German, or a French Huguenot), and that only 40 per cent are English. The few Englishmen of any consequence in South Africa, these days, are content to restrict themselves to their business interests in Cape Town, Johannesburg, and Durban.

As a result, the continual bickering within the South African Parliament along racial lines is a fight among the "Dutch" *about* the English, rather than against them. Were some English personalities present, these debates might serve as a safety valve. Without this escape, these discussions only tend to embitter the Nationalist feeling.

The whole tendency of South African politics has been toward a "super-Nationalist" Party, splitting off from a Nationalist Party. General Hertzog left Botha, demanding a republic. Dr. D. F. Malan, perhaps the most dangerous figure (to the British), left his pulpit and joined Hertzog. When Hertzog cooled down on the republic idea, Malan left him, to form another super-Nationalist Party, and led the Parliamentary opposition up to the outbreak of this war. When in this present war General Smuts brought South Africa in on the side of the British against Germany, and Hertzog fell, Malan drew Hertzog further away from the commonwealth idea, although, at this time of writing (January, 1940) Malan and Hertzog have not fused on the republic idea. And there is no real reason to believe that Hertzog has abandoned his political belief that to remain within the British Commonwealth of Nations is, in spite of Nationalism, the best life-insurance policy for the Union of South Africa.

Malan, even his worst enemy will tell you, is the man to be watched. He is intelligent, honest, and fanatic; an easily comprehensible comparison would be to say that he is the South African De Valera. By birth, training, profession, and political attitude, he appeals to the majority of South African instincts. To begin with, he is an ex-predikant of the Dutch Reformed Church, and to most Afrikanders on the veld the Bible is still the one and only book. Finally, he is almost insanely determined to take South Africa outside the British Commonwealth, and there is an alarming number of South Africans who are pro-anything, as long as it is anti-British.

Malan has but to capitalize these two strongest appeals to the South African temperament.

He was born 65 years ago, at Reibeck West, the farming town where Smuts was born. He studied for the church at Victoria College, Stellenbosch, and finished his studies at the University of Utrecht, Holland. His first district, at Montague, S.A., in 1906, was in a rich wine-growing province; yet the young Malan preached, if not strict prohibition, then rigid temperance. His probity was so passionate that his wine-growing religious Dutch congregation forgave him even that. When, before the war of 1914–18, General Hertzog began preaching his advanced gospel of Afrikanderism, practically demanding a republic, and quarreled with Botha, Malan took Hertzog's side. After the World War, when an Afrikaans newspaper was established to help Hertzog's Nationalism, Malan resigned his pulpit and became editor of that. When General Hertzog became premier, Malan became minister of interior in his cabinet. He was the best minister of interior, even his enemies admit, that South Africa ever had.

When, in 1933, for the safety of South Africa, General Smuts and General Hertzog merged their two political parties together (a union which lasted until the outbreak of this last war), Malan split off and organized a purified Nationalist Party of his own. Malan's party demands:

1. A republic for South Africa.
2. Total segregation of the native and colored races, both territorially and industrially.
3. Complete stoppage of Jewish immigration.

And, as a philosophy, Malan's party holds that there is room in South Africa for one language only, Afrikaans.

There is not one of these demands that does not appeal, strongly, to the heart of the majority of South Africans of "Dutch" extraction.

The violent anti-Semitic program throws light on a curious facet of the South African mind. Its opponents try to deride it by declaring that this sentiment is back-veld. They are wrong.

The anti-Semitic bill itself, which the Malanites brought before the South African Parliament of 1939, was introduced by none other than Mr. Eric Louw, the first South African minister plenipotentiary to the United States.

Before that, Mr. Louw was South African High Commissioner in London; afterwards he was minister to France and Portugal, then minister at Rome. After this "twelve years' pioneering abroad," as he called it (during which he engaged in a bitter controversy with Lord Passfield, Dominions Minister, over the status of the South African High Commissioner at London, Louw claiming wider privileges), Louw resigned his ministership and returned to the Union to side with Dr. Malan.

He is known as the best dressed man on the Nationalist benches.

His anti-Semitic bill rivaled Hitler in its blind harshness. Known as the "aliens amendment and immigration bill," it proposed, among other things, that no person of Jewish parentage (and this is made to include all naturalized British subjects) should be allowed to enter the Union of South Africa for permanent residence. It refuses even a temporary sojourn to anyone whose passport provides that he would lose his nationality within a specified period or prohibits his re-entry into the country where the passport was issued. This seems to include every possible refugee of Jewish origin.

Moreover, it declares that Yiddish is not a European language. This clause was undoubtedly inserted because the knowledge of at least one European language was a strict requirement of the present immigration act. Louw's act was attempting to block every loophole.

The bill even proposed that all aliens in South Africa would have to carry pass cards (the way the Negroes do now), and that firms employing aliens would first have to obtain official permission, then publish the names on signboards and documents, giving any previous names that these aliens might have held. This retrograde bill was so ruthless that it would require all Jews who had entered the Union under the 1937 aliens act to surrender their permits and take the tests again.

That this anti-Semitic bill had no chance whatever of getting passed, Malan admitted to me himself, when I saw him in Cape Town, in February, 1939.

"The Government members will assure us of their support in the lobbies," he said, sarcastically, "and then they will go in and vote against it out of personal loyalty to Smuts and Hertzog and party politics. We know that. Nevertheless, a large number of them will, in their hearts, wish that they could have voted for it. *And that is what we want to show them.*"

I have heard few unpleasant things put in a more sinister fashion!

Cape Town papers were uniting in calling the bill "contemptible."

They declared it only emphasized the racialism that is always an unfortunate side of Union politics. But that was merely another thing that Malan wanted to make apparent. Its opponents also said that it was a low appeal, that it was playing up to the sentiments of the 300,000 "poor whites" in the Union, who are below the "bread-line" status. The more Jews you displace, the more jobs you provide for needy Afrikanders. And that was just another thing that Dr. Malan, expredikant of the Dutch Reformed Church, wanted to make known to everybody.

For he is a politician.

In 1932 a Carnegie Commission visited South Africa, and, after a careful study, reported that 22 per cent of the population of the Union was "poor white"; 34 per cent were below the normal sustenance level; 20 per cent had not risen to the taxation class; and only 3 per cent could be classed as well-to-do.

It is said that the Jews have never been so happy anywhere else in the modern world as they were in Johannesburg. It was literally their golden age, and many an aristocratic British name today is being supported by the money earned by the early, adventurous British Jews on the Rand or in the Kimberley diamond mines.

Today, one person in every sixteen in Johannesburg is a Jew. And one-third the Jews in the Union of South Africa (78,000) live along the Witwatersrand, the gold reefs.

Similarly, as they knew their segregation bill would also meet defeat, the Nationalist Party was merely circularizing it as a "petition" to be presented to Parliament. This bill would make all natives and colored people live outside the towns, or in special areas in the towns. And it would legally bar the blacks from certain occupations.

They are already barred, by the equivalent of a law, from practically every one of the skilled trades or professions in South Africa. And the term "colored" is not a polite name for a Negro, as it is in the United States; it means someone who has a detectable amount of black blood in him. If Sarah Gertrude Millin is correct, then this debars from all the professions and trades over one-third the entire population of the Cape Province.

In South Africa they say, "You are just as white as you can get away with!"

Malan would risk antagonizing even this large bloc of voters. (The "coloreds" have votes in Cape Province.) For he said to me, "Even if those bills can never be passed, I want to show the majority of South Africans where their hearts lie, and this way will do it."

He then made the statement by which his party hopes to ensnare the white labor vote in the Union:

"Unless white labor is protected against black or colored labor, the white race will go down."

This is the equivalent of saying, "South Africa must be a white civilization, therefore the black man must not be allowed up." And when I pointed this out, Malan made the staggering remark that "the *intelligent* section of the native and colored community would welcome segregation."

In order of importance among the aims of the Nationalist Party, I would say that this holding down of black and colored competition was the chief. It is nothing less than legalized repression. To break with England is really not an aim for many Boers; but advocating political jingoism which may always be counted upon to get plenty of votes at election time—votes from people who know they can play with this fire without ever getting burnt; England will always protect them, if only for her own interests, they feel.

But the South African universities, the intelligentsia, and many honest politicians, like Malan, are working day by day to get a republic; they want to break with England as quickly as possible.

General Smuts assured me that this was all very well; a great number of South Africans liked to "play with this idea"; but, he insisted, the minute the menace of Germanism became apparent, these people would rush for cover within the British Commonwealth. He did not extend this to Malan and the other leaders of the Nationalist movement, but he indicated that it went for about 99 per cent of the intellectuals.

If you study these aims against the "racialism" that is always the background for South African politics, this feeling between Afrikaan and British, you will see many things come into focus that, at first glance, seem quite incomprehensible in far-off England.

The chronic racialism in South African politics, both local and national, arises from something more tangible than the fact that it is a frustration, a hang-over from the Boer War; a great many South Africans sincerely believe today that they *could* exist as an independent state. Not so many, perhaps, now that Germany has shown her attitude towards small neutral states. But, as Hertzog has shown by his speeches, quite a representative section of South Africans believe they could, and should, keep out of Europe's (England's) wars, and that they would not lose their freedom by doing so.

To people of this belief, to cut the painter with England would be the first step to guarantee immunity.

But the desire for a republic comes from something deeper in the heart than that. "It's this," said a group of South African journalists to me in Johannesburg; "we people, whom you choose to call 'Dutch,' are the only real South Africans. We have no other homeland outside this country. When our people came out here from Europe, they came to found a new country—*and this it is!*

"Now, with the 'English' South Africans, they always have one foot in England. They don't place all their allegiance here. 'There is always England'; that's what's in the back of their minds. They are only half-hearted South Africans. They want South Africa for the empire; we want it for South Africa."

"Well," I asked, "what *real* difference to you does that make?"

"Only this: South Africa, the way things are now, is a machine, with strings attached to its levers, and those strings go to England. Every time we think we are running the machine ourselves, someone in England pulls a string."

"We don't *own* our country!" said another one. "It's not wholly ours."

They said they did not want me to leave South Africa without forming the right impressions. They asked whom I had seen at the Cape. I told them: Smuts, Pirow, Malan, etc., giving them quite a list of personages.

"My God!" gasped one, unconsciously; "why, he's seen *all* the wrong people!"

But that is just where the chronically untenable situation in South African politics comes in. Personalities.

The personalities of General Smuts and General Hertzog, the two outstanding national figures of South Africa, were so strong that a large part of their former United Party followed the *personal leadership* of one or the other. Until the outbreak of this present war, it was the combination of these two men which was the strongest influence holding South Africa within the British Commonwealth.

But, in January, 1940, Hertzog made a speech which shocked his followers. Formerly a man with a "single-track" mind, whom South Africans always believed they understood much better than they did the subtle Smuts, he suddenly revealed an attitude towards European politics that came as nothing less than alarming. In a speech which Smuts characterized on the floor as reading like *Mein Kampf*, Hertzog demanded that South Africa withdraw from the war, declare a state of peace with Germany, and remain perfectly neutral. Smuts said that Hertzog had shamed South Africa. And even the Malanites (who detest the name "Malanazis," as they have come to be called in the Union) recoiled from the wreckage that single speech of Hertzog's made of the Opposition tactics.

On January 27, 1940, Hertzog's "peace motion" was defeated by 81 votes to 59 in the Cape Parliament. The English hailed this as a great victory for Smuts; and it was—for Smuts. But the fact should not be overlooked, or its importance minimized, that 59 members of the South African Assembly thought it right, in crucial times like these, to cast their vote *not* to help England. They numbered 42 per cent of the Assembly. And, in a strange way, this reverses the "racial" composition of South Africa, which is 60 per cent "Dutch" and only 40 per cent "English." The London press, perhaps unconscious of the significance of the vote, declared that the "*personality of Smuts* [my italics] had never reached a higher point in South African politics."

Five months after this war began, when Hertzog and Malan were both in violent opposition against Smuts, Hertzog still refused to accept Malan's bitter program for a republic, with immediate separation from England. Hertzog was still sticking to his conviction that it would be wisest for South Africa to remain within the Commonwealth.

When I talked with Malan in February, 1939, it was the common saying in Cape Town that if Smuts were not alive Hertzog would swing over to the Nationalist movement. This would be an invaluable help to Malan.

"But it would be much better the other way," Malan said to me, seriously. "If Hertzog died, the men who follow him would desert Smuts. There would be so many of them that I would probably have a majority against Smuts."

As the events have shown, Smuts was able to carry the Parliament, voting South Africa into the war on England's side, against both Malan and Hertzog.

———

Malan is a pale, heavy man, nearly always dressed in black, with intense, brown eyes, behind spectacles, so fanatic that they seem to smolder when he is pressing home some point. His mouth is the stern, dogmatic aperture of the prelate who believes implicitly in the righteousness of his cause. It is said that he never laughs, never makes a joke; but he gave an unconscious heave when I said to him: "To the English, your ideas must seem horrible!"

"I believe that we shall have a republic within our time," he said, solemnly. "I am doing all I can to bring it about. I won't ask for it merely because I shall have a Parliamentary majority; I shall put it to a special vote of the people—a straight vote on whether or not they want a republic. No other political question will be allowed to be mixed with it."

He said he did not fear that a small Republic of South Africa would be attacked by any nation. When I countered by pointing out German rapaciousness, he replied:

"Look at Holland! Look at Belgium! Look at Denmark, Norway, Sweden!"

(That reply reads rather differently now. "Do," I feel like telling Malan; "look at Holland, Belgium, Norway, and, in particular, France!")

But it was substantially the same thing that Hertzog said in Parliament, just one year later; he, too, asserted he did not believe that Hitler was a menace to the small states. He said this five months after this war had been on!

But on July 17, 1940, when Dr. Van der Merwe, Nationalist, a strong supporter of Malan, was trying to organize a mass meeting "to consider active constitutional steps to establish a republic," Hertzog gave a statement to the Afrikaans paper, *Die Vaderland*, in which he said:

> I regard the purpose of it in the present circumstances as extremely undesirable and foolish. I therefore express my strongest disapproval, and decline to be a party to it in any way. I wish to warn the people against irresponsibility.

In reply to my request for his reasons for having a republic, Malan said that it was the same desire for full nationhood that had motivated the United States and the Irish Free State, and which the British were repressing in India. He declared it was the natural evolution of all component parts of the British Commonwealth. The right of appeal to the Privy Council, he declared, would soon be abolished in Canada. He was even more specific in indicating certain immediate steps that should be taken to prevent South Africa being drawn into any war of England's.

Simonstown, the British naval base at the Cape, he said, should be put on a different basis. The Union of South Africa should not and could not be asked to defend it. "As it is, if we give shelter to British ships, and no others, in time of any war we are *automatically* drawn into it. South Africa cannot have neutrality with Simonstown the way it is."

He elaborated the analysis I had just been getting from Dr. Karl Bremer, the deputy leader of the Nationalist Party. Bremer, far from being a back-veld South African, went to London University, finished his medical studies at Cornell University, and then served as an intern in St. Bartholomew's Hospital, in London.

"If Germany were able to beat the combined British and American fleets," said Bremer, "and South Africa had taken part on the losing side, then it is our country which would be handed over. In the event of a defeat on the part of, say, Britain, France, and America, then, *if we have not taken part in any war*, we retain our independence."

"Germany would never take a white man's country in Africa," said Malan. "She might take a native country, but not a white country, unless we fought against her. The English are the only country which has made war in Africa against a white race."

I said that his position seemed to be that South Africa was banking on the protection she would get because England would never willingly let her Cape route be menaced by Simonstown falling into foreign hands, but that the South African Nationalists were not prepared to make any sacrifice. If the combined fleets of England, France, and America were *not* defeated, then South Africa was sitting safe, anyway.

"You mean that we should go in on the side of the 'democracies'? That ideology is not enough. The fact that the world seems to be working up to war is not enough. You, the democracies, are quite prepared to ally yourselves with the worst form of dictatorship of all, the Communist.

"On the side of patriotism? Patriotism for England? There is none. As I have said before, the only country which has made war against a white civilization in Africa is Great Britain. There are many Afrikanders in the Hertzog-Smuts United Party today who want a republic for South Africa with all their hearts, but they are playing for safety, for self-interest. They think they will secure this by remaining under the protection of England.

"On the other hand, there is just as much to be said for another fear that is growing stronger every day here; and that is, *that if we are drawn into another European war we shall lose all.*"

I would have been much more impressed by Malan's arguments were it not for one of them. He declared that the large settlements of salmon-colored people in South-West Africa, the Bastaards, the Cape Whites, and the undefinable number of people in the Union, who are known as "coloreds," are *not* the mixture of Boer and Bantu.

"No," said Malan, piously, "they are the racial mixture of Bantu and Hottentot."

If Malan can believe *that*, I can also readily understand why he can believe that South Africa would never be endangered if she became a republic. Malan can believe anything.

"BLACK ZOOS"

LIFE IN AFRICA IS LIKE LIFE IN A SHIP—AND THE white men are the passengers.

It can be taken as an axiom that a white man never intends to do any heavy-duty manual work in Africa. His life's job, as he considers it, is to supervise black labor. He is dependent upon the native for all the manual work in the mines, on the farms, and for all the labor in connection with urban civilization. Until he is willing to do this work himself, he will never be able to free himself from the black man. The black man must, therefore, be kept under control. This reservoir of black labor must be preserved. More than that, it must be made to work. Left to himself, the native would do only the barest minimum of work, merely enough to keep himself alive, if that. Therefore a system of taxation, to make a native work, was invented long ago. Whether it is head or hut tax, the result is the same; a large number of natives must be absent from their Reserves a certain number of months every year, in order to earn enough money to pay this taxation. And any *surplus* of labor which the white man feels he may reasonably do without may be segregated in Reserves.

That, in rough outline, is the position of the black man in South Africa today. This does not apply to Tanganyika, where the British administration is holding the country in trust for the natives, and tribes like the Masai would never labor for the white man. Nor has it any connection with the British West African coast, where all cultivation is in native hands, and the white men are merely Government officials or traders. It holds good, however, to a large extent for the Belgian Congo and French Equatorial Africa; for while there may be no Reserves in these last two territories the natives are being, one by one, caught up in the mesh of taxation, put on a revolving belt of progress, and made to acquire a money urge, in spite of themselves. With Kenya, it is about half true.

Both Kenya and the Rhodesias are in transition, and seem to be heading towards the South African model.

The chief scandal of these Reserves is the overcrowding. In Natal (always strongly under English influence), 43 per cent of the land has been set aside for the natives; 8.75 per cent in the Cape Province; 3.56 per cent in the Transvaal; 0.2 per cent in the Orange Free State.

In the Transvaal 70 per cent of the population is on 3.56 per cent of the land; in the Free State, 67 per cent is on 0.2 per cent.

These are the "black zoos" which the white man has set up for the Africans.

The Transvaal and the Orange Free State are the most "Dutch" of the South African provinces. Here not even a "colored" man may buy a drink, and all natives (unless they live on the premises of their master) must be in their locations by 9 P.M. Johannesburg and Pretoria have "pick-up" vans, police patrols which pick up and arrest natives found after that time in the streets.

But there are 300,000 natives in the mine compounds on the outskirts of Johannesburg!

If you have seen a recruiter at work, you will remember it for the rest of your life. You will never forget the sight of scrambling, stinking black man power.

"I'm sending down a hundred boys today," said the medical officer in Ovamboland. "Want to watch it?"

Now, Ovamboland is the one place within the South African jurisdiction where the black man need not do any work, if he does not want to. The tax there is only five shillings a year; it may be paid in either cash or grain; it is all put into a tribal trust fund, and spent back on the native.

Yet there were over four hundred "boys" scrambling outside the employment shed for these jobs.

The scene afforded a diluted impression of forgotten slave markets; like a cattle fair; like the selection of vegetables at Covent Garden. Only, this was a river of black flesh that was banking up outside the door of the Northern Labor Company—a black cargo for the waiting motor lorries.

"Africa's richest asset!" said the doctor. "About half of those 'boys' out there are Portuguese Angolas. They've already walked over four hundred miles to get here. They're much heavier and stronger than the local Ovambas, but their chests are weak; they die like flies in the copper mines."

The local Ovamba "boys" did not want to go to the Tsumeb copper mine, 180 miles below; the deaths had been averaging eight natives a day there, only a few months before. At one time it mounted to as high as 10 per cent of the labor corps. The situation was so bad that the Government had stopped recruiting for ten days, until it had been investigated.

It was then discovered that the mine authorities had been giving the "boys" raw, uncooked food. They had to cook it themselves, after their work was done. One "boy," interviewed by the Government medical officer and the native affairs official, had, on coming off shift, not eaten for twenty-two hours. "I have no time to work, and then cook my own food," he said. As the result of the investigation (which had been made just before I got there) the Tsumeb mine had now installed a kitchen.

This Tsumeb mine was about a 100 per cent German concern, with the bulk of its capital held in Berlin. There were 240 Europeans in the mine, of whom only one was not a German. He was a South African, an electrical apprentice, married, and he was being paid £4 a month.

Many of the "boys"—those who did not die—would return from the Tsumeb mine ruined for life, from sulphur fumes, lead poisoning, and, until this particular date, from the atrocious food.

"It seems a damned shame to send him down there," said the doctor, having just passed a magnificent Angola "boy." "Break him."

The local Ovambas both did and did not want to go to the fields of the Consolidated Diamond Mines, at Lüderitz. They did not like the tales that the other boys had brought back, of the cold fogs along the South-West African coast, and of the alternative blazing suns. But they knew they would thrive there, for the Lüderitz diamond field feeds its "boys" like fighting cocks. What frightened them most was the new X-ray apparatus which the mines had installed to prevent the natives from smuggling the stones out in their bodies. There had been a big strike in the fields when the machine was first used; the natives were afraid the X-rays would sterilize them!

It was on the damp islands off that coast that the Germans had put their Herrero captives during the rebellion of 1904–07, knowing full well that the natives would die of exposure. The sea was full of bodies being washed up on the mainland. Five hundred, at least, died from cold there.

Outside the "boys" were fighting to be passed.

The doctor who was examining them was supposed to be the medical officer for 25,000 square miles and 150,000 natives; and, as he is always examining recruits, it can be seen what attention he can give to the other natives. He was being assisted by two native clerks, and a German known as "the rodent man" because his particular job in the district was to stamp out the bubonic plague. His macabre little office was full of flea-diagrams, stuffed rats, mongoose, and civet cats.

The "boys" came in stripped.

There was a strange, dank, sour smell about them that became sinister as it began to flood the room. It was not like white man's sweat; this was different. The doctor made them jump towards him in two enormous leaps, like frogs. This was done to expose the hernia (very common, from faulty cutting of the umbilical cord); it comes down when they jump. The "boys" made every effort to conceal the hernias, putting their hands over the places.

Each "boy" was made to demonstrate that he did not have a common venereal disease. It struck me that they were particularly clever in their effort to evade a revelation. There was an astonishing number of malformed, or not fully formed legs, varicose veins, and the beginnings of elephantiasis. The doctor refused to pass any with roughness on the skin. "This fellow might very likely be a starting leper."

Regarding them, as the hundreds passed before me, I realized the truthful saying that Africa is not a healthy country, even for the native, and that the great majority of African natives have something wrong with them. It wasn't the white man who had debased these bodies; it was the vile climate. Most of the Portuguese "boys," when asked why they were so anxious to go "South," said, "Because I am hungry, master."

Considering the death rate (and "boys" must have brought the tale home), it was amazing how anxious they were to go. A healthy "boy" will try to substitute for his weaker brother; be examined, then pass on the card. For no "boy" may leave Ovamboland without a pass card. In the scramble to be examined, two who had just been rejected succeeded in getting into the room for another examination. The doctor told one by his spotted behind. "I won't look at those with spots on them!" And the other was blind in one eye. It was amazing, the deftness and celerity with which the doctor examined them. He held his hand over one eye of this "boy," then held up the fingers of the other hand. He asked how many fingers he had raised. But the "boy" could not tell.

When the doctor had passed one, he marked, with yellow chalk, the letter A, B, or C on his naked chest. Then the "boy" stepped to the left, and two native attendants clapped a cord around his neck, and sealed it with a lead "plomb." The A's and B's were sent to the copper mines or diamond fields; C's were considered only good enough to work on the farms. Thus was this black humanity graded.

An A "boy," going to the mines, begins at 8d. a day for a shift of nine hours. Their average earnings are 25 shillings a month. (A white miner gets over £1 2s. 6d. a day.) A B "boy" gets the same as an A, if working in the mines. But on a farm he starts at 10 shillings a month, for the first four months; then 11 shillings and 12 shillings for the next two blocks of four months. But not many B's go to farms; it is usually the C's. These start at 8 shillings a month; and, as far as I could make out, that is about all that they ever get.

A year later these "boys" would come back (some of them) to Tsumeb with the usual £5 earned by a year's labor, and, as I have said, buy trinkets for their wives and sweethearts before they began their long trek back into Ovamboland and up into Portuguese Africa. While there is no stipulated tribute, each "boy" would have a few shillings, kept strictly in reserve, which he would give to his headman or chief. Very few "boys" fail to do this. No harm comes to them if they do not hand over this token of fealty. But, as the medical officer pointed out, it was comforting to find savages who willingly gave "money that hurt" rather than break with their old tribal loyalties.

Whenever a naked "boy" hopped before us with a ring of ostrich shell beads around his neck, we knew that he was going South to get the money to be married. This necklace showed that he had just become "engaged."

The records of the Northern Labor Company's recruiting office showed that about 90 per cent of the men who have once been South try to go back again. Some re-recruit the minute they get back to

Ovamboland. But the doctor said that the average "boy" remained at his kraal for four or five months. The doctor wanted to make this an obligatory eight months, so that the native would be ingrained with his old customs again, and not become detribalized.

Every one of these natives had perfect teeth. I looked down several hundred throats that day; I have never seen such superb molars. They were not even discolored. But all the local Ovamba boys had the middle lower tooth knocked out—so that they could spit properly. And a great number of the Portuguese West Africa boys had their teeth filed. Why? To get a good grip on their meat? Or for beauty? None knew. They said that it was done with a knife, and that it did not hurt to do it. I examined several sets of these filed teeth closely, and I couldn't discover any discoloration, even where the dentine must have gone, nor was there any sign whatever of any decay setting in. Their smiles were appalling.

There came before us, this day, two proud Herrero "boys." They were much taller than the others, some five feet eight or nine inches. They were "Ovatjimbas," descendants of those Herreros who had fled from the Germans, in the rebellion of 1904–07, into the unexplored Kaokoveld.

They had skins like satin, and the medical officer said they had the finest spines he had ever seen.

When the required number of "boys" had been passed, they were reassembled again in a long line, and passed before the doctor, who gave each an injection of anti-cholera and typhoid serum. Then they romped off, congratulating each other like schoolboys who had just passed an examination. They were then addressed by the recruiting officer.

He told each group of A, B, or C "boys" where it was going; what would be a day's work, and what they would get for it. He told them that food, shorts, shirt, blankets, and medical service would be given to them free. And then he turned over the job to the Government clerk-interpreter. His was the most interesting address. He said:

"If you have any complaints to make over your treatment in the South, if you have a row with your *baas*, or something like that, you must make your complaint to the Native Affairs Officer, or the Magistrate, *at once!*"

"You see," one of the white men at the recruiting office explained to me, "the 'boy' really ought to see the Magistrate while the blood is still showing from any cuts or bruises."

"And yet most of them want to go back?" I said, wondering.

"Yes; but damned few of them ever want to go back to the same master. Their optimism about us white men is humiliating. They always think they'll find a better one!"

H. V. MORTON

Pietermaritzburg, Durban, Zululand: 1947

"THIS WAS NOT A BIT LIKE MY IDEA OF ZULULAND. . . . THERE WERE GENTLE
DOWNLANDS, ROUNDED HILLS, LONG SWEEPING VALLEYS THAT REMINDED
ME NOW OF DORSET AND AGAIN OF DEVONSHIRE, SOMETIMES OF THE
YORKSHIRE MOORS AND OFTEN OF SCOTLAND."

Reviewing one of H. V. Morton's books in the New York Times, *Orville
Prescott wrote that Morton is "English, urbane, immensely cultivated, a
man with a lively curiosity and an indefatigable interest in people, places
and the historical past." And Harold Nicolson, writing in* The Observer,
called him "an ideal travelling companion."

*From the twenties through the forties, H. V. Morton's fifty or so books
made him the most widely read travel writer of his time. He began his
career as a newspaperman in England and soon had a position with the
Daily Mail. In later years, he wrote, "I have no hobbies except travelling
about and learning things, meeting people in village pubs and on village
greens, talking to them and putting down as faithfully as I can what they
say to me, coloured, of course, by my own mental background and by my
conception of their places in the social history of these islands, or lands."*

*His books covered the world, and their titles show clearly his point of
view as an informed and thoughtful observer. Many of them begin with
In Search of . . . , or A Traveller in . . . , or A Stranger in . . . , making
his work a perfect fit for these Reader's Companion volumes.*

*A selection from his classic In Search of Ireland, published in 1930,
is included in The Reader's Companion to Ireland.*

*Many readers, otherwise unfamiliar with South African history,
will recognize the names of Isandhlwana and Rorke's Drift from two fine
movies. The 1964 Zulu, written and directed by the American director*

*Cy Endfield, vividly depicts the battle of Rorke's Drift on January 23,
1879, when a small British garrison at an isolated mission station and field
hospital successfully held off an attack by overwhelming Zulu forces (later
winning eleven Victoria Crosses, the most ever awarded for a single engagement). The glory of the film is Endfield's evenhandedness in picturing
both sides of the struggle with courage and dignity. Endfield became fascinated by the subject and in 1979 cowrote* Zulu Dawn, *about the battle of
Isandhlwana, the first battle of the Anglo-Zulu War, which took place the
day before Rorke's Drift.*

*Both sites can be visited today. The mission station still stands at
Rorke's Drift.*

THE PLACE THAT INTERESTED ME MOST IN PIETERMAR-
itzburg was the Church of the Vow, now the Voortrekker Museum.
It is a modest little building, devoted to the relics of that not so far off
day.

I saw the only organ used on the trek, which I suppose came down
the Berg with Erasmus Smit. There is the footrule used in laying out
Pietermaritzburg in 1839. There are several early Nineteenth Century
dresses, which show how charming the mooi meisies must have looked
on Sundays. Then there are some fine and impressive waistcoats, wedding
veils, and, in an inner hall, a complete trek-wagon.

To me the most interesting object in the Museum is a dark green
glass flask found on the body of Piet Retief. In raised relief on one side
is an American eagle and a wreath containing the initials "J.K.B."; on the
other side are a number of Masonic emblems used in England and America during the early part of the Nineteenth Century. Such flasks, which
are not common, are a puzzle to Masonic antiquaries. Although the Museum calls it a "water bottle," I believe most authorities believe that these
bottles originally contained gin or whisky. The double of Retief's bottle,
bearing the same initials, which are those of the maker, is to be seen in
the Grand Lodge Museum in Freemasons Hall, London, and other specimens are known to exist in the United States.

The Director of the Yale University Art Gallery tells me that these
"J.K.B." bottles are believed to have been made at the beginning of the
Nineteenth Century at Keene, New Hampshire, a time when discussions

on Masonry had reached a peak in America. "J.K.B." is thought to be a combination of makers' marks at the Keene works.

Who gave this American flask to Retief, I wonder? So far as I know, he was not a Mason. The problem is confused by a picture of an entirely different flask with silver mountings illustrated by Dr Godée-Molesbergen in his *Zuid-Afrika's Geschiedenis in Beeld*, who says that this was given to Retief by the Freemasons of Grahamstown and that it is in the Pretoria Museum. He wrote in 1913. But it is not there, nor, so far as I can find out, was it ever there! Where is it? The Pietermaritzburg flask was presented by the Theological Seminary, Stellenbosch, and there is no reason to question its genuineness, but it would be interesting to know how this mysterious object came into Retief's possession. It is possible that the American missionaries who were established near Durban at that time gave it to him. But if he already possessed one from the Freemasons of Grahamstown, why should he have been given another?

It must have gratified the Voortrekkers to know that their hero went to his death with the American eagle in his pocket.

Pietermaritzburg is a fine-looking city which wears its air of grace and quality with becoming ease. The summer heat can be like that of an oven and there is no relief from it at night, when the semi-tropical trees stand in the thick air and one longs for a breath of wind. The inhabitants refer to the city as "sleepy hollow," and make jokes about their indolence that are contradicted by the number of shops which sell tennis racquets, golf clubs, polo sticks, cricket bats, and footballs.

There is a fine City Hall which is called Renaissance, but is really a massive bit of pure Edward VII, a distinct little period in architecture and dress. I was taken to the much finer Provincial Council Building, where the Parliament of Natal assembled before the Union. It was a strange sight to see the shadow of Westminster falling so far from home. In an airy, classical chamber I was shown the bar of the House, the division bell, and, in a glass case, the ruffles, mace, cravat, and sword of Black Rod. There is also a war relic of Westminster in the form of a stone from the Houses of Parliament.

Not unnaturally in a young country, public statuary in South Africa is an expensive civic indulgence which has as yet produced few masterpieces, and I was therefore impressed by the Natal Volunteer Memorial of the South African War, which stands in a little garden. I thought it a notable piece of allegory, crowned by a lovely figure of a Winged Victory in the act of sheathing her sword.

Every evening as dusk begins to fall you will hear the sound of wings over Pietermaritzburg. From every point of the sky flocks of birds are seen flying towards the city. Some come in formation like duck, others come in enormous flocks, like starlings, and they settle among the trees in the Bird Sanctuary.

A five acre lake in a well planted park has been devoted to the birds, which might be classified as permanent residents, such as the water-fowl and the stately cranes, and more numerous lodgers, like the egrets, who fly off every morning to earn their keep in distant fields. It is fascinating to watch their homecoming in the evening. I was reminded of Trafalgar Square, where much the same thing occurs when the thousands of starlings come home to roost round the National Gallery and St Martin-in-the-Fields. Here in Pietermaritzburg the egrets return in their hundreds of thousands, but more gracefully and with better manners than the London starlings.

The egret is the cow's little white companion, whose patient, statuesque figure is one of the memorable sights of the South African countryside. He is called the tick-bird, and, having adopted a cow, his life is spent in standing beside it all day long, seizing insects disturbed by the animal's feet and, it is said, in picking up the gorged ticks which fall from its body. Sometimes an impatient egret is seen standing upon its cow.

It is as a lonely, devoted individual that you think of the tick-bird, a creature seen in ones and twos throughout South Africa. As you observe his little upright figure in the fields, it occurs to you that perhaps he accompanies the object of his devotion to bed. But this is not so. In the Bird Sanctuary it is proved that the tick-bird is as gregarious as the swallow or the starling. Each one belongs to a flock. As it grows dark, each tick-bird says good night to its cow and joins the great homeward flight, which settles like a snowstorm upon the trees round the lake.

On my way to Durban I paused to admire the Valley of a Thousand Hills, which is, after Table Mountain, perhaps the most talked of view in the Union. It is a view of Natal that may be seen by any casual visitor to Durban with an hour or two to spare, and it is indeed a panorama of green mountain country stretching away to Zululand that is not easily forgotten.

1

A LINE OF GLEAMING BUILDINGS, THAT REMINDS THE TRAVELLER OF
Miami in Florida, rises from the sea and shines in the hard sunlight. The
waves pound upon sandy beaches, the tide rises and falls in a great lagoon
which is one of the finest harbours in Africa. And from a hill above the
town at night you can look down and see the lights of Durban sparkling
for miles.

There is an air of musical comedy or of a film set about this place.
The light is just a little too strong and white to be sunlight, the flowers
are a little too bright to be real, the flamboyant trees seem too exotic to
be genuine, yet against this sunny, lotus-eating background the tramway
system operates, motor omnibuses run to time, people go down to offices
and earn their living, typewriters tap, cables are sent off to every part of
the world; and in a huge municipal palace the mayor sits in an air-
conditioned parlour, with several cooling pictures of New Zealand on the
walls, and administers the affairs of what is, in spite of everything, a real
city.

Like all South African ports, Durban is a delightful mixture of business and fun. Its streets are always filled by residents and visitors, so that
in saying that the girls of Durban at once strike the observer with their
charm and beauty, one is paying a compliment to the womanhood of the
Union, for one may have been gazing with admiration upon the maidens
of Pretoria or Bloemfontein. And where else in South Africa can you see
a more provoking mixture of white and brown and black and yellow? You
leave the main street and find yourself looking at a mosque or a Hindu
temple. You see Moslems wearing the fez, and Indian women, in youth
as frail as spectres, drifting along in clouds of mauve chiffon. Then in the
next street you come to the more earthy Bantu market, where huge
bronze-skinned native men are putting back municipally brewed Kaffir-
beer with enormous heartiness. And on the wayside, a few steps from a
spotless chemist's shop in which a man in white overalls will make up
the most hieroglyphic of prescriptions, a native wizard sits offering for
sale the paws of monkeys and the fat of the hippopotamus.

Among the tramcars, the motor buses, and the American limousines
stands the barbaric figure of the Zulu rickshaw "boy." Upon his head
topples a fantastic structure of bull's horns and feathers, coloured beads

hang about, his fine body, and with a rhythmic, leathery sound of bare feet he trots between the shafts—the oddest-looking human taxi in the world.

Durban Europeans have their yacht club, a country club, and polo, swimming, golf, and cricket, and some are fortunate enough to live in imperial Roman villas upon hills where, between the snowy columns of their pergolas, they can watch the distant Indian sea. Great showers of brick-red and blue bougainvillea droop from the white pillars. In the still gardens, which have a warm, snapping, crackling life of their own, lizards bask and flash. The earth is ochre-red, and from it spring hot-looking flowers. Jacaranda trees hold bunches of blossom as blue as Kew in lilac time, and the Flamboyant, lit with its great red stars, is sometimes taller than an elm. In these exotic gardens I would come to a row of hollyhocks and a border of delphiniums with the feeling that I had been handed a glass of cool spring-water.

The first evening I was in Durban, I was invited to dine in a restaurant. The electric fans were working, for was it not December? There were mangoes with the dessert. My host, addressing the Indian waiter, said:

"It's a long time since I've seen you. How have you been keeping?"

The Indian at once adopted an expression of the utmost misery. He cast down his eyes and said that Fate had been cruel to him, for he had lost a son. My friend said how sorry he was, and asked if he had any other children.

"Now," replied the waiter with an air of lugubrious loneliness, "I have only sixteen."

2

It is not easy to surprise Durban in that slipshod, half-awake condition so familiar to the early riser in London and Paris. When seven o'clock strikes in the morning the place is fairly humming with activity: by eight o'clock not only can you buy almost anything, but you can also ring a man up at his office. By nine o'clock you begin to seek the shady side of the street and to understand why Durban begins its day so early.

An institution which gave me a great deal of pleasure is Durban's large and beautifully run Museum. What the Stone Age, the Bronze Age, Celtic, Roman, Anglo-Saxon, and so on, are to us, animal life is to the museums in South Africa. The bewildering variety of life on wings, crawling on its stomach, and walking on all fours, fills one with astonishment.

The South African birds which you begin to know very quickly are the egret, or tick-bird, the secretary bird, the big eagle, the lammervanger, who is sometimes seen sitting on a rock brooding, or more often gliding about the sky on unmoving wings, the cranes, and wild duck; but the great number of smaller birds remain unidentified until you go to a museum of this kind. One of the strangest birds I have ever heard of is the Honey Guide. It is not much larger than a sparrow and is greyish-brown in colour, with a spot of yellow on each shoulder. Its habits were described by Andrew Sparrmann in 1772, but no one believed him.

This bird, which is found in many parts of Africa, guides men and animals to bees' nests, and, when they have taken the honey, the bird expects to be left a portion of the comb as a reward, preferably a piece containing larvae.

"When I was trekking in South Rhodesia some years ago on a collecting expedition," the Director told me, "I noticed a small bird following me and obviously calling to attract my attention. One of my natives told me it was a bird that led people to honey. I decided to follow it. It would wait until I came close, then it would fly on and wait for me, calling to me all the time. This continued for an hour or so, and I began to think of giving up!

"Soon, however, instead of continuing its flight, the bird began to fly round in a most excited way giving an entirely different cry, and I noticed that bees were leaving and entering a hole in the ground. I had the nest dug out and left the comb containing the brood, which the bird immediately claimed. The natives say that should you leave nothing behind for the Honey Guide, the next time it will lead you to a cobra, a puff adder, or a mamba!"

The Director told me the story of a friend who was led by a Honey Guide on a long chase which, to his irritation, ended near the starting-place, but on the far side of a ravine. When he had taken the honey, he decided to go the short way back, but found it impossible. After several attempts, he realised that the Honey Guide had taken him along the only possible route for a human being.

One of the most interesting objects in the Museum is a skeleton of that extraordinary and now extinct bird, the Dodo. I was told it was bought about thirty years ago from a French naturalist of Port Louis, Mauritius, the island on which the Dodo used to be found. Durban's

Dodo is more complete than those possessed by the British Museum, the Cambridge University Museum, or the Natural History Museum in Paris, and a feathered reconstruction of the skeleton shows what a poor, fat, silly, and entirely delightful bird it was.

It was really an ancient type of pigeon that settled on Mauritius in prehistoric times and, taking to the ground, lost the use of its wings. It was as large as a turkey and became heavy and duck-shaped, with little, useless wings and an absurd tail-tuft; at the same time its pigeon's beak was enormously exaggerated, while its eyes remained the same size, so that the poor Dodo became an object of ravishing unloveliness. The Portuguese called it the Dodo, from doüdo, a fool or simpleton, and the Dutch used to chase it about Mauritius and club the poor creature to death with pistol-stocks or anything else, just for fun, apparently, for the Dodo was not good eating. The Dutch called it the nasty bird—walgvogel.

Those Dodos which survived the Dutch in the Seventeenth Century were exterminated when dogs and cats and other animals were introduced on the island. The poor creature was not fitted for modern life, and you can see him sitting up in his case in Durban Museum wearing a placid expression, as though entirely in favour of extermination.

3

The Old Fort at Durban was built by British troops in 1842, but is now such a rampageous tropical garden that you can only with difficulty follow the line of the earthworks. It has been planted with trees and flowers by the Durban Light Infantry Old Comrades Association, who have settled a number of old soldiers and widows of others in the barracks.

The garden enshrines a number of early Durban memories. The first white men round the bay were British adventurers and ivory traders who, under two naval officers, Farewell and King, managed to make friends with the Zulu tyrant, Shaka, and obtain from him a large grant of land. That was in 1824, thirteen years before the Voortrekkers appeared in Natal. The little group of Englishmen was in the heart of enemy country. What is now the Transkei was then a wild and hostile native territory which separated them from white civilisation at Grahamstown. The gallant adventurers hoisted the Union Jack and repeatedly, but vainly, begged the Colonial Government to make Natal a British possession.

An alert young Jew, Nathaniel Isaacs, who was with them, has left a fascinating and vivid account of the rough Robinson Crusoe–Swiss Family Robinson life round Durban Bay in those days. By the time Retief arrived in Natal both Farewell and King were dead and Shaka had been assassinated by his half-brother Dingaan. In the forays with the Zulus that followed many of the original English settlers lost their lives, and after Blood River the Boers established a Voortrekker republic of Natalia, with its capital at Pietermaritzburg.

The Colonial Government, at last roused by these stirring events and alarmed by the idea of a state on its borders with a sea coast, sent troops to hold Durban. A clash between these troops and the Boers in 1824 led to the famous ride of Durban's hero, Dick King, to get reinforcements from Grahamstown, six hundred miles away, through wild and hostile country. King was the son of an 1820 Settler and at the time of his ride was a young man of twenty-eight. He knew the country well and had spent his life driving ox-wagons and collecting ivory from the Zulus for the traders. He completed the six hundred mile journey in ten days.

His famous ride is a good example of the room for disagreement about an event which occurred only a century ago, for hardly two accounts agree in all details. Some say that he started from the Old Fort, or from the bottom of Gardiner Street, where his fine mounted statue is to-day, or from elsewhere; some say that he rode a white horse, others say a bay; some claim that he rode the same horse all the way, others that he frequently changed horses at mission stations.

What is unquestioned is that he followed the coast for the first hundred miles or so, then struck inland and on the last hundred and fifty miles passed through Morley, Ibeka, Butterworth, and King William's Town. Of the innumerable rivers, some, presumably, he could ford in the saddle, others he had to swim. Sometimes he hid by daylight and pressed on in the night.

I do not know whether any similar feat of horsemanship has ever been recorded; if Dick King rode the same horse for six hundred miles—which hardly seems credible—there is nothing with which to compare it. The greatest ride in English history, so far as I know, is Sir Robert Cary's four hundred mile gallop from London to Edinburgh to tell James I that Queen Elizabeth was dead. Cary left London at about ten in the morning on a Thursday and was kneeling by the royal bedside in Holyrood Palace on the Saturday night, telling James that he had succeeded to the throne. His four hundred miles had been completed in three days, but he was not in dangerous country, he had a relay of horses, and there were no rivers to ford.

Dick King saved the garrison in the fort. Reinforcements immediately embarked and were sent to Durban by sea, and the little Republic of Natalia was forced to submit. So Natal became a British Colony in 1843 and, like everything else in South Africa, its story is so surprisingly recent. It was the year Nelson was placed on his column in Trafalgar Square!

Even those historians who may consider that Natalia would in any event have ended in bankruptcy, or in disagreement and more trekking, admire the men who made it and their efficiency in action. The achievement of the Boers in clearing within four years so vast a territory as that between the Orange River and the Limpopo, and the Province of Natal, for white settlement is surely one of the great romances of colonial history.

4

I left Durban early one morning and passed through smiling suburbs to the road that leads northward into Zululand.

The approach to this native sanctuary was unlike anything I had expected. I might have been in India or Trinidad. All the way out of Durban I ran through little townships and villages which swarmed with Indians and their enormous families. Hindu temples and mosques were to be seen in what presumably had once been white towns. The Indian traders and merchants who stretch down the east coast of Africa culminate in Natal with a tremendous population of some two hundred thousand. Once the lowest of the low in their own country, they now dominate many branches of trading and some, I was told, have made large fortunes. That they can undersell the European, have a lower standard of living and, when rich, wish to live side by side with the Natalians, constitutes part of what South Africa knows as "the Indian Problem."

These people were imported in 1860 to cultivate the sugar, tea, and other crops in Natal, and they continued to be brought into the country until 1911. When their period of indenture ended, many were allowed to stay on as market gardeners, hawkers, and domestic servants, and, together with traders who arrived from India, multiplied and increased, as they obviously continue to multiply and increase.

I went on through the sugar country and came at length to the town of Stanger, which was once a great centre for the ivory hunters and traders on their way back from Zululand. Standing in a little garden just off the road is a memorial erected by the Zulu nation to the Bantu Napoleon, Shaka.

The creation of the Zulu military state is surely one of the most remarkable events in the history of South Africa, and one wonders how it came about. Legend says that towards the end of the Eighteenth Century a chief named Dingiswayo went into exile and wandered about for years, coming eventually to Cape Colony. There he was impressed by the sight of European soldiers drilling in uniform.

Zulu tradition recounts how one day Dingiswayo returned to his people riding upon a horse and grasping a gun, the first horse and gun seen in those parts. But more interesting still, he is said to have been accompanied by a white man whose identity is one of the enthralling mysteries of Africa. Who was the white man who helped to launch the Zulu nation upon its career of conquest, and what happened to him? This unfortunately we shall never know.

Dingiswayo, who had assumed the chieftainship, began to organize the tribe on a military basis. He introduced conscription and imposed discipline, forming his men into battalions on the European pattern. When he launched his well-trained warriors upon the surrounding tribes, his victories followed one another, but during one of his expeditions he was captured and put to death. He was followed by the terrible Shaka. That was about the year 1818.

Shaka was a born conqueror and despot. His nation, like Sparta, was now an armed camp. Every boy went into training and was eventually admitted into the army, and no man was allowed to marry until he had washed his spear in blood. Regiments, which numbered about two thousand men, were split up into companies, and each one was distinguished by a special uniform and a name. Some wore skins of otters, some of leopards, some had crests of ostrich feathers, others wore the plumes of the blue crane and the feathers of the Kaffir finch. The cow-hide shields were either red, white, black, or spotted. Certain regiments of proved valour were royal regiments and formed a Praetorian Guard.

Zululand was now covered with military kraals, each one the station of a certain regiment. After every engagement there was a ghastly ritual, when those who were said to have shown cowardice in action were put to death upon the command of Shaka. Upon one occasion a whole battalion which had not distinguished itself suffered the death penalty, each man having the point of a spear thrust beneath his armpit until it pierced his heart.

One of Shaka's first innovations was to limit the number of assegais carried into battle and to force his troops to rely upon a short stabbing-spear. His plan of battle was the pincer movement of modern mechanised warfare. The Zulu army advanced in the form of a half moon, and when the right and left wings had surrounded the enemy the main body advanced and delivered the attack. While the battle was in progress a large body, the reserve, remained seated with their backs to the fray.

The memorial at Stanger is placed upon the site of Shaka's great military kraal, Dukuza—the Labyrinth—where Farewell and King, Fynn and Isaacs visited him. It is possible to gain from these observers a clear idea of those great military camps, where the king lived with a host of concubines and surrounded by thousands of mostly celibate Janissaries.

Thousands of beehive huts spaced with military precision formed a circular band round the kraal, and each group of huts were the quarters of a particular regiment. Like a queen in a hive, the Zulu monarch was the central figure, accessible to his subjects, and on occasions only too visible in transports of ungovernable rage. He exercised absolute power over the lives of his people. The organisation of the Great Place was perfect. At a moment's notice the army commanders could call out whole regiments in full war-paint to dance, to display cattle, or to go off to war or to hunt. Everything the King said was formally approved by thousands of yes-men shouting in chorus. That Shaka saw through it all is perfectly obvious, but he throve on a reputation for inhumanity and based his power on fear; in which, of course, he was not alone in the ancient or the modern world.

When Fynn saw him first, Shaka was wearing a turban of leopard skin from which a crane's tail-feather rose two feet into the air, cubes of dried sugar-cane were let into the lobes of his ears, his shoulders and his body from waist to knee were covered with a fringe of twisted monkey skin, and at his arms, elbows, and knees were bunches of white hair from the tails of oxen. He was over six feet high, muscular, and active.

Isaacs tells how every morning the king would bathe and then rub his body with balls of pounded raw meat. Sometimes he would spend most of the day reclining in his hut surrounded by the royal girls, who knelt on mats. At night he would curl up on a reed mat and place his head upon a wooden neck-rest. Anyone who asked for an audience had to comply with etiquette as rigid as that of a European court.

His cruelty took extravagant forms, such as his massacre of thousands who did not appear to him to show sufficient grief when his mother died, a slaughter that was ludicrously extended to calves, so that the cows should appear to join in the universal lamentation. Once, suspecting infidelity, he made a clean sweep of the whole harem. His judicial functions seem always to have ended in the wretched defendants being hurried away, their necks broken by a sudden sideways jerk in transit, and their bodies beaten with knobkerries.

The white men were a great pleasure to Shaka. He did not know enough about them to fear them, as Dingaan did. To him they came at a time when life was boring, when a million Bantu had been slain in war and there were no new worlds to conquer—when in fact there was nothing to do but to gloat over the cattle and spend days in the company of a tedious harem. These white visitors were new and exciting, so were the stories they told of a brother monarch named George far across the sea, in whom the Zulu chief took the keenest interest.

The few years before his assassination were brightened by the gifts of macassar oil and purgatives, by a razor—a bold gift to offer him—and a mirror. With flawless logic he argued that if one pill were good, twenty must be twenty times as good, so that his court frequently suffered from overdoses of popular remedies. The muse of history would have been in one of her most playful moods if Shaka's desire to travel across the sea and meet his fellow monarch in London had been gratified. One wonders what George IV would have made of him, and he of the First Gentleman of Europe! George's tastes were catholic, and they might have got on famously. It would also be delightful to be able to report a subsequent attempt to recreate the Brighton Pavilion upon the hills of Zululand!

But Shaka's life was cut short by the assegai of an assassin, and he was buried where his monument now stands. Rising upon a series of stone plinths is a tablet surmounted by a draped urn that might more fitly commemorate John Wesley.

5

My surprise grew as I approached the capital, Eshowe, for this was not a bit like my idea of Zululand. I was prepared for something lush, tropical, and threatening; in other words, Congo country. But instead there were gentle downlands, rounded hills, long sweeping valleys that reminded me now of Dorset and again of Devonshire, sometimes of the Yorkshire Moors and often of Scotland.

It was surprisingly green, and less congested than the Transkei. Huts dotted the hills and the slopes, different from the white mud-walled huts in the other reserves; these were made of plaited basket-work and thatch that came down almost to the ground, giving them the appearance of old-fashioned bee-skeps.

The natives also were different. The men looked infinitely finer and taller, and I thought more young men were visible than in the Transkei. I passed them marching across the land or resting beside the road, and those not dressed in European clothes had skins that shone as if polished with blacklead. The women were performing the same eternal tasks, carrying burdens and drawing water; and they too, I thought, looked slightly more vivacious than the Xosas and the Pondos: in grace of move-ment, however, there was nothing to choose between them.

Eshowe is another of those beautiful onomatopoeic words—perhaps the best of them all—which describes the wind passing through the for-est. The town stands high and is surrounded by forests. It is fairly cool, and within twenty miles of the sea. You could go there and see little except the excellent hotel, a trader's store, and a few shops, but scattered all round about are many buildings which if brought together would form quite a respectable little township. There are at least four churches, a court-house, a hospital, a police station, a swimming-bath, an agricultural college, and a building in which the *Zululand Times* is printed.

Confidently expecting by this time to be lost in darkest Africa, I found myself instead in a sophisticated little hotel full of people who would have fitted into the background of Boscombe or Ilfracombe. There was even the same elderly woman knitting the same ambitious garment whose progress I have been watching all my life. Lunch included Scotch broth and the best steak-and-kidney pie I have encountered for years. When I asked the manageress whether the cook was English or Scots, she replied: "Oh no, he's a Zulu. Would you like to meet him?"

In the kitchen outside a rotund little bearded Zulu was introduced to me, wearing on his head a peculiar cone-shaped chef's hat like a dunce's cap. His name was Mzwayi. When I complimented him upon the pie he was pleasantly modest, and said that years ago he had been cook to a "most particular English missus" who had taught him how to make it.

I was lost in admiration for that unknown woman. Are not such women the true standard-bearers of civilisation? Posterity bestows its laurels upon people who have never done anything half as useful as teaching a Zulu to carry a perfect steak-and-kidney pie into the future. I thought I would like to have met Mzwayi's "most particular missus" and to have congratulated her upon her contribution to civilisation.

I was so tired that I went to bed at nine o'clock. The next moment, it seemed, a Zulu maid was gently finding room for a tea-tray on the bedside table, the sun was invading the room, and the usual South African bird was saying "Ho-ho" from an adjacent tree; for no one has taught these birds to sing.

6

Sixty-five miles away to the north-west of Eshowe are Isandhlwana and Rorke's Drift, and the place where the Prince Imperial was killed. I wonder how many people in these days could give off-hand an account of Isandhlwana? Yet it is only eighty-six years since that disaster horrified our great-grandparents and created an outcry in Press and Parliament.

It happened thirty years after Blood River, when the Zulu nation had recovered from its defeat and under a new military patriot, Cetewayo, was ready to fight the white man again. The Government, finding war inevitable, sent out an army from England in all the splendour of European military pageantry. There were lancers with fluttering pennons, brass bands, and gun teams with pipe-clayed drag-ropes. It is clear that the folly of fighting a frontier war in the European tradition was obvious to Boers like Kruger and Joubert, who warned Lord Chelmsford, the commander, that the only way to fight Zulus was to put scouts out ahead, form laager, and wait. But that was not the way things were done at Aldershot.

So the army marched into Zululand with bands playing, and one of its columns was surprised by a force of twenty thousand Zulus, who massacred eight hundred British soldiers and five hundred native auxiliaries. The tents were discovered still standing as if nothing had happened, and all round lay the disembowelled corpses of the defenders, the dead horses and oxen, and the rifled stores and ammunition boxes. That was Isandhlwana.

Cetewayo was eventually defeated at the battle of Ulundi, when the army formed a square, as at Waterloo, which was in effect a living laager with the cavalry in the centre. As at Blood River, the square opened at the critical moment and the cavalry rode out. This battle broke the military power of the Zulus and Cetewayo became a captive.

I would like to have seen the place where the Prince Imperial died. I am told that there is a rough stone cross erected by Queen Victoria in "affectionate remembrance of Napoleon Eugene Louis Jean Joseph, Prince Imperial, to mark the spot where he, while assisting in a reconnaissance with the British troops on 1st June, 1879, was attacked by a party of Zulus and fell with his face to the foe."

The Prince Imperial, son of Napoleon III and the beautiful Empress Eugénie, was an embarrassing addition to Lord Chelmsford's troubles in South Africa. He was a young man who, at the tender age of fourteen, had been taken by his romantic parent to witness the triumph of the French army in 1870 and, instead, he was returned to his mother before Sedan. His father was now dead, and as Prince Imperial he had already heard the intoxicating cry of "Vive L'Empereur!" rising into the English air from the throats of French royalists; for to them he was already the Emperor Napoleon IV and the hope of the Third Empire. He was thus a heavy responsibility for any commander-in-chief, especially in a country where any patch of tamboekie grass might conceal an assegai.

He was twenty-three, romantic like his father, headstrong and brave, and it was natural for him to see in the Zulu War an opportunity to distinguish himself as became the son of Napoleon Bonaparte's nephew. Might not a brilliant career in South Africa end amid fluttering handkerchiefs, the tossing plumes of cuirassiers, and the blare of fifes and trumpets in the Champs Élysées? Where but on a battlefield might a Napoleon reach a throne—and Zululand at that time was the only available battlefield.

The British Government, with the Isandhlwana despatches newly in the files—for the Prince came out with reinforcements after the disaster—firmly opposed the young man's wishes. But his mother went to see the Queen. That entente was irresistible.

"I did all I could to stop his going," said Disraeli after the tragedy. "But what can you do when you have to deal with two obstinate women?"

The Prince had passed high in his class at Woolwich—too high at least for a prince—and no one knew quite what to do with him. Little jobs like sketching and mapping were found for him, but the great thing was to keep him away from dongas and patches of mealies.

One morning in June he rode out with Lieutenant Carey, six troopers, and a Kaffir guide to inspect a camping site. While they were making coffee, a party of Zulus hidden in a donga opened fire. The horses plunged, and only five of the horsemen managed to scramble into the saddle. Two horses broke loose and two men ran about to try to catch them. The Prince Imperial, who was riding a mettlesome grey standing sixteen hands high, could not get his foot into the stirrup-iron. Hearing the other horses galloping past, the grey plunged and swung round, attempting to follow them, the Prince made a desperate effort to leap into the saddle with the help of a holster, which snapped and flung him off his balance so that he fell to the ground. His excited horse trampled on him and galloped off after the others.

He was now alone. The two unmounted troopers had been stabbed to death. He scrambled to his feet, drawing his revolver, and faced fourteen Zulus. Later that day a cavalry patrol was still able to recognise the naked body of the young man who, to many Frenchmen, was the Emperor Napoleon IV.

In April of the following year a strange procession moved through Zululand and picked its way carefully over the rough country that leads to Itelemi Hill. An escort of some twenty Natal Mounted Police surrounded a civilian spider driven by General Sir Evelyn Wood. Behind rode a groom with a led horse saddled for a lady, and farther back were baggage-wagons and a vehicle in which the startled faces of ladies' maids gazed out at the grim landscape. When they reached the place where the cross is now, Sir Evelyn Wood gave his arm to a lady in deep mourning whose lifted veil revealed the lovely face that for a little time had smiled in the sunshine of the Second Empire. What Eugénie thought as she knelt at her son's grave will never be known. She had been Empress of France. It must have seemed to her that the glittering adventure, begun so long ago in Corsica, had ended for ever in this lonely grave in Zululand, slain by the assegai of a black Napoleon.

7

The Chief Native Commissioner had kindly arranged a Zulu dance for me at a kraal far over the mountains. We set out in the afternoon, and travelled for a long way until we came within sight of a mountain top which I was told was four thousand feet above the sea.

The kraal was evidently a large one, but we lost sight of it as we turned off the road and began to ascend a steep track. As we came in sight of it again, it was clear that we had been observed, and a large group of Zulus was gathering to welcome us. Even at that distance, seen against the sky, I could tell that they had put on their war-paint. I could see tossing headdresses of feathers, and I was reminded of the descriptions of Nathaniel Isaacs as he approached the Great Place of Shaka.

This was, of course, nothing like Shaka's vast military town, but it was nevertheless one of the largest kraals I had so far seen in Zululand. A stockade of thorn bush and cactus enclosed several acres in which stood perhaps thirty or forty huts. They were all of the old-fashioned beehive type with the thatch touching the ground, and an entrance so small that you would have to enter on hands and knees. Within the main enclosure was a smaller cattle kraal constructed of wickerwork, where the milking was done and where the cattle were kept at night.

As we drove up into the entrance a crowd of some hundreds of Zulus, men and women, surrounded the car. I did not see one old hat, football jersey, or pair of trousers. The sight reminded me of the African village in some exhibition I had seen when a child. While I was admiring the fearsome and barbaric assembly, an old Zulu dressed in a white over-all, riding-breeches, brown leather gaiters, and a sun helmet strode up in a stately manner and saluted the Commissioner, then, taking off his hat, he uttered the royal salute, "Bayete eZulu!," which was echoed by all his followers. He was the chief.

He led the way into the cattle kraal where the dance was to be held. A few chairs had been placed for us, and no sooner had we taken our places than three cows were driven into the kraal. The chief made a speech to the Chief Commissioner, who rose and critically examined the beasts before selecting one. The chief then presented this cow to the Commissioner, who expressed his thanks in Zulu and returned the gift to the chief. The animal was driven away and immediately killed and flayed. All this, I thought, was running remarkably true to type! I began to wonder which of the onlookers would be hurried away to a Hill of Death!

The dancers, a startling sight, gave me a good idea of the scene witnessed by our ill-fated men at Isandhlwana as the impis swarmed towards them. From caps and rings of leopard skin, tall black plumes waved like the ostrich-feather bonnets of a Highland regiment. Their necks and shoulders were covered with leopard-skin corselets, which hung down in front of their bodies in a V shape. The tails of animals hung from their waists, and some more bushy tufts of white hair above the elbow and below the knee. Each man carried a shield—some of them small dancing-shields—and everyone carried a blunt stick.

The same atmosphere of anti-climax and hiatus, which is also inseparable from any Arab ceremony, then pervaded the enclosure, and the dancers drifted off in ones and twos until I began to wonder whether anything would happen. Leaving the Chief Commissioner and the chief in earnest talk, I took a stroll into the village. The delay, I gathered, was caused by the women dancers, who were not ready. They were sitting outside their huts clothed only in beads and bands of beads, busily engaged in greasing one another's legs and bodies until they shone like oiled bronze.

I had been told that the old chief possessed twenty-one wives and I wondered whether the dancers were young wives or elder daughters. With such a domestic establishment, it was obvious that what I had assumed to be a village made up of many different families was really only one family, and that most of the population must be the sons and daughters of the old man in the sun hat.

No woman preparing for a presentation at Court could have taken more pains before her mirror than the dancers as they crouched on the earth greasing themselves, seeing that every bangle and bead was in place, and especially that the elaborate hair-dressing was properly arranged. They were not wearing the high Nefrititi-like mud-pack of the married Zulu woman, but had arranged their hair in thin plaits, each plait ending in a bead or a charm, and the whole fringe falling round the face in front as well as back. At last they arose and, giving a final pull to necklaces and hip-bands, walked slowly towards the cattle kraal.

The dancers now formed up in a wide half-circle, the women in the front row, and began shuffling and stamping their feet to the sound of a low, mournful chant. The warriors brandished their sticks and knobkerries and waved their ox-hide shields and, as the dance progressed, the chanting became sharper and louder. A little old woman beating a tin can ran rapidly in a crouching attitude in front of the dancers, shrieking a word or two at them and inspiring them to greater stamping and shuffling.

This dance was called the Inkondhlo, and is one often performed at weddings and on other festive occasions. It was monotonous, and once having started there seemed no end to it.

The old chief, whose name was Nkantini, sat in state with the Chief Commissioner, facing the dancers and occasionally pointing with his stick to anyone who in his opinion was not giving of his best. I heard an amusing explanation of the name Nkantini, which is, of course, a corruption of the word canteen. This man's father, Siteku, had taken part in the attack on Isandhlwana, and after the battle took possession of a canteen, or quartermaster's stores, in which there was a large quantity of paraffin. Mistaking this for whisky, Siteku and his followers drank so deeply that some of them are said to have died. The effects of paraffin so impressed Siteku that he called his young son Nkantini to commemorate the event!

When the dance petered out I went for another walk round the kraal, and was delighted by the dignity and good manners of the people. They were in a very happy mood. The beast that had been slaughtered was ready to be roasted, so that everyone was looking forward to the feast which would begin as soon as we had departed. Outside one of the huts I saw two young married women helping one another to build up the peculiar cocoa coloured head cone, the isiChola, which is as distinctive of Zululand as the women's white eye paint is of the Transkei. First, the woman's hair is drawn up to its full length and plaited with grass into long spikes which stand upright from the crown of the head. The hair is then built up with certain fibres and treated with fat and red ochre. The finished effect bears a close resemblance to the high crown of Akhnaton's queen, Nefrititi.

We had a tremendous send-off, and the inhabitants of the kraal departed hastily to prepare for their feast.

8

Among those sights which have impressed most travellers in South Africa from the earliest times until well into the Nineteenth Century were the enormous herds of game which roamed all over the country. Nothing like it had ever been seen elsewhere in the world. The great herds of bison in North America, impressive as they were, could not be compared with the variety of wild life to be seen in South Africa.

When the white men first landed, hippopotami and lions roamed round Cape Town, then, as man and his guns advanced, the animals retreated, but even in the first few decades of the Nineteenth Century there were gigantic herds of migratory buck mixed with zebra, ostriches, and all kinds of other animals in regions now cultivated and settled.

A vivid idea of the sights seen by Nineteenth Century hunters may be gained from the illustrations in two accessible books which once had great popularity in England, Cornwallis Harris's *Wild Sports of Southern Africa*, and *The Lion-Hunter of South Africa*, by Gordon Cumming. The frontispiece in Harris's book shows a horseman galloping beside a great herd of antelope, wildebeest—or gnu—zebra, and ostrich, while in the distance other herds are calmly grazing, undisturbed by the tumult. Gordon Cumming shows a man firing from the saddle into a herd composed literally of thousands of blesbok.

What has happened to the once vast animal population of South Africa? A mass slaughter took place in the Nineteenth Century, as the heads and horns in castles and mansions all over the world, and in the glass cases of natural history museums, prove, and, as the human invaders pushed their towns and their railways forward, the game retreated, and might by this time have been almost extinct if South Africa had not established game reserves.

Large tracts of land have been set apart in many districts throughout the country, where the game are allowed to breed in natural conditions. No one is allowed to shoot them and Nature is encouraged to establish its own balance, as in the days before the coming of the white man. Lions and leopards are allowed to prey on buck, zebra, and giraffe, with the result that the species are kept strong and healthy. The two most famous reserves are the Kruger National Park in the Transvaal, celebrated for its lions, and the Hluhluwe Game Reserve in Natal, celebrated for the black and the elsewhere extinct white rhinoceros.

South Africans love nothing better than to spend a holiday in the rest camps at these reserves, where they sleep in huts and go out by day to see the wild animals in their natural surroundings and shoot them with a camera. Nearly everyone in South Africa has some startling story of a lion met face to face in the Kruger Park, or of a rhino that charged them in Hluhluwe.

When Mr D. E. Mitchell, the Administrator of Natal, offered to drive me up to Hluhluwe for a few days with the rhino, I accepted with alacrity, for there could be no better guide.

We left Eshowe after lunch. The journey before us was one of a hundred miles to the north into the more desolate coastal regions of Zululand. We passed through the beautiful green hill country, where the beehive huts had the mournful look of lonely cabins in Connemara. Sugar-cane grew on each side of the road, and once we had passed through the little town of Empangeni the road stretched ahead devoid of town or village for mile after mile.

Hluhluwe—another lovely word—means "Sweet waters," and you can hear them lapping if you pronounce the h's as l's. At first sight unpronounceable, this word may easily be rendered correctly, as in Zulu, by any Welshman, and indeed by anyone who can say Llewelyn. Mr Mitchell told me that the Hluhluwe Reserve covers sixty square miles of country, and it is the only place in the world where you can see the South African white rhinoceros, for the white rhinoceros of the Uganda is a sub-species.

We crossed the Black Umfolozi River on a long, rickety bridge and saw, far below, a trickle of warm brown water flowing eastward to St Lucia Estuary, where crocodiles and hippopotami are to be seen and where men go to catch sharks. The country now became wilder than ever. A place that looked quite important on the map turned out to be a trader's store with a petrol pump and a few chickens pecking round outbuildings near a cactus hedge.

As we went on, I saw another aspect of Nature's attempt to turn South Africa into a wilderness. Here was a problem of land degeneration almost as difficult to fight as soil erosion. It is called bush encroachment. We passed through mile after mile of recently good grassland, but now bush country in which nothing can grow. Between this point and Swaziland to the north there are tens of thousands of acres of good land degenerating into bush. You can look back and see the grass like an outgoing tide.

We passed imperceptibly into the Game Reserve, where I saw a glorious wild land of green rounded hills and dense valleys, and far off line after line of blue mountains. There is a profound difference between wild country, no matter how desolate, in which man is living, and utterly primitive country that has never known his fires, his huts, and his ploughs. The Hluhluwe Reserve was primitive Africa, incredibly primitive pre-Bantu Africa. I could have imagined that any rock near the road concealed the pigmy people, who, according to Zulu tradition, were an older, smaller race even than the Bushmen. Then there was a sudden gallop, a frisk of tails, and right across our path streaked a dozen zebra like fat, painted ponies. The grass grew high beside the road and I saw a movement in it. We stopped the car. One by one several melancholy snouted faces appeared, and then, bounding on their knuckles, turning every now and then towards us, a family of baboons, the little ones bringing up the rear, crossed to the other side.

We came to a dell as green as any wood in Surrey. The trees arched overhead and the watchful stillness of woodland lay all around.

"Look!" I cried, "the animals I've been longing to see—springbok!"

"No," said Mr Mitchell. "Impala."

And almost before we had had time to watch, six exquisite red-brown bodies had curved like divers through the air across the road, six bodies with curving horns, six deer-like muzzles, each with a little white mark near the eye; and they vanished noiselessly, like a dream, into tall grass.

We came out of the wood to the shoulder of a hill. A notice-board stood there as surprising and laconic as "Unexploded Bomb." It just read: "Danger. Rhino." We scanned the hillside eagerly, but could see nothing.

9

The rest camp at Hluhluwe stands upon the top of a hill. There are a number of circular white rondavels standing in lines upon grass, a welcome and cheering sight. There is a smell of wood smoke as Zulu servants fire the stoves for hot water. The huts are civilised places; mine had a small kitchen and a bathroom and also electric light.

About eighty visitors can be housed in the camp, and they must bring their food with them. The camp provides beds, bedding, cooking utensils, cutlery, crockery, firewood, and large, silent, competent Zulus, who do the housework and the cooking. Like so many things in South Africa, I thought the price—four shillings a night—amazingly cheap.

After a bath we went off to dine with Captain and Mrs Potter, the Game Conservator and his wife, who live at the far end of the camp in a house among trees. The Potter mansion touches the highest point of improbability. Standing upon a hill in Zululand, surrounded by many strange African trees and shrubs, it has the air of having flown straight over from Sussex. It is one of the houses advertised every week in *Country Life*: solid, stone-built, leaded casements, and all modern conveniences. One expected the door to be opened by a London stockbroker.

Upon a parquet floor covered with lion and zebra skins stood Captain Potter, wearing a safari shirt and khaki trousers, tall, lean, brown, and observant—just the type you would choose if you were writing a play or a film about life in the back of beyond. The things that worry so many people—stocks and shares, money, the deplorable state of the world— meant nothing to him in this solitude. More important than Russia and America and anything else was the sick rhino calf in Umfolosi.

Captain Potter was born about sixty years ago in Staffordshire, although, like so many South Africans of sixty, he looks no more than fifty. When he was a schoolboy at Berkhamsted, he remembers seeing Lord Rothschild emerge from the gates of Tring Park behind a team of zebras; but he had no idea then that his knowledge of these animals was later to become more profound than that of his lordship. He came out to South Africa, where eventually his love of animals and solitude led him to Hluhluwe.

We had dinner as if we were in a house in Cape Town, the well-trained servants in white jackets moving noiselessly over the lion skins. The talk was all of wild animals—of rhino, buffalo, zebra, buck, but always back to rhino, the pride of Hluhluwe. I gathered that the average visitor arrives by car and spends his time looking for rhino, generally with a camera. He can go in his car along the few roads that traverse the reserve, where he frequently meets these animals round a corner, or he can go on foot, but should he do this, he must take a game guard with him.

It is not uncommon for a visitor to be "treed" during his visit, and this has happened to many distinguished and dignified persons; for when it sees you, the rhino will either lumber away or instantly charge. Two policemen upon a recent visit to the reserve had been forced to spend a night in a tree while a rhino patrolled beneath.

There are a hundred and fifty of the ordinary black rhino in Hluhluwe and two hundred and fifty to three hundred white rhino, mostly in the adjacent Umfolosi Reserve, the only remaining white rhino in the world. The difference between these animals is in size and habit, not colour, for the white is much the same colour as the black. But he is, after the elephant, the largest of land mammals. A good-sized male will stand six feet six inches at the shoulder and may weigh about five tons. White and black rhino have two horns, the larger of which is between four and five feet in length.

"How can you tell a white from a black rhino?" I asked.

"The white rhino has a square lip, and the black has a pointed, prehensile upper lip," I was told.

I asked if there are any other signs that might be observed from a greater distance.

"Yes. The white rhino lives on grass and carries his head so low that it almost touches the ground; the black rhino lives on the leaves of trees and bushes and carries his head higher."

The white rhino, although larger than the black, is not so aggressive. Both animals have such poor sight that they can see nothing farther away than about thirty paces, but the senses of smell and hearing are highly developed. The black rhino never utters a sound. When angry, his grunt can be heard only for about ten yards, but the shout of the white rhino can be heard for half a mile. Both white and black rhino calve only once in three years.

During the day-time the rhinoceros often sleeps, and feeds at dusk and in the early morning. He is so frequently met with at night that visitors are cautioned to arrive at the reserve in daylight.

1 0

It was not yet five on a sharp, chilly morning. Mist lay in swathes in the valley. There was utter silence. I shivered as I put on a bush shirt, but I knew that in two hours it would be almost unbearably hot. Just as I had loaded a camera, I heard the sound of a car outside. Mr Mitchell and Captain Potter were looking keen and resolute.

The road from the camp winds steeply down into the reserve, passing round a tall hill; the ground falls away on the left to grassland dotted with bush; to the right is the steep hillside. As we turned a corner, Mr Mitchell braked and brought the car to a stop.

"Look!" he whispered. "What a bit of luck!"

Forty yards away, right in our path, a female rhinoceros and her calf were asleep on the road, snuggling into the hillside. We had the sun behind us and it shone on them.

"I say, Potter, she's big, isn't she?" whispered Mr Mitchell.

"Yes, she is pretty big," said Captain Potter.

I thought she was colossal. She lay in the road like a broken-down tank. Her body was elephant-grey with a hint of pink, and the immense mass heaved slowly as she breathed. The calf was the size of a big pony. I had not yet seen a rhinoceros move, and was feeling fairly courageous. I suggested that I should get out and take a photograph.

"Be quick," said Mr Mitchell, "for we may have to reverse if she charges."

Taking a few steps on the road, even though accompanied by Captain Potter, my heroism began to ebb. The rhino's main horn was at least four feet long and her sharp little ears were like the knot in a handkerchief which people make to assist memory. As we tiptoed towards her, those small ears twitched independently, and suddenly, with a stupendous lurch, she was on her feet looking at us. It was a most surprising movement. The calf rose, too, and stood beside its mother. I decided not to bother about a photograph and went back to the car.

"We'll just creep a bit nearer," said Mr Mitchell, slipping forward yard by yard.

Having heard us, smelt us, and now having seen us, the rhinoceros moved to face us squarely. She lifted her head with its two horns and watched us. The sun shone in her eyes, lighting up two spoonfuls of black malice. As we slowly advanced, she stood her ground squarely. We were now about thirty yards away. I looked round to see if Captain Potter had brought a gun. He had not. I looked back and thought it would not be easy for us to reverse uphill at a sufficient speed. I already saw the engine of the car speared on her horn and began to wish that Mr Mitchell's nerves were not so good.

"Look out," whispered Captain Potter.

"It's all right—I'm watching her," whispered Mr Mitchell.

The malicious vegetarian lifted and lowered her head as if scenting us, and made a slight stamping motion with a foot.

"Here she comes!" said Mr Mitchell, putting the car in reverse, as the ponderous mass came lightly towards us, then as suddenly swerved off the road into the bush, accompanied by her calf.

She paused when a hundred yards away and again faced us as we continued down the road. At the next bend, we encountered a small car puffing up the hill towards the camp, packed with a laughing family party, who waved to us and shouted cheerfully as they went past. Little did they know what game we had flushed from their path!

After breakfast we motored off again in search of rhino. We repeated the process after lunch. We counted twenty-seven rhino in the course of the day, which I believe is almost a record bag. We saw also kudu, impala, inyala, buffalo, bush buck, zebra, wart-hogs, and monkeys.

I noticed that every one of our twenty-seven rhino carried a red sore about the size of a saucer on its body. Captain Potter told me that these sores appear only during the breeding season, and his theory is that they are musk glands.

"If you returned here in two months' time," he said, "I would give you a fiver for every sore you could find. They will all have healed up. If you should examine the body of a young rhinoceros, you would see on its side an indentation where the musk gland will develop in adult life.

You will not find this theory advanced in any zoological work. It is my own theory, based on observation and contact with these creatures. Also, during this time of year I can smell the rhinoceros musk."

We spent an enchanted afternoon among hills and valleys, coming suddenly upon pastures where zebra and wildebeest grazed together. With a tribe of monkeys running, stooping, and turning before us, we climbed hills and came to cool forest paths, full of furtive movement as buck hid from us, all save one, a tall kudu bull who stood beneath an arch of leaves and faced us eye to eye. The only movement in his body was an inquisitive trembling of velvet nostrils until, the engine starting up, his resolution snapped and he was gone, with nothing to show that he had ever been there but a waving bough.

The great thrill of our day was waiting for us, unsuspected but not unsought, at the top of a hill as we were returning to the camp. We came slowly up the hill and, turning a corner, had just changed gear for the flat when we saw a rhinoceros charging at full gallop, with his horn aimed at us. Automatically Mr Mitchell pressed his foot on the accelerator, the rhinoceros pulled up at a small bush on the side of the road and worried it with his horn, and in that second we were past him!

It happened so quickly. There was no time for alarm.

"Well, did you ever see anything quite like that?" said Mr Mitchell. "That old Punyana heard the car and was waiting for us at the top of the hill, and—if it hadn't been for that bush he might have got us!"

The Punyana is a slightly smaller type of rhino, bad-tempered and savage, as we saw only too well. The extremely clear impression I had of him was that he was moving with the speed of a horse and was attacking us out of sheer ingrained malice.

The following day we set off by car from Hluhluwe and were in Pietermaritzburg in the evening.

MARTIN FLAVIN

Johannesburg and a gold mine: late 1940s

"DOWN WE WENT—FIVE THOUSAND FEET OF SWIFT DESCENT WITHOUT
A PAUSE, A DROP SIX TIMES GREATER THAN FROM THE TOP OF THE RCA
BUILDING TO THE GROUND."

*The American writer Martin Flavin was known in his time primarily for
his novels and more than a dozen plays, but he also wrote two really excellent books recounting his travel experiences.* Black and White: From
the Cape to the Congo *was published in 1950 and covers his travels in
South Africa, Bechuanaland (now Botswana), and the Congo (until 1997
known as Zaire and now the Democratic Republic of the Congo). His
1962 book* Red Poppies and White Marble: A Journey on the Riviera of
Antiquity *is an insightful tour of the southern coastal regions of Turkey.*

*Flavin is an observant and thoughtful traveler, qualities particularly
useful for a foreign visitor in South Africa. He sees clearly through the
facts and figures, as when he notes in his introductory comments: "I have
said that the wealth of South Africa is gold, but the statement should be
carried a step further: the real wealth of the country is cheap labor, deprived of which the Union would be bankrupt overnight."*

*Throughout the narrative, his tone is reserved and understated, and
he opts more often than not for irony over rant. In noting that black
South Africans have "Jim Crow busses" available to them, he adds that
they are also permitted to ride the trolley cars "if they are accompanied by
a white man," calling this "a generous regulation which enables the white
man to keep his servant near him."*

*And always he hears the clock ticking for South Africa. Writing of a
makeshift Johannesburg township called Meroka, which he calls "the*

plague spot of the country—of the world perhaps," he notes that "there has been trouble in Meroka, and there will be again."

Much more than a tour of a gold mine, this excerpt from Flavin's book offers a troubling insight into the heart—or the several hearts—of South African society.

MR. BROOKS OF VACUUM OIL CALLED FOR ME AT 7:45 A.M., at my hotel in Johannesburg, to take me to a gold mine.

I had come up from Cape Town a day or two before on the "Blue Train," a miniature "Twentieth Century," of which the residents are justly proud. It runs twice a week and does the thousand miles in twenty-seven hours, ten hours faster than the ordinary trains, which isn't very fast, but fast for Africa. It's Continental in design, air-conditioned, and equipped with most of the gadgets to which we are accustomed in America. Unlike most African trains it has soap, towels, and toilet paper. Incidentally, it is almost impossible to get on it—like those exclusive schools for which you must be entered when you're born. But the Ministry of Transportation came to my rescue and got me a cute little coupe all to myself. It's a good train, and I was glad to get on it and very sorry to get off. The only place in South Africa where I was equally comfortable was a hospital in Johannesburg where I spent four wonderful days.

Johannesburg, or Joburg as they call it, is an urban island in the midst of nowhere, a pin point in the vast, sad wilderness of Africa: a city of nearly a million population, about half of which is black and lives on the wrong side of the tracks—really outside the town, in sordid Jim Crow areas to which it is restricted. The white people refer to themselves as Europeans, and call the Negroes Natives. Strictly speaking these designations are ethnologically unsound, but they serve the purpose of the color line. The South Africans are very proud of Joburg. Some of the more enthusiastic and less well-informed say it is like New York. But they are mistaken about that. It's more like Detroit, with a dash of Butte, Montana, and a pinch of Houston, Texas—a kind of composite of the three. It's a mining town in fact, without any other excuse for its existence, built on a gold mine—or rather, on a lot of them, on a narrow seam of gold-bearing rock, known as the Reef, outcropping from a flat and broad plateau, six thousand feet above the sea.

The city is three years younger than I am, and on the whole, I think, is less well preserved. The core of it is an ugly, throbbing, congested business section, sprawling planlessly, and glutted with traffic, depressingly unequal to its present needs; fringed with residential sections in process of, or threatened with, absorption; thinning out into attractive suburbs—expensive homes with well-kept lawns and gardens, and winding tree-lined streets; country clubs, and bowling clubs for bowling on the green, tennis courts and swimming pools, cricket grounds and soccer fields; the whole ringed round for part of its circumference, at a respectful distance antipodal to the suburban area, with wretched Native slums— the most appalling slums I've ever seen. Finally, there are the mine dumps, rearing from the landscape—ocher-colored hills growing into modest mountains, pyramids of powdered stone geometrically designed, not devoid of beauty of a cold, forbidding sort, certainly impressive against the deep blue sky, which seems deeper and bluer in Africa than elsewhere: the monuments of Joburg, night soil of successful enterprise, excrement expelled in sixty years of eager, unremitting gluttony.

Gold, not diamonds, is the wealth of South Africa, in a ratio of 10 to 1 for gold. Even wool is far ahead of diamonds. But gold is at the top, far ahead of everything. The average annual production is 12,000,000 ounces, which at $34.50 per fine ounce has a value of $414,000,000. There are 2,335,460 European (white) men, women, and children in the Union of South Africa—or were alleged to be the last time they were counted. If the gold were divided equally among them, each man, woman, and child would receive about $200 yearly. But it's not divided among them; and there is no good reason why it should be, since they take little part in the production of it. There are 7,735,809 Native (black) men, women, and children in the Union; and, in addition, 905,050 so-called Colored (mixed breeds), plus a handful of Asiatics. Or say, to summarize, almost 9,000,000 non-Europeans—four blacks for every white. If the gold were divided among the dark-skinned people, they would each get something less than $50. But it's not divided among them either, though they are the ones who actually produce it, who perform all the hard, menial labor of the mines.

Some 300,000 Native workers are employed in the gold mines of South Africa: contract labor, with an average term of fourteen months' employment, which of course can be repeated, and usually is. This labor is largely recruited from the Native Reserves, which comprise only 12 per cent of the Union's total area of 472,550 square miles. It is worthy of note that although there are four times as many blacks as whites, only one-eighth of the country has been allocated to them, wherein they may maintain some semblance of their natural tribal life and culture, and hold up their heads like men. To make the picture a little more graphic, let's put it this way: 5½ Europeans to 1 square mile; 160 non-Europeans to 1 square mile. But the blacks are not confined to reservations; they are everywhere of course, and for one excellent reason: the Native Reserves will not support the Native population, not even on the bare subsistence level to which it is conditioned. They must get out or starve. No good to say, as is so often said—if they were skilled, efficient cultivators of the soil (which they are not)—if they had the proper mechanized equipment (which they haven't)—if they didn't spend their money buying cattle to trade for working wives (which is their way of life)—if this, if that— The fact remains that, being what they are, they must get out or starve.

Hence cheap labor for the farms and for the mines, for every menial task. The labor unions and the law effectively debar them from skilled occupations and economic progress. Hence the dreadful, festering urban slums; hence disease and poverty and crime. Hence $400,000,000 per annum worth of gold. But recruitment of labor for the mines is not confined within the borders of the Union, suggesting that the mining occupation is not as popular as sometimes represented. Labor is recruited from Portuguese East Africa, from Bechuanaland, even from as far away as the Rhodesias.

The South African lives in terror of two things. One is a decline in the price of gold, which he is helpless to prevent. For gold is not an ordinary commodity, like a cabbage or a motorcar, on which you can raise the price if your cost should be increased. The implementing sources of the price of gold are political rather than economic, and at all events remote from South African control. The other dread that haunts their sleepless nights is fear of an increase in the cost of labor—the labor which must produce the gold, if it is to be produced. I have said that the wealth of South Africa is gold, but the statement should be carried a step further: the real wealth of the country is cheap labor, deprived of which the Union would be bankrupt overnight. Without ruthless exploitation, and suppression, of a vast, subsistence-level labor pool, the economy of the country would be incapable of functioning. And in this day and age, that should be enough to keep a sober man awake.

The mines are at the apex of the general situation, and thereby serve as a focus of attention: what happens in the mines will happen elsewhere.

Their position at the moment is said to be precarious. The mines are deep—the deepest gold mines in the world; only black men can, or will, work at these levels. And the deeper down you go the more difficult it gets, and the more expensive. And Native labor, as yet unorganized, unacquainted with and not yet equal to such complicated undertaking as collective bargaining, outlawed by statute from most of the rights which we regard as inherent civil liberties—Native Labor is nonetheless awakening, slowly and painfully, to its wretched situation. Faint echoes from the outer world are coming to its ears in the galleries underground, and in the urban centers. The gold mines may indeed turn out to be volcanoes—almost any time.

The thoughtful citizen is not unaware of this, and is doing what he can, with what light he is endowed, to avert, or to postpone, a day of reckoning. With the Nationalist party in control of the government—a recent, unexpected political upset—repression and coercion should gain fresh impetus. But it would be a mistake to ascribe these policies to cruel and ruthless men. The European, like the Native, is the victim of a situation which he has inherited, which has grown slowly through a hundred years, for which no one can be said to be responsible. He is facing a problem which seems to him insoluble on any other terms than the present status quo; his purpose is to keep the problem where it is, not to let it worsen—which is of course impossible. He believes he is fighting for his life. And so indeed he may be—a losing fight, I think; but there is wide divergence of opinion about that. At all events he is neither a monster nor a brute, but an average, decent fellow—or as decent as any of us are. He wants to do the right thing, just as much as you and I. He may be stupid and shortsighted, and I rather think he is. But the problem isn't mine, and tolerance grows with distance. I don't know how I'd feel if I were in his place, and I'm equally doubtful about you.

It should be noted that the European population is by no means united, politically or socially. In the region of the Cape the atmosphere is British; but the interior of the country is largely dominated by the Afrikaners, as the Boers are called, descendants of those hardy Dutch and Huguenot pioneers who were original settlers of the land, with an Afrikaans language of their own, and highly separatist and reactionary tendencies. Politically, they are the Nationalists, isolationist by instinct and tradition: South Africa for the South Africans; and by South Africans, they mean themselves, the Boers. The unsuccessful war they fought with Britain for their independence has not been forgotten, nor have their objectives been relinquished. The wounds were deep and much bitterness remains. In personality, the Afrikaners are not unlike our Texans: a shade less rough and noisy, but friendly and informal, rugged individualists accustomed to big country.

I HAD A LIMITED TIME TO SPEND IN JOBURG, AND I WANTED to see the inside of a gold mine. I had thought there would be no difficulty about this, but it turned out otherwise. Gold mines are open to visitors twice a week, a designated mine on a designated day. The mines rotate among themselves the responsibility of entertaining visitors. A certain number of applications are accepted for each occasion, and when the quota has been reached the list is closed. There was a day which fell within my scheduled time, but I was too late to be accepted. At this point Vacuum Oil comes into the picture. I had a letter of introduction to the managing director, and, as it turned out, they had made application for some visiting employees, one of whom was kind enough to retire in my stead, saying he could arrange to go another time. And so, for the day, I assumed his name and place.

Hence Mr. Brooks, at 7:45 A.M., in a baby Peugeot car, the back seat of which was already overloaded with two young visiting oil men from the Free State, who welcomed me with easy hospitality. I had brought with me, as I had been instructed, a bath towel and a change of underwear, and, with this bundle underneath my arm and an inconvenient camera hung around my neck, I climbed into the seat with Mr. Brooks. We crawled down the street, already thick with traffic, past the railway station with its stand of dilapidated rickshas—the only ones I saw in Johannesburg, and exclusively for Natives, I suppose, since I never saw a white man riding in one. There are Jim Crow busses for them, but at infrequent intervals and hopelessly inadequate; and they may ride on the trackless trolley cars, if they are accompanied by a white man—a generous regulation which enables the white man to keep his servant near him. And the black man may walk freely on the streets of Joburg, with his luggage on his head, until nine o'clock at night—and even after that, if he has a pass signed by a white man. There are many aspects of the South African color line which are painfully reminiscent of those we have at home. But there is one important, fundamental difference: every step the black man is able to take forward in America has the support of law—

of National law at least; in South Africa every step he takes is in violation and defiance of it. The cards are stacked against him.

We emerged out of the city onto a broad, paved highway, flanked with mine dumps; and, in the distance, with Native areas: Sophiatown, a squalid slum of 60,000; four-room houses with one family to a room, water from a faucet in the yard, bucket privies which are emptied at night into disposal wagons. Farther off, Orlando, a community of 90,000, in a treeless, sun-bleached, wind-swept plain; fairly decent housing, but the same overcrowded, intolerable conditions; no facilities for recreation or entertainment, scarcely any shops; schools to accommodate only a fraction of the children; medical dispensaries utterly inadequate to the population. A poor, sad place. But they do the best they can: there are yards with pretty flowers, and crowded rooms as clean and neat as can be, with curtains at the windows and pictures on the wall and teacups on a shelf. The workers of Orlando trudge back and forth to Joburg to their jobs, a round trip which may well consume five hours of the day. If they waited for busses it might take them longer. Still farther is Meroka, the plague spot of the country—of the world perhaps: a settlement of 60,000 squatters, in a kind of no man's land; shelters made of odds and ends of everything—tin cans and rags and sacks and scraps of wood, not even approaching the dignity of hovels. And it can be bitter cold on this high plateau of Africa, and sometimes it rains for days. There has been trouble in Meroka, and there will be again.

It was a fine midsummer day, near the end of February. Billowy, white cloud racks drifted slowly through the sky, very high above the earth, seeming somehow to emphasize the vastness of the landscape, to widen and expand the rim of the horizon till it melted into nothing at the very end of nowhere. Not even on the sea have I felt the world so big as it seems in Africa—nor so lonely and so sad. Mr. Brooks, himself an affable young man, remarked that we were lucky: the mine which was open for visitors on this day was the Durban Roodepoort Deep—one of the really deep ones, near nine thousand feet, he thought, which was about the limit they could work and make a profit on it. He was well acquainted with the mines, he said, had worked in one himself when he was a boy. "Not a bad job for a youngster," he reflected, but engineering was his line and he preferred the oil business, which at least had the virtue of the open air. "And the Natives?" I inquired. "How do they like working underground?"—"Oh, they love it," he assured me. "They're better fed than they ever dreamed of being. They come in like scarecrows, and go out like fancy cattle. They work a few months and save their money, and then they can go home and buy themselves more women."—"And then?" I queried.—"Then?" He thought about it. "Well, they sit around, till they're hungry, I suppose; and then they leave their wives to till the ground, and come on back and have another go."—"It doesn't seem to get them anywhere," I said.—"No," he agreed, "I don't suppose it does. But then you see they haven't really anywhere to get."

He stopped the car and pointed out a low brick wall around a narrow patch of naked ground—formal gateposts, and an iron gate opening into nothing, as if someone had started to construct a house, beginning with the garden wall and not going any farther. "There!" he said. "That's supposed to be a monument, but they never finished it. There's a plate on the gatepost, and that's all." And there was a tarnished plate, undecipherable from where we sat, across the road from it. The boys in the back seat looked out languidly. "That's the very spot," Brooks said, "where the gold reef was discovered." He drove along, relating the circumstances of it—

The sixty-mile gold reef of the Witwatersrand ("Ridge of the White Waters" in the Dutch language) was discovered in 1886. Among the occasional gold seekers who wandered through the country was a prospector named Fred Struben. The region of high veld was a desolate, barren one which had yielded little profit to the Dutch pioneers of half a century earlier, most of whom had perished fighting at their wagon wheels, slain by Matabele warriors who sought to bar their way. But in 1886 there was no great danger from hostile assagai, nor determined competition for possession of the bleak and inhospitable country, which the natives indeed had never greatly valued. Fred Struben could wander at his will, in peril of no greater hazards than exposure to the weather and starvation, with both of which he acquired some acquaintance. He found gold here and there in negligible quantities; but he didn't find the reef, though it seems he was convinced that it was there, and kept on searching for it with dogged, dauntless courage—which in any other line of human undertaking would deserve a designation of psychotic.

A man named George Walker had been employed by Struben to supplement his efforts, at a spot some miles distant from what is now Johannesburg, and which was then a village of about 100 people. But Walker was a more fragile vessel than his employer, and presently grew weary of the gold-seeking life. So in due course he resigned from Struben's service and went to look for work of a more rewarding nature, at a settlement called Langlaagte, where he found employment with a farmer. His eyes were sharp enough to notice, unelatedly perhaps, that the doorway of the barn, which was built of conglomerate stone, contained indubitable specks of gold. And shortly afterwards, while idly strolling about, the toe of his boot struck and dislodged an outcrop of the gold-bearing rock. He went directly to the owner of the farm, saying simply and briefly these historic words, "I have found the main reef." And so in fact, as it turned out, he had. There is nothing more to chronicle of Walker, save that in the fine tradition of great discoverers, he died obscurely and in abject poverty.

AS MR. BROOKS CONCLUDED HIS ACCOUNT WE TURNED OFF the highway, on a tree-lined road, at the end of which was a group of neat brick buildings, one storey high, containing the managerial offices of the Durban Roodepoort Deep. Behind the buildings, at some distance, was an ocher-colored dump of sizable proportions, and less far off the ugly structure of a hoist. Motorcars were parked around a patch of lawn, and from some of them the visitors of the day were now alighting. There were, on later counting, twenty-four of us, about equally divided as to sex, of a wide variety of ages, and representing several nationalities. The only Americans besides myself were three determined women from Los Angeles. We stood around and waited, the usual procedure on excursions of this sort. It was hot in the sun and some of us went in and waited in the hall. The boys from the Free State were sizing up two unaccompanied girls and Brooks had strolled away in search of information.

A young Anglican cleric with a thin, ascetic, sensitive face and a cultured British accent exchanged a word with me and introduced himself. He told me he had been in Africa five years, had come out direct from Oxford. He was now at the head of a mission in Sophiatown—of a school which began with kindergarten, and went on through grade and high school. But they could only take one child in three or four, in the district that they served; there were so many children; conditions were deplorable. He said it was at the age of adolescence that the Native boy or girl was in desperate need of help. Before that they seemed unaware of the color line—or at least of its more crippling implications. But with adolescence, frustration came to torture them—awareness that the white man's way of life, which had been forced upon them, had no place in it for them; that there was no future for them, no matter where they turned; no youthful ambition they could hope to gratify; no road they could follow without quickly coming to a sign which read, KEEP OUT.

He gave me this example: in a school, with which he had acquaintance, a young preceptor newly come from England had introduced a modest business course—really nothing more than shorthand and typing, but which promised some vocational opportunity. The teen-age boys and girls had been elated, had gone at the undertaking with a will. At the end of the term some of them gave promise of being expert typists, or even secretaries. But then it turned out that there were not any jobs for Native typists, no positions they could fill. The young preceptor hadn't thought of that, or hadn't thought that far. One girl had killed herself, and the class had been abandoned. "Things like that," he said.

I asked a question: "In what way are the Natives different from the rest of us?"—"There is no real difference," he replied. "What appears to be a difference is actually a lag, due in the main to deficient opportunity."—"You mean they have the same potentialities—for technical skills, for intellectual speculation?"—"Exactly. With the same individual variations."—"What about their moral character?"—"Morality," he smiled, "is a question of geography."—"Yes, I know," I said. "But, to be specific, are they less honest than the white man?"—"No." He shook his head. "They are by nature simple, gentle people—hospitable, kind." He paused with a shy look in his eyes, as if he were afraid he might be shocking me. "I like the Natives. I would rather live among them than among the Europeans."

Brooks came hurrying back with information. There was a treat in store for us, he said, something that visitors rarely had a chance to see, as it only happened at infrequent intervals, and very seldom on a visiting day: they were casting ingots in the smelter—ingots of pure gold; and that was the first thing we would have a look at. The excursion began to come to life. Someone instructed us to go into a room where a man behind a table checked our names against a list and took our signatures on a document of some kind, presumably a waiver of liability. But the name I signed was not my own, so it didn't seem to matter what I might be signing and I didn't stop to read it. We were now directed to get back into our cars, and to follow a lead car through the gate.

There was nothing much to see when we got inside: a considerable enclosure, with the mine dump and the hoist as its most conspicuous features; and some shedlike buildings here and there, neither numerous nor imposing. We stopped in front of one of them, and a pleasant-faced young fellow, of the engineering type, directed us to go inside where we would be equipped with coveralls and helmets like those that he was wearing. He glanced at my shoes and said I should have worn older ones. And I said I would have, but the ones I had on were the only ones I had. The hoist was clanging up and down, and ore was being dumped, rattling into something; but there were scarcely any workers to be seen, no suggestion of a great industrial undertaking. And I remarked about it.—"The business of a gold mine is underground," he said, and added patiently that the Durban Deep employed 10,000 men, housed in two compounds of about 5,000 each, one of which we would be shown in due time. The mine operated on three shifts, eight hours each, six days in the week. But the night shift was a small one, not a mining shift in fact, but a clean-up and repair crew. I asked him if the Natives were satisfactory workers.—"Oh, they're all right," he shrugged. "Of course they're bloody stupid, and they're lazy. But they're all right, if you tell 'em what to do and stand by and watch 'em do it."—"Do they like their jobs, working in the mine?"—"I wouldn't know," he said. "I never asked 'em." And he added that I better hurry up and change my clothes or I might not find any coveralls to fit me.

There were two dressing rooms for visitors, one for men and one for women. The men's was like a locker room in a modest country club, with hooks on the wall to hang your clothing and benches underneath, and two old-fashioned showers behind a wood partition. In a corner on the floor was a pile of blue denim coveralls; and though they'd been picked over by the early comers, I found one I could wear, albeit rather snug. I stripped to my undershirt, and afterwards regretted I hadn't stripped that, too. Brooks had thoughtfully reserved a helmet for me, of shiny steel, with a hooded light bulb fastened on the front. It was heavy and uncomfortable, and steadily grew more so. My clerical acquaintance was hanging his clothing on the next hook to mine, and I remarked that a visit to a gold mine was probably no novelty to him. On the contrary, he told me, he had never paid a visit to a mine before, though he had long intended it; and he added rather sadly, "In Sophiatown we live in the shadow of the mines."—"You mean that labor is recruited there?"—"No, not that," he said. "The urbanized Native is too smart to take the bait, and most mine labor is recruited far away, in the country districts. The workers come alone; there is no provision in the compounds for their families. And so, when they go home, at the end of the period for which they have contracted, some of them leave souvenirs behind."—"Souvenirs?" I questioned.—"Yes, souvenirs," he smiled. "Babies they have fathered. And we have many of them in Sophiatown."

Brooks interrupted, calling from the door. We went out and joined the ladies, who were similarly garbed in coveralls and helmets; and walked to the smelter which wasn't far away—housed in a modest building, with the general appearance of a country blacksmith shop. As I stepped across the threshold, out of brilliant sunlight into semidarkness, some Native workmen, stripped to their waists, wearing thick asbestos gloves and eyeshades, were in process of removing a brick of solid gold from one of several small furnaces which occupied the end of the room. The ingot was in a mold, suggestive of a bread tin, only somewhat larger. It was drawn from the furnace on a paddle, like a baker's. Except for the blinding orange glare in the oven's mouth, and the golden halo round the mold and avalanche of sparks, it might have been no more than a big-sized loaf of bread. It was the last loaf of the day, and was quickly cooled and dumped from the mold onto the earthen floor, where there were several more of them, already cold and black and unimportant looking.

"About $400,000 worth of gold," a superintendent told us, as we gathered round in an awed, respectful circle. Somebody suggested that it looked a simple matter to get away with one. "Pick one up and try it," the superintendent said. So we had a go at that, picking up a gold brick weighing sixty pounds; it was too small for its weight or too heavy for its size; anyhow, there seemed no convenient way to hold it. The Native workers, of whom there might have been about a dozen in the place, went on about their business, exhibiting no interest in what was going on. They didn't laugh or smile, or seem aware of us. In a corner of the room there was a vat, or washtub, presided over by a European; and I walked over to see what he was doing. He was cleaning the gold bricks as they were carried to him, scraping off the crumbs and blackened scale. He said I needn't worry that any of the stuff would get away: every grain of it was caught in fine mesh screens in the bottom of the tub. The bricks began to look like gold when he got through with them.

He asked me where I came from and I told him from America. "From America?" he chuckled. "That's where we send the gold; you chaps buy it from us. We dig it up and ship it overseas; and you take it off to some place called—Kentucky, I believe, and bury it again."—"That's right," I said.—"It doesn't seem to make much sense," he grinned. "Might just as well leave it buried over here." He paused to scrape the surface of a brick with a wire brush. "It takes five thousand tons of rock to smelt out one of these; and that's a lot of digging, and a lot of sweating, too." I asked him what the Natives thought about it. And he answered, with a twinkle in his eye, that he didn't think they'd heard about it yet. "When they do," he said, "I expect they'll laugh their heads off."

The tour was departing and I started for the door, but he called after me, "What sort of place is this—Kentucky?"—"It's a state," I told him. "Like what you call a province."—"Oh—" He nodded. "Is it near the place where they make the atom bombs?"—"Right next door to it," I said.— "Well, that's good," he chuckled. "Keep 'em close together. One won't be much good without the other."

We walked a short distance to the hoist, where, while we waited for the cage, we were equipped with batteries for our helmet lamps—flat, rather heavy boxes belted to our waists. The Native boys who brought and strapped them on were quick and deft about it, but not talkative or friendly. They disappeared, and presently returned with armfuls of over-coats—thick, heavy ones, like army issue. "When you come up you'll need them," our conductor said. "It's hot down there and you're likely to get chilled coming up the shaft." We had several guides by now—six or eight of them, young fellows for the most part, competent and friendly, taking watchful care that none of us should come to any harm. The cage came clattering up: a narrow iron box roofed with heavy mesh, with double gates at either end, hinged to open inward. We crowded into it, about thirty men and women, including our conductors, and there was no room to spare; indeed, to close the gates, we had to push and wriggle. But at last they were banged shut, and down we went—five thousand feet of swift descent without a pause, a drop six times greater than from the top of the RCA Building to the ground. When the cage came to a stop some-one remarked that there were hoists in the mines which traveled at a speed of thirty-five hundred feet per minute (forty miles an hour); and which, he added, was two and one-half times as fast as the fastest sky-scraper elevator in New York. I don't know if ours was one of these, but it went down pretty fast. Opening the gates was a difficult affair, since we were packed against them like sardines. With a lot of squirming we opened them a crack, wide enough to enable some of us to dribble out, until finally there was room to push them back. I suppose they dare not have them open out, lest they should come open while the cage is moving. At all events I thought them ill-contrived, wasteful of space and time-consuming.

WE WERE IN A SPACIOUS CAVERN, ILLUMINATED WITH ELEC-
tric lights, with a narrow-gauge track along one side of it, which disappeared at either end into galleries in the rock. At this point we were
mercifully relieved of our overcoats, and informed they'd be waiting for
us later on, at another shaft. There were several other shafts, they said,
and we would not return by the one we had descended. There was not
much activity in sight, and indeed there wasn't much anywhere they took
us. Perhaps that was designed; perhaps they avoided the more active
operations, for fear of interfering with the work, or of injury to us. It is
possible, of course, there were things they didn't care to have us see,
though that I doubt. In any case it was difficult to believe that 4,000 men
(an average day shift, I suppose) were working in the mine. If they were
they must have been where we were not, or spread very thin in the
network of galleries.

There was a rumble of approaching cars in the dark depths of the
tunnel, then the winking lights on the helmets of the men; and presently
the train came into sight: little dump cars filled with rock and pushed by
hand, two workers to a car, young fellows for the most part, stripped to
their waists and their bodies sleek with sweat, the whites of their eyes as
white as fish belly. They barely glanced at us as they trudged slowly by,
not chattering or laughing or kidding one another, and not cursing or
complaining, but silent and impassive—yes, and sad; like oxen pulling
plows, without knowing what they're doing or any reason for it, and ill at
ease about it, uncomfortable, embarrassed by an unnatural task; yet docile
and resigned. That was the expression in their eyes, when I thought about
it afterwards—the basic aspect of it, sometimes tinged with sullenness,
with deep unvoiced resentment—in the eyes of most of them, in the
mine and on the ground, wherever they are laboring in the service of the
white man: in the eyes of houseboys passing cocktails at a party, and of
stevedores working cargo on the docks at Cape Town, docile and resigned,
alien and sad.

It was hot and humid, like a tropical conservatory: hot and close
enough to make me feel a little faint, though there were blowers pumping
in fresh air, and standing underneath one, it was fairly comfortable. But
a few steps away the air was like a wet and sticky blanket wrapped around
your head. We snapped on our helmet lights and set off into the tunnel
where the cars had disappeared—a straggling procession, escorted by our

guides. Brooks and the Oxford man and the two boys from the Free State walked along with me, and the engineering fellow who had criticized my shoes kept close beside us. He asked me if I felt all right and I said I did, which was trifling with the truth. I was thinking to myself: if I take it easy and am careful not to hurry, I may survive this trip. I'd been down in mines before, I don't know how deep, but this was the hottest and the wettest. My coveralls were soaked with sweat already, or maybe with water condensed out of the air. It was wet underfoot: puddles in the space between the tracks; and water dripping from the roof and trickling down the walls, which looked like granite and were not heavily timbered. Drip, drip, drip—you could hear it everywhere. I asked our guide how they got rid of it, for I saw no sign of pumps. "We drain it farther down," he said, "and pump it out from there." I ventured to inquire if we, ourselves, were going any lower. He said he didn't know, but probably we would—maybe as far down as seventy-five hundred, which was not far from the bottom. "I hope we will," chirped Brooks. I hoped we wouldn't, but I kept it to myself.

Presently we overtook the string of dump cars. They had stopped and were unloading—onto the floor of the tunnel, it appeared. But this was not the case; they were dumping the rock into a chute which went down somewhere. I had trouble understanding this until it was explained that the cars which would be hoisted to the surface were on a lower level, and the ore was being fed directly into them. "Sounds silly, I suppose," our guide remarked. "But gravity is what we use whenever we can do it. It's easier to drop things than it is to lift 'em up." I let it go at that, but I still don't understand it very well—nor how you'd ever start a mine that way, for in the beginning there would be nowhere to drop things. But I was too hot and uncomfortable to care.

We stood for a while to watch the dumping. There was a European foreman on the job, not performing any labor, but watching and directing, as indeed there always was when Natives were employed at anything. This one, for our benefit perhaps, was being brisk and sharp, shouting snappy orders in some Bantu language. It seemed a very simple operation and I asked why it required a white man to direct it. The answer was the usual one, that you couldn't trust a Native to do anything correctly by himself. To illustrate his thesis our conductor told a story which I'd already heard a dozen times, and which, with variations, goes like this: there was a fire somewhere and a Native bucket brigade went into action, for which its members had been scrupulously trained; the blacks ran back and forth in perfect order, some distance to a stream, with buckets full of water on their heads. One of them had no bucket, but he ran with the others, in his proper place, with a sardine tin of water balanced on his skull. Brooks and the Free State boys laughed heartily. I glanced inquiringly at the Oxford clergyman, but he smiled and shook his head, as if to say there was no use discussing it.

"How much are the Natives paid?" I asked.—"Two bob (fifty cents) a day," our guide replied. "And of course their food and housing. That's the basic pay."—"You mean that some earn more?"—"A little more," he said.—"And what's the basic pay for the white man in the mine?"—He named a figure which amounted to eleven times the Native wage.—"But the white man has to feed and lodge himself," amended Brooks. "The Native's better off a lot of ways, what with medical attention and everything he needs." He elaborated on it as we walked along: if the Native stuck it out for fourteen months, an average term of contract, say roughly around 350 working days; if he saved his money, which he could do if he wanted, he would wind up at the end with $175. "And that's a lot of money for a Native," he concluded.—"But they don't save all their money," the Oxford man objected. Brooks tossed that off. "It's up to them," he said.

We tramped on through the tunnel, which was reasonably spacious, with ample head room save now and then for timbers arched across it. There was nothing to suggest that gold was being mined, nothing to be seen except the dripping walls, gleaming wetly in the light we flashed upon them. The tunnel curved and angled here and there, aimlessly it seemed, though perhaps it had followed an erratic seam of gold which had been dug and finished. But that was pure conjecture on my part. At last it widened out into another cavern, like the one from which we'd started. And here we overtook the balance of the party, grouped around a staging, climbing into something which startlingly suggested a small flat-bottomed boat, almost standing on its nose. "A kind of chute-the-chutes," our guide explained. And so indeed it was: a shaft sunk at an angle, with iron boats that slid, or rolled, upon a track—like little landing craft (it took three of them to hold the thirty of us)—like baking dishes really, with iron lids that clamped across the tops. The tourists were having fun about it. There were no seats in the boats; and, sitting on the floor, when the lids came down, there was no room for their heads. They had to flatten out, on top of one another. Then the lid would be banged shut, and down they'd go—like traveling in a coffin on a roller coaster.

I was in the very front of my boat, which was not the place to be, as all the other passengers slid down toward my end. Fortunately there was little room to slide; we were packed too tight for that. When the lid came down I ducked my head, but it jammed my helmet hard and almost tore my ears off. I was wedged between the two boys from the Free State, with the elbow of one of them digging in my throat and the knees of the other jabbed into my stomach. They asked solicitously if I was comfortable; and I told them I was fine, which was a lie. Somebody pressed a button, or did something, and down we went, with that old devil Gravity dancing on our backs and ramming us together till I thought I should be smothered. How fast? I have no notion; but in next to nothing we were there. The lid clanged up and we crawled out—like the fabled birds emerging from a pie. We were in another cavern, similar to the others, but a thousand feet closer to the center of the earth, and six thousand feet below the surface of the ground—just level with the sea. It was hotter and wetter, but otherwise unchanged.

I sat down in a puddle on the floor to catch my breath and straighten out my ears. Then off we trudged again, the five of us at the tail of the procession, into another tunnel, with neither tracks nor dump cars, less spacious than the last one and with more timbering in it. The dripping water trickled along the sides of it; here and there, in dead-end caves, it stood in still, black pools, fenced off with wooden railings—abandoned pits of unknown depth, filled to overflowing. There was no sign of life; the tunnel seemed deserted, until at last we heard the muffled chatter of a pneumatic drill—a welcome sound in the silence of the place. And suddenly we came around a corner on the workers: two Natives, and a foreman who was standing idly by. They were in a narrow alcove in the tunnel wall; and the man with the drill was working in a hole in the ceiling of it, standing on a step cut in the rock, all of him out of sight except his legs. The other man was standing near, holding the heavy air hose. When we paused to look, the foreman cut the air off, and the deafening racket stopped. They were mining gold, I thought. But I was wrong. It turned out to be another gravitational matter: digging *up* a chute to connect another tunnel. I felt cheated and disgusted. "Why don't you dig them down?" I asked him irritably. "If we dug them *down*," he said, with admirable forbearance, "how would we get the rock out of the hole that we were digging?"—I hadn't thought of that.—He went on to explain they were drilling for a blast; when the rock was loosened it would come tumbling down and could be hauled away.—"Okay, that's clear," I said.

"But how did this thing get started, before it had a bottom, before there was a place from which you could dig *up*?"—"I wouldn't know," he grinned. "That was before my time."

The man with the drill had climbed down out of the pocket in which he had been working. He was a Zulu. I could tell this by his tribal decoration: flat, white discs of bone inserted in his broad, distorted ear lobes. He was naked to the waist, with goggles on his eyes and a helmet on his head, and so thickly smeared with powdered stone and sweat that his coal-black skin was gray. He was young, in the flood tide of his strength— a Zulu boy, descendant of a proud and warlike nation which the white man had subdued with long and painful effort. He stood beside his helper, with the drill clasped in his arms, crouching with the weight of it, staring at us dully, half blinded by the light we focused on him. And then he raised his hand and pushed his goggles up; and his eyes were like the others—alien and sad.

His ragged jeans were ripped in a revealing place, and someone made a laughing reference to the fact, without, I'm sure, intent to give offense. The Oxford man turned away and walked on by himself. People in South Africa are prone to make remarks about the Natives in their presence, as if they were not there. At a dinner table, for example, I have heard them discuss the Native Question in its most alarming aspects, in the hearing of the servants, even to the point of anecdotes which reflected on the boys engaged in serving them. Once or twice I had ventured to inquire how they dared to be so frank, though "frank" was not exactly what I meant. What I really had in mind was "so callous and unkind." In reply I had been told that the Natives never listened to what was being said, that they didn't understand and didn't care. But I had seen them listening, seen it in their eyes, and seen them care. And this Zulu boy had listened and had cared.

WE WENT ON THROUGH THE TUNNEL, AND IN A MOMENT heard the drill begin again. Our guide was describing the technique of blasting—a white man's job, he said; no Native was allowed to use explosive, under any circumstances, anywhere.—"Why not?" I asked.—"Because they'd blow themselves to hell."—"What makes you think they would?"—"Because they're made that way; they haven't got the know-how. It simply isn't in them."—"Have you ever tried them at it?"— No, he never had, he said; and the day that they were tried he would quit the mining business. We overtook the Oxford man, and, walking at his side, I put the question to him: would he trust the handling of explosive to a Native?—"Of course," he said. "Why not?" And he added with a smile that in the recent war they had handled plenty of it with considerable effect. "It's like this," he said. "When a white man does a stupid thing he is said to be a fool, and it's let to go at that. But when a Native makes a slip it's because his skin is black, and the whole race is condemned by implication."

We emerged abruptly into another cavern, in which there was a shaft and waiting cage. The rest of the party were already tucked inside it, and calling us to hurry. As I wedged myself through the crack between the gates, I thought with fine relief that this must be the end, that we were going up. But I was wrong about it. The iron gates clanged shut and down we went, another fifteen hundred—a mile and a half below the surface of the ground, or nearly that; more than a quarter mile below the level of the sea. And nothing at the end but another dripping cave, hotter and wetter than the last one. My iron hat encased my head like an instrument of torture, and the battery box dragged at me like a lump of solid lead; my knees sagged with the pressure. The atmosphere seemed thick enough to swim in, if one could make the effort. Perhaps we had arrived at the bottom of the mine, at the end of gravitational undertakings; I didn't think to ask. Anyway, they were pumping water out of it; there were big pipes in sight, and the sound of sucking pumps. And there was a blower, with something that resembled air gushing from its mouth. I sat down under it and lit a cigarette.

"Bit rugged down this deep," our guide remarked. "But gold is where you find it."—"You really mean there's gold down here?" I asked, ironically I hoped.—"Right there, around the corner, a hundred yards or so." He nodded toward a tunnel into which the visitors were already straggling. Half of them were women, and some of the men were older than myself. If they could take it, I could. "Okay," I said, "let's go." And I threw my cigarette away and climbed back on my feet. The members of our group applauded feebly, and off we went once more. "Let's get this straight," I said, when we'd walked along a way. "Do men really work down here, without compulsion, for fifty cents a day?"—"Natives," said the guide. "And there's no compulsion."—"Do their contracts say how deep they'll have to go?"—He didn't think so but he wasn't sure. "Anyway," he added, "they get along all right. Why, they get fat on it."—"And eight hours isn't long," Brooks commented cheerfully. But a minute was too long, an hour was a nightmare, and eight of them beyond imagination.—"Ask him," the Oxford man whispered in my ear, "how many hours they spend waiting for the cage to take them up." I asked but I didn't get an answer, beyond that they were lifted as rapidly as possible. "I am told," the Oxford man said, in my ear again, "that they often spend twelve hours underground." And I repeated this. But our guide was vague about it.

Still, I reflected to myself, all sorts of undertakings were subject to abuses. The mining occupation was not confined to black men; and a mine was a mine, whether deep or shallow; and while fifty cents plus keep seemed a very modest wage, in the modern world, for doing anything, still, the wage of the worker was a variable factor, differing widely with location and conditions. No, it was none of these things, nor all of them together, which made it seem so ugly: not the depth and discomfort of the mine, nor the pitiful reward for working in it. Nor was it this I saw, reflected in their eyes, not the hardships of their tasks. It was something else entirely: the vicious, devastating, and degrading color line.

We turned out of the dark and silent tunnel, through a narrow entrance, into a good-sized chamber, hewn in the rock. And here at last were signs of life: a score of Natives, armed with picks and shovels, desisted from whatever they were doing and grouped against the wall, out of the way, with their European bosses close beside them. The tourists were assembled in the chamber, perched on heaps of rubble with which the floor was littered, their headlights and attention focused on the wall— on something in the rock which the master guide was tracing with a pocket flash, which was hard to see at first, since it looked but little different from the rock through which it ran. But then I saw it was a different color, rather greenish: the seam which held the gold, scarcely wider than my hand, and in places not so wide. It seemed incredible that anyone could find it, or, having found it, could pursue it through the earth—like a microscopic vein in the carcass of an elephant.

"There it is," the guide kept saying. "That's the stuff we're after. And we have to move a lot of rock to get it." The visitors crowded close, with murmured exclamations in half a dozen languages, reaching up to touch the seam, picking crumbs with eager fingers. But the guides invited them to help themselves. The rubble on the floor was full of it, they said, and they crawled on hands and knees, finding samples for their guests. Our guide selected a good-sized chunk for me. He examined it with care and said it was a splendid specimen, and would be a first-rate souvenir to keep; but it looked to me like any other rock. I thanked him warmly and stowed it in my pocket, where it jabbed me in a tender spot every time I took a step. The Native workers grouped against the wall took no part in the proceedings and gave no indication of interest or amusement. As we straggled out I heard their foreman barking orders, and the scrape of picks and shovels—cleaning up the mess perhaps. On the way back through the tunnel I lost my souvenir. It weighed about two pounds, and when no one was looking, I sneaked it from my pocket and dropped it in the dark.

We were back on the surface in two jumps—straight up, no chute-the-chutes. But part way up we changed from one shaft to another; and at the final loading point our overcoats were waiting in a dump car, with Native boys at hand to help us on with them. We were warned to put them on, no matter how we felt, which was good advice, I guess; for the air in the shaft felt like a polar blast. But when we squirmed out of the cage the sun was shining brightly amid the drifting clouds, and the day was warm and fine, as we had parted from it. I glanced at my watch: we had been about three hours underground.

Our guides took leave of us. We would have time to change our clothes, they said, and then we'd be conducted to the compound, to see for ourselves how the Native workers lived. In the dressing room we hastily stripped and crowded in the showers; and in the midst of this boys rushed in with trays of tea—the inevitable complement of every under-taking in South Africa. You are waked with tea at dawn, on trains or boats or anywhere, nor is there any way I discovered to prevent it; all protests are ignored. Again, at eleven in the morning, tea is compulsory, with supplementary, unpalatable cake, more often stale than not—just in time to spoil your appetite for lunch, which is not a bad idea, for the food is unexciting, monotonous, and dull; and then of course there is ritualistic tea at four o'clock. Three teas a day is the statutory minimum, and dodg-ing any one of them is regarded with suspicion. I was not in a bank or business office where there was not a teacup on the desk of every clerk; they were either taking tea, or getting ready to, or had just finished with it. In the so-called skyscrapers of Johannesburg, which are not imposing structures, the elevator cages are equipped with little shelves, designed to hold the operators' teacups. Anyway, they brought us tea, and littered the benches with cups and bowls and jugs. There was no room to sit down, and when I got my clothes on I escaped out of the place and went to work to clean my shoes which were caked with sticky mud. A new conductor was waiting at the door, and he called a passing Native boy to help me. The boy kneeled down obediently and scraped the mud away, polishing the leather with his hands. He said they were good shoes and he asked how much they cost.—"About five pounds," I told him.—"Five pounds!" He shook his head and his eyes were big with wonder. I thought about it then: it would take him fifty days to earn that much—four hundred hours underground; and the shoes, however good, would be long worn out before he paid for them. I gave him a shilling, and he seemed surprised and pleased, glancing doubtfully at the guide from the corner of his eye, as if to make certain such things would be permitted.

THE TOURISTS BEING REASSEMBLED, WE WERE DIRECTED TO get into our cars and follow a lead car to the compound. The Free State boys declined; they had had enough, they said, and someone else was leaving, who would drive them back to town. So Brooks and I crawled into the Peugeot and followed the procession—several hundred yards through deserted, littered grounds, beyond the lofty, ocher-colored dump. And there we came abruptly on the entrance to the compound: a gateway in a long, one storey building, through which we drove into a spacious yard, two or three acres in extent—a quadrangle in fact, bordered with rows of small brick houses, boxlike little structures with narrow space between them. The area enclosed was an open court of lawn and flower beds, nicely landscaped and well cared for. At the far side of it, opposite the entrance, were some even smaller houses, which afterwards turned out to be latrines and showers. And at one side was a building of good size, of skeleton construction, with walls of glass or screen, widely open to the air. There was a patch of paving in the lawn, for playing some sort of ninepin game; and, as we drove in and parked our cars, there were several Natives playing—perfunctorily, the thought went through my head, as if they had been told to get out and show the visitors that they were having fun, though I have no shred of evidence to support such an idea. Perhaps it was the gateway that suggested it, or rendered me susceptible to such a train of thought. Though the gateway was in no sense formidable: there were no gates or bars, none that I was aware of; no guards and no formality. Yet the feeling was of an institutional entrance—of a place, when once you got inside, it might be hard to leave.—"Beautiful!" said Brooks, standing at my elbow, as we looked across the garden with its beds of brilliant flowers. And it was beautiful, in an institutional way—somehow reminiscent of a modern penitentiary. "I wouldn't mind living here myself," he added. I made no comment, but the bare suggestion of it sent a shiver down my spine.

We were taken to the commissary first, the building with the glass and screen, open to the air. I noticed, as we passed the ninepin alley, that the players had already disappeared, as if they'd done their stunt and could now go back to bed, or wherever else there was to go. There was little sign of life inside the compound; perhaps a day shift lived here, now at work beneath the ground; or a night shift, now asleep. Some workers passed us, going to and fro, clad in faded jeans, clumping on the pavement in their heavy shoes, going on about their business, barely glancing at us. There is nothing picturesque about the black man in South Africa—nothing savage or unique. They have lost all that, or buried it away with the costumes and customs of the past, to be resurrected now and then on state occasions—when the King of England comes to visit them, or when they stage a tribal dance for the benefit of tourists—perhaps more genuinely in their own reserves, when they are alone among themselves. But where they are in contact with the white man they look and seem like poor black people anywhere. Visibly at least there is little to distinguish the Native in South Africa from his brother in Harlem or New Orleans.

The commissary was a sanitary dream, efficiently designed and immaculately clean. At one side was a railed-off passageway, in cafeteria style, where the customers could pass in single file, with pans into which the food was ladled by Native cooks in spotless aprons. There were half a dozen of them attending on the cauldrons, and even fewer diners; while we looked on only three or four passed by. I inquired about this, assuming that it couldn't be a normal eating hour, and was told they came for food when they were hungry, that it was provided for them twice a day. There was no place in the building where it could be eaten—no tables, chairs, or benches; the big room was a kitchen, nothing more. It was explained that they took the food away, to eat it at their leisure in their houses. As for the contents of the cauldrons: there was one big vat of mealies, a sort of corn meal mush, which is the basis of the Native diet; another filled with beans; and a third which at first defied analysis, but turned out to be a messy looking stew of hashed-up vegetables. Our guide said the Natives had no use for vegetables; and so they disguised them in this fashion, dicing them so small they could be with difficulty recognized, and not readily separated or rejected. The sort of subterfuge one employs in feeding children; and, indeed, I have done the same with dogs. There was no meat in sight. They had it twice a week, our guide explained. It was given to them raw, as they preferred to cook it for themselves, on stoves inside their houses. "They like it tough," he said.

I watched a man, as he paused to fill his pan, a big one like a wash basin—like the pan I use for a Norwegian elk hound; and it was ladled full of beans and mealies, with a scoop of vegetable stew to top it off, poured on like gravy: an unsavory looking mess, with a sickening, musty odor, though no doubt titillating to the Native nose; in any case more bulk than it seemed remotely possible a single human being could consume—at one sitting, anyway. "Forty-four hundred calories a day," our guide said proudly, somewhat as a breeder might have spoken of prize cattle. "We build 'em up," he added. But the man with the brimming pan was neither big nor fat. He was in fact a scrawny little fellow; and he did not look hungry, nor as if he were intrigued by his Gargantuan platter and trembling with impatience to be at it. Again I had the feeling—with no foundation for it, and which I'm sure wasn't true in any literal sense—that the man had been told to bring his pan and fill it to the brim, in order that the visitors might be witness to abundance. He walked away unhurriedly, with the pan held out before him, and a sorrowful expression in his eyes. But perhaps the source of that was the vegetable gravy, which could never be unscrambled from the mealies and the beans.

We went up a flight of steps onto an open mezzanine where there were numerous vats and troughs of trickling liquid, all spotless, chromium steel; and some aproned Native boys attending on them. "It's the brewery," said the guide, "where they make their beer." Kaffir beer, it's called; and it has a decent alcoholic content, which, if it be reduced beyond a certain point—and I judge, from what was said, that had been tried—there is a storm of protest. About their beer, it seems, they are fussy and determined. "We give them what they want," our guide declared expansively. "We try to make them happy." He poured some beer in glasses and invited us to try it. It didn't taste like beer, nor much like anything; it was sour, flat, and tepid. We went down the stairs, into a good-sized room where the meat was stored: carcasses of beef hung up on hooks—and not just the carcasses, for most of their insides were hanging up beside them. "Those are titbits," said the guide. And so no doubt they were, to Native taste; but not a pleasing sight to Western eyes. There was no refrigeration, and the smell was pretty thick. The tourists did not linger in the meat house.

We went out of the building and followed a path beside the garden, past the row of neat, brick cubicles in which were housed the showers and latrines, to the open door of one of the small structures which lined three sides of the enclosure. The house was too small for all of us to enter at one time; and so, half a dozen in a group, we crowded in. It consisted of a single room, about sixteen feet square, with a narrow open space before the door, in the center of which was a little iron stove, to furnish heat in winter and to cook their meat. The rest of the room was taken up with bunks, tiered to the ceiling, and shrewdly staggered to economize the space. I counted twenty-four, but it was hard to see them and I may have made an error. The place was clean and in perfect order, suggestive of a barracks—blankets smoothly spread, in military fashion. And the lodgers were at home, some of them stretched out, or sitting, on their bunks; and others standing, a bit like raw recruits in the presence of an officer, uneasily at attention, not quite sure what to do. I don't know why they were at home; or, since they were not working, why they were not asleep. I had the feeling—as by now I had it of almost every-thing—that their house had been selected for inspection, that they had been warned to have it shipshape, and relieved from their jobs to set the stage. I should have liked to ask the guide about it, but I didn't think he'd tell me; and anyway he had said his say and gone before I got inside. I lingered in the room to take a picture, until all the other visitors had gone out. And when the black men saw me opening my camera they seemed to come to life, exchanging words about it; and several grouped themselves, with smiling faces, edging to the front to be sure to be in it. They struck self-conscious poses, and were motionless and silent. But when I'd snapped the shutter there was a lot of chatter, and one of them stepped forward—a stalwart, handsome boy—to ask in careful English, with timid eagerness, if I would send a picture they could pin up on the wall. I told him I'd be glad to if he'd write his name for me. But he couldn't write it, nor could any of the others.

Brooks and the Oxford man were waiting for me. The rest of the party was already far ahead, retracing its steps toward the entrance to the compound, to the building which contained the administrative offices. I asked Brooks if he still thought he would like to live here. And he laughed and said he'd changed his mind. "Though actually," he added, "it's not very different from the way I lived when I was in the army."—"That is probably true," the Oxford man agreed. "But when you were in the army you were fighting for your country, for the preservation of your way of

life. The position of the Native is not analogous." And certainly it isn't.—
As we walked along I kept telling myself that these black men were not
prisoners, but were there because they chose to be, and free to go away
if they so elected—though not entirely free, for they were signatories to
a contract which was binding in the law; which, though they could not
read it, they had signed, or made their marks. At all events the contract
had been explained to them—if indeed it had been, and if they could
understand it: a rigmarole of unfamiliar words recited to a black man in
the bush, who had never been away from home before, from the simple
tribal customs of his group; who lacked the education and experience to
grasp its elementary implications. But some of them had been before,
and had signed and gone again; and those who had returned could describe what it was like; and the bush boy must have heard—or could
have if he wanted. And they were not prisoners; they were under no
restraint. They could walk out if they chose and not come back—though
where were they to go?—where without a pass?—and how obtain a pass
if one were in violation of his legal contract?

We overtook the balance of the visitors, already halfway through the
administrative tour and going pretty fast; perhaps the visiting period was
drawing to a close. We were told there was a playing field for football
and cricket, on which Native teams contended; that sometimes on Sunday they would stage a tribal dance, to which members of the public were
invited; that occasionally a motion picture would be shown, though the
subjects must be chosen with great care, since most of the pictures were
far beyond the reach of Native comprehension and likely to be strangely
misinterpreted—as for example: European love scenes, as depicted on
the screen, represented to the black man offensive and incredible behavior. Somewhere, we were told, there was a hospital, with two European
doctors in attendance; but we were not taken to it. We walked through
a first-aid room, which appeared to be all a first-aid room should be. We
were taken to an office where the workers' cards were kept—many files
of them; and good big cards they were, with fingerprints and history, and
full record of demerits, if such had been incurred.

I held one in my hands, which was written nearly full with infrac-
tions of the rules, and was obviously the record of a rebellious rascal. He
had been absent many times and frequently drunk; had engaged in numerous brawls and beaten up his fellows; had been accused of theft,
though the charge had not been proved. He was lazy and incompetent,

according to report, and repeated reprimand had not improved him. He had disappeared for days and then turned up, to continue his career of crime and disaffection, unchastened and unchanged. I asked a young official who seemed to be in charge, where this ruffian went when he was missing. But he only smiled and shrugged, as if to say my guess would be as good as his. "Probably Sophiatown," the Oxford man said dryly.—"And what do you do with such hoodlums?" I inquired. He said there were minor punishments they could inflict: offenders could be fined, or even locked up, for brief periods of time.—"There is no corporal punishment?—no flogging?" I suggested.—"No, nothing of the sort," he answered warmly. "When they are guilty of serious offenses, they are of course turned over to the police authorities." He added that they tried in every way they could to reform the few bad characters who were bound to turn up in any good-sized group—to salvage them if possible. "We do the best we can for them," he said. "And if it seems hopeless, in the end we send them home." He took the card out of my hand and scanned it. "On such evidence as this," he smiled, "we can scarcely be accused of being either ruthless or impatient."

I had a final question in my mind, which I had been saving to ask someone who wasn't just a guide. "Tell me," I said, "how do these men get on in the absence of their women—most of them young fellows in the prime of sexual life? What do they do about it? How do they get along?"—He frowned and hesitated, and then he told me carelessly that they got along all right—or anyway, most of them; they didn't seem to suffer from the absence of their wives, and were maybe glad to get away from them. "They get along all right," he repeated firmly; and there was something in the way he said it that did not invite discussion.

The excursion appeared to be completed; the visitors were departing, and Brooks was waiting for me in the Peugeot. The Oxford man strolled with me to the car. "I would wager," he remarked, "though I cannot prove it, that within walking distance of this place, it would be hard to find a Native girl, past the age of puberty, who has not got a baby or is not expecting one."—I said it seemed to me like a reasonably safe bet.—"As for these compounds," he went on, in his cultured, gentle voice, "the truth is they are reeking hives of sodomy, of every variety of sexual perversion; and the facts are known to many people. What else could they be, unless the laws of nature were suspended?" He paused and added wearily, "The conditions that exist are only tolerated because their skins are black."—I nodded my agreement; we shook hands and said good-by. As I crawled into the Peugeot he leaned upon the door to say a final word. "But of course," he smiled, "you're familiar with these matters; you have a color problem in the States."—"Yes, we have," I said. "Or anyway I thought so before I came to Africa."

JAN MORRIS

Durban: 1958

"DURBAN REMAINS CHIEFLY A PLACE OF THE SEA. IT STANDS LIKE A GRANDEE
UPON ITS BAY, SURROUNDED BY DOCKS AND INSTALLATIONS, AND THE SHIPS
SAIL IN PAST THE HOTELS AND MAKE THEIR SIRENS ECHO IN THE HILLS."

*James Morris was born in England in 1926. During World War II, he
served with the Ninth Lancers in Italy and Palestine. After the war, he
began working as a journalist, traveling the world as foreign correspondent
for the* Times *of London and later for the* Guardian. *In 1953 he was special correspondent to the British Mount Everest Expedition, and it was his
dispatches that brought England word, on Coronation Day, of Edmund
Hillary's successful climb.*

*In 1956 Morris gave up newspaper journalism to write essays and
books, primarily of history and travel. The volumes of the* Pax Britannica
*trilogy, completed in 1978, are a brilliant and broad-ranging history of the
British Empire. Individual books and essays have covered Venice, Oxford,
Sydney, Hong Kong, Manhattan, and many other places, including more
than a hundred of the world's cities.* Fifty Years of Europe: An Album,
published in 1997, captures a world about to change forever.

*In 1972, James Morris underwent a gender change and became
Jan Morris, an experience she wrote about in the autobiographical*
Conundrum.

Jan Morris is also included in The Reader's Companion to Ireland.

In 1957 the Manchester Guardian *sent Morris to South Africa, resulting in a book called* South African Winter, *published the following
year. This was a dark time for the country, and Morris saw as much
shadow as sunshine.*

IN THE MIDDLE OF THESE BIG SOUTH-EASTERN RE-
serves lies the seaside city of Durban, where the summer is raucous
with the holiday-makers of Johannesburg, and the winter is illuminated
by the running of the July Handicap, the smartest event in the Union's
calendar. When people think of Durban, indeed, they usually think of
Zulus, for the city is full of these virile people, and their great black bodies
and ornate fineries give an exciting edge to its activities.

This conjunction of the tomtom and the *Tatler* is often piquant. If
you sit on the veranda of one of the great hotels, eating a dainty tea and
listening to the string quintet behind you, you will be pleasantly surprised
to find the Zulu women sauntering along the pavement beneath your
table, offering their trays of trinkets and souvenirs, gaudy bracelets and
ebony elephants, and inviting your custom with dazzling toothy smiles.
Up the road from the railway station, where the grand expresses steam
in from Jo'burg, the Africans have their market and their beerhall: a raw-
boned, muscular place, where there are handsome black faces everywhere, and courteous manners, and hordes of small boys eating steamy
lunches, and piles of wild-cat skins, and heaps of mealie, and hanger
upon hanger of loud nylon petticoats, in every shade of orange, red and
outrageous pink. There are some famous ju-ju shops in Durban, stocked
with extraordinary assemblies of charms and talismans: stocks of old twigs
and dried leaves, animal guts, fungi, bundles of bones, strange minerals,
jars of powders and rough grey pills. In Durban you can buy hippopotamus fat, which makes you irresistible if applied properly; or buffalo's
eyelid to rub on your head; or hyena eyelash, a commodity potent in many
ways, I forget exactly how; or crocodile fat, a protection against violent
weather; or elephant's liver; or delicate braided tassels, made from the
hair of baby monkeys.

And everywhere, a gay link between the cultures, there are the famous rickshaw men, the city's mascots, dragged out mercilessly at the
drop of a royal hat, the first clink of a lens-hood or the merest suspicion
of a public festivity. They range the streets stylishly looking for custom,
from the Coee T. Rooms to the grandiose Town Hall, whistling and shouting and grinning ingratiatingly. Their plumes and feathers wave grandly,
their movements are magnificent, but their voices are often incongruously
squeaky: and all their rickshaws, I am assured, are made in the United
States. ("How marvellously they move," I once remarked to a lady at my
hotel, as two of these massive figures came prancing by, now running
gracefully, now leaping easily into the air and tossing the horns of their

head-dresses. "It's rather like how you feel in a dream, when you can fly downstairs, or levitate." The lady turned and looked at me severely. "Young man, did you not know that the Astaires themselves came to this city, and saw our rickshaw men, and that's how they got the idea for their celebrated entries and exits, as for example in *Holiday Inn*, which you are probably too young to remember anyway, or *Showboat*? Dreams indeed! They're real enough, young man, believe me!" And as she said this, with scathing sibilance, I noticed the dread gleam of lunacy in her eye.)

For myself, though, Durban remains chiefly a place of the sea. It stands like a grandee upon its bay, surrounded by docks and installations, and the ships sail in past the hotels and make their sirens echo in the hills. The sea, its splendours, and its mysteries are never far away. It was from Durban that the liner *Waratah* sailed one day in 1909 with her 300 passengers, never to be seen again; and when I was in the city research chemists were examining a piece of old metal, washed up on a nearby beach, which people thought might be a relic of that baffling tragedy. Vasco da Gama is said to have sighted the bay of Durban on Christmas Day, 1497, and named this country Natal: Perestrello charted it in the next century; countless old adventurers, merchants and voyagers landed here for water or trade; and almost every great British warship has put into Durban at one time or another, on her way to Trincomalee or Hong Kong or the forgotten China stations of the British heyday. If you wander along the quay you will find three or four neat little whalers tied up alongside: each morning they sail from this city of pleasure to go a'whaling, returning to Durban in the evening hauling their catch behind them. (During my South African winter they caught a white whale some eighty miles out; it weighed sixty tons and had fiery red eyes, like Moby Dick.) Best of all, Durban is a port for the magnificent packet-boats that bring the mails from England, and play a persistently intrusive part in the affairs of South Africa. In Durban everyone seems to know when the mail-boat is due, just as in the American West any shopkeeper can tell you when to expect the Rocky Mountain Rocket. "The mail-boat's in," you hear people say, and at the hotels there are often knots of elderly passengers at the reception desks, fresh from the steamer, cluttered with lap-rugs and golf-clubs, like figures in a pre-war travel poster. One of the great experiences of the Union, to my mind, is to see the mail-boat sail from Durban in the dusk of a winter evening. The gay promenade is lavish with light, its phalanxes of tall buildings ablaze, its strings of fairy lights stretching above the sands, with a glitter of teashops and amusement parks, and the glint of the wheels of rickshaws, and a stream of cars rolling along the corniche, and a distant juke-box, and the whistle of the Jo'burg train. Then, out in the bay, the mail-boat appears beyond the harbour mole, and slides silently away into the night. You can just make out her slim purposeful lines, and the thin stream of vapour from her funnel, above the fuzzy lights of her superstructure; and if you listen very hard, ignoring the cars and the juke-box, you may perhaps hear the smooth unruffled pounding of her engines. For years the mail-boat was the lifeline of South Africa, the only link between this remote outpost and the parent civilization in Europe. To a people surrounded by barbarians, at the tip of an unknown continent, 3,000 miles from a university or a great library or a fine dressmaker or a symphony orchestra or a turkish bath, only the mail-boat brought the promise of support and sympathy. No wonder, when that elegant ship sails nowadays, to vanish so dreamily into the southern ocean, there are often a few South Africans to run across the road and see her go, and wish her a metaphorical *bon voyage*: and if you are susceptible to this kind of thing, the last twinkling of her lights will bring home to you what the Afrikaners mean when they say, in their plaintive moments: "Man, we've nowhere else to go. This place is all the home we've got!"

Indeed, Durban often feels a long way from Europe. Its façade is a little like Brighton or Atlantic City. Its great occasions are instinct with the snobberies and ill-considered chiffons of Ascot. Cheerful women drive many of its taxis, and bring to the city some slight suggestion of austerity, as though it has just survived the blitz. Hundreds of retired Englishmen live in the comfortable heights that surround the place, and there is a plethora of the usual over-acted Scotsmen. Nevertheless, in Durban you often feel nearer Asia than Europe: and this is scarcely surprising, for so you are. Great fields of sugar-cane surround the city, and the climate is sticky and heavy and semi-tropical, scented with rich exotic flowers, and spattered (if you go to the right place) with the chattering of monkeys and the screams of tropical birds. There are flaming jacarandas, poinsettias, flame-trees, pawpaws, pineapples, mangoes, bananas, oranges and innumerable minor fruits and strange flowers. A third of Durban's population is Indian, imported by the British in the nineteenth century to work the sugar plantations, and these active, acquisitive, litigious people give some parts of the city a sense of constant querulous motion. If you drive to the north, towards Zululand, you will find suburbs so hot and palm-shaded, so crowded with ornate pillared houses, so bright with saris, so thick with thin brown faces and bicycles and mosques and domed temples and incense and gongs, that you might very well be in Madras or Bombay. Gandhi lived here, and launched his first passive resistance campaign in Natal. There are many highly intelligent Indians in Durban, and many rich ones, and a great number whose commercial instincts are impressively refined and sharpened.

So, of course, there is an Indian problem. There are Indians elsewhere in the Union, though immigration is banned: but most of them live in Natal, and Durban is their capital. None of their neighbours, alas, much like them. The British Natalian finds the beggars too clever by half, and distrusts their competitive abilities. The Afrikaner segregates them, thus forcing their leaders into the camp of the political discontents. The ordinary African loathes them, for he has often felt the lash of their tongues or the extortions of their commerce or the sharp end of their writs of attachment. Most of them have never been to India, and find it difficult to cherish much patriotic pride in Mr. Nehru's achievements. The Indian Government offers to pay passages home for those who want to go, but hardly anybody does; and the South African Indians feel themselves apart from the perennial feud that embitters relations between Cape Town and New Delhi (in one of the Indian airports there used to be a notice forbidding the entry of dogs or South Africans into the dining-room, and a Jo'burg citizen once told me that a prime purpose of the South African Navy was "to prevent an Indian invasion, of course"). South Africa is a land full of neuroses—the complexes of peoples snatched from their homelands or subjected to diverse alien influences—and the Indians are among the most embittered of all. The Africans cannot yet, in all honesty, claim many citizens of real distinction; but among the Indians of Natal there are a thousand men eminently capable of sharing in the processes of national government, but ineluctably prevented from doing so. They are brown-skinned, and therefore second-class citizens.

The presence of this fertile community in Durban gives the city an extra dimension in racial relations, and the alignments between its various peoples are curious and often complicated. The English-speaking Natalian, by and large, rather likes the Zulu, so long as he is not too westernized. "He's a decent fellow, the Zulu, as straight as they come. He's a sort of—how can I put it, now?—he's a sort of natural gentleman, you know." On the other hand, as we have seen, he intensely dislikes the Indians. "They're a lot of quibbling monkeys, like so many second-rate lawyers—and you should just *see* how they cheat our poor Zulu boys, it really is a shame." As for the Afrikaner, slowly gaining numbers in Durban: "The Dutchman? It's like spending your life with a paranoiac unitarian who insists on talking Gaelic. You understand me?"

Many of the Indians are no less contemptuous of the African, as you will observe if you hang around the Indian shops of Durban, and watch the blanket-wrapped primitives sidle in to buy their blazing cottons or their hyena eyelashes. The Indian shopkeeper can be very hard. Other Indians, though, have frankly thrown in their political lot with the black men. Many Indian liberals are active in South Africa, and some of them have appeared at the treason trial in Johannesburg: if ever a concerted, organized resistance movement arises to fight apartheid, the argumentative Indian barrack-room lawyers will no doubt be among its generals.

This is, of course, a direct result of the Nationalist Government's racial attitudes, which cast a stigma upon anyone whose skin is not white, and inevitably throw all these different peoples into each other's arms. When I was in the Union controversy raged about a visiting Japanese seaman who had been discovered drinking a milk shake in a white café. "We welcome our brothers of Asia," said an Indian broadsheet I was shown, "and all our brothers who do not share the lily-white skin of the Herrenvolk." About the same time an African life-saver who had rescued another African and an Indian from drowning was sent £10 by the Government in recognition of his courage: the authorities said regretfully that it would have been £20, one for each life saved, except that unfortunately one of those rescued was an Indian, not a black man. (This reminded me of the Mississippi ferry-boats, where some lifebelts are reserved for white passengers only.)

Why, remarked one of the newspapers caustically, that life-saver misjudged the situation—he should have swum straight past the Indian to look for another drowning African. "He should have considered the problem from an essentially ethnic standpoint."

This is the kind of nonsense that occurs when a city is forcibly divided into the compartments of racial segregation, and the whole emphasis of social intercourse is on the differences between peoples rather than the similarities. There are, Heaven knows, economic disparities enough in Durban: from the magnificent hillside villas of the Berea, swamped in fragrance and bougainvillea, to the unspeakable black slum of Cato Manor, one of the worst in the Union. But in a more advanced society, less subject to the fallacies of racial theory—in one of the razzle-dazzle states of the American continent, say, there would be a marvellous bubble and fermentation to Durban. It has the assets of a Rio or a Buenos Aires: a glittering seashore, a wonderful country setting, flourishing trade, bold history, vigorous inhabitants, all the promise of prosperity. It ought to be stimulating, adventurous, provocative.

But alas, most of the verve of Durban comes with the ships or the holiday-makers. Suspicion and resentment dampen the effervescence of the place, and occasionally erupt into bloodshed. The fibres of the city are coarsened by mistrust—between black and white and brown, between Briton and Afrikaner and African and Indian. Scarcely an eyebrow was raised, during my visit there, when a native location was raided by the police in the small hours of the morning, and 1,500 Africans were arrested, most of them on niggling petty charges. Bright may be the silks of the July Handicap, and extravagant the coiffures; but some people say that the most inflammable, the most potentially vicious of all the South African cities is Durban, where the rickshaw men glide like dancers past the grand hotels, and the mail-boat slips away to sea in majesty.

ALAN MOOREHEAD

Kruger National Park and Swaziland: 1956

"IF YOU CAME TO A HERD OF ELEPHANT YOU STOPPED, TURNED OFF THE
ENGINE, AND WAITED UNTIL THE LAST BEAST HAD GONE BY."

*Australian journalist and writer Alan Moorehead had already won atten-
tion with* Gallipoli *and* The Russian Revolution *before* No Room in the
Ark, *a book about his travels in Africa, was published in 1959. Huge success followed the next year, when* The White Nile *appeared, and Moorehead followed up with his own vivid brand of history in* The Blue Nile,
Cooper's Creek, The Fatal Impact, Darwin and the Beagle, *and other
books.*

*Kruger National Park covers 7,700 square miles and has more than
1,600 miles of roads. Named for the nineteenth-century president, it was
first established in 1903. Today, the annual number of visitors is approaching the million mark.*

*Swaziland, now an independent monarchy sandwiched between South
Africa and Mozambique, is actually smaller than Kruger National Park,
with an area of 6,700 square miles. Once administered by the Transvaal
and South Africa, Swaziland became independent on September 6, 1968.*

COMPARED TO THE OLD FLYING-BOAT DAYS THE PRES-
ent journey by air to South Africa is rather a humdrum affair, and
Johannesburg itself has a sobering effect on anyone who arrives, as we

did, with somewhat highly-charged ideas about the primitiveness of Africa. We had not been in the city twenty-four hours before we found ourselves being disillusioned on two quite definite points. There were, we were told, very few large wild animals in South Africa any more—wild, that is, in the sense of roaming about the countryside at will. As recently as eighty or ninety years ago they teemed in millions; on the very place where the new city of Johannesburg now stands (it is barely seventy years old), the early farmers record seeing hordes of springbok half a mile wide that took four hours to pass. They were shot down by the wagon-load, and the carcasses sold off for sixpence apiece. The springbok is a lovely antelope that proceeds in times of danger with a series of immense bounds into the air, and it is the national symbol of South Africa. Today, however, you would be lucky to see even a single specimen anywhere around Johannesburg; along with the other wild animals the species has only been preserved in the game sanctuaries and the National Parks. Other creatures like the quagga, the Cape lion and the blue buck are now altogether extinct.

Our other disillusionment was concerned with the primitive African communities we were so anxious to see: the noble naked huntsman with his bow and arrow, his war dances and his witch doctory. I consulted an Englishwoman who had been living in Africa for many years about this. "I doubt," she said, "if you will find many Africans going *naked* any more. Up north in Uganda you may come across a few tribes where the women wear only a clump of leaves tied around their waists. But there are not very many of them. All Africans prefer to wear European clothes if they can get them, and to hunt with rifles and shotguns instead of spears. As for the dancing, the best place to see it is at the gold mines here in Johannesburg. The miners put on a show on Sunday mornings—but not naked of course. They wear their miners' helmets and the shirts and trousers in which they work."

"But the bushmen," I said. "The primitive bushmen in the Kalahari desert?"

"Well yes," she replied, "they *are* rather primitive, but unless you are an anthropologist I don't think you would find them very interesting. They don't actually do anything, you see. Most of the time they sit around in a circle grubbing for wild melons in the ground. Just occasionally a man will get to his feet and shuffle around in a kind of slow dance for a bit, but that is the only thing that ever happens. They don't even breed any more."

All this was very disappointing, and I confess that as my wife and I wandered about Johannesburg and the neighbouring countryside for the first week or so we saw nothing that would have seemed really remarkable in Manchester or Birmingham. This was a world of tenements and office blocks, of golf-courses and suburban gardens, of shanty towns and gas stations; and it is only occasionally that something happens to remind you that this is still Africa, and that it hasn't yet been altogether overtaken by the outside world. One hot evening my host and I went for a walk, and we might have been in any pleasant garden suburb anywhere except that, as we turned a corner, we found ourselves in the midst of a stampede of young negro boys. They ran past us with frantic staring expressions on their faces, and two African policemen came after them, shouting as they ran. We soon saw what had been happening: the young negroes had been breaking the law by playing cards in the street. There, scattered on the grass, were the cards, a straw hat and a jacket abandoned by their owners in their haste to get away, a wallet that had fallen to the ground. When the police saw that there was no hope of catching the young men they stopped and picked up these fallen objects. Then they went back to their prison van and began calling out softly: "Here's your wallet. If you want it come and get it. Here's your jacket."

The young men turned round and stood uncertainly in the roadway. Obviously it was quite unbearable to them to see their precious things dangled before them in this way, and soon one of their number, more childish and perhaps less courageous than the rest, began to shuffle forward. His was the straw hat and he wanted to get it back. He stopped for a moment but the police called to him once more, reaching out the straw hat to his hand, and the boy came on again. Then the whole group started to move slowly forward. One by one the police clapped handcuffs on their wrists and pushed them into the prison van.

Later that evening we were driving out to a dinner party a few miles out of Johannesburg with a woman friend, and since it was still daylight and we were early I suggested we might stop on a hilltop and smoke a cigarette.

"Not here," she said.

"Why not?"

"People get murdered here."

"In the daylight? On a hilltop? With other cars going by?"

"Yes," she said. "Let's wait till we get back to the main road."

At the dinner party (and we had dressed in dinner jackets for it), it was the usual thing: directly the meal was over we began to play games, liar dice, poker, canasta, bridge—any sort of game so long as everyone was occupied. Such conversation as we had turned on sport (racing chiefly) and political events abroad. In the rooms the furniture was European and so were the pictures and the carpets; nothing was African. In other words, Africa was being deliberately excluded, and it had the effect of making one feel that one was on an island, that we were not merely the few rich shutting ourselves off from the many poor, but that we were white and the rest of the people around us were black. In South Africa there are still only two and a half million whites in a sea of eight or nine million coloured people, and if you take the larger area—the whole of black Africa below the bulge—the discrepancy is even greater. Then it is something like three million whites against sixty million blacks. One begins to see why Europeans in Africa make such a point of asserting their Europeanness, of wearing their formal clothes and emphasizing *their* tribal customs; it is one way of maintaining their authority and independence.

This was a theme that kept cropping up on our journey from this time onwards; this feeling of isolation among the white communities; and however placid the outward scene might have been one was always conscious of an undercurrent of uneasiness. After all, it is not so much more than sixty or seventy years since this was the dark continent and Dr. Livingstone was the one white man in existence for many thousands of miles around.

I used to enjoy watching the negroes on the roads outside Johannesburg. They still walk in single file as though they were on a jungle path, and often one of their number will be playing a guitar or a mouth organ softly as he moves along. Then, when the moment comes for the group to split up, each man taking a different path across the fields, their conversation still continues; apparently they cannot bear to break off contact entirely and be on their own again, and so, without looking back, they keep on calling out chance after-thoughts to one another until at last their voices are lost in the distance. It all looks artless and innocent enough, a vague recapitulation of one's own childhood, of long-forgotten summer evenings when one strolled idly home from school, gossiping and playing with one's friends along the way. And yet, just because these scenes are so natural and friendly, they contain a sharp reminder to the white man that he still remains an outsider here, that *he* could never walk quite so unself-consciously about Africa, that he is marked, in fact, by his own feeling of superiority.

It is the same thing at the mine dances on Sunday morning. The audience sits in tiered seats around a sort of bullring, and just as in Spain, there are two kinds of seats—those in the sun and those in the shade. The Europeans sit in the shade. The miners love to dance; it is their big blow-out of the week, and in groups of a dozen or more the different tribes come in to do their turns. It is a pity of course that their traditional grass skirts and leopard skin capes should have got so mixed up with the ragged European shirts and the aluminium miners' helmets, and that the drums should so often beat out a completely non-African tune (they were very keen on that ancient number "I want to *be* happy/But I can't *be* happy/Till I make *you*/Happy too"). But the true rhythm does break through quite often, the slow shuffle through the sand, the sudden blast of the leader's whistle and then the leap into the air, the fantastic shudderings and stampings. Then one can easily imagine that a lion is being hunted down and killed, that the huntsmen are returning in triumph to their women in the kraal, and that some tormented ancestral spirit is being laid to rest at last. Not far from me in the sunshine a negro spectator was busily knitting himself a pullover as he watched. He was wearing the back portion which he had already completed, and was now knitting his way, row by row, across his bare black chest in front. The needles, I noticed, kept time with the drums.

The dancers clearly were delighted that white tourists were there to watch them, but one had the strong impression that they were really dancing for themselves and their own people in the sunny stands—the true *aficionados*—and that they were responding to instincts which white men have long since regarded as much too crude and childish to be brought out and displayed like this in the open.

So much, then, for our hopes of seeing the primitive tribal life of the Africans, at any rate in the south, so we decided instead to concentrate on the principal object of our journey, the wild animals. Friends in Johannesburg willingly mapped out a route. It was to take us mainly through the great game parks that have been established within the last forty years or so, beginning with the Kruger and Hluhluwe reserves in South Africa and then taking us gradually northwards until we reached the sources of the Nile in Uganda and the Belgian Congo.

The Kruger Park, our first objective, is somewhat older and larger than most of the other game reserves. As far back as 1884 President Kruger began to take up the cause of protecting wild life in South Africa, and by the end of the century an area of 1,500 square miles had been marked off as a sanctuary on the borders of Portuguese East Africa. But it was not until 1926 that the park, with a number of large additions—it now covers 7,340 square miles, roughly the same area as Wales—really began to get under way. Its objects were commendably simple: to stop, in part at least, the wholesale slaughter of animals that was still going on, and to give both scientists and the public a chance of studying wild life in its natural surroundings. In practice, however, the policing of the park turned out to be difficult. There was no fence, of course, and the local farmers on the edge of the reserve were not easily mollified when the animals emerged at night to trample their crops and even attack their workers. Among the meat-hungry Africans who regarded all animals as their natural enemies anyway, poaching developed into a minor industry. There were such matters as forest fires, droughts and diseases to contend with, and even the increase of the carnivora, especially the lions, presented a problem; their main prey, the antelopes and the zebras, began to disappear at an alarming rate at times, and some of the lions had to be shot. Even more threatening was the pressure from political groups who argued that the park lands were needed by the expanding human population for agriculture and for grazing.

It was the tourists who probably saved the day. From the first, ordinary people in Johannesburg, Durban and other cities liked to drive out to the Kruger for a few days holiday—not to shoot, often not even to photograph, but simply to enjoy the experience of living for a little in the kind of wild surroundings which are rapidly disappearing from the earth. The money they paid in entrance fees and for their accommodation was enough to keep the project alive through its experimental years. Now in the nineteen-fifties all the original problems still exist, but it is hardly likely that the South African government will allow the park to fail. Some ninety thousand tourists passed through it in 1956, and the numbers have increased since then.

It was a lovely summer day in February when my wife and I set off by car from Johannesburg across the high veldt. The widow birds with their fantastic black tails a foot or more in length were everywhere fluttering about like pennants in the breeze. A tremendous landscape dotted with clumps of eucalyptus trees and occasional farms unfolded, and we ate a picnic lunch beside a stream. Then as we went on eastward through the afternoon we entered hot groves of semi-tropical fruits, oranges and grenadillas, pineapples and bananas. I ran over the rules of the park in my mind as we drove along. No fire-arms or dogs were allowed. Once inside the entrance gate you kept below a maximum speed of twenty-five miles an hour, and if you came to a herd of elephant you stopped, turned off the engine, and waited until the last beast had gone by. Buffalo, hippopotamus and even lion you could afford to be more casual with, and in every case you were perfectly safe, so the book of instructions said, provided you remained in your car; apparently the oil and petrol fumes obliterated the human smell, and in any case the animals had grown used to cars and no longer associated them with danger. Finally, you had to be inside your fenced-in camp in the interior of the park before darkness fell, and there you remained shut in all night until the gates opened again at first light in the morning.

All this was very well in its way, and yet one wondered. What happened if the car broke down in the park before we got to the camp? Did you simply sit there all night? The book of instructions had nothing to say about this, nor did it indicate what you had to do if you lost your way along the forest tracks. What happened if you turned a corner and suddenly found yourself in the middle of a herd of elephants? Suppose too they changed course and came in your direction? It was reassuring, of course, to know that ninety thousand people had made this trip the previous year, but in the back of one's mind one remembered very vividly all the stories one had heard of big game in Africa, the ambushes, the sudden charges of the wounded buffalo. I don't think we were actually afraid; still, the conversation lapsed and we drove up to the entrance of the park very quietly in the late afternoon.

Here at least there was nothing alarming. A pole across the road. A couple of African park attendants hanging about. A white game warden in a kiosk surrounded by coloured postcards. We signed an agreement that we would do nothing to injure the animals, paid the modest fee of ten shillings a head and the same amount for the car, and then drove on. A gravelled roadway stretched directly before us into the bush, with high grass and shrubs on either side. Pretty soon we turned a corner, the kiosk vanished from the rear-view mirror, and we were on our own.

It was astonishingly quiet. We kept gazing ahead, and to either side, but nothing moved, not even a bird, and there was no sound except for the soft crunching of the tyres on the gravel. We still had five miles to go, and after a bit I accelerated a little to twenty miles an hour. Neither of us spoke. And then all at once it happened. There, not fifteen yards away, under a group of low trees stood a kudu bull. He was casually reaching up to nibble the leaves on a branch, but he stopped when he saw the car and with his moist eye full on us remained absolutely rigid. I on my side was so surprised that I stalled the engine and then hastily got it going again. And still the animal never moved. For perhaps three minutes he stood there silently gazing at us, and then with a sideways movement of his head he turned and walked away. At once a female came out of the shadows and joined him and there were sounds of other animals in the bush beyond.

I am trying to describe this incident precisely as it happened because this first sight of wild animals in their natural surroundings really is something of a revelation, and although a thousand more lively scenes may overtake the traveller later on it is the first impression which will probably remain most clearly in his mind. The colours of the animals are brighter, their outlines clearer and their eyes more sprightly, than anything one could have previously imagined. There is a kind of tense vitality in their movements, an element of challenge in their glance, that immediately diminishes you, the observer, to a much smaller stature than you thought you had before. That sense of privilege and superiority with which human beings approach another species suddenly forsakes you—you are simply another intruder in the bush on the same level as the animals themselves—and in a moment you comprehend how much human contact distorts wild creatures and destroys their proportions. While the zoo keeper forces on them an appearance that is much too soft and tame, the hunter (and incidentally the artist, the photographer and the taxidermist too) almost invariably makes them out to be too fierce and dramatic. Few animals in a natural state spend their lives in a state of panic or rage or in violent motion. They may be constantly on the alert, but for the most part you find them simply standing there under the trees, like this kudu, quietly munching leaves; and as a spectacle it is superb.

We were lucky, of course, to have met a kudu bull at this first contact, for he is a large beast with fine spiralling horns, and he is generally conceded to be one of the noblest sights in the African bush. But it was the same with a pair of impala that bounded across in front of us a little further down the track, the same marvellous grace and suppleness of movement; and even the unlovely baboon that met us at the gateway of the camp had a positively *soigné* air. His fur looked as though it had been freshly cleaned and brushed.

The camp where we spent the next three days was called Pretorius Kop, and has been used as a model for such camps in many of the African parks. It is a queer atmosphere. You might be living in an American motel except that here your hut is a circular affair with a thatched roof called a rondavel, and that the black boy who comes to cook your provisions calls you Bwana, and that you are deeply conscious of the fence that divides you from the surrounding bush. There is a considerable amount of come and go as the carloads of other visitors return from their evening drives around the park (they have to pay a late fee if they arrive after the gates are closed), and presently you discover that there exists here too, as at a ski-ing chalet or even in a country golf-house, a local jargon and an expertise. One soon gets used to it. You exchange stories of the day's experiences with the other visitors, and you tend to overplay your hand a little, though in a deprecatory way, so as to keep ahead of your opponents. You call across to the people in the next rondavel who have just come in: "See anything?"

"Nothing much. Just a few warthog and a couple of giraffe."

Warthogs are pretty common, but the giraffe are somewhat unusual at this end of the park, and so you counter this with: "They say there's a pride of lion up on the Sabie River road. Fellow I met saw a kill up there today."

Hardly anyone ever sees a lion making a kill, and your neighbour now has to think fast if he is going to go one better. Possibly he will make some such remark as: "Yes, I know about those lion. I got within ten yards of them yesterday." Or perhaps, "You didn't miss the wildebeest and the zebra on the Skukuza track, did you? There must have been a hundred of them there this morning."

And so on.

Then too, there is a certain *cachet* in having visited the other game parks as well—and usually any park is better than the one you are actually in. "You can't see much here in the summer," we were told, "the grass is too high. If you want elephant—and they're the best of the lot—you have to go up to the Wankie in Southern Rhodesia. I suppose we must have run into a couple of hundred of them there last year." Or again: "Well, of course if you haven't seen the White Rhino down at Hluhluwe you haven't seen anything yet. They're dangerous too."

This is the point. Danger, or at any rate the illusion of it, seems to be required to give a sparkle to the visitor's curiosity, and he is constantly being reminded by the authorities that, despite the matter of fact way in which he is allowed to drive about for quite long distances on his own, a danger does exist. At Pretorius Kop notices warn you in Africaans: *"Bly in die pad. Bly in u kar. Spoedbeperking 25 m.p.u."* "Keep to the road. Stay in your car. Speed limit 25 m.p.h." And more explicitly: *"Olifante is ge-vaarlik. Pasop!"* "Elephants are dangerous. Keep your distance!"

Gladly at first you keep your distance. You are not reassured by the photographs showing lions crouching on the bonnets of cars and peering placidly through the wind-screen at the occupants inside, nor by the fact that they will sometimes walk alongside the traffic on the roads, using it as a screen to approach their quarry. You are indignant at the fools who occasionally will drive up to a lioness resting with her cubs in the midday heat beside the track and throw beer-bottles to stir her up. On this first night when all is quiet within the camp you sit on the porch of your rondavel, and you hear—or think you hear—some distant roar in the jungle, some night-bird brushing past in the sky, and you are overtaken with a quite genuine sense of adventure and excitement. And in the morning with the first white light of dawn you drive out very cautiously to see what you can see.

Often for quite long periods nothing happens. You drive up hopefully to each corner, and still the empty silent scrub expands before you. But there is always another corner ahead, and so you keep going and you make a virtue out of the fact that at least you have seen a lilac-breasted roller perched on a tree stump and the tracks of some large animal around a water-hole. In this way perhaps half an hour goes by, and like a dis-appointed fisherman you feel your sense of expectancy gradually draining away. Then when the animals do appear—and sometimes they fairly crowd upon you, as many as half a dozen species feeding together—you experience an almost childish glow of satisfaction. You stop the car, au-tomatically you talk in whispers as you get your field-glasses into focus. Even though the herd may be barely thirty or forty yards away it is only gradually that the individual animals insinuate themselves into your view among the patches of shade and sunlight, and it is not until you have looked again a second and a third time that you become aware of a group of waterbuck on the left, the sprinkling of impala among the zebras, and the bright beady eye of some small cat-like creature surveying you from the branches overhead. Despite the general air of watchfulness the ani-mals give the impression that they have been quietly grazing there for a long time, and as a rule nothing very dramatic occurs. The outlying mem-bers of the herd look up sharply when you first arrive, move off a little way into the scrub, and then begin grazing again.

The things that really startle them—the whiff of a hunting lion in the long grass, the warning flight of some bird above their heads—are usually too subtle for you to notice. All you are aware of is a sudden unnatural stillness in the bush. Every head has been jerked erect and turned in the same direction, every animal has frozen into the rigidity of a statue. For perhaps a minute or two they remain like this, and then, apparently reassured, they relax again. At other times the herd is seized with an ungovernable panic, and in a second the peaceful pattern is shattered by a wild commotion, the guinea fowl scuttling into the undergrowth, the zebra running together in a pack with their tails flying out behind them, the antelopes every ten yards or so making immense jumps into the air in the hope of catching a brief glimpse of the approaching enemy; and in a moment you are entirely alone in the clearing.

After a day or two of this one begins to realize that one must reassemble one's ideas about the wild animals in Africa. Somewhere in the tangled background of one's education something seems to have gone wrong; and now it is not the strangeness of the things that one is seeing that is so impressive—it is their false familiarity. Like most of our generation (the lost one dating back to before the First World War) my wife and I had grown up with the legend of Africa, the danger-legend of the explorer and the white hunter, of Rider Haggard's tales and many a movie star on safari. The lion springs, the elephant charges with a terrifying bellow, and it is always some poor human devil who is going to get the worst of it unless he shoots quick.

Here in the Kruger Park, however, we were confronted with something quite different, the legend, as it were, within the legend: the animals reacting not to human beings but to themselves and to the surrounding forest. In other words, once you remove the human element—and in particular the emphasis on human danger—an entirely new world emerges. You see that an elaborate and subtle skein of influences is at work; that, for instance, there was a very good reason why those zebra and impala and other antelopes should have been grazing together; one species excels in hearing, another in smell, and another in sight, and together they establish a very effective warning system against their common enemies, the lions, the leopards and other carnivora.

These discoveries tend to create in one a simple unaffected pleasure. It is, of course, an obvious escape-entertainment, but there is nothing really synthetic about it because one quickly realizes, however calcified and disillusioned one may be, that this is a world that we knew very well when we were young; the dream world of the jungle stories to which we listened in a trance of sympathy and fear and quite definitely *wanted* to believe. And although this world has nothing to do with human beings it is often more moving, more entertaining and much more terrible than anything which has been dreamed of in the movies or the sportsmen's notebooks.

I found myself especially attracted to some of the lesser species, mostly I suppose because nobody had ever bothered to tell me about them before. Who, for example, ever writes about the warthog? Yet you find him everywhere in this part of Africa; he has a small trotting-on part in every other scene. The warthog is the clown of the jungle, and he has a certain awful charm. He is an extremely bothered animal about the size of a small pig, and he is furnished with two enormous tusks, a lion's mane and a tail and hindquarters which are quite uncompromisingly bare. He roots about the ground in family groups, and if surprised he stands and stares for a moment with deep concern written all over his appalling face. Then with a flick of his head, his tail rising like a railway signal bolt upright behind him, the father of the group is off into the scrub. The rest of the family follow in line, the biggest first and the smallest drawing up frantically in the rear. The warthog is not really ugly—it is the sort of countenance that is covered roughly by the French phrase "une jolie laide"— yet by his mere appearance he has been known to stampede a herd of buffalo.

There were a lot of warthogs around Pretorius Kop while we were there, and we were told that they had a passion for a little wild green apple called a Marula that falls to the ground in summer. In this African heat the fruit ferments quickly and the warthogs sometimes become quite drunk. Instead of bolting in the usual way they stand and gaze at the intruder with a bemused and careless eye. Then the instinct for self-preservation dimly asserts itself, and they turn and make a befuddled rush for a few yards, stop, change direction and then plunge off again. Finally they subside to sleep on the ground to awake to heaven knows what sort of primeval hangover in the morning.

With the giraffe, at the other end of the scale, much the tallest creature in the bush, it is quite different. Here is the least demonstrative of animals (it has no vocal cords and utters only the smallest of sounds, a sort of sighing snort in the throat), and in all Africa it is certainly the most decorative thing alive. We came on a family one day in the Kruger Park—just the two parents and one half-grown child—and for a long time, with their heads thrown slightly back, they surveyed us across the tops of the acacia trees. Giraffes have a slightly affronted air when they are disturbed; somehow they contrive to make you feel as though you have just said something in particularly bad taste, and they sniff the breeze reproachfully. The skins of this group were superb: smooth and bright and glossy, so bright indeed that they stood out plainly against the bush, as plainly as the stripes of the zebras do. Clearly this pattern of jagged brown squares is meant to camouflage the animal by breaking up its outline, but it didn't seem to be very effective at a range of thirty yards; not, at any rate, with those ten-foot necks swaying above us like vast asparagus stalks among the trees. And then abruptly they were off. No living creature in this world runs as the giraffe does. It moves its legs in pairs on either side, first the right side forward then the left, and this imparts a singular undulating motion to the huge beast. It flows across the countryside with the delayed rhythm of a film in slow motion, and it is perfectly wonderful to watch.

Later on, in other parts of Africa, we saw many giraffes and learned a lot about them, and it was always something rather pleasant and out-landish. In parts of Kenya, for example, they have had to raise the tele-phone lines a clear six feet or so to allow the big bulls (they grow to 17 or 18 feet) to pass beneath; and at Hluhluwe there was the strange story of the giraffe who simply could not believe in itself. It was a baby just a few days old that had been abandoned by its mother (possibly because she had had two offspring and could not feed both), and a farmer had picked it up and brought it to the game warden's house. For three and a half years the warden looked after the orphan; it was brought up with his own children and played with them every day. When it grew too big to come into the house it kept mooning through the windows at the warden and his family while they were eating dinner, and it followed them around to their bedrooms through the garden when they went to bed. Finally it was decided that the moment had come when the animal, now fully grown, should join his own kind, and he was taken off to a herd of wild giraffe that had recently come into the park. But one look was sufficient. The small brain was quite unable to register the fact that such extraor-dinary animals could exist, and that he was one of them: he turned and bolted. They took him back half a dozen times with the same result, and in the end they gave it up. A little lonely and reproachful, the tame giraffe lives now in a specially constructed paddock near the warden's house.

All the animals in the parks are of course in the process of adapting themselves to human beings, and an uneven but quite definite evolution is being observed as the years go by. At Kruger Park birds still cannot always estimate the speed of approaching cars, and they occasionally smash themselves into the wind-screens. Sometimes herds of impala (those charming small antelopes with lyre-shaped horns that are impossible to dissociate from Walt Disney's Bambi) are seized with the frantic desire to stampede at the sight of a vehicle on the road. One animal with a mighty bound into the air starts it, and the others follow. The leaders get across the road safely, but the others coming on behind, their vision obscured by dust, are likely to crash into you. Giraffes too will sometimes rush blindly forward in this way, and one kick from that tremendous fore-leg can smash the radiator of a car.

On the other hand, elephants and some of the larger carnivora have quickly got to know the limits of the park, and they realize they are safe from human interference there. If they stray over the borders at night into the neighbouring farms in search of food they take good care to be back again inside the park before morning breaks.

There is, in fact, a constant nocturnal warfare going on along the frontiers of every park, the animals going out and the poachers coming in. African game rangers armed with rifles and posted every quarter of a mile or so along the more populated boundaries of the Kruger Park do a certain amount towards keeping the situation under control, but they are not always effective; it grows lonely on your own in the bush, there is an immense temptation for a man to try a bottle or two of the local home-brewed beer, and after that to sleep. And while he sleeps the poachers come creeping in with their spears and wire snares.

I had imagined that it might be an exciting experience to drive about the park at night, that the bush then became alive with staring eyes, and that all sorts of horrendous shrieks and cries resounded in the under-growth; but the game rangers told me it was not a bit like this. One rarely saw or heard anything at all. Just occasionally, they said, some of the smaller beasts would dart across the road or an antelope of some kind would become transfixed in the headlights. The impala were very easy to catch in this way; they simply stood there, utterly demoralized, gazing into the lights, and you could walk up and grab them by the horns.

For my part, I felt very little desire to break the rules and sally out of the camp at night. More than once when we were returning at sunset from some outlying part my wife and I debated what we would do if the car broke down. We agreed that if it were only a matter of a mile or two back to camp we would walk and risk it; further than that, no, we would wait until morning.

It was absurd of course. In Africa pythons don't drop on you out of trees, and it is only by the most random accident that a man will be trampled by an elephant or attacked by a hungry lion at night. But nothing will stop the imagination working. One looks at these rolling endless hills of scrub as the night closes in, one pictures oneself lost out there in the blackness, and at once one recognizes the characters in the Ancient Mariner's vision:

> Like one that on a lonesome road
> Doth walk in fear and dread,
> And having once turned round, walks on,
> And turns no more his head;
> Because he knows a fearful fiend
> Doth close behind him tread.

The man on the lonesome road is you, lost in the park, and the fearful fiend is a leopard lying in wait in the branches above your head.

These visions had a powerful influence on one unlucky visitor to Pretorius Kop, not long ago. This man was driving alone, and by some mischance, just as night was falling, he turned down a side track which had been closed to visitors because the bridges along it had been washed away. Darkness still found him wandering about, and in something of a panic he rushed at one of the little streams in his path. Half-way across the engine flooded and would not start again. With the water flowing just an inch or two below the floorboards he waited there all night. The game warden at the gate was only a couple of miles away, but even in the morning the man still did not care to walk. He waited in his car all through the day and the next night, and it was only by chance that an African park attendant came bicycling down the deserted track on the second morning. He found the man in a state of mild hysteria, and it was some little time before he could be induced to get out of his car and wade over to the bank.

There have been very few incidents in the history of the Kruger Park to justify such extreme fear. Game rangers do get mauled by lions from time to time; occasionally a female elephant that has been separated from her young will make a charge, but the truth of the matter is that large wild animals will not usually attack human beings. Their instinct is to escape from men whenever they see them, and, with odd exceptions, it is only when they have been hunted and wounded that they become dangerous.

"In the old days," one veteran sportsman told me, "rhino, buffalo and elephant always used to charge, but that was because we were always out shooting them. I have still never seen a rhino in any other position except coming at me head on. It is only recently and only in the game reserves that the animals have become relatively tame." And he went on to speak of a kind of glee for killing which used to possess the early settlers in South Africa; just to see an animal was enough, they *had* to kill it. He remembered one farmer telling him with delight how just that day he had succeeded with five shots in wiping out the last five survivors of a rare species of antelope.

And so an endless spiral is created: the huntsman—the native with the poisoned arrow, the sportsman with the rifle—deliberately creates danger for himself by attacking the animals, and this danger, this created risk, then becomes the justification for his hunting.

At Kruger Park they tell a story of a noted game warden named Wolhuter, who was clawed from his horse by two lions one day, and although terribly mauled managed to survive. Wolhuter's son is now a ranger at the Kruger Park, and he continues to ride on horseback. "My father had bad luck," he told me. "Nine times out of ten no lion will molest you even if it's hungry. Sometimes the younger lions—the two- and three-year-olds—will chase a man on horseback but they only do it for fun, and you can easily get away. Whenever we have had a serious case it has always been because the animal has been in pain. I remember not long ago an African game ranger was knocked off his bicycle by a lion and killed. Afterwards when the animal was shot it was found to be in agony from a thorn in its foot. But that was a very rare case."

After three days at Pretorius Kop my wife and I turned south to Hluhluwe (Sushloo-wee is about the nearest I can get to the correct pronunciation) in the hope of catching a glimpse of the rare and allegedly dangerous white rhinoceros. This involved a journey of some hundreds of miles through the British protectorate of Swaziland. Swaziland is the Rider Haggard country; these are the hills that Allan Quatermain and his friends trudged across in search of King Solomon's Mines. At Mbabane (another phonetical snare—Imbabarn seems to be the local usage) the proprietress of our hotel took me out on to the veranda one evening and pointed to the west. "Look," she said, "Queen Sheba's Breasts." There they were, two pointed peaks on the skyline, just as Haggard had described them, and the track that wound down through the pass was obviously the track that Quatermain had followed.

The rest of Swaziland, a green and lovely countryside, was almost as romantic. We called on Sohhuze, the reigning chief, a man who speaks English but lives in a kraal of native huts and on occasion receives visitors mounted on the back of a warrior. He was unable to see us, however; a polite message was sent out saying that the country was suffering from drought and that he was making rain.

It fell that night—four inches, to be exact—and it turned half Swaziland into a quagmire of impassable black mud. It was in the tail end of this cloudburst that we drove down to the shores of the Indian Ocean and thence to the Hluhluwe reserve in Natal.

At Hluhluwe, a much smaller park than Kruger, the main camp of thatched huts perches on a ridge. You see it from a long way off, but the last few miles are rather difficult going on a steep and winding road; and it was here that our car burnt out a coil and came to a dead stop. Two days of thrashing about in the Swaziland mud had been too much for it. There was still half an hour of daylight to go, and since the camp was just above us we decided to walk. As it so often happens, however, we underestimated the distance and the sun set very quickly. I don't think that either of us were very disturbed about the animals at that moment; we were too tired and dishevelled at the end of the long day, and we would probably have reached the camp without giving them a thought had not some people driven up behind us. They asked: "Aren't you frightened to walk at night with the rhino about?" The white rhinoceros! He was beginning to sound like the white whale in Melville's *Moby Dick*, and certainly we would have been frightened had we remembered him.

Next day, however, when we went to see the huge beasts it turned out that the white rhinoceros is hardly dangerous at all, not at any rate as rhinoceroses go. The African ranger who was with us calmly got out of the car we had borrowed and walked up to a group of half a dozen of them. We followed gingerly, choosing a path along a line of easily climbable trees; and there they stood, not twenty yards away. As far as I could see they were like any other rhinoceros except that the colour of their hides was dirty grey. They mooned about through the bush with a fine antediluvian deliberation, and although they were perfectly well aware of our presence—a rhinoceros has very bad eyesight but its sense of smell is acute—they seemed to be neither annoyed nor surprised.

It is the ordinary black rhinoceros that is dangerous, and when on the following day we came on a large female with its young our guide would by no means allow us to get out of the car. Instead he instructed me to keep the engine running and be ready to move off at speed. The black species (it is actually light orange in colour when it has been rolling in the mud, a thing it often does) is the most unpredictable of African animals. Occasionally it will charge a car, and nearly always it will go for a man on foot if he approaches too close. With over a ton weight coming at you at twenty miles an hour you don't stand much of a chance. Among themselves the rhinoceroses are constantly fighting, the females included, and it is not the two horns, the front one perhaps three feet long and sharply pointed, which do the damage; it is the terrific lunging blow delivered by the animal's shoulder. This sets up internal injuries in his opponent.

At Hluhluwe we heard much argument about how these and other large wild animals which have always been regarded as the prerogative of the hunter are going to be preserved. Once you have got them into the park do you allow nature to take its course and achieve its own balance? Or do you shoot off a few lions, leopards and cheetah when you find that they are making too much havoc among the lesser game? Do you burn off the grass each year to bring on the new spring growth, or again do you let the natural vegetable process have its own way? These and other technical questions, we discovered, are debated all the way up and down East Africa, and there does not appear to be any general agreement in sight. Each park makes its own rules.

But it is the question of disease which is the really dominant issue. Wild animals, though not usually affected themselves, are carriers of a parasite called Trypanosome, which is spread by the tsetse fly. It is disastrous both to cattle and to human beings (it carries sleeping sickness) and there are other plagues which they also help to spread. Until recently the usual remedy was simple: exterminate the wild animals. The slaughter was fantastic and was not confined to Africa. In 1924, for example, there was an outbreak of foot and mouth disease in the Stanislaus National Park in the United States. Some 22,000 deer were shot, and both disease and animals were exterminated together. In Zululand, close to the Hluhluwe, there was a much more drastic affair in the nineteen-forties. Nagana, the tsetse fly disease, took hold, and a systematic destruction of all wild animals began. Between 1942 and 1950 138,329 head of big game were shot. And still the disease was not stamped out.

Nowadays more imaginative methods are being tried: spraying from the air is one answer, and in some places the tsetse fly is kept back by lopping the foliage of the bigger shrubs. But these are expensive experiments, and it is still general practice for governments in Africa to order the destruction of large numbers of game whenever disease threatens a settled area. Only in such remote places as the Kalahari desert in Bechuanaland are the animals really safe—at all events for the next few decades. Here in the Kalahari, where the only roads are the dried-up courses of rivers that flow just once or twice a century, vast herds of gemsbok (an antelope with a white blazed face and two horns like spears) roam about; and the lion, the kudu and the springbok are still left pretty much to themselves. In the Gemsbok Park the only human inhabitants are those lamentable bushmen, some forty of them in all, who do nothing but lie in the sun all day.

As for the other parks, it seems to be everywhere agreed that they will all have to be fenced off one day if they are going to survive, a vast project requiring millions upon millions of pounds. Up to date fencing has only been tried out on a small scale in South Africa to protect the Addo elephants, a special breed that lives in an impenetrable jungle near Port Elizabeth. These elephants used to trespass on the citrus fruit farms nearby, and they were shot at until only eleven beasts were left. Then the government stepped in and constructed a fence of tramlines and lift cables, eleven and a half miles in length, its posts sunk six feet into the ground; and behind this barrier the elephants have slowly begun to breed again.

At Hluhluwe, however, one is not much aware of any of these problems. Poaching seems to be at a minimum, and there are no lions to eat the smaller beasts or elephants to trample the neighbouring farms. It is the prettiest park in Africa. During the long wet summer it blooms with such flowering trees as flamboyants, frangipani and mimosa, and there is a refreshing greenness everywhere. Unlike the Kruger Park where, for the most part, you drive along bush tracks on a level with animals, here the ground is broken up into small hills and valleys; and since the roads run along the ridges you look down on the game from above and see them not individually but in herds and in constant movement. In one short early morning drive we saw rhinoceros, buffalo, wildebeest, nyala (an antelope which is distinguished, in the male, by a coat of gunmetal blue with an unusually bright white stripe down the back), warthog, impala, baboons, monkeys, zebra and one solitary ostrich: quite a bag to mention casually to our neighbours in the next rondavel when we got back. An ostrich seen close-to in the bush looks like nothing so much as a preposterously enlarged chicken, and there is something a little indecent about its huge bare legs. I had been told that ostriches sometimes swallow stones and pebbles as an aid to digestion, and unless I am much mistaken our specimen was doing precisely that. He was pecking at a patch of gravel when we came by, and I saw him raise his tiny head and gulp awkwardly a couple of times before he paced away. Incidentally, it is quite untrue that ostriches bury their heads in the sand at the approach of danger. They may bend their necks down to the ground, but they do this so that they will not be seen from far off across the plain.

In Hluhluwe too we first began to observe the storks. They come down here to the Cape of Good Hope in great flocks around October every year, and then at the end of February begin to assemble for their long six-thousand mile flight back to Europe. This is a delightful thing to see. Just a few birds appear in the sky one day, slowly spiralling around, and from hour to hour newcomers add to their numbers. Then again on the following day still more storks arrive to join the slow circle in the sky, and the same process may go on for a week or more. Finally all the members of this particular flock are gathered together; by some mysterious means the signal for the start is given and in mass formation they wheel away to the north. April and May find them repairing their crude nests of sticks on the cottage chimneypots in Alsace-Lorraine and Holland. Just a few of the older and the weaker birds don't feel equal to this journey, and often, I was told, you will see them loitering about in the swamps and the marshes in South Africa through the winter, like elderly holiday-makers who linger on in half-deserted seaside hotels long after the season is over.

ILKA CHASE

Johannesburg, Kruger National Park, Cape Town: 1964

"AT SOUTH AFRICAN AIRPORTS . . . THE EUROPEAN TOILETS ARE TENDED BY
BLACK WOMEN. THE THOUGHT THAT, WHEN ALONE, THERE IS NOTHING TO
PREVENT THESE DARK-HUED LADIES FROM SEATING THEMSELVES UPON THE
SACROSANCT WHITES' POTS HAS A PLEASING ELEMENT OF LUNACY."

At mid-century, Ilka Chase was a familiar star on the American stage and
on radio and television. But she also wrote some of the most engaging and
charming travel books in the literature, with such titles as Second Spring
and Two Potatoes, The Carthaginian Rose, Around the World and
Other Places, and, perhaps the most intriguing title, Elephants Arrive
at Half-past Five. All, alas, are out of print.

When I saw her on television as a child and read some of her books
as a teenager, I thought her a Grand Lady, i.e., multitalented, professional, independent, and withal charming and graceful. Rereading her
books now confirms my earlier impression.

Chase was among the last representatives of an earlier age of travel.
She and her doctor husband, Norton Brown, lived in New York and
knew, it seems, everyone—or, at least, everyone who mattered. They
moved in a world held together by an international web of friends and
acquaintances and the friends of friends, so that, no matter where they
came to earth, there was always someone there to greet them and to in-
troduce them to someone else.

They were intrepid travelers and crisscrossed the world many times,
moved always by an eager curiosity and a desire to see what was good in
every place they visited. The doctor, as Chase usually refers to him, took

the pictures. Her account of a solo visit to the Maya ruins at Chichén Itzá in the Yucatán is included in The Reader's Companion to Mexico.

In 1962 Chase and her husband visited and very much enjoyed East Africa, where they met Joy Adamson and her lions of Born Free fame and traveled widely in Kenya, Uganda, and Tanzania. So in 1964, when they planned a trip to the South Seas and decided to go west all the way around the globe, they once again included Africa on their route.

This was an ambitious itinerary, even for people armed with money and privilege. They would head west first to San Francisco and then on to Honolulu. From there to the South Seas: Fiji, Tahiti, Bora Bora, and Moorea. Then back to Fiji and on to New Zealand, and then on again to Australia. It took some vigilance on Chase's part to keep the travel agency and tourist office people who worked out the details from giving them a schedule that wasn't too exhausting. The first plan had them leaving Ayers Rock in central Australia at dawn, flying all day to Perth on the west coast, changing planes on a tight schedule, and flying all night and the next day well into the afternoon before reaching Johannesburg. It was too much, and a revised plan gave them a night and a day to rest in Perth.

After Johannesburg, their intention was to visit the Rhodesias (now Zimbabwe and Zambia) and then continue northward to Nairobi. And after that they would fly to London and so to home.

Five hours out of Perth, their Qantas Electra Mark II prop-jet landed for refueling at the Cocos Islands. And, true to form, even at such a remote spot and at 1:30 in the morning, there, standing on the tarmac to greet them, feed them, show them around, and keep them entertained for the ninety-minute layover, were two couples who had been alerted to their arrival by a mutual friend in New York.

Back aboard the plane, the next flight was nearly eight hours across the Indian Ocean to Mauritius, two hours on the ground there, and then four more hours to Johannesburg.

But, in fact, they had already had some contact with South Africa before leaving New York. When they had applied for visas at the South African Consulate, they found some of the questions on the form quite disturbing.

Chase writes:

" 'Have you ever been known by any other name?' The chill begins.

" 'Racial origin.' Were you once a Negro, I suppose.

" 'Do you contribute professionally or otherwise to newspapers, publications, radio, television, or films? If so, please give details.'

"Obviously. Who wants tattletales and reporters on the premises?

" 'Kindly furnish the following particulars in respect to any person known to you in South Africa: Name, Relationship, Address.' Guilt by association?"

Perhaps most disturbing of all, Chase reports, "We later discovered they had tapped a couple of sources to obtain information about us" before issuing the visas.

By the time they finally reached South Africa, it was late September, the beginning of spring.

THERE ARE THOSE WHO SPEAK OF JOHANNESBURG AS Jo'burg, but I do not call Philadelphia Philly nor Los Angeles L.A., and if I am not on terms of intimacy with cities of my native land I am that much less so with the South African metropolis. For me it is Johannesburg and from the air the most striking feature of its landscape is the enormous mine dumps, the sand-colored slag that has been hauled from the mines and piled up around the countryside in mesas and mountains. They are scarifying and ugly, and as they contain cyanide no verdure can survive as cover. South Africans are experimenting with special grasses and one must hope they succeed, for the slag heaps are depressing.

Industrial installations sometimes have a skeletal, fierce beauty of their own. Sometimes, looking at them, we experience the satisfaction inherent in functional economical design, or sometimes flame and steam combine to create spectacular effects—this may be classified as beauty if of a notably non-human kind, but the slag from the gold mines of Witwatersrand is exsanguinated dross, empty and flung away, barren and sad.

We touched down at two forty-five in the afternoon, having been in transit for twenty hours and fifteen minutes. It is a crushing journey and we were exhausted, but despite our fatigue Norton and I had been laughing in the plane. "This was the flight the travel people back in New York had planned to preface with that ten-hour job from Ayers Rock to Perth." It would have killed us.

As it was we were groggy and could barely comprehend what was happening when we were met by a charming couple whom we did not know, the Tilden-Davises, and a large bunch of glorious sweet peas was thrust into my hand. Driving to the hotel our fuzzy-mindedness began to clear.

New York friends, Yvor and Leila Smitter, who had lived in Johannesburg for three years, had written letters and a friend of theirs, Mrs. Kenneth Anderson, with whom I had been corresponding on our way around the world, had invited us to dine the night of our arrival and had apparently planned to meet us at the airport. Unfortunately she had been ill and had had to go out of town for a few days' rest, but so thoughtful and courteous was she that she had asked two friends to take her place, and so thoughtful and courteous were they, they had agreed. This struck us as regal hospitality, which was increased by an invitation to dine.

They dropped us at the Hotel Langham, where we rested and bathed, and shortly after seven picked us up again. Another couple, the Hugh Traceys, joined us at dinner at the Cafe Royal in the Park Royal Hotel. Like the Esplanade at Perth, it was cozy Victorian and we had a good dinner and a good South African wine.

Glancing over a list of people Leila Smitter had given us thinking we might possibly be able to get together, Mr. Tracey murmured, "Ah yes, Alan Paton, one of our romantic writers." Being so freshly arrived I felt it too soon to ask if he said that because he considered sympathy for the black African cause moonshine but I thought it a provocative comment. Hugh Tracey is a tall, gray-haired, handsome Englishman and an authority on native African music. He has lectured all over the United States and has a famous record library which he invited us to visit.

Our host, Iain Tilden-Davis, was half English and half American and our hostess, Pamela, was a full-blown Irish rose; rounded, warm-hearted, and candid. "I thoroughly enjoy living in a country where there is a subject race," she said cheerfully. "I dislike housework and enjoy having someone else do it for me." So do we all, but in most countries domestic help is not a subject race. Quite the contrary! Any subjects involved are likely to be the employers who, despite high wages and abject catering to the whims of the empress in the kitchen or the nursery, are walked out upon at the drop of a hat.

It is hard, but morally speaking I suppose it is better for the employers' characters, if not their dispositions, to be so situated that they cannot take advantage of an underdog. All I ask is not to be the underdog myself.

As we learned, the Tilden-Davis sense of responsibility was stronger than their light-hearted comments might lead one to believe. Sometimes the going had been hard for them and then it was hard for their neighboring Africans too. They would come silently and sit in a circle around the door hoping for food. When that happened, what the Tilden-Davises had, they shared.

Pamela, we discovered, was a horoscope enthusiast and like many people addicted to astrology tended to regard her friends as an Aries or a Taurus, which may not be inaccurate but it does make for a somewhat impersonal relationship.

As it is, we are daily becoming more and more disembodied digits. I did not even know that besides my Social Security and bank account numbers and a phone where more numbers will shortly usurp our pleasant Plaza exchange, I had an identification number as well. It was the New York State Department of Motor Vehicles which enlightened me. On top of all those, to be thought of as rams or bulls or crabs instead of as us adds to the dehumanization. Although Pamela Tilden-Davis herself is singularly cozy.

She and Iain took us to call on Nadine Gordimer, the writer, best known in this country for her contributions to *The New Yorker*, and that book of quality, *Not for Publication*. She is a distinguished woman, small, with rather aquiline features, her dark hair piled on top of her head in a coronet braid. That afternoon she wore a short straight dress, a kind of Chinese cheong sam, greeted us hospitably, and showed us around her charming old house and big garden. We met her young son, obviously an extremely intelligent child as well as being very well mannered, and we also met her Weimaraner. She was devoted to him but her true loves, we gathered, were bulldogs. She had crossed a bull and a Weimaraner who, judging from their photographs, were irresistible, and called them the Weimar Bulls. When I said that the name made me think of *The Bull from the Sea*, she said, "Oh, if you're going to Cape Town be sure to look up Mary Renault, she lives there." We said we would.

Unfortunately Reinhold Cassirer, Miss Gordimer's husband, was away so we did not meet him, but those who know him think highly of him. In Germany, before the war, he was an art dealer and would often send pictures out on loan or consignment to galleries and museums in the United States. When he began to realize that Hitler's ascension to power was inevitable he wrote his colleagues urging them to retain the pictures for safekeeping, and thus preserved a good many works of art for their rightful owners and from the acquisitive clutches of Herr Goering.

The Cassirers had a nice Daumier over the fireplace and a charming Degas ballet dancer.

Nadine Gordimer and Alan Paton are among the tiny number of South African whites who stand firm for the blacks, believing that the conditions under which they are obliged to live are scandalous, and she and Mr. Paton are thoroughly and frequently taken to task for this attitude by the great majority of the white South African press.

Feeling differently about the situation, the Tilden-Davises are nevertheless devoted to her. "But there you are, you see," said Pamela, "Nadine will give a party for her African friends, a barbecue, let us say, Friday night and Sunday morning they are still there, drunk on the front steps. Now I don't like that, I care too much for discipline."

WHILE IN JOHANNESBURG WE LUNCHED AND DINED WITH hospitable people to whom mutual friends in New York had written letters, and wherever we went the entertaining seemed effortless. As any hostess knows this is the result of hard work and meticulous planning, but in South Africa helping hands are more readily available. One hostess told us they had three servants and paid the three together forty-two dollars a month. It is not altogether surprising if "the natives are restless tonight."

One evening dining with the Donald Agnews of the American Express office we met Doris Trace. We had a letter to her too and she asked us to lunch at the Englehards' the next day. They themselves were away, but Doris runs the house for them whether they are there or absent and is a capable and charming woman.

The Charles Englehards are Americans, proprietors of enough lettuce to enable them to adorn their lives with attractions such as race horses, ocean-spanning private planes, spacious houses in assorted countries, and the delightful Mrs. Trace.

While lunching in the garden we commented on its beauty and Doris laughed. "This is the season of the year I always get fired. The accountants are coming out this afternoon and I know just what they're going to say. 'Doris, this watering is costing a fortune.' I'm sure it's costing a guinea a minute but we've got to hold till the rains come." As in American cities of the Midwest few people live in town, they are nearly all in the suburbs on properties commensurate with their budgets. We were grand and visited some quite large budgets.

Doris spoke of guineas and we had assumed that the money of South Africa was pounds, but our eyes had been opened on our arrival. It is rands and cents, and one rand is worth $1.40.

The other luncheon guest was Mr. Jack Robb who, in the course of much marrying, had one time drawn the young English actress Virginia McKenna as a stepdaughter. We were interested because she was playing the part of Joy Adamson in the filming of *Born Free*, and we would be meeting her in Kenya. When Mr. Robb said he understood the picture was almost finished our spirits were dashed. We wanted to meet Miss McKenna and her husband Bill Travers, but the real lure was the lion cubs and the baby elephant Joy had written us about.

Thinking it over it seemed to me improbable they could be so nearly finished, for shooting had started in mid-August and we were only at the end of September, but possibly an ex-stepfather knew? To our vast relief he did not. As matters developed they finished around the first of March and were lucky to make it then.

Doris Trace showed us through the house and one painting in particular caught my eye: a colorful scene of cane fields, a red and white railway signal, and a round black head peering through bright green grass. It was by Felix Kelly, and I hope some day to meet the gentleman and see more of his work.

Doris' own quarters were like a flat in a London mews. A small living room with an open fire, lots of family photographs, a tiny bar amusingly decorated by her daughter, cozy and gay. "Gets rather crowded at times," she said. "The Engelhards come in here and their friends and if my kids are visiting . . . we're like a Marx Brothers movie."

After luncheon driving back to town in one of the family cars, we were surprised to see a rank of pedicabs drawn by men as they had been in the Orient. Somehow they didn't fit. We did a bit of souvenir shopping at Ivy's and Gainsborough Galleries, and found the merchandise to be hides, carvings, fertility charms, beaded dolls, and baskets.

We had been offered tickets to the mine dances but turned them down. I wish now that we had seen the dancers, for they are peculiarly characteristic of Johannesburg. Held on Sunday mornings in the compounds of various gold and diamond mines, the performances are contests between native dancers in tribal costume and are apparently entertaining and colorful. More colorful, let us hope, than their weekday lives.

Very early one morning en route to Rand Airport at Germiston where we were catching a plane for Kruger National Park we passed through an area known as the Eastern Native District Township. It is an appalling ghetto-slum, a shanty town of crowded shacks made of flattened tin cans with tin and corrugated iron roofs and rickety chimney pots. The ground is mud and slag and shale and supports not one tree or blade of grass. The entire area is surrounded by a high iron paling fence and the inhabitants must carry passes and be inside by nightfall. When we asked why the fence, our driver assured us it was to protect the children. "As you see, the township is on a main highway and the children run out into the road. This way they are safe." We said that African children must be exceptionally big and strong if a fence of such proportions was required to keep them inside. In Cape Town when we asked why a high barbed wire fence—the kind that bends inward at the top—surrounded another African district, our man replied, "They like it. We were going to put up a wall but they said, 'we don't want a wall,' so of course we didn't."

I do not know if they have brainwashed themselves to the extent that they believe these fictions or if they are hopeful that the visitor will but, I suppose, they are to be commended for keeping a straight face when making their explanations. In fairness one must say that the whites themselves admit that the Eastern Township is a wretched place. "But it's old," they say—new it must still have been pretty horrible—"and we're moving them out as quickly as the new developments are ready."

We were told that sometimes Africans are reluctant to leave their neighborhoods, sordid though they be, because they are in sections where they may own property. I believe in the new districts they are only allowed to rent.

In the early morning as we drove past, Africans by the thousands were pouring out of their hovels on the way to work. We thought many of them looked sullen and apathetic, which seemed natural. Brightness was the surprise.

At the small airport things were reasonably disorganized and so were we. Having been told it would be frightfully hot as we were only going to Phalaborwa—the Kruger National Park stop—Norton was in safari clothes and I wore shorts. Gradually other passengers began assembling, all men in business suits, and we felt distinctly out of place. A sign on the counter said Welkom Passengers which we took to be a greeting in Afrikaans, but that turned out to be the destination of the business suits.

We finally got our proper plane and once aloft I went into the lavatory and changed into slacks as the temperature was well below freezing.

Things warmed up considerably later on, and the captain said he hoped we would be able to see the dramatic landscape where the escarpment drops four thousand feet to the veld, but maybe there would be a cloud cover over it. There was.

Arriving at Kruger National Park after a flight of an hour and a half, we were met by Louis Bothe, a good, well-informed driver, who guided us to a Volkswagen and we set off to see the animals. At the gates of the park we came upon two or three of our old enemies, bulldozers, and sure enough they were scalping the land for a development that will be cheek by jowl with the reserve. Kruger sounds large, about eight thousand square miles, but in actuality it is a long, narrow strip along the Mozambique border. It is not fenced and the poaching is vicious, but there is little reason to suppose that a fence would keep poachers out. They encroach over the western or Transvaal boundary just as much. With a housing development I should think the situation can only deteriorate.

The day was cloudy but the visibility was unlimited. Normally, when traveling, one does not hope for rain but we hoped hard. The need was desperate. The whole park was gray, dry scrub grass and dry, twisted trees. From May 1 till October 15 the entire reserve may be visited, the rest of the year only a limited area in the southwest (Pretoriuskop and Skukuza are open), but although we were there on September 29 and theoretically there were two weeks to go, Louis Bothe said they might have to close to prevent forest fires. June apparently is the best month.

Our plane had been late in taking off so it was nine-thirty when we arrived and late for the best results. Animals are usually seen in greater numbers in the early morning and around sundown but in any case, after the magnificent reserves of East Africa which we had visited two years before, we found Kruger disappointing. One may not turn off the roads and although it was a weekday there were a good many cars and we progressed slowly in single file, hoping that game would come to look at us. In the course of the morning we did spot seven giraffes and a frieze of exquisite impala leaping across the road as well as a kudu in his chalk-striped gray suit, two ostriches, and my slabfaced love, the warthog, with his curling little tusks and periscope tail. I appreciate that warthogs are not everybody's cup of tea but I fell in love with them when we first saw them, and I find them endlessly amusing.

We passed a fever tree with four great eagles' nests but there was nobody home. They are lovely trees, yellow with spreading branches and lacy green foliage. They were so named by the Boers, who frequently came down with malaria and who cherished them because when they saw them they knew they were near water. The Letaba River rewarded us with several tons of hippo and a few somnolent crocodiles. There were baboons and steenbok and peering hard we could discern a sandy reed buck in the dry river bed so one could not count the day lost. But the elephants and lions, alas, had taken to the hills.

We lunched at the Letaba River camp which can accommodate over three hundred people in the modern, sand-colored concrete rondavels and had a quite good oxtail stew, although Norton complained that his was all bone and no meat. "But sir," said the waiter proudly, "it is oxtail," as though having no meat was its virtue. "Oxtail very good." "I am a doctor," said the doctor coldly, "and I know that on the sacrum there is no meat."

On our return flight we were lucky. The clouds had lifted and the captain had been right. We saw the great escarpment dropping abruptly four thousand feet to the plain, and the marvelous dark mountains and ridges and the long, long road that passes through a small tunnel to avoid an even longer journey around the entire range. The legend that Africa wins the heart is true.

Although it had not been on our itinerary originally, we had heard so much of the charm of Cape Town we decided to go. Speaking of Howard Clark, the president of American Express Company, Donald Agnew had said, "You know how he is, a few hours, maybe, in a place. In Cape Town he and his wife liked it so well they stayed a day and a half!" Jean and Howard Clark knew what they were about. Cape Town is a joy.

Our own feeling was that in Johannesburg it would have to be friends who made one's happiness. The atmosphere of the city itself was, to us, oppressive. There was too much dark misery, but in Cape Town there is an almost palpable lifting of the spirit. Not that *apartheid* isn't practiced, it is, but there is an illogical quality about it in Cape Town that renders it less grim.

At South African airports, there are signs over the lavatories: Europeans. Non-Europeans. But the European toilets are tended by black women. The thought that, when alone, there is nothing to prevent these dark-hued ladies from seating themselves upon the sacrosanct whites' pots has a pleasing element of lunacy.

The hygienic arrangements throughout the country have a complexity that would put the most abstruse bureaucracy elsewhere to shame.

Non-European means black African. It also means Chinese but not

Japanese, an unexpected subtlety. I suppose it means Indians too, Red or East but I am not sure. Perhaps, god-like, they are above bodily functions. Since, in the strictest sense of the term an American is not a European, Norton and I hesitated, but being white we knew what was expected of us. If South Africans were logical they would have three categories: Black, White, Colored.

For the record, however, I will say they are not without provocation. I have experienced rural African lavatories and they are horrifying. The Tahitians' aren't much better. Personally I would like to see us relax about the moon and devote some of that effort and wealth to more and better plumbing on the planet earth.

Driving from the airport we saw that spring had embraced South Africa as well as Australia. Golden wattles, mustard and daisies blazed against the dark green stone pines, and an immensity of blue water sparkled in the sunlight.

On the way to our hotel we passed a new African housing development in the process of construction. They were building eight thousand units for which the tenants would pay the equivalent of ten dollars and eleven dollars a month rent. The houses themselves were bleak but they were new and clean, and the inhabitants would at least have sun and air in abundance.

The Mount Nelson Hotel is not bleak. It is a large pink stucco building of irregular shape and many white balconies, situated at the foot of Table Mountain and surrounded by terraces and gardens, tennis courts, a bowling green, and a small swimming pool. We had an L-shaped bed-sitting room with pretty flowered chintz, comfortable chairs, and good lights. In the lounge a cheerful fire crackled and we decided that the *Cape Argus* was the best newspaper we had seen since leaving the New York *Times*.

The honeymoon soured a little at luncheon in an exchange with the Indian waiter, who asked us how long we were staying. We said several days.

He: (brightly) Seven?

We: No, several till Saturday. (Waiter looks relieved.) We leave early in the morning. (Waiter looks angry and harassed.)

He: Tomorrow is my day off.

The implication of a tip was clear but as we were only at the soup of our first meal we felt he was a bit premature. I suppose their wages are small and their need is great but so is their nuisance value.

In the course of our afternoon drive we saw the Glenn, a saddle between Table Mountain and Lions Head—some people call it Rump, take your choice—sweeping up to Signal Hill. One can ride a cablecar to the top of Table Mountain, which we would have liked to have done, but although the weather was clear there was a high wind and on such days the little car would swing like a basket, so the ride was closed down. We did however gaze upon the Twelve Apostles, twelve headlands sweeping in a vast majestic curve around the bay.

In the course of the afternoon we visited the South African Museum, which is not madly fascinating but does have a collection of lifesize casts of Bushmen leading simple bushy lives against a vivid diorama. Drop five cents in the slot and you get five minutes of recorded native music. I have a weakness for this kind of display so felt grateful to the Peabody Harvard Kalahari Expedition who had so kindly set it up for me.

Cape Town and its environs is the place par excellence for driving, as at every turn the views are breathtaking.

It lies a thousand miles by road from Johannesburg and our chauffeur, Owen Clark, had recently covered it under circumstances not felicitous. He was driving a seventy-five-year-old woman who insisted on a hundred miles an hour and kept announcing at intervals that she would in all probability die en route and kept giving him instructions as to where to deliver her body. "We finally get there," he said disgustedly, "and out she hops and off she goes without so much as a 'Thank you, Owen.' I was deader than she was."

Travel bureaus are always pretending that you are going to need far more time than is actually the case to admire the local splendors but the next morning, per instructions, we started out punctually at nine for the day's junketing as I had one or two errands to do before leaving the city.

In the store where I was shopping there was a book department so I asked if they could tell me where I might find Miss Mary Renault.

The saleswoman knew at once and said, "I'll look up her telephone number for you."

"Oh," I said, "I've tried that, she's not in the book."

"What name did you look under?"

"Mary Renault."

"Ah, that explains it. Her name is Mary Challans." I thought the *nom de plume* had gone out long ago.

We got the connection and at first a guardian dragon said I could not speak to Miss Renault, she could not be disturbed. I explained that I was from New York, that I was a devoted fan, that I would greatly appreciate. . . . The dragon relented and Miss Renault came to the phone. Further amplification of the above and how much I admired and enjoyed her books and "I write myself" and it was all beginning to sound pretty fatuous so that although I had secretly been hoping she might invite us for tea I could hardly blame her when she said, "I am at work on a new book and you will understand I can't see anyone." I wished her well with it and hung up. If it is of the caliber of *The Last of the Wine, The King Must Die*, and *The Bull from the Sea*, I will have been doing her army of readers and myself a service.

When I told Norton of my disappointment he asked if I had told her that it was her friend Nadine Gordimer who had suggested I call. "Oh, Lord! I kept wondering what I could say that might make her change her mind. What a fool I am. How *could* I have forgotten!" Norton sighed. But so often the obvious is the last thing one remembers.

We photographed the flower market, an explosion of color in an alleyway between two big buildings, and visited a couple of museums. The Koopmans–De Wet is a delightful eighteenth-century private house, with the slave quarters in good repair, and the rooms filled with beautifully waxed furniture, delft, and glassware.

Old Town House, built in 1755, shelters the Michaelis Collection, which was presented to the city by Sir Max Michalelis in 1913—a collection of seventeenth-century Dutch and Flemish artists. They have an interesting if not first-quality Rembrandt, a good many of his etchings, and a Frans Hals portrait of a woman.

The cultural department taken care of, we started another tour of the city, passing fine park land that had been given to the nation by Cecil Rhodes, and drove by Groot Schur, his old property. A handsome, substantial house with whitewashed walls, red roof, and the typical Dutch gables, it is now the residence of the Prime Minister when Parliament sits those six months at Cape Town.

From where Mr. Rhodes lived to where he is memorialized is not far. His memorial is warmly regarded and certainly it is large. Set on a hillside, the shape of an E without the center arm, its spacious open façade of sandstone columns overlooks the city. Eight bronze lions guard it, and forty-nine steps, one for each year of the statesman's life, lead up to it, the whole spearheaded by a vigorous bronze horse, a vigorous bronze rider astride him. The rider's name is "Energy," of which the late Cecil must have had an abundance.

What Cape Province has done for her former Prime Minister is imposing, but with the exception of the Lincoln Memorial and possibly the Taj Mahal, which I have never seen, I am allergic to recognition by monument. At least dead monuments. They make the recognized seem pompous which, with the truly great, is not so. The memorial Rhodes left to himself through the scholarships he made possible honors him more than the official pile of masonry. Beautiful parks or gardens, a great avenue of trees, a wild area preserved, these living things seem to me more worthy tributes to the distinguished dead. Part of the Rhodes memorial is a park, that is true, and it is the better part.

A ravishing garden, although I do not think it commemorates anybody, except that Rhodes bequeathed the land, is the National Botanic Gardens at Kirstenbosch, about seven miles from town. In the spring, late September and October, twelve hundred acres of mountain slopes are carpeted with hundreds of thousands of wild flowers. The day we were there the sun reigned in splendor from a cloudless sky splashing over rocky peaks, tree-filled hollows, and a blazing sea of pink and orange, purple, yellow, white, and lavender bloom.

In an unaccustomed burst of liberality even non-Europeans were allowed to enjoy the glory, and many of them were doing it, walking quietly about on the grass, good strong stuff that could stand the gaff.

We were surprised that people were allowed to walk across it—one of the earliest memories of my childhood is the signs in Central Park abjuring me to Keep Off—and we were even more surprised by the absence of Do Not Pick The Flowers signs. No one seemed to be doing it and we later discovered they had learned the hard way. People used to pillage the wild flowers along the dual carriageways—two-lane highways to us—and the authorities decided to clamp down. Police blocks were set up along the road and anybody found to be secreting even one blossom was fined thirty rands. Forty-two dollars. That came high and the picking ceased.

Continuing on our way from Kirstenbosch, we passed wild calla lilies that are called pig lilies because there are so many they are fed to pigs, who fancy them as delicacies. We were in vineyard country and noticed that the vines had been drastically pruned. Owen observed that the grapes grown on trellises are used for the table, those closer to the ground are for wine. Dr. Brown questioned this. The grapes at the top being as ripe as those at the bottom, he thought that if they did use the lower ones for pressing it might be because they experienced less temperature change at night.

Our destination was Groot Constantia, a famous old Dutch Colonial homestead that in the late seventeenth and early eighteenth centuries belonged to Cape Colony's Governor Simon van der Stel. The house, of whitewashed plastered stone with handsome gables, a meticulously clipped black thatch roof and finely proportioned doors and windows with natural-colored wood moldings, stands at the end of a long avenue of trees. In 1925 a fire destroyed the interior but the outer walls and gables held. It was restored and is today a charming and exact, if not original, example of the architecture of the period. The interior is airy and spacious, furnished with many authentic period pieces, and the kitchen and small storeroom are a delight, with copper and brass gleaming and twinkling pink and gold.

The estate still produces wine, and a few enormous kegs are kept in a long narrow building across the courtyard at the back of the house. It is called the cellar but most of the storage seemed to be on the ground floor. It is redolent of its joyous produce and noteworthy for the quite beautiful pediment designed by the eighteenth century sculptor Anton Anreith.

We wandered around the property for some time, in and out of the house, obeying the admonitory sign *Nie Rook Nie* (No Smoking), and then started for Muizenberg for luncheon. This is a small seaside resort, and the place where Cecil Rhodes died in 1902. It is situated on False Bay, so called because mariners blown there by storms, approximately aware of their location, used to think they were in Cape Town Harbor in Table Bay. Unhappily the long, beautiful beach is desecrated by unusually ugly overhead power lines and the gaunt scaffoldings that support them.

We ordered curry for luncheon and it arrived with something mysterious on top of it. Rice? No. Chutney? No. An unusual assortment of condiments? Guess again. Light unsweetened custard. It sounds deranged. It tasted marvelous. Its name was Bobotie curry and I recommend it. We washed it down with a Nedeburg cabernet. South African wines are better than those of Australia, but they have been at it longer and the Cape's settlers numbered not only Dutch but Portuguese and French

Huguenots and it is not unnatural to suppose that they brought along some of the lore of the motherland.

The food was delicious but the service so speedy we had to hang on to our plates lest they be snatched from us in midbite. We forgot that with the British the knife and fork placed side by side indicate one has finished.

We sometimes play a game about what deep-ingrained-from-childhood-habits one would have to unlearn if acting as a spy; pretending to be of another nationality.

There is a story, for what it is worth, that during the war, in a crowded gathering, the British occasionally had reason to suspect the presence of a German Army man. If that was the case someone would suddenly shout loudly "*Achtung!*" and sometimes, so inbred was the response, a man would snap to attention.

As far as British habits and customs are concerned we felt one could learn to look to the right rather than the left when stepping from the curb in British territory fairly quickly.

With discipline and repetition one would remember to leave the knife and fork spread eagle, but I suspect the act that would send an American spy to the firing squad would be giving a number into the telephone and then standing there like a triple-crowned imbecile expecting the connection.

I made a spectacle of myself that very evening. Back at the Mount Nelson I thought I would put in a call to Johannesburg. A thousand miles away, yes, but still not overseas or hurdling a language barrier. I got the operator, gave the number, and stood in the booth waiting. The hotel porter who had been watching me came forward.

"Can I help you, Madam?"

"Thank you no, I'm just waiting for my call."

"Oh, I shouldn't do that, Madam. Why don't you go and dine? I'll let you know as soon as the call comes through."

"But surely it will only take a minute or two?"

"I should dine, Madam."

Madam dined, Madam drank coffee in the lounge, Madam was deep in an elevating book when the porter appeared. "There has been no connection, Madam."

"Thank you. Will you be good enough to ask the operator to cancel the call?"

A drive of spellbinding beauty is the one that circles the peninsula, winding along the sea and mountains between Cape Town and the Cape of Good Hope. One of the great drives of the world is the French corniche along the Mediterranean, but I should say that in a sense the corniche of South Africa is even more striking. It does not have the picturesque clustering villages nor the feeling of an ancient civilization—it is wilder, grander. It does not border a limited sea but is the threshold of an ocean that sweeps to the South Pole and on around the world.

Part of the time the tide was out and flat combers spread over the sand, gigantic white scallops edging pale blue water. Owen spoke of the Japanese fishermen and told us about their long lines which, supported by glass floats, extend for fifteen and twenty miles. Every thirty feet they let down a line with a baited hook and after that they simply weave up and down and back and forth to see what Santa Claus has brought them. They move a little more sharply than it sounds because fish left on hooks attract sharks and that is not good for business.

At frequent intervals during the drive we stopped to absorb the view and so Norton could get his pictures, and when we did friendly baboons jumped up on the car the way they do at Nairobi National Park in Kenya. We passed colonies of weaver nests hanging from the branches of the trees looking like small bottles of Chianti in their straw jackets, but there were communal dwellings too, enormous nests where each family had its own entrance, like an apartment house.

We came finally to the gateway of Cape Point Reserve, about thirty-three square miles of parkland on the southern tip of the peninsula. Here elands roam and peacocks trail their feathered splendor and here are picnic grounds fragrant with gorse overlooking the unsegregated ocean but the grounds are divided into European and non-European areas and they are exactly alike and one would be hard put to it to discern a boundary line were it not for the signs which enlighten the ignorant as to which is which. No human soul was to be seen in either preserve but it is important to keep the record straight.

We climbed a steep hill for a better view of the Cape of Good Hope itself and there it was, a few jutting rocks, not very big yet one of the great landmarks of the world and of history. Sir Francis Drake, when he rounded it in the *Golden Hind* in 1580, is supposed to have called it "The most stately thing and the fairest Cape we saw in the whole circumference of the earth." Here he differed from its discoverer, Bartholomeu Diaz, who nearly a hundred years before had dubbed it the Cape of Storms. It was his king, John II of Portugal, apparently a member of the So Much Good in the Worst of Us School, who must have said "Come, come, not that bad, surely," and named it Good Hope. The old optimist turned out to be right too, because Vasco da Gama sailed past it and kept going until he reached India, the dream of one and all.

The Cape, by the way, is not the southernmost point of the continent of Africa as people sometimes assume. It's way down there but to the southwest. The actual southernmost is Cape Agulhas, which lies about one hundred miles away. Leaving Cape Point we returned by way of Chapman's Peak, Hout Bay, and Sentinel Park. In the bay is a small factory that processes those South African lobster tails, so popular in the deep freezers of American supermarkets.

We were sorry to leave Cape Town for it is a beautiful spot. The air is cool, the sunshine warm, the sea, the sky, and the flowers a fabulous panorama of color. There is brilliance in the atmosphere and the climate is virtually a year-round delight with May, June, and July the months to be wary of for they are the rainy season.

Inevitably, however, the moment came and the next day, having better luck than I had met with on the phone, we were able to raise Johannesburg after only two and three-quarter hours. By air. We remained at the airport for a little while and then in the same plane of South African Airways—a fine line with good food and service—we flew on to Bulawayo, Southern Rhodesia, where we changed our rands back into pounds.

MICHAEL WOOD

The Blue Train from Cape Town to Victoria Falls: 1979

"IT IGNORES THE OUTSIDE WORLD. AT A SEDATE FORTY MILES AN HOUR IT
TRANSPORTS ITS PAMPERED PASSENGERS SMOOTHLY AND SOUNDLESSLY
BEHIND WINDOWS TINTED WITH PURE GOLD TO KEEP DOWN THE GLARE."

*Journalist and historian Michael Wood has been a writer and on-air pre-
senter for BBC television since 1976. In 1979 he presented one segment of
the enormously popular* Great Railway Journeys of the World *series, traveling to South Africa to ride the Blue Train.*

*The train's name recalls the luxurious Blue Train from Victoria Sta-
tion which, in the twenties and thirties, transported passengers overnight
from the chilly, fog-dim streets of London to the palm-lined promenades
of the Riviera. It is this train that Henry Green's fog-shrouded characters
hope to board in his 1939 novel* Party Going, *and Agatha Christie used it
as a setting in* The Mystery of the Blue Train.

*South Africa's Blue Train has the same sort of cachet, with the dif-
ference that it is itself a destination just as much as either of its termini.
It first went into service in 1939, replacing an earlier luxury train, the
steam-powered Johannesburg–Cape Town Union Limited. It carries its
passengers in considerable comfort from the suburban ease of Cape Town
to the wild beauty and drama of the Zambezi River and Victoria Falls—
and, looked at the other way, from the interior of the continent to the last
point of land at the Cape and the meeting of two mighty oceans.*

*For other comments on the Blue Train, see the selection by Michael
Palin.*

For an earlier view of Victoria Falls, see the selection by Frank G. Carpenter.

IN THE AUTUMN OF 1979 I WENT TO SOUTHERN AFRICA in the privileged position of a journalist and traveller. I was to retrace Cecil Rhodes' railway route from Cape Town to Victoria Falls, from the mother city of the whites in Africa to Lobengula's indaba tree. The railway had been Rhodes' dream, part of a strip of British Empire red right up Africa. He it was who financed the push to the Zambezi in the 1890s, where (having disposed of Lobengula, king of the Matabele) he founded a country and named it after himself: Rhodesia. My journey, then, was his: into the heart of Africa.

And what a time to do it! That November Rhodesia was teetering on the edge. Fifteen years after a UDI which was intended to inaugurate 1000 years of white supremacy, the illegal and racialist regime of Ian Smith had very rapidly come face to face with History. For eight years now the black nationalists of the Patriotic Front had been fighting a full-scale guerilla war against the white settlers to win back the land seized by Rhodes in the 1890s. Declaring themselves Lobengula's heirs by proxy, they consulted the spirit mediums of the people; they swore their oaths on the dead freedom fighters of the failed revolt of 1897; they had even determined that their new country would bear the name Zimbabwe, after the great stone city which is the supreme architectural achievement of the ancient black races of Rhodesia (an achievement which hard-line whites denied them). Now, despite heavy losses, the Patriotic Front controlled much of the countryside. And now, around the conference table at Lancaster House in London, they were negotiating with the British government and the Smith regime to obtain a free election.

The war had already displaced hundreds of thousands of people into protected villages and the black townships around Salisbury. A quarter of a million more had fled to refugee camps in Botswana, Zambia and Mozambique, where they were living in destitution. A million head of cattle had been lost. There was devastation, disease and malnutrition. When I set off on 16 November from Cape Town, the war was still being fought while the PF talked. It might be over by the time I reached the Falls. If it ended, where would that leave South Africa, Rhodesia's chief ally, and their illegally held colony in Namibia, where another guerilla war was increasing in severity? And if talks broke down, would war eventually engulf the whole of southern Africa, drawing in all Rhodesia's neighbours? Such thoughts gave me a sharp sense of anticipation at the start of the journey. Whatever happened, the next weeks would be unrepeatable.

Cape Town 16 November 1979. "You must take the Blue Train," everyone said, "it's the most luxurious train in the world." That had never struck me as a reason to travel. Quite the reverse, in fact: I always seem to have chosen the most eccentric and decrepit ways of getting to places. But South Africa is a land of the most violent contrasts, and somehow with its vaunted luxury the Blue Train seemed an appropriate way to begin this venture into the interior.

Twice a week the Blue Train runs the thousand miles from the Cape to Pretoria. In the old days it used to meet the Union Castle liners, and it preserves that vanished air of pre-war gentility. It is a diesel train with absolute self-confidence. It ignores the outside world. At a sedate forty miles an hour it transports its pampered passengers smoothly and sound-lessly behind windows tinted with pure gold to keep down the glare. There is a private suite with lounge and bathroom; a bar in whose leafy corner one might see a bridge class in progress; a pince-nez *maître d'hôtel* whose fastidious regard would do credit to Claridges. This, in short, is a train on which travel itself is the destination.

The first hours of the journey pass through the fertile, temperate plains of Cape Province with their vineyards and oak trees in the lee of the grandiose spurs and fairytale peaks of the Drakenstein. This was the heartland of the original Dutch settlers of the seventeenth century, who built their farms in the delectable valleys around Paarl and Stellenbosch. Their descendants—Afrikaners, Africans, as they call themselves—have formed the ruling élite in South Africa since 1948. It was they who re-gularised forms of racial separation already practised in British colonies south of the Zambezi into apartheid, the total separation of black and white races. Of course they are now a state under siege. If not yet phys-ically, then certainly spiritually.

You would not know it from the wealth and self-confidence of the Blue Train's clientèle. To them events beyond the Limpopo are a mote in the mind's eye. But at the lunch table Willem de Clerc, a tenth-generation Afrikaner who farms near Paarl, shook his head sadly: "We are not a strange people, we are a very human people, but they thought they could change the world. This is a reformed society. Like the English revolution, or the communists, or the Jacobins in France, they thought a political system could provide all the answers in human life. It's like Hamlet—you know how that ends—the bodies piling up around him."

A state under siege. At Paarl there are three massive, pale-coloured granite boulders, like debris from some planetary ice age. The largest is a mile in circumference. A mile! It was named Paarl, "pearl," in 1657 by an early Dutch settler who thought it glistened like a pearl in the sunshine after rain. On the top, reaching far into the blue sky, is the Taalmonument, the Language Monument. "It symbolises the origin and development of our language here over the three hundred years," said my lady companion in the cocktail bar. "We say that Afrikaans is *'n Perel van Groot Waarde,'* a pearl of great worth," she added. In what other country could you find a monument to a language erected by the people who speak it? You might expect it to have been erected in the heroic days of the nineteenth-century struggles with the British, or maybe in 1948. But no. It was built in 1975. When you become hated by most of your fellow citizens in the world, you have to define very clearly what it is you are fighting for.

The route which the train now follows is the route by which the whites penetrated into the interior, first by ox carts through a precipitous and almost trackless mountain terrain, on the trail of the transhumant Bantu; later by the railway tracks which were laid up the Hex River in the late 1870s and early 80s, rising from the orchards of Worcester (750 feet above sea level) to the top of the pass at nearly 3600 feet, higher than the summit of Table Mountain.

The Blue Train climbs the Hex River Pass by an extraordinary series of curves, some only 100 yards in diameter, so that at one point the front and rear of the train are parallel to each other, going in opposite directions! At the top there is a spectacular view of the 7000-foot peak of the Matroosberg on the one hand, and stretching back below us the rich vineyards of the Hex valley. Then, within a couple of hours, there is a dramatic change in the landscape. We enter a wilderness like nowhere else on earth. The Great Karroo, the Hottentot "Land of Thirst."

Into this "worn-out emaciated land without soil or verdure" (as a nineteenth-century traveller put it) the Afrikaners made their Great Trek in the 1830s, away from the British overlords of the Cape to find a new promised land. They called it New Eden: a land of baked wastes broken by sills of ancient rock and protruding kopjes blazing hot by day and cold, black, starry brilliant by night. Here hardy farmers of Dutch and British stock still make their living from this intransigent soil, scratching fertile oases in an immensity of scrub. Treeless, dun-coloured and crumbling, the soil of the Karroo comes alive only infrequently when the rain makes gullies run with water and a carpet of red and blue flowers springs overnight, as from nowhere. But in some places in the Karroo there has been no rain now for three years.

Life cannot be viewed through gold windows. At five o'clock the Blue Train stopped at Touws River to change engines. I decided to get off there, to see something of the people who live by the track. From the conditioned air of the Blue Train I stepped on to the platform and into a sunlight that falls like a heavy weight on the head and shoulders; the eyes narrow with the glare; the air is dry and hot and smells of the surrounding mountains, of gorse and (is it?) thyme. No one else gets off. The Blue Train's doors hiss shut, and soon its last coach disappears in the heat haze in front of the red hills towards Lainsburg.

The familiar images of the Karroo: the wind pump, the white farmhouse with its cluster of pepper trees out of sight of its neighbours' chimney smoke. A perpetual frontier country; a drought-stricken land where the landlords make their money from sheep or nothing. The Afrikaners are fond of saying that their oldest tradition is their feel for the land, and out here everything has a biblical simplicity: the throat-cutting of the sheep for the owner's monthly gift to the workers; the weekly hand-outs of water, meal, coffee and sugar; the poverty of the workers themselves, most of them itinerant, earning thirty or forty Rand a month; their stoical resignation.

"We hope the Lord will help us so that life gets better than it is now," Maria said to me, sturdy wife of a deaf mute farm hand, "then I might like the Karroo. As it is, we have to work in the Karroo because only some bosses understand my husband: it's the bosses here who know him. I've no choice. I've three children still at school. I must stay here now. He's my legal husband. If I'd been alone I would have gone somewhere else. It may be better for my children. White people we've worked for say I bring them up well. My daughter wants to be a welfare worker. The boy wants to be a carpenter. The baby—he's nine—says he will work on the railways. They earn good money there."

Here too is the larger-than-life figure of Oom Dan, the "old boss," the foreman who rules this farm with a paternal iron rod for the absentee landlord.

"The workers I treat like children, they look on me as their father. I've told them they can call me 'meneer,' *Mr* Van Vuuren, but they have always called me 'baas' and now they want to call me 'oubaas.' They prefer that. I don't work with them any more, but I go with them wherever they go. Where they work, I sit with them. When they go to the veld they want me with them. Ask them. They'll tell you they haven't got a 'radio.' They need me because I am their 'radio'. . . . As for the life here in the Karroo, I never go to town. Take me to a town, take me away from the farm, and within two months you can bury me."

Above Dan Van Vuuren's living-room door there is a portrait of D F Malan, the nationalist architect of apartheid. I suppose his compatriots would consider Oom Dan a typical Afrikaner countryman—the man who knows sheep, who knows the veld; a red-necked bull of a man, devout and intolerant, hard as nails; the ruler of his roost. Such were the original Trekkers, one imagines, hard-bitten frontiersmen building their society on traditional Afrikaner virtues—self-sufficiency, a refusal to kow-tow to outside authority, Old Testament fundamentalism and a belief in the divinely ordained supremacy of white over black.

In the next few days I wound my way slowly through the centre of the republic. First from Touws River up to Ladismith on a delightful slow train which starts at two in the morning and can take up to eight hours to do eighty miles. It is an old "24" class built at the Hyde Park Works of the North British Locomotive Company in Glasgow, a smart little branch line engine which chugs slowly up and down this one line twice a week. A pleasant life for a train, I suppose. Its job is to ferry workers to the vineyards of the Ladismith valley, to carry supplies to isolated farms in a region with no made-up roads, and to bring domestic water to tiny, one-horse halts in the long dry season. The locals call the train Makadas. I could not discover why. "Muck and dust" someone suggested (plausible enough). "Make a dash" said another (surely not?).

The train was already two hours late by the time dawn came up over Hondewater. But on the Makadas time has no meaning. The traveller must simply sit back on his wooden seat and watch the splendid sunrise touch the far-off tips of the Oudtshoorn range with gold. Then, as the still morning air becomes warmer, listen to the explosive whoosh of steam echoing in the crags of the Little Karroo. On this train a local farmer responded memorably to my comments on the efficiency of the service.

"Well, this is an old-fashioned system for sure," he said, "but so are we. Diesel is surely not fitting with our mountains. We've just got to have this steam locomotive." Later on in the journey I would understand his remark.

The Makadas stops at Ladismith. The line was never driven through to Oudtshoorn to join up with the coastal route and the Indian Ocean. The last station on the Oudtshoorn side of the mountains is called Protem, "so far." But, in fact, it goes no farther. Ladismith was thus left at the end of the line and nobody goes there today. So, to return to the main line north you must either go back from Ladismith the way you came, or you can cut through the Seven Weeks Pass under "Magic Mountain" and back by road to Lainsburg.

From Lainsburg it is possible to take any number of trains through the desert northwards. One, the Trans-Karroo Express, is still pulled by steam engines, the 15Fs. Some of these are "stars," kept in immaculate condition by their crews with whitened wheel rims and cab roofs, coloured number plates, burnished pipes and personal brass emblems: an eagle, a horse, a star. In South Africa the railways are the biggest employers and among the best. Pride in the locomotive is expected and fostered.

At Beaufort West, on the way to De Aar, we are overhauled by a Garratt steaming free at full speed, charging north with no load. "We are lending several of them to the Rhodesians," the conductor said in a confidential tone in answer to my question, "diesels too, and technicians." A black smudge of smoke hung over the horizon to the north long after the engine had whirled frantically out of sight.

De Aar is not a place you would visit for the fun of it. Central rail junction of the republic, like Crewe and Swindon it is an out-and-out railway colony. It stands in the middle of a hot, howling wilderness, said an early traveller, and it stands there simply because of the railway. Here the main lines go north and south, east and west, carrying minerals, the arterial wealth of South Africa: iron ore, copper, manganese. The distances are terrific: the eight o'clock evening train from De Aar to Windhoek in Namibia, 800 miles away, takes two days. The railyards are all smoke, grime and coal dust, with hundreds of steam locomotives and thousands of black and coloured workers to service them. These people live in townships which are literally on the other side of the tracks. For them there is a curfew in the white town.

In De Aar it is easy to see why steam has survived in South Africa. The republic has no natural oil deposits of its own. But it does have ample coal. And an almost limitless supply of cheap African labour to maintain the labour-intensive steam locomotives. Cleaning and greasing, but not driving—there are no black drivers in South Africa—white railwaymen do that. "An old-fashioned system," said the man on the Makadas. And this is why.

I travelled the next 150 miles to Kimberley on the footplate of one of the giant freight trains going north. The two coupled class 25 giants, *Maria* and *Jennifer*, whose names belie their devastating power, pour columns of black smoke hundreds of feet into the air as they roar at 50 mph past the kopjes of the northern Karroo. Here the landscape is a vivid orange desolation, a place of mirages. This line from De Aar to Kimberley is the steam buff's paradise. Thirty freights a day pull up the long incline to Krankhuil huffing and puffing, shooting unburned coal into the sky. We pass mineral trains going south ("We're pulling it out of Namibia as fast as we can," someone would later tell me in Kimberley); moving north we saw armaments: for Namibia, Rhodesia, who knows?

We cross the Orange River, the historic dividing line between the original Boer republics and the British imperial possessions in Cape Province. In fact we do not enter the Free State here but skirt its southwestern edge, reminding us that the British built this railway to outflank the Boers, via Kimberley through Bechuanaland and on to Rhodesia. While the crew boil their coffee on the end of a rod thrust into the furnace, we pass over the Modder River where the British suffered a humiliating disaster in the Boer War, and then on to Kimberley past a reassuring litany of English and Dutch country stations: Chalk Farm, Heuningneskloof, Spytfontein, Wimbledon—names for an Afrikaner John Betjeman to conjure with.

Kimberley. Those backwoods republics across the Orange and the Vaal rivers might have remained quietly in their inhospitable landscape and never made their mark on history had it not been for the accident of the discovery of mineral wealth: diamonds in Kimberley in 1869, and the subsequent finds of gold on the Witwatersrand in Transvaal in 1887. The conflicts by which the British tried to dominate the Boers and control this wealth—the Boer Wars—have been the determining factors in the politics of South Africa ever since.

Kimberley bears few signs of the rush now. But this was where Rhodes, then Prime Minister of the Cape, made his fortune, signing the biggest cheque ever for the rights to the main mine, the Big Hole. This is what enabled him to finance the construction of a railway 1000 miles to the Zambezi, to found Rhodesia, and to conceive his kingmaking visions of a southern African federation. The Big Hole is his monument. A pit of Babel. It is silent now, filled with water. Like a meteorite crater gouged in the veld, it goes down a thousand feet. "When I'm in Kimberley," said Rhodes, "I often go and sit on the edge of the mine and reckon up the value of the diamonds and the power they conferred. Every foot of that blue ground means so much power."

History has passed Kimberley by. Rhodes' company, De Beers, still have their head office here, but their operation has moved elsewhere, to the Joburg gold reef and the new diamond mines of Botswana. Kimberley just sits and swelters with its wild west sidewalks, waiting for the one blessing of the African summer, the torrential downpour which comes here punctually every day at five and leaves the awnings streaming, main street aflood with a momentary monsoon.

The go-getters have got up and gone. But behind them is left a strange flotsam. It is a sight you might have seen in the days before the rush—a handful of poor white prospectors, men and women, licensed by De Beers to hand-sieve for loose diamonds in the stony hills above the Vaal river. The temperature is 114 degrees, but men like Lou Bothes still work here as he has for fifty years. An archetypal prospector, Lou lives in the same hut he has had for all that time. At seventy-three he still puts in a full day of backbreaking toil in a claim hole with no corner of shade. He still dreams of finding the big one (and after all, the Cullinan itself was a loose diamond, missed by the diggers).

It is a strange world, the diggers' world. Ruled by dreams, omens and superstitions. It is considered bad luck to have women on a claim; they abandon it altogether if they find a snake in it. Men in white shirts are a good sign, so are dreams of silver fish, of "dog diamonds" and especially sheep's heads. A diggers' legend here at Noitgedacht has it that the biggest diamond of all will be the shape of a sheep's skull. The sheep's skull drives them on.

"I began this when I was fifteen," said Lou Bothes. "I once left and took another job, on the railways, but I soon came back. I'm a digger at heart. The biggest diamond I ever found was fourteen carats. I wanted a thousand pounds for it" (Bothes still counts in the old Cape Colony currency), "but they would only give me five hundred. I gave the money away: I had my 'auntie' to look after, you see!"

"What's so good about this digging life that you stick at it?" I asked. "I just don't know what it is, man: I've worked myself to death, but I just can't stop this business. I have to go on. I can't go anywhere else now."

Dawn in the brilliant immensity of the high veld. There is a clarity which was unimaginable to this traveller from the cold north. From a dozen miles away, the plain of Kimberley stretches towards the Kalahari in the palest wash of white sky and white earth, ash of the exhausted volcano in whose heat the diamonds were fused in the blue ground. An immemorial flatness save where the lip of Kimberley kopje marks the site of the ancient convulsions. The place seems extraterrestrial; it creates illusions in the air and in time. At Barkly West, derelict Victorian workings mingle with artefacts from the Stone Age; miners were here before History. Everywhere there are great spoil mounds marked with weathered claim tickets; at Pniel you walk on a river terrace heaped with gravels, tiny gemstones and semi-precious pebbles: agate, jasper, jade. It would be no surprise here, one feels, to stumble on the bleached bones of dinosaurs.

By the middle of the day the temperature was nearly 130 degrees and the mirages were growing more insistent. The polished limestone rocks melted the rubber on my shoes. I fled back to Kimberley with the first signs of heatstroke.

That was a Saturday. The next Monday morning, a week out, I left Kimberley and diverged from the northern route to follow the Blue Train's track into Transvaal. To Johannesburg. Joburg was not on Rhodes' historic railway to the Zambezi—in fact in the 1890s it was hardly a town at all, just shanties—a drinking, whoring, spending, mining camp; the African Klondike. But it is now the political, commercial and racial hub of South Africa, and along with its black satellite towns, it is a magnet to the traveller who wishes to understand what is happening in South Africa today.

You arrive in Joburg past yellow spoil heaps, made from gold workings which go down 11,000 feet below the skyscrapers, so deep as to feel the inner heat of the earth. Joburg is literally and figuratively built on gold. It shows. The place oozes surplus wealth and purchasing power, and has a standard of living unknown elsewhere in Africa. Where else in the western world would you find the lights of skyscrapers blazing top to bottom throughout the night? Here consumption is conspicuous.

Joburg is ringed by black townships which provide the service labour for this wealth. In these townships also live the black migrant gold workers who come from all over southern Africa to the Witwatersrand to make their living, 6000 from Rhodesia, and thousands more from Botswana, Mozambique, Zambia. They live out of sight of white eyes in all-male hostels where violence and death are commonplace.

The biggest of the townships is Soweto. Or rather, So/we/to—South Western Townships—is several rolled into one. It is the home of a million and a half people, and is the largest city in Africa after Cairo. Now the name of Soweto is known throughout the world and has become a rallying call for the oppressed black peoples of South Africa. Here in June 1976, riots which began as a protest about the teaching of Afrikaans in black schools ignited a cry of rage against the treatment of blacks throughout the republic. Soweto, with its urban vitality, aggression and sheer energy, provided the fuse. And of seven hundred killed by the police, four hundred died here. Out of sight of Joburg, on the far side of the buffer zone required by apartheid, Soweto is an hour's journey from Joburg by train; it lies in a shallow bowl of hills which are hung with sulphurous fumes even on a clear summer's day. Soweto is made up of endless lines of identical brick-asbestos bungalows. Miles of them. To go there I needed a special permit, for apartheid works both ways.

Wednesday 5 December. Dube Station, Soweto, soon after dawn. Here too the railways reflect the life of the community. At this ungodly hour while a cold wind whips up the rubbish in the streets, thousands of the people of Soweto are rushing to the trains to take them into Joburg. There are not enough trains, and every one leaves with scores of people hanging on the outsides for dear life, clutching buffers, couplings, window frames, all desperate to get to work. If they are late there are plenty more who will be happy to take their jobs. It is a nightmare scene this, fingers clawing the door frames as the train moves off; crowds of people running across the track; the incessant drone of the loudspeaker drowning all conversation.

I had arranged to meet a journalist friend whom I had met in Joburg, and who covers Soweto affairs for the black edition of the *Star* newspaper. Derek was standing on the platform looking snappy in a light grey suit. In his voice humour, reason and anger were mixed in equal measure. But humour in particular, which is one of the great qualities of the people of Soweto.

"It's all a question of giving a man his human dignity," he said, "his right to vote. They've got to give us that now. I can remember seeing my father bowing and scraping before a white fat cat—'yes boss, no boss, anything you say boss'—cringing—and it really hurt me as a child to see my daddy who I loved and revered stripped of his dignity as a man. When I grew up I once did that too. But not now. They must give us our rights. You must understand that the people here in Soweto are temporary."

"What do you mean, temporary?"

"They aren't permanent," he replied. "Everyone who works here has to be registered in a homeland where he can be returned. He has to renew the permit each year. You belong to Transkei or Bophuthatswana, not here."

"Do the people of Soweto feel temporary?" I asked.

"No, they feel quite permanent." He grinned a wicked grin.

Despite all the "wind of change" publicity blowing around that autumn, Derek remains unconvinced. He feels that if there have been minor changes in "social" apartheid, the political structure is as rigid as ever.

That night he took me to Lucky's club in Orlando, Soweto, the only real *club*, as opposed to a shebeen, a drinking house. Lucky is a gentle giant of a man, a man who works hard for his community but who also possesses that Odyssean cunning needed to survive in the jungle of Soweto.

We arrived early, before sunset, and as the light slanted across the billboards at Orlando station, we heard beautiful mellow jazz—Duke Ellington—being played in the room next to Lucky's fish bar. A group of men of all ages was getting it together on battered but cherished instruments. That night we all got drunk and everybody wished to talk about everything—from Charlie Parker to what we British were doing in Northern Ireland, a story even more tortuous than the Afrikaners and the blacks.

Rhodes pushed his railway a thousand miles from Kimberley to the Zambezi in a few years in the 1890s. "If there be a God," he said, "I think he would like me to paint as much of Africa British-Red as possible." To return to his route from Joburg you must journey west overnight on a standard diesel to a rail town whose name used to appear on every schoolchild's atlas: Mafeking.

I suppose I came here expecting that somehow the Boer War siege would still be tangible. But today another siege is on everybody's lips. And this time there will be no relief for Mafeking. In 1980 the town will be assimilated into the black homeland of Bophuthatswana and henceforth exist only as Mmabatho.

Formerly capital of the British protectorate of Bechuanaland, Mafeking owes its existence to the railways. It is a major junction linking Rhodes' northern route with the gold reef. It was for this reason that the Boers besieged it in the Boer War. Now the railway workshops have gone, Bechuanaland is independent, and if the whites here resist incorporation they will lose all their custom to the neighbouring black "capital." "We'll become a ghost town," someone said, a *spookdorp*. But in a way that is precisely what Mafeking is, and its real ghosts lie in the cemetery by the railroad track, in a corner of a foreign field that does indeed remain for ever England. For King and Empire, it says on the crosses. By the end of that distant war, Kitchener had in South Africa the largest number of British troops ever sent abroad on any expedition. "We're not forgetting it/we're not regretting it/we're not letting it fade away or gradually die . . ." So they sang in 1901. Now these young men from Lincolnshire and Staffordshire lie forgotten, passed only by the antiquated steam engines in the sidings which shunt up and down all day and pass the weeping willows with a chuff of steam and a mournful whistle.

The fate of Mafeking is the destiny of Mmabatho. To get to Mmabatho you leave Mafeking past the cemetery, then out over drab empty scrub for a mile or two. There the line stretches away to Botswana, Rhodesia, and the copper belts of Zambia and Zaïre. There is nothing else here but thornbushes, and mud-walled huts roofed with corrugated iron sheets weighed down by boulders. Here, the South African government has determined, will be the "capital" of this new so-called independent homeland. Above the red ant hills, three new buildings have gone up: a block of brown-brick service flats, a stadium of scaffolding, and the crowning glory, the symbol of Bophuthatswanan national prestige, the administrative centre of President Mangope's Bantustan, the Mmabatho Sun Hotel. The architecture is what might be termed Tijuana-Tswana: in front there is an ornamental pool which my caustic friend Frankie insists on calling Lake Mangope within earshot of the chief of police. In the air-conditioned casino ranks of one-armed bandits are being plied by a crush of South African whites in short-sleeved shirts. They're "abroad" here, you see—there's even a South African Embassy down Lucas Mangope Highway to prove it. So they can indulge in all the delights forbidden them in the republic proper, notably gambling, and wining, dining and dancing with black girls.

The way Derek Thema sees it, the Afrikaners feel that if everyone had the vote, then that would be the end of a culture which has lasted for over 300 years here. So there must never be a non-white majority. The answer they have dreamed up is to separate the races territorially and allow the non-whites to "develop" with their own culture in their own areas. Basically then, the idea is that two-thirds of the population get about an eighth of the land; they have their own government under men like Mangope, whose decisions can be overruled at any time by Pretoria; they have no control over arms, right of entry, the presence of South African police, post offices, roads, railways, harbours, aviation, entry of aliens, currency, loans, customs and excise. So if the Mmabatho Sun Hotel, this mini Las Vegas, strikes you as a little bizarre as the "capital" of a non-existent state, as a focus for black civil and political aspirations, it plainly serves to remind us that political aspirations for blacks do not yet exist in South Africa.

In the Mmabatho Sun Hotel I had to keep pinching myself. But unbelievable as this white playground is, there is more to come. In the foyer of the hotel I opened my *Mafeking Mail and Botswana Guardian* to read that only days hence Bophuthatswana will play host to a "galaxy of stars" for the opening of Sun City. My patient reader, if he has followed me this far, may wish to skip this. I record it solely in the thought that in a couple of hundred years, when the whites here have grudgingly let themselves be assimilated into Azania (as Derek tells me the republic will be renamed), some Fellini may wish to know what follies the late twentieth century got up to. For Sun City, as its name implies, is nothing less than a self-contained city, providing escape for thousands of people, a place, says the *Mail*, where,

> Day and night will have no meaning—no natural light but thousands of reflected and refracted beams to illumine the mind-blowing vista. Set in an ancient volcanic crater on the slopes of the Pilanesberg near Rustenburg, it's a fantasy world, a conceit of the imagination which makes time and space fade into the cosmos . . . 80,000 bricks have been laid every day for 18 months . . . an entertainment bar hangs over the central slot machine area like a Star ship, its amber mirrored Perspex sending down sunbursts of light . . .

And the dark cloud beyond the Limpopo was no bigger than a man's hand.

I left Mafeking on 7 December bound for the north. From here, Rhodesia Railways took over, and we passed from the racially segregated system of South Africa to the good old British class system. This stage of the journey was a 24-hour, 500-mile ride on the daily train to Bulawayo through the spacious and exhilarating veld of Botswana. Rhodesia Railways have run this service for many years now, but it was still curious to consider the presence of Botswanan customs on a Rhodesian train. After all, there was a war going on up the line, and Botswana was a front-line state sheltering guerillas of the PF. But in Africa railways transcend politics. This line is Botswana's lifeline; they would like it for themselves, and are negotiating to that end. But in the meantime they are very gentlemanly about it.

Larger in area than France, with a mere 750,000 people, Botswana is poor and unexploited. For many years after independence in 1966 this former British protectorate was one of the world's poorest nations (albeit one of the few democratic ones). But there has been a dramatic increase of wealth and urban population in the last fifteen years. Now that new copper, nickel and diamond pipes have been discovered, the bush awaits the exploiters.

The train winds through the beautiful hills beyond Lobatse, and I witness a glorious sunset. The dark veld to the south-west gained a faint milky-white opacity; in the amber sky floated single clouds tinged with blood red and purple; the sun disappeared with astonishing speed in a blaze of vermilion, leaving a line of golden brown clouds along the horizon. Then just before it actually goes dark, looking up from the red band above the hills, the sky shaded into a violent deep blue where the first stars stood out. Magnificent. Now this is what I call train travel! Forget about air-conditioning and gold glass. Open the windows.

And there's the evening meal to look forward to, cooked on a coal-fired Aga in a tiny galley. And after dinner, what sensations to sit back to. The sounds and smells of the fringe of the Kalahari desert: bush fires, cattle trails, sweet grasses of the veld, the chatter of distant voices. Every small halt bringing its quota of new travellers and their goods, new bustle and talk.

It is eight o'clock and we arrive at Gabarone, the capital of Botswana. The platform is crowded with children and baggage, women in bright print dresses, miners in cowboy hats, pedlars and sellers of sweet corn and beer. It's Friday night and a lot of people want to go home for the weekend. The conductor is allocating sleepers and bedding in First and Second Class. He is surrounded by a struggling throng, most of whom are waving booking forms at him: Friday night is always packed and there's usually a fight for beds.

"Mr Jongwe? To Palapye, yes sir, three berths. We get there 3.15 in the morning. Mr Ubongwe? Motloutse River. Coach 18b. Mrs Chikerema? Are you Mrs Chikerema? Let's see: Francistown. Right, this way thank you."

"Watch out for the girls if you're on till Francistown," my Glaswegian steward grins a wicked grin, leaning out of the open window. "It's pay night, you see. Ay, these girls come down the corridors in First and Second knocking on the doors. Keep it locked. *And* sleep on your wallet. Fourth is full of ragamuffins and pickpockets."

And of course the delight about the Bulawayo slow train is that, unlike South Africa, you and your fellow travellers are not segregated. You can spend the night meeting Khama princes, politicians, students, guitar players, card and dice hustlers, *and* ladies of fortune.

It's only ten o'clock, but people go to bed earlier than in Britain. I read for a while. Alex, a friend in Joburg, lent me Stanley's *Travels through the Dark Continent*. In 1879 Stanley wagered that the Europeans would carve up the whole of central Africa in twenty years, dividing it all neatly with boundaries. And they did. But could he have possibly foreseen a hundred years ahead? In his wildest dreams?

At six in the morning the steward brought round tea in Rhodesia Railways liveried tea cups, and a jug of water with which to wash. I lifted the blinds to see the bush still stretching interminably. For five hours the narrow single-track line runs through this thickly wooded country for mile after mile dead straight; a thread so tenuous and insubstantial that the traveller is in constant expectation of finding it washed away, or ceasing altogether in a pile of sleepers and the whitening bones of Victorian railway navvies!

There is time for egg and bacon before we get to Francistown at about 7.30. Francistown was the old capital after Mafeking. This was the centre of Africa's very first gold rush in the 1860s. It was over in ten years, though the last of the town's forty-five gold mines only closed in 1964. Now, those with the expertise work in South Africa.

At Francistown a group of about a hundred get off, men from the

Joburg reef, with their bags, their wide-brimmed hats, their transistors and their swagger. As the train pulls out, they are dancing on the platform. Africa!

By 9.00 there is a different atmosphere on the train. The crew are armed. We are approaching the Rhodesian border. "Jesus is Coming! Are you ready?" says the huge placard at the frontier post at Plumtree. There I meet my escort, Craig. Young, fit, trimly bearded with a gold chain round his neck and carrying a stubby sub machine gun, Craig is a typical "Rhodie," a formidable drinker of Castle lager and a tireless chatter-up of women.

"No, we never get blasé," he tells me over the first glass of the day, "people who get blasé usually get buried. You can never pin them down to a man-to-man situation because it's a guerilla war: they could be out there now, taking a pot shot at my beer. In fact if they hit my beer I'll be more annoyed than if they hit me."

Typical Rhodie bravado. The bar is now mainly stocked with middle-aged men in shorts, fit and embittered. There is a fragile Dunkirk spirit among them as they wait for the end of their country.

The line has ascended to Plumtree and the border. Just into Rhodesia, at Coldridge, you catch a glimpse of mysterious pyramidal hills far away to the right above the bush. Then the track enters a region of enormous stones, some arranged in weathered piles precariously balanced on top of each other in gravity-defying pinnacles. This is the south-west edge of the Matopo Hills. We are almost at Bulawayo.

"Room 224, thank you Sir." The "boy," who was about forty, put down my suitcase. He wore an immaculately pressed white shirt with lapels, white shorts, socks and pumps. He came back with tea in old Victoria Hotel silver and insisted on taking away my crumpled shirts for ironing. Outside the window lay the flat green landscape of Bulawayo, a city of parks, palm trees, teak and jacarandas. Banks of black cloud were building up from the east. Big drops of rain struck the window panes. A crackle of lightning flashed over the perimeter and down to the darkening bush on the horizon. The electricity seemed to hang in the mouth like a premonition, sharp and acrid. On the bedroom desk was a copy of *Bulawayo This Month*: I opened it to read of the Toastmistress' Club; Scottish Country Dancing; the Matabeleland Dog Training Club. We cling to these reassuring arrangements of society. But how fragile they are. "Refrigerated candles burn longer," says the handy hints page. Rhodesia is still keeping its chin up. The main story in the *Bulawayo Chronicle* tells of the expected fears about the now agreed ceasefire; the adverts show the underlying drift—the property columns are full of bargains ("4 servants qtrs, s/pool . . . chalet with bar, huge wendy house . . ."); the "jobs wanted" page too ("housemaid, clean honest and v. reliable worker; present employer emigrating").

Bulawayo still has the feel of a pioneer town with its wooden sidewalks and its streets wide enough to turn a four-yoked ox-cart. In 1893 this was the site of the royal kraal of King Lobengula of the Matabele. But Rhodes coveted his mineral wealth—more perhaps than a through route to Cairo, though Rhodes' map in Bulawayo Museum shows his red crayon doodle right up central Africa. In 1893 the Matabele were overthrown and in 1897 the railways arrived here, 800 miles from Vryburg. So swiftly did the exploiters open up the heart of Africa. It is difficult to imagine the significance this had for the whites. It meant real contact for pioneers camped in hostile land, "the beginning of civilisation in its entirety," said the *Bulawayo Chronicle*, a new era for "the men who have led England's advance into the heart of the Dark continent." The commissioner for South Africa, Alfred Milner, called it a "great day in the history of South Africa and the empire." Three cheers for Joe Chamberlain! The banners said, "Forward Rhodesia" and "Our two roads to progress, railroads and Cecil Rhodes." The omens were propitious. Even without the immense goldfield they hoped for, there was the greatest coalfield in Africa, and the magnificent soil of Rhodesia.

As for Lobengula, that "naked old savage" as Rhodes called him, he died within a year of the conquest. Of smallpox, it was said, but if you read his disillusioned pleas to the great white queen in London, you may think like me that he died of a broken heart. Beaten in battle by Rhodes' mercenaries, the British South Africa Company Army, he was compelled to sign away his land in a famous peace parley celebrated by white Rhodesians as the founding of their nation. "Their eyes wear a discarded look," said a contemporary, "their past is gone and they have no future."

The Sunday after my arrival I was driven out to the Matopos by friends in spite of the restriction of petrol rationing and a four o'clock curfew. The place we sought is called "view of the world," Rhodes' name for it. It is a great granite whaleback surmounted by huge balanced boulders. From the top there is a view round the whole circle of the horizon, the jagged rocky ranges of south-western Rhodesia. The Matabele thought it a magical place, the home of benevolent spirits. Here on the top now are buried Rhodes, Jameson and Coghlan (the first prime minister), a trio of troubled spirits. At the bottom of the hill is a lodge which has a display of Rhodes' life in it, including a framed picture of Oriel College, Oxford, Rhodes' college and mine. "Boss went to the same school as Mr Rhodes," said my guide to the warden, helpfully. He nodded blankly. How long, I wondered, before the memory of Rhodes and his eponymous state vanishes here? (In fact, within a month of the election of 1980, his statues would be smashed all over the land.) Rhodes never saw his railway to the Falls completed. Here at the graveside Kipling spoke his epitaph: "Living he was the land, and, dead, his soul shall be her soul." And so it was to be—for as long as his Rhodesia lasted.

7.30 A.M., Tuesday 11 December. I came down to Bulawayo station to take the daily mixed goods and passenger train north to Thompson Junction. With me was Graham from Government Information. The emergency laws meant no journalist could go anywhere unsupervised. But Graham was a companion rather than a guard; middle-aged, laconic and discriminating, he had seen it all. The train was late. Under a veil of drizzle I watched a Rhodesian Garratt shunting in the sidings, a really spectacular sight this, 220 tons of locomotive giving out ferocious explosions of steam. By July 1980 steam here was to have been a memory. But in the last two years of the war the trend has been reversed. Rhodesia has large coal reserves, and steam engines are being rebuilt. In this way the Rhodesian government has been able to fight the shortage of foreign currency and oil under sanctions. There is even talk of building new steam engines, though the Manchester firm who made them, Beyer-Peacock, is long gone. Standing here in the rain on the day UDI was due to be lifted was a time to reflect on the position of Rhodesia's railways. They lie at the centre of the systems of southern Africa. From Bulawayo lines reach to all points of the compass: to the copper belts of Zambia and Zaïre through Victoria Falls, and on to the Atlantic at Lobito by the famed Benguela railway of Angola; to Lusaka and Dar on the Tan-Zam railway; to Beira and Maputo in Mozambique; into South Africa through Botswana and over the Limpopo at Beit Bridge. Most of these lines are now closed due to the war. With a black majority in Salisbury they could all operate again.

Our engine has arrived. It is a Garratt loaned by South Africa. Perhaps the one I saw all that time ago at Beaufort West? It carries extra water, and the passenger wagons are separated from the engine, for if the boys in the bush attack, they'll go for the driver first. We will make the 220-mile journey during daylight because of ZIPRA attacks; the guerillas have infiltrated much of the countryside by now. The train also carries troops. There is only a handful of passengers. But they all know what to do in an emergency. The women too.

"I know how to fire a machine gun," said the pretty girl with the steady eye. "I can take it apart, clean it and put it together again." She seemed amused by my admiration: "A lot of us have lost friends in this war. The bitterness between black and white won't be an easy thing to overcome. But in time we will. We've got to." It was the most sensible thing I had heard so far.

Mid-morning we stopped at a place called Sawmills, sixty miles into the bush. There had been a derailment upline. So we just sat and waited. For six hours. We whiled away the time with the staff, Len (a Cockney) and Brian (a Yorkshireman), playing cards and discussing the merits of Yorkshire beers and holidays in Wakefield.

After the long delay at Sawmills darkness was coming on as we moved again. Another forty miles and we were on the Dett straight, the longest straight track in Africa which takes us seventy miles through the Wankie game reserve. As night came on and we slowly clattered along, animals appeared everywhere in the growing gloom: zebra, kudu, buffalo, sable, jackals, warthogs, giraffe and elephant. Looking out, the train appeared to be a tiny corridor of dimmed light in the vast velvet dark of the bush. For the first time I felt a sensation of the physical presence of Africa in all its mystery. I leaned back against the open window. An elephant trumpeted with a great screech yards from the train. I started. Graham smiled.

"In the old days," he began, "we used to take hampers of food and rifles and walk and camp in the Eastern Highlands around Inyanga and Leopard Rock. Now that is beautiful country. The Troutbeck Inn at Inyanga, or Mrs Hardy's old place at Rusape—she cooked the finest food in Rhodesia. Still does, though the 'ters got her housekeeper and put a grenade into her bar. One day you must see the east. Take the road from Chipinga to Umtali on the Mozambique border. In the spring the mountains are covered with red, musasa and mahogany; with yellow lilies, proteas. . . ." His eyes narrowed. "Never be able to do that again, camping in the bush. Never in my lifetime at least. Mark my words, there'll be 'ters in the bush for ten years after this war. This is a bloody hateful war. If the PF win—which they will—he'll never make them put down their guns. It's been their life for too long. . . ."

He looked up and blinked behind his tinted spectacles in the dim light of the saloon. He sipped his pink gin and shifted his battered old Browning into the corner. Outside, the train's headlight penetrated far into the night. The whistle blew a single long high blast.

It was midnight when we reached Wankie. Outside the carriage the rain was falling in torrents on a deserted platform; the end-of-November rains which reduce Wankie's stifling humidity to sodden jungle and streaming roads; November rains which bring an end to the killing season, as the Rhodesian army calls it, affording relief to the guerillas in the bush. Graham's driver was a lone figure in the pouring darkness. He drove us up to the promontory over Wankie where a giant baobab tree marked our hotel site.

In the morning in teeming rain I walked out almost naked to the end of the promontory to look over the drenched landscape of Wankie; coke ovens, cooling towers and pit heads dotted about the vegetation; a Barnsley in the bush, surrounded by undulating ranges of wooded hills under a low cover of grey cloud. Beneath me, skirting the hill, lay the line to Victoria Falls which I hoped to take the next day. There I caught a sight of another of the famed Rhodesian Garratts, a monstrous black engine with its detached front boiler like a bulbous nose, pulling a coal train towards the Falls which lay away in the rain and mist seventy miles to the north through the jungle. There was no longer a passenger service that way, because of the war. The line seemed tiny, dwarfed by the elements.

Wankie is southern Africa's biggest coal outcrop. It provides the government with the coal it needs to run industry and the railways and continue the war. It is a company town. Owned by Anglo-American, the overlords of De Beers, and therefore part of a big-business mineral empire which rules right up this railway line from the Big Hole at Kimberley, the Joburg gold reef, the diamond pipes in Botswana. This land went to De Beers as part of the deal for funding Rhodes' seizure of Matabeleland, and passed to Anglo-American in 1953. More than any other place, perhaps, this sustained the fifteen years of UDI.

That night Christopher Soames arrived to lift sanctions and pave the way for an election. He made a speech on the radio, prefaced by martial music and a full list of his honours to the last CMG. That night in the

Wankie Miners' Club we watched *Coming Home*, a film about the Vietnam War. The audience applauded the patriotic sentiments of Jane Fonda's husband and hissed Jon Voight, the anti-war veteran. The love scene was cut by the censor. Afterwards in the bar miners from Sheffield and Doncaster supped their Lion lagers while a mine captain from Barnsley buttonholed me.

"Bloody great country this, lad. God's own country. Come back to England? You must be joking. Gone to the dogs, mate." He looked me up and down. "They don't know how to work there any more, especially the young 'uns." Like many Rhodies this man had come out after the war, disappointed by the turn in English politics ushered in by Labour's victory in 1945. We didn't fight the war for that, they said to themselves. So they came out here to preserve the virtues they thought they were fighting for. Rhodesia still has the feel of fifties Britain. And it's true: if most Rhodies came back today they would be dismayed by what they saw. Now they are on the end of the plank.

In the bar while a pianist played "My Way" Craig was holding forth in front of the girl we'd met on the train. He was depressed because a convoy car had been hit and four men killed near Vic Falls. Tomorrow while Graham and I rode an armed freight, he would be in a convoy.

"Look, man," he said. "I guarantee we will get hit: no way we will not get hit tomorrow." He still had his Rhodesian-made replica of a short Israeli tommy gun: "I'll sit up front tomorrow, next to the driver, 'cos if the 'ters attack I'll want to spray 180 degrees, and if you boys are in the front seat I don't want to have to blow your effing heads off, man." Suddenly I was glad I was going to be on the footplate.

Next morning in the yards at Thompson Junction by Wankie I boarded the footplate of class 15a number 395, a Beyer-Garratt bound for the Falls with a cargo of coking coal for Zambia and Zaïre. On the plate with me was a soldier, Bruce (a real gentleman, quiet, dignified), and the three-man crew, the furnace being hand-stoked. Graham was in the guards van with the guard and two black troopers of the Rhodesian army ("trust them with my life," whispered Bruce). The most exhilarating journey of my life began at about 10.00 on 13 December, the day after Soames' arrival. The war was still going on. The previous night in Thompson Junction a shunter had been wounded and a train sprayed with bullets. In Wankie town a policeman had been killed. None of us really knew what to expect.

There are a dozen little halts between TJ and the Falls. Now they are deserted. One by one we passed them, Sambawizi, Nashome, Lo-bangwe, and not a sign of life at any of them. At midday we stopped at Matetsi to take on water and rake out the fire box. The previous day I had visited the military command for permission to go to Matetsi, and I knew that it lay in the heart of a guerilla zone. When we got there we found the army post sandbagged in at the river crossing. There was a small radio station behind high wires, and the water tank. Two men had been killed here last week. Bruce tied a bandana round his forehead to keep the sweat out of his eyes. The driver's mate perched on top of the engine and swung the gantry pipe round to the boiler, while Graham and the troops fanned out facing the silent bush. The sun was really hot by now, and the burning ash showering out of the fire box made it impossible to stand near the locomotive. The bush was invitingly green and shady, but Bruce said the paths were booby-trapped. I sat down on the rails until it was time to climb back aboard.

On the last stretch, the thirty miles to the Falls, we touched fifty miles an hour through beautiful broken country, vivid green bush with rocky gulleys traversed by water courses. Some trees were covered with blossom, others dotted with red fruit; there were baobabs, palms, and some trees which looked like oaks, elms and chestnuts. *Et in Arcadia ego!* Momentarily all thoughts of war receded. Then, at about five miles distance, we saw the tell-tale cloud of spray beginning to be distinguishable from the clouds. Exactly what Livingstone had seen in 1855.

We came in sight for the first time of the columns of vapour, appropriately called "smoke," rising at a distance of five or six miles, exactly as when large tracts of grass are burned in Africa. Five columns now arose, and bending in the direction of the wind . . . the tops of the columns at this distance appeared to mingle with the clouds.

We sped into the Falls zone past the wire fences of the minefield, under the blockhouse with its oil drums and sandbags on the road bridge checkpoint. Victoria Falls was then a defended zone—a "protected village" for whites, as it were. Ironic to think of the white hoteliers and shopkeepers huddled round the Falls for safety. When the Falls were first discovered by Livingstone, no natives were found to be living within a radius of ten miles, as if respectful of its primordial force.

Vic Falls Station: neat, well-kept, overflowing with bougainvillaea and jacarandas, flower-boxes and mimosa. The white sign says Cape

Town 2651 k/m, Beira 1534 k/m. Engine 395 wheezed to a halt. We staggered on to *terra firma* black-faced, unburned coal in our hair, hot, shaky and exhilarated. The journey was almost over.

The railways reached the Falls in 1904, and the tourist industry rapidly followed to make the most of the scene. The Edwardian Falls Hotel, where I was booked in, still preserves the old style: huge electric fans swishing in the dining-room: be-fezzed waiters, misanthropic monkeys munching mangoes in the palm court, bougainvillaea, mosquito nets, barbecues, sundowners, planters punch, marimba bands, tribal dancing, tea, toast and marmalade, egg and bacon. And always the roar of the Falls, invisible from the hotel but for the smoke merging with the sky above Rhodes' railway bridge.

The place was virtually deserted. Tourism was by now non-existent. Not surprising really, for there were only two ways of getting there now the trains didn't run: either you careered by convoy from Wankie, guns at the ready, or you took an old Viscount from Bulawayo and twisted down like a falling leaf from the cloud cover in tight circles on to the airstrip, constantly veering away from the Zambian side to cut down the risk of SAM missiles and sniper fire. Such precautions were taken everywhere after a Viscount was hot down over Kariba.

That evening before dinner the station master drove me up the Zambezi to the edge of the minefield. Gingerly, for after dark hippos walk the river road. We passed three big American-style motels, all deserted, musty, mildewed in the humid tropical air, their carpeted dance floors the haunt of snakes and insects. The Elephant Hills casino lay empty, hit by a stray SAM missile from Zambia. At sunset impala teemed at the water hole, temporarily returned to Africa.

We walked down to the river. The Zambezi looked like a great dark ocean. Harry picked up strange husks and fruit and told me how they grew. About to retire, he was weary and could not disguise the bitterness he felt about the fall of his country. He would not stay in Rhodesia if the PF won. I reflected that after all these years of war, the white Rhodesian nationalists lived in what was to all intents and purposes a police state. All their news was censored, for example. They had never heard Robert Mugabe speak! Harry shrugged and looked at me as if I was personally responsible for the Lancaster House sell-out, as he called it. We stood silent there in the forest like the characters in the Conrad novel, confronted by the stillness of the forest "with its ominous patience, waiting for the passing of a fantastic invasion."

There remained one last walk to complete the journey. The curfew lasted till 6 A.M., but I went down to the Falls at five to savour the moment. Dawn here rises over Zambia right behind Rhodes bridge, shooting streams of sunlight through the cascades and forming rainbows in the water vapour, above you, below you and all around you. One of the few places on earth, perhaps, where you actually can be over the rainbow! By the gorge the rain forest grows out of itself, tangled creepers and saplings pushing through the sodden trunks of their dead progenitors: a mulch of rotten bark and leaves dotted with red aloes and dozens of orange butterflies. Wild animals are here too, warthogs, impala, gazelles, though all retire at dawn. In this fantastic moment I felt the ecstasy of a rain king, but my reverie was broken by the muffled boom of a landmine.

"Usually game, sometimes a 'ter," said Craig when I got back for breakfast. "The elephants break down the fences. Sometimes you get a whole herd of impala blowing themselves to pieces."

Rhodes' graceful bridge still spans the Zambezi gorge, four hundred feet above the swirling maelstrom of the Boiling Pot. It was built by the Cleveland Bridge and Engineering Company of Darlington in 1903–4, prefabricated and pre-erected on their premises before being shipped out to Africa. The railway reached the Falls in 1904, and the bridge itself was opened the next spring. By then Rhodes had been dead three years. He had asked that the bridge be built so close to the Falls that the spray would wet the carriage windows. It does, I am told. But in December 1979 the only trains to pass over the bridge were Zambian, picking up our load of coal and maize. Like everyone else I was forbidden even to step on the bridge. In December 1979 this was the front line in Africa.

Over the gorge the Zambian frontier post surveyed us with binoculars. Had it not been for the war, I could have crossed the bridge and followed Rhodes' route northwards through Livingstone to Lusaka, Dar-es-Salaam, Mombasa, Nairobi, Lake Victoria, Kampala, Rejaf, then eleven days by boat to Juba and back on the train at Khartoum, Wadi Halfa, Aswan and Cairo. Rhodes' dream never actually became reality, though you can still travel 6500 of the 8000 miles by rail. Maybe I'll do it one day.

Now it all seems so long ago. The Blue Train still carries its cosseted passengers from the Cape to Pretoria. But steam is to end on the line from De Aar to Kimberley. The South African government has announced plans to give Soweto full city status and its own university; so Derek and

Lucky will no longer be "temporary." Mafeking is no more. Rhodesia is now Zimbabwe, and Rhodesia Railways are the National Railways of Zimbabwe. You can travel once more by passenger train to Victoria Falls.

It is hardly a hundred years since the Falls were first seen by a white man. "A scene so lovely," Livingstone said, "that it must have been gazed on by the angels in their flight." In that time the tide of white colonialism has advanced and receded. It may already be too late for South Africa to respond to that tide. Like the Falls themselves the current of history is remorseless, unswerving and deaf to persuasion.

P. J. O'ROURKE

South Africa: 1986

"ALL THE PEOPLE WHO LIVE IN HYDE PARK ARE WHITE, JUST LIKE BEVERLY
HILLS. AND ALL THE PEOPLE WHO WORK THERE . . . ARE NOT WHITE, JUST
LIKE BEVERLY HILLS. THE ONLY DIFFERENCE IS, THE LADY WHO DOES THE
LAUNDRY CARRIES IT ON HER HEAD."

A reviewer in the Wall Street Journal *once called P. J. O'Rourke "the
funniest writer in America." O'Rourke's personal style of outspoken journalism has appeared just about everywhere, from* National Lampoon *to*
Car and Driver *to, perhaps most often,* Rolling Stone. *His books include*
Modern Manners, The Bachelor Home Companion, Republican Party
Reptile, *and* Holidays in Hell, *a collection of his magazine pieces on a
wide variety of subjects, on all of which he holds strong opinions. The following piece, based on a month-long visit to South Africa, was originally
titled "In Whitest Africa" and was published in* Rolling Stone.

DECEMBER 1986

I'D BEEN TOLD SOUTH AFRICA LOOKS LIKE CALIFORNIA,
and it looks like California—the same tan-to-cancer beaches—the
same Granola'd mountains' majesty, the same subdeveloped bushveldt.
Johannesburg looks like L.A. Like L.A., it was all built since 1900. Like
L.A., it's ringed and vectored with expressways. And its best suburb, Hyde
Park, looks just like Beverly Hills. All the people who live in Hyde Park

are white, just like Beverly Hills. And all the people who work there—who cook, sweep and clean the swimming pools—are not white, just like Beverly Hills. The only difference is, the lady who does the laundry carries it on her head.

I was prepared for South Africa to be terrible. But I wasn't prepared for it to be normal. Those petty apartheid signs, NO DOGS OR NON-EUROPEANS, are rare, almost tourist attractions now. There's no color bar in the big "international" hotels or their restaurants or nightclubs. Downtown shopping districts are integrated. You see as many black people in coats and ties as you do in Chicago. If I'd really tried, I could have spent my month in South Africa without noticing any hint of trouble except the soldiers all over the place. South Africa is terribly normal. And this is why, I think, we get so emotional about it.

Everywhere you go in the world somebody's raping women, expelling ethnic Chinese, enslaving stone-age tribesmen, shooting Communists, rounding up Jews, kidnapping Americans, setting fire to Sikhs, keeping Catholics out of country clubs and hunting peasants from helicopters with automatic weapons. The world is built on discrimination of the most horrible kind. The problem with South Africans is they admit it. They don't say, like the French, "Algerians have a legal right to live in the sixteenth *arrondissement*, but they can't afford to." They don't say, like the Israelis, "Arabs have a legal right to live in West Jerusalem, but they're afraid to." They don't say, like the Americans, "Indians have a legal right to live in Ohio, but, oops, we killed them all." The South Africans just say, "Fuck you." I believe it's right there in their constitution: "Article IV: Fuck you. We're bigots." We hate them for this. And we're going to hold indignant demonstrations and make our universities sell all their Krugerrands until the South Africans learn to stand up and lie like white men.

Forty miles from Jo-burg is Pretoria, the capital of South Africa. It looks like Sacramento with soldiers, like Sacramento will if the Chicanos ever rebel. And on the tallest hill in Pretoria stands the Voortrekker Monument, a 120-foot tower of shit-colored granite visible for twenty miles in every direction. The Voortrekker Monument is to the Afrikaners, the controlling majority of South African whites, what the Salt Lake City Tabernacle is to Mormons. It commemorates the Great Trek of the 1830s when the Boers escaped such annoyances of British colonial rule as the abolition of slavery and pushed north into the interior of Africa to fuck things up by themselves. The Voortrekker Monument's rotunda is decorated with an immense, heroic-scale bas relief depicting the entire course of the Great Trek from Bible-kissing sendoffs in Cape Town to the battle of Blood River in 1838 when 3,000 Zulus were killed vs. o dead Boers.

It was with unmixed feelings about Afrikaners that I climbed the wearyingly dramatic steps to the monument. One stroll through central Pretoria and one walk through the memorial's parking lot were enough to see that they're no-account people—dumpy women in white ankle socks and flower-print sundresses, skinny, quid-spitting men with hair oil on their heads and gun-nut sideburns. Their language sounds like a Katzenjammer Kids cartoon: *Die telefoon is in die sitkamer* ("The telephone is in the living room"). *Die dogter ry op n' trein* ("The daughter rides on the train"). And their racism is famous for its high degree of international deplorability. Liberal pinkteas, unreconstructed Stalinists, cannibal presidents of emerging nations and fascist military dictator swine all agree on this point.

Therefore my heart sank when I saw the Great Trek sculpture. It was, God help me, "Wagon Train" carved in stone. There was no mistaking the pokey oxen and Prairie Wagoneers parked in a circle for a combat-ready campout. The gals all had those dopey coal-scuttle bonnets on and brats galore doing curtain calls in their skirts. The fellers all wore Quaker Oats hats and carried muskets long as flagpoles. Horses pranced. Horizons beckoned. Every man jack from Ben Cartwright on down stared off into the sunset with chin uplifted and eyes full of stupid resolve. Every single give-me-a-home-where-the-buffalo-roam bromide was there, except the buffalo were zebras, and at that inevitable point in the story where one billion natives attack completely unprovoked, it was Zulus with spears and shields instead of Apaches with bows and arrows. The Zulus were, of course, doing everything Apaches were always depicted as doing before we discovered Apaches were noble ecologists—skewering babies, clobbering women and getting shot in massive numbers.

South Africa's bigoted, knuckle-headed Boers turn out to be North America's revered pioneer forefathers. And here I was, a good American descendant of same, covered with gore from Indian slaughters and belly stuffed to bursting by the labor of kidnapped slaves, ready to wash up, have a burp and criticize the Afrikaners.

Now, if the horrible Afrikaners resemble us—or me, anyway—what about the English-speaking white South Africans? They're better educated than the Afrikaners, richer, more cosmopolitan. They dress the same as Americans, act the same as Americans and, forgiving them their Crumbled Empire accent, speak the same language. What are they like?

I'd heard about the sufferings of the blacks in South Africa. I'd heard plenty about the intransigent racists in South Africa. And I'd heard plenty more than enough about the conscientious qualms and ethical inconveniences that beset whites who go to South Africa and feel bad about the suffering blacks and intransigent racists there. But I'd never heard much about the middling sort of ordinary white people with Mazdas to keep Turtle Waxed and child support payments to avoid, the ones who so resemble what most of us see when we brush our teeth. What's their response to the quagmire of apartheid? How do they cope with the violence and hatred around them? Are they worried? frightened? guilty? bitter? full of conflicting emotions?

I stayed a month in South Africa, traveled five thousand kilometers, talked to hundreds of people and came back with a two-word answer: they're drunk.

The South Africans drink and open their arms to the world. Before I left the States I phoned a lawyer in Jo-burg, a man I'll call Tom Mills, a friend of a friend. I called him to see about doing some bird hunting. (Just because you're going to a place of evil and perdition is no reason not to enjoy it.) And when I called him back to tell him what hotel I'd be staying in, Tom said, "The hell you are. We've got a guest house and a swimming pool. You're staying with us." This was a sixth-generation white African, no radical or pal of the African National Congress. He knew I was an American reporter and would do to South Africa what American reporters always do and which I'm doing right here. And he didn't otherwise know me from Adam. But Tom insisted. I was his guest.

"It isn't like you thought it would be, is it?" said Tom as we walked around the lawn with enormous whiskeys in our hands. "It's like California, isn't it?" Except the sparrows are chartreuse and the maid calls you Master. "That doesn't mean anything," said Tom. "It's just like saying 'boss' or whatever." And that barking noise, that's jackals on the tennis court. "Mind your step," said Tom. "This is where the yard boy got a cobra in the power mower."

The South Africans drink and make big plans. Tom's plan was to put a property qualification on the vote. "Do away with apartheid and the Group Areas Act and all that. Let anybody have whatever he can afford.

If he can afford political power, let him have that, too. That's about how you do it in the States, isn't it? It doesn't change things much."

Tom's friend Bill Fletcher had a plan for splitting up the whole country into little cantons, like Switzerland's, and federating it all back together again some way or other—*togetherheid.*

Tom's wife had another plan, which I forgot. We watched the TV news and mixed more drinks. Down in the black townships the "comrades" and the "fathers"—the young radicals and older moderates—were going at it with necklacings and machetes. But this wasn't on the news. New regulations had been issued by the government that day, forbidding any media coverage of civil disturbance. The lead story was about sick racehorses.

The South Africans drink and go on the offensive. Tom and Bill and I and some other bird hunters went to Jim Elliot's house for drinks. Jim was a dentist with a den made up almost entirely of animal heads and skins and other parts. The bar stools were elephant feet. "A man can live like a king in this country!" said Jim, petting a Labrador retriever named Soweto. "Like a goddamned king! I've got my practice, a house, a couple of cars, a shack down on the beach and the best goddamned hunting and fishing in the world. Where else could I live like this?" He hauled out a five-kilo bag of ice. "I know you Americans like your ice." He stuffed in as many cubes as my big glass could hold and filled it with Scotch to the brim.

"The blacks live better here than they do in the rest of Africa, I'll tell you that," said Bill Fletcher.

"We like the blacks," said Tom. "They don't deserve to be treated the way they are."

"We all like the blacks," said Jim.

"Though they're a bit childish," said someone and told a story about the new maid at his house who tried to make tea in the steam iron.

"But they don't deserve to be treated the way they are," said Tom. And he told how last year he'd seen a white motorist run into a black man and knock him across the road. The motorist stopped but wouldn't get out of his car. Tom called an ambulance and tried to get the white man to help, but the man just drove away. "He was a British tourist," said Tom with some satisfaction.

Later Jim said, "We fought alongside everybody else in World War I and World War II, and now they all turn their backs on us. The minute we're in trouble where are our friends?"

And a good deal later somebody said, "Thirty days to Cairo," by which he meant the South African army could fight its way up the whole length of Africa in thirty days. It's probably true. And it would certainly put the South African army thirty days away from where it's causing trouble now. But I didn't point that out.

The South Africans drink and get serious. Tom and I were shooting doves and drinking beer with a Greek car dealer named Connie. Connie had lived in the Belgian Congo and had been trapped there with his wife and little children in the horrors of '60 and '61. Sitting out in a grain field at sundown, Connie talked just a little, just obliquely about people mutilating each other, about the rape of nuns "by the very ones which they were ministering," about cattle left alive with their legs cut off at the hocks. "It makes me shake to even think what I saw."

That night Tom and I drank with Carlo, who'd come out to Africa in 1962, a teenager from a little village in Sicily carrying his mother's whole savings, one English pound and fifty pence. He'd made his way to Angola, "so rich, so beautiful. You put a dead stick in the ground, it would grow." He'd prospected for minerals, gotten rich, started a big-game hunting operation that had, at last, eighteen camps. Then the Portuguese left. He talked about corpses hanging in the trees, about men castrated and fetuses hanging out of the slit bellies of women and, like the Greek, about cattle with their legs cut off. He abandoned all his mineral claims, dynamited his hunting camps—"not even the stones were left in one piece"—and came to South Africa to start over.

I wondered what I'd think if I were South African and looked at the rest of Africa and saw nothing but oppression, murder, chaos, massacre, impoverishment, famine and corruption—whereas in South Africa there was just some oppression and murder. "You think the blacks can't govern themselves?" I said to Carlo.

He shrugged. "It was the East Germans, the Cubans who did the worst things I saw."

"You know Jonas Savimbi?" he said, naming the head of the more-or-less pro-Western UNITA guerrillas fighting Angola's Marxist government. "I would cut my arm off, here, to put Savimbi in power." And he pointed to the same place on his limb as the cattle had been mutilated on theirs.

South Africans drink and get nostalgic. I spent the Christmas holidays on the Indian Ocean in Scotboro—a sort of Southampton or Hilton Head with its peak season at South Africa's midsummer Yuletide. There were a lot of old people there, members of the "Whenwe Tribe," so called because most of their sentences begin with "When we were in Nyasaland . . . ," "When we were in Bechuanaland . . . ," "When we were in Tanganyika . . ." It seems Africa was a paradise then, and the more that was drunk the more paradisical it became. Though it must have been an odd kind of Eden for some of its residents.

"You can see why the blacks steal," said one old man, ex of Rhodesia. He'd been captured by the Germans at Tobruk. "In the POW camp at Breslau we worked in the post office—stole everything in sight. Only natural under the circumstances." He flipped his cigarette out onto the lawn, the way everyone does in South Africa. There's always someone to pick up the butts.

"The only reason blacks have bones in their skulls is to keep their ears apart," said a startlingly ugly old lady just as the maid, with expressionless face, was passing the cocktail weenies around.

"Now, wait a minute . . ." I said.

"Well, of course *your* blacks have white blood." The ugly woman shook her head. "I've never understood how any man could be attracted to a black girl," she said, helping herself to several miniature frankfurters and looking right through the very pretty maid. "That kinky hair, those fat noses, great big lips . . ."

I would be drummed out of the Subtle Fiction Writer's League if I invented this scene. The old woman was not only ugly with the ugliness age brings us all but showed signs of formidable ugliness by birth—picklejar chin, mainsail ears and a nose like a trigonometry problem. What's more, she had the deep frown and snit wrinkles which come only from a lifetime of bad character. All that day I'd been driving through KwaZulu, through the Valley of a Thousand Hills in the Natal outback, driving through little villages where the Zulu girls, bare-breasted to show their unmarried status, were coming to market. Burnished skin and dulcet features and sturdy little bodies like better-proportioned Mary Lou Rettons— I had fallen helplessly, fervently, eternally in love thirty or forty times.

And the South Africans drink and grow resigned to fate, at least the younger ones do. At a dinner party full of junior business executives, the talk was about the olive-colored South African passport that most countries won't accept as a travel document. "We call it the 'Green Mamba,'" said an accountant, "because you can't take it anywhere."

The guests discussed countries the way people their age in Manhattan discuss unfashionable neighboorhoods where they might be able to find a decent-sized apartment.

"We're looking at Australia," said an estate agent.

"Oh, Christ, England, I guess," said a law clerk from Tom's office. "My grandmother is English."

"The 'Florida option' is what most people are thinking about," said an assistant hotel manager. "Same weather, strong economy, and that's where everybody else goes when their governments fall apart."

They didn't talk about money or careers. They didn't even talk about apartheid as much as we do.

"If the United States were serious about fixing the situation here," said the law clerk, "all they'd have to do is give every young professional in South Africa a green card. Nobody would be left." At least nobody they knew very well.

"When you don't work with people and you don't live with people, you don't know them," said the accountant. "Just the help."

And the help's attitude, lately, has been, as they put it, "shifting."

"Who can blame them?" said the law clerk.

"They say it's those of us who've been moderates," said the estate agent, "who'll have our throats cut."

"What about the Afrikaners? Do you blame them?" I asked.

Helpless shrugs all around. "A lot of us are part Afrikaans," said the assistant hotel manager. And he told a Van Der Merwe joke, the South African equivalent of a Polish joke, about an American, an Englishman and Van Der Merwe the Afrikaner. They can each have a wish. All they have to do is run off a cliff and shout their heart's desire. The American runs off the cliff and shouts, "Gold!" A pile of gold bars appears at the bottom of the cliff. The American falls on top of it and he's killed. The Englishman runs off the cliff and shouts, "Silver!" A pile of silver coins appears at the bottom of the cliff. The Englishman falls on top of it and he's killed. Then Van Der Merwe runs off the cliff, but as soon as he gets over the edge he looks down and yells "Oh, shit!" A huge pile of shit appears. Van Der Merwe lands in that and walks away unscathed.

Those Afrikaners drink a lot, too, though it looked like just plain drinking as far as I could see. I spent an evening in a dirty little bar in a farm town called Humansdorp in the Cape Province. At first I didn't think the locals even noticed I was there. Then I realized they had all been speaking Afrikaans when I came in, but, after they heard me ask for more ice in my whiskey, they switched their conversations into English—still not saying a word to me. The bartender regaled one customer with the details of a practical joke he'd played, putting cayenne pepper in somebody's snuff. The rest of the bar was trading stories about bad and foolish black behavior.

A kid who'd just gotten back from his two-year army hitch was saying that Namibian girls smear menses mixed with mud all over their bodies. (For all I know it's true but no weirder than some of the ingredients I've noticed in my girlfriend's shampoo lately.) Somebody else said he kept building houses for his farm families, and they kept tearing holes in the roofs to let out the smoke from their cooking fires. There was concerned clucking over the neighborhood black teens. After they're circumcised they're supposed to spend a month alone in the bush, but instead they spend it begging beside the highway. Finally one of the Afrikaners turned to me and asked about sheep farming in the United States. By that time I'd had enough to drink to tell him, although I don't believe I know which end of a sheep you're supposed to feed.

Then everyone wanted to have a chat. "Was it difficult figuring out the South African money?" (There are 100 cents to the Rand.) "Did people try to deal [cheat] you around here?" "Does America have a lot of blacks?"

"I want to go to America," said the young ex-soldier, "to see how you do it."

"Do what?"

"Get along with the blacks."

What a strange place America must be—land of sanctuary for all beleaguered oppressors, with simple money and endless sheep-farming opportunities, where blacks behave somehow because they've got white blood. Mike Boetcher, the NBC correspondent in Jo-Burg, told me his baby's nurse, a beautiful girl of nineteen, wants to go to Harlem "because everybody is young and rich there" and because no one in Soweto has enough cows to pay her bride price. Mike said he tried in vain to tell her most guys in Harlem don't have a lot of cows. And in the Transkei "homeland" I talked to a black divinity student who'd visited America. "The most wonderful place," he said, "so wealthy and beautiful and with perfect racial harmony."

"What part of America did you visit" I asked.

"The South Side of Chicago."

I was pretty drunk myself by the time I'd been in South Africa for three or four weeks. Not that I'm not usually, but there was something white African in this bender. I was fuddled. My head boiled with clichés. I was getting used to being confused. I was getting used to hearing the most extraordinary things. From this Irish couple who'd been living in Africa for three decades, for instance. "There hasn't been apartheid here for years," said the wife.

"One of the problems is that that word was invented," said the husband.

I was becoming South African—used to having people all around me all the time doing everything for me and not doing it well.

I went in to dinner at my resort hotel in Mosselbaai, on the spectacular Big Sur–like "Garden Route" along the coast between Port Elizabeth and Cape Town. I'd had my six or eight whiskeys with the Irish couple in the lounge and was ready for one of the elaborate, big, bland and indifferently cooked meals that constitute South African cuisine. The restaurant was turned out in red plush and crisp linen. Candles glittered in cut-glass sconces. But when I sat down at my table there were three teaspoons, two water glasses, one dirty wine glass, no forks, no knives and no napkin.

"I need a dinner fork, a salad fork, a knife and a napkin," I said to the waiter, who stared at me in dull surprise and then headed out across the dining room at the speed of a change in seasons. His feet were sockless below the tuxedo pants and he was standing on the backs of his shoes with just his toes stuffed into the unlaced oxfords.

He returned with another spoon.

"I need a knife, a fork and a napkin!" I said.

He came back twenty minutes later with the water pitcher and filled my wine glass.

"LOOK HERE," I said, "DO YOU SPEAK ENGLISH?"

He thought about that for a long time. "Oh, yes." He disappeared and came back in half an hour with one more water glass. "Is the master ready to order?"

He was without recourse, voteless, impoverished, unpropertied, not a legal citizen in his own nation, yet he had me reduced to a paroxysm of impotent drunken rage. I left him a huge tip and ate my chicken with a spoon.

It's always hard to see hope with a hangover, nowhere more so than at the butt-end of this continent in a country that's like a nightmare laundry-detergent commercial—makes whites whiter, coloreds brighter.

They're building themselves a gigantic Cinerama, Technicolor Ulster here. And the troubles in Ireland have been going on since my own relative Tighernan O'Rourke, prince of Breffni, had his wife stolen by Diarmuid MacMurrough, king of Leinster, and O'Rourke got so mad that MacMurrough had to call on Henry II of England for help. That was in 1152. I think we can expect the same swift and decisive resolution to the problem in South Africa.

Divestment and sanctions—I guess those are the big answers proposed in the States. Well, economic sanctions sure nipped the Russian Revolution in the bud, made the Ayatollah Khomeini's Iran fold like a hideaway bed and put Chiang Kai-shek right back in power on the mainland.

The whole time I was in South Africa I only talked to one person who was in favor of sanctions and that was the divinity student in Transkei who'd visited the South Side of Chicago. He cited biblical example ("When the Pharaoh hardened his heart, God had to find another way"), but he also told me the Bible requires polygamy. So I'm not sure whether he was in earth orbit or not. Of course, there were a lot of people I didn't talk to. The comrades, busy performing "the necklace"—that is, putting flaming car tires around people's necks (actually, down over their shoulders in order to pin their arms to their sides)—were hard to chat up. And I never bumped into Bishop Tutu. Most of the blacks I did talk to would be considered, by South African standards, middle class, even sellouts— Uncle Bantus. They told me "political power grows from economic power." They saw sanctions as hurting one of the few black chances to get a leg up the ladder.

I have no idea whether they were right or wrong. But when I was in Ulundi, the administrative capital of the Zulu tribal lands, I was hanging around, drinking beer and talking to people, and a young political organizer leaned over to me and said, "It's really very simple why we are against sanctions. If we have money, we can buy *guns*." So maybe we should factor that into our next U.S.-Out-of-South-Africa rally.

The South African government's own solution, the homelands, is a hideous joke. I traveled through the Tswana tribal homeland, Bophuthatswana, in the north; KwaZulu in Natal where the Zulus refuse to accede to "independence"; and through the two Xhosa homelands, Transkei and Ciskei along the Indian Ocean. They're all the same. Everyplace is littered with windowless huts that you couldn't tell from latrines if there were any latrines to tell them from. The garden plots look like Grateful Dead fan beards. People are dumped into these rural wastes, far more people than the land can support. So the men have no choice but to go off to the rest of South Africa and work as "foreigners." The homelands are on the worst land in the country, scorched foothills and prairies on the verge of desertification. Raw trenches of the red African soil have eroded in webs across the pastures. Every foot of ground is overgrazed.

The tribal economic system, like that of ancient Europe, is based on cattle. (The word "pecuniary" comes from the Latin, *pecus*, "cattle.") The cows aren't often eaten or sold or even milked. They are the bank account, the measure of the clan's and the family's wealth. They're also an ecological nightmare in these cramped precincts.

I used to have eight head of Hereford beef cattle at my place back in the States. I asked some people in Ulundi what kind of wife these would get me.

"Oh," said one, "probably a girl who's lived in the city for a while and had a couple of kids."

"But," I said, "these are pure-bred Polled Herefords, going a thousand pounds or more."

"No, no, it's like Rand notes, it's the *number* of cows that counts."

I did see one homeland that worked, beautiful and severe bushveldt taken back from Boer farms and restored to its natural state with blesbok and gemsbok and springbok boking around all antlered and everything and herds of zebra—art deco on the hoof—and packs or gaggles or whatever-they're-called of giraffes (an NBA of giraffes would be the right term). This was, however, a homeland for the animals, the Botsalano Game Park in Bophuthatswana.

Tom Mills and I were riding in a Land Rover with his wife and two kids when we came right up beside five rhinoceri—four really enormous gigantic ones and a calf that was pretty tremendously huge itself. It's not easy to describe the effect that the first sight of a wild rhino has on a not very brave author from Ohio. It's like taking your four-year-old on a surprise visit to the Mesozoic era. I felt a vaulting thrill combined with some desire to start crying and crawl under the jeep. Tom, in what I felt was an extremely foolhardy move, turned off the engine.

"There are two kinds of rhinos," said Tom. "White rhinos are fairly docile. They don't usually bother you. But black rhinos are very nervous and aggressive. They'll charge."

"These rhinos are gray," I said.

"White rhinos and black rhinos are actually about the same color," said Tom.

"How do you tell them apart?"

"White rhinos have a square upper lip. The black rhino's is pointy."

I looked at our rhinos. Their upper lips were square, in a pointy sort of way. "How else do you tell them apart?"

"I forget."

The rhinos, who are very nearsighted, finally noticed us. They cocked their heads in this Godzilla way they have and began to amble in our direction. A rhinoceros ambles at about 60 mph. There was a moment of brief—but nonetheless high—drama while the Land Rover engine went ugga-ugga-ugga before it caught.

The rhinos made South Africa more depressing, if that's possible. The big game is disappearing from Africa. Most Africans have never seen a rhino in its natural state (which is a state of mild pique, I believe) any more than we've seen the prairie black with bison. And, to be fair, the white South Africans are the only people on the continent returning any land to the wild. Whatever's going to happen in South Africa will be bad for the rhino, too. And rhinos only occasionally kill for fun and never go to the U.N. afterward and say they did it because of American imperialism or communist subversion.

We drank as much as usual that night, sitting outside the tents with Botsalano's game warden. While baboons goofed off in the shrubbery and frogs sounded in the water hole like ten thousand little boys with sticks on an endless picket fence, Tom's wife Sally talked about her father, an Edinburgh grocer who'd come out to South Africa when she was a little girl. "He was looking for a healthier place to raise a family, where my sisters and I could grow up with more of a future than we'd have in Scotland."

The game warden told how the leopard was coming to extinction in South Africa. The leopards used to be hunted as trophies, mostly by Americans and Englishmen. Any farmer who had a leopard shot on his land received a trophy fee of several hundred Rand. So whenever a farmer had a leopard around, he was careful to preserve it until some rich guy came looking to decorate the rumpus room. Even if this cost the farmer a few lambs or calves, it was worth it. Then the animal rights people, the "bunny-huggers" as the warden called them, got legislation passed forbidding the import of all spotted fur, including stuffed heads, into the U.S. and the U.K. Now the farmers just shoot the leopards—mothers, cubs and everything—as pests. "So fucking bloody much for good intentions," said the warden.

A couple days later, driving with Tom in his Mercedes sedan through the perfectly empty Sunday streets of Jo-burg, I put it to him about South Africa. "There aren't *that* many Afrikaners. What, three million *vs.* two million English and other real Europeans? And you guys control the economy, almost all the major industries, right?"

"Mostly, yes."

"You've got the money. You've got forty percent of the white vote. And you've got twenty-four million blacks, coloreds and Indians who'd back you up. What's keeping you from taking the Afrikaner National Party and snapping its spine like a chopstick?"

"That's just not how the English are, you know," said Tom. "Most of us aren't very political."

"A couple of Chicago ward bosses and you'd have this country in your pocket."

"I suppose people think it wouldn't be cricket."

I'd never heard "wouldn't be cricket" used seriously before. Interesting what "cricket" means if you think about it—boring, insanely complicated and riddled with snobbery and class.

We'd pulled onto the N-3 freeway. Jo-burg's office towers shone behind us. Flat-topped artificial hills from the gold mine tips rose in the distance. I was staring out the window at South Africa's admirable highway beautification when we came over a rise, and I caught a glimpse of what was beyond the screen of trees and shrubs.

Thousands of tiny, slatternly huts were pressed together in a jumble stretching for miles. And every one of those hovels seemed to be on fire. Smoke drifted in an ominous smudge across the highway. "Riots!" I thought, trying to fasten my seat belt for the high-speed evasive driving we'd have to do through hordes of angry comrades who would, no doubt, come roiling across the freeway at any moment, stones and firebombs in hand.

"If you look over there," said Tom, "you can see Alexandra. It's one of our older black townships."

Maybe he hadn't noticed it was on fire. "Isn't it on fire or something?" I said.

"That's from the cookstoves. They don't have electricity."

And then Alexandra slipped back behind the decorative landscaping and was gone.

Tom and I had been out that afternoon shooting doves again with Connie the Greek car dealer. We were shooting near Sharpville, site of the famous 1960 massacre, a sleepy farm town, nobody's picture of a killing ground. All around were huge Afrikaner grain spreads, completely up-to-date and identical to big mechanized American farms except they weren't going bankrupt—thanks, in part, to worldwide bans on selling grain to South Africa. But out in the middle of these homesteads, invisible from the pretty country roads, are the people who work the land. Their one-room, cinderblock, tin-roofed shacks are set in the fields with wheat growing right up to the doors—not even room for a garden, just a communal well in a muddy dooryard. There were half-naked kids all over the place. We took some of the kids along to run after the dead birds and pluck and gut them—"curly-headed retrievers," the South Africans say. The kids got a Rand apiece, about fifty cents, U.S., plus cigarettes. One of the boys, who said he was fifteen but looked an undersized twelve, was fascinated by Tom's Mercedes. He'd never been in a car before. Tom and I gave him a ride up and down the dirt track by his home. The boy kept sniffing and poking at the air conditioner vents. "*Where* does the cold air all come from?" he asked.

"Um . . ." said Tom and looked at me.

"God, I don't know," I said. "Something gets heated and that, uh, makes it cold." So much for the educational benefits of superior civilization. Tom flicked the electric sun-roof switch to change the subject.

The kid watched the roof panel slide back and forth. "Now I've seen everything," he said.

Tom had a client named Gilead, a man of sixty or seventy who'd started out selling coal from a sack in the black townships and was now one of the richest men in Soweto. Save for a bit of melanin, Gilly was the image of my Irish grandfather—close-cropped hair, a build like a Maytag's and fingers thick as my wrists. He even had the same gestures as my grandfather, pulling on the old-fashioned pointy lapels of his banker's stripe suit, then planting his thumbs in the pockets of his vest and toying with the thick watch chain that ran across his belly. Gilly's skull bore four or five large hatchet scars from the gang quarrels of his youth. When I first met him, in Tom's office, he was telling about one of the stores he owns being "off-loaded" by the comrades.

"The gangs, they set up at either end of the street, you know. They are just boys, some no more than ten years old. Some of the boys come into your store and buy a pop. Then they throw the bottles around to create their diversion and begin to empty the shelves. And you just stay quiet if you don't want to be necklaced."

"Yes, but *you* weren't in the store when that happened," said Tom.

Gilly began to laugh. "No, I was not in there the first two times it happened."

"Well, he was in there the third time," said Tom to me, "and he chased them down the street with his pistol."

"Oh, ho-ho-ho-ho," Gilly laughed and rocked back in his chair as though the comrades were the best joke in the world. "When I was young, ho-ho-ho-ho, there were guns everywhere in the townships. And these little fellows, all they've got are stones."

"You know what we have to do," said Tom when Gilly'd left, "we have to get Gilly to come out to our house for dinner and bring his wife and some of his friends. It would be interesting for you to talk to them."

But the riots in Soweto kept anyone from getting in or out after dark and, even in the daytime, there were too many barricades and stonings to bring the women along. So Gilly and three of his black friends, young men in their twenties, came to an afternoon *braai*, a barbecue, at Tom and Sally's house. A Christmas-week strike had begun in Soweto that day and Gilly, Bob, Carswell and Nick arrived in a rusted Datsun, although Gilly owns a BMW.

We all sat on the patio for a stiff twenty minutes while the Millses' maid peeked around the doorpost with an expression of intrigued disapproval. But then a few beers were had and the steaks and the *boerewors* sausages began to spatter on the grill, and one more of the hundred thousand endless discussions of South Africa's "situation" began.

The strange thing is that when I look in my notes now, if I cover the names, I can barely tell who said what or if the speaker was black or white. Carswell, Bob (and me, I guess) favored one man, one vote. Gilly, Nick, Tom and Sally felt Tom's idea about property qualification had merit. There was a general denunciation of the Group Areas Act, which dictates where what race can live, and of U.S. sanctions, too. "Politics is dirty," said Carswell and there was unanimous disparagement of President

Botha and Winnie Mandela. Everyone agreed moderates would come to the fore if they just had a chance. Bob described, with considerable anger, how the riots and strikes in Soweto were controlled by anonymous pamphlets and unsigned ads in the *Daily Sowetoen*. He blamed outside agitators, just like the Reagan White House does. "They call you up in the night," said Carswell, "and ask what size tire would fit you."

"We need more black police and black army forces," said Nick. Nick, Bob and Carswell had small children and were furious about the black school boycott. They said the ANC leaders were pushing a public-school strike while the leaders' own children were being educated in private schools. They feared, they said, "the intentional creation of a black underclass." Of course, there's one of those already but, anyway, everyone praised capitalism for a while and Bob made a poetic appeal for whites to stay in South Africa, although perhaps he was just being polite in response to the hospitality.

Then Nick said something that shocked me, and that I could see surprised Tom and Sally. "I'm angry that South Africa is singled out," he said. "Why should Senator Kennedy come here and tell us our troubles? We're not the only country in the world where bad things happen."

"I have just this one fear," said Carswell. "Attack from the outside— South Africa has no friends."

After the meal Gilly waxed historical and told a horrifying story about seeing three men crucified by the Spoilers gang in Alexandra in the 1940s. "One man was still alive, nailed up to this post. He was screaming but his mouth was dry and no sound came out. I will never forget it."

"What are you guys going to *do*?" I asked Nick, Bob and Carswell. "How are you going to get rid of apartheid?"

"Such meetings as this are valuable," said Carswell, as though something had been accomplished that afternoon.

"That was a real eye-opener," said Tom when Gilly and his friends had left.

"Incredibly interesting," said Sally. "We've got to do that again."

And it dawned on me—they'd never had black people as guests in their house before.

"We've seen Gilly and his wife at office parties," said Sally. "And there are black and Indian students at the kids' schools. We've seen the parents at school functions."

We were going to the Fletchers' house that night for dinner. "Let's not say anything about this," said Tom. "I'm not sure how Bill and Margaret would feel about it. They're a little old-fashioned about some things."

"Yes," said Sally.

But at one that morning when we were all good and drunk and passing around the Afrikaner Witzend brandy, Tom couldn't resist. "You'll never guess what we did this afternoon," he said to Bill and Margaret. "You know my client Gilly, who owns all the stores? Well, we had him and some of his young friends out to a *braai*. They had some extraordinary things to say. It was a real eye-opener."

"Incredible," said Bill. "What a great idea. We ought to do that, Margaret. With some of my subcontractors. That's a great idea."

"We really should," said Margaret.

I had the most peculiar feeling in my woozy haze. I was present at the birth of a fundamental, epochal realization of human fellowship. But I was sure the birth was coming too late to save the baby.

I'd walked Gilly out to the Datsun when he was leaving Tom's house. And he took me by the arm and said, "Apartheid is the evil thing. Apartheid must just stop. If those laws are removed, no more policemen will be needed." He glanced toward Tom and Sally. "They all know it's wrong."

I said, "They don't seem to know how to get rid of it."

"They know," said Gilly. "They just don't want to give up the advantage they have on the black man."

"Is it too late?" I said.

"What man does man can fix."

Maybe. On my last day in South Africa I drove through Soweto— probably not a good idea for a person as putty-colored as myself in a shiny red rent-a-car. Also, it was illegal. No white person is allowed to go there without government permission. Even white police and soldiers don't enter Soweto unless the "situation" gets so out of hand they think they have no choice. But I'd been in South Africa for a month and had not met one white person who'd been there. It's just outside Jo-burg, a huge adjunct taking up the whole southwestern quadrant of the city's outskirts. But I hadn't talked to any white person who'd ever even seen Soweto.

And then I couldn't find the place. A city of two million people and when I looked at my rental car map it wasn't there. I drove around the N-1 beltway and there were no signs, no exits marked Soweto. I got off in the southwest and headed in what I thought must be the right direction. I took a couple of gravel roads, navigating by the sun. Finally I saw a Soweto sign, the size that might say "PICNIC AREA 1 MILE." And on the other side of a hill was Soweto, as big as the San Fernando Valley, a vast expanse of little homes.

It was not such a terrible-looking place, by Third World standards. It was littered and scruffy and crowded, but most of the houses looked like what you'd see on an American Indian reservation. Each modest dwelling was set on a small plot of land. There was electricity and no raw sewage stink.

Soweto was almost rich as riches are measured in Africa. And there was plenty of economic power here for political power to grow out of it if that were the way things worked in South Africa. But it wouldn't have mattered if each of those houses had been Graceland. People would be just as oppressed. South Africa is one of the few places I've ever been where things are not a matter of dollars and cents.

I locked my car doors, adjusted my necktie and drove through the place in a sweat. Soweto is like discovering arithmetic. It is an epiphany about what "83 percent of the population" means. Until then I hadn't *seen* the blacks in South Africa, not really, not even in the overpopulated homelands. Now they pressed in on every side in the slow jam of bicycles, trucks and foot traffic. I hoped I had something in my wallet, some left-over receipt from a United Negro College Fund donation or some damn thing to save my pink ass when the comrades got to me. Everyone was staring in my windows. Everyone in the crowd was looking at my pale, stupid face.

And then I saw that they were smiling. And here and there was a happy wave. There was laughter from the little kids. I drove through Soweto for nearly an hour without so much as a bad look tossed in my direction, let alone rocks or firebombs.

Maybe I'd caught them by surprise and they didn't know what to make of me. Maybe they thought I was so crazy to be there that it was funny. I didn't know.

Months after I got back I was giving a lecture on journalism at some little college in the middle of Pennsylvania and I told the students about driving through Soweto. One of them came up to the lectern afterward. She was from Soweto, an exchange student. "Don't you know why the people were smiling and waving at you?" she said. "They thought you were great."

"But why?"

"It's *illegal* for you to be there. How did you ever get in?"

"I don't know. I was lost. I came in through some back roads."

"The government isn't letting anyone in there and when people saw you, that you had managed to get in some way. . . . They figured you must be somebody good, an organizer, or from some international group, that you would even be there."

"Even though I was white?"

"*Because* you were white."

There *is* some hope for South Africa, for the souls of the people there anyway. I mean, personally, if I'd lived my forty years in Soweto and I saw some unprotected honky cruising down my street on a Saturday afternoon, I would have opened that car like an oyster and deep-fat fried me on the spot.

ADAM HOCHSCHILD

Summer Folk: 1988

"SWAMI YATIISHVARANANDA WILL LECTURE ON MEDITATION AND SELF-
REALIZATION. CHARLIE PARKER'S FULLY LICENSED RESTAURANT AND DISCO
WILL PRESENT THE MISS SA WET T-SHIRT CONTEST. IN THE CENTER OF THE
CITY, A FEW BLOCKS FROM PARLIAMENT . . . WHITE SCHOOLBOYS ARE
PLAYING CRICKET."

Adam Hochschild, cofounder of Mother Jones *magazine, has had a long
interest in South Africa. While he was in college in the early sixties, he
spent a summer there, working on an anti-apartheid newspaper. In later
years, his reports on South Africa won awards from the World Affairs
Council and the Overseas Press Club of America.*

*In 1988 he returned again to South Africa, partly to observe ceremo-
nies marking the 150th anniversary of the Battle of Blood River—between
the Voortrekkers and the Zulus under their chief, Dingane—and partly to
reexamine a country he had known for years that was about to change
dramatically and forever.*

The Mirror at Midnight, *from which the following excerpt is taken,
was published in 1990.*

THE MOST UNEXPECTED THING ABOUT GOING TO
South Africa is that the plane is full. I had hoped that a half decade
of well-publicized bloodshed would discourage enough travelers so that I
could stretch out across a few empty seats and get a good night's sleep.
But every seat across on my 747 from Europe to South Africa is occupied.

One of my seatmates is a cheerful German who visits the country twice a year on business, but whose real enthusiasm is for its hunting:

"Springbok, antelope, an incredible variety! The professional hunter takes along his boy; they're out in the bush together all day; they've been working together for years. No race problems there. . . . Politics? Oh, South Africa just needs *time* to solve its problems."

Judging from the tennis racquets they carry, many other passengers are tourists, among the several hundred thousand, I later learn, who visit South Africa each year, heading for the country's beaches and game parks. And judging from other statistics, some of my fellow passengers must be immigrants. Years of upheaval have reduced that number, but some ten thousand newcomers still arrive in the country each year, lured by skilled jobs and good pay, and black house servants at $30 a week or less.

After my plane lands at Cape Town, the pilot announces, "The safest part of your journey is now over. On leaving the airport, *please* drive carefully." There is a burst of nervous laughter from the passengers: the road between Cape Town and its airport runs past a number of black townships, and at times in the last few years when tensions have been high, black youths have stoned vehicles driving past. At the airport, an armored car with the bright yellow paint of the South African Police is parked on the tarmac; its hull, high and V-shaped to deflect the blast of land mines, gives it the look of a steel sailboat on wheels. On the freeway into the city, some buses have wire mesh over the drivers' windows, against the stones. How do builders overcome a brick shortage? runs one South African joke. Answer: They send a couple of buses through a township. But today things are quiet, and from the freeway I can see black teenagers playing soccer on gravelly patches of dirt.

Cape Town is heartbreakingly lovely, its setting, as the intrepid traveler Anthony Trollope observed in 1877, "one of the most picturesque things to be seen on the face of the earth." The flat-topped Table Mountain looms above the city, its famous "tablecloth" of fog rolling off the top and dissolving into the air. The mountain throws a protective, tree-covered spur around Table Bay, a beckoning arm of land which welcomed ashore the first Dutch settlers more than three centuries ago. To the south stretches the rocky, surf-fringed Cape Peninsula, pointing downward like a finger toward the junction of the Atlantic and Indian Oceans. Surely it was not only the Cape's strategic location that made those sailors stop here, but also its uncanny beauty.

This hillside sea-city's charm haunted me when I lived here for part of that summer twenty-six years ago, and it still does so today. Perhaps because it is in such contrast to what goes on here. For the full panoply of apartheid has been legislated into being in a setting of transcendent loveliness. By night the lights of the Alpine cable-car station on the summit of Table Mountain twinkle like an earthbound star. By day a wash of brilliant sunlight covers arcaded nineteenth-century streets, stately public buildings, statues of white statesmen and generals, and a Botanical Gardens with palm trees and aviaries full of chirping birds.

At the edge of all this greenery stands the majestic Parliament building. One afternoon I sit in the press gallery and listen to a "reading" (a formality; almost anything the President wants is passed) of a bill asking for some $100 million worth of extra funds for the police, army, and prisons. All the members rise in silence as a white-gloved functionary carries in a huge gold mace, preceded by other officials in black tailcoats. The Speaker wears a black gown, and the building's walls are filled with gilt-framed paintings of other white men in wigs or old high-collared uniforms. Pages in green jackets with gold braid carry messages. Later, Honorable Members from here or there rise to ask questions of the Minister of this or that: is such-and-such an item covered by the supplementary appropriation or the general appropriation? So solemn is the sense of ceremony, so dark and cathedral-like is the wood paneling of the chamber's walls, so respectfully hushed are the white schoolchildren in shorts and blazers who watch from the visitor's balcony, that for a moment you can almost believe that the whole thing is legitimate.

Outside Parliament, trees shade the streets from the summer sun; a few blocks away, the air is filled with fresh smells from open-air flower stalls near the cobblestones of Greenmarket Square. Immaculate parks are laced with walking paths. At first glance there is little to remind you that the scene is not some exceptionally unspoiled city in southern Europe.

For most whites, it *is* Europe. "Read Gorky's *Summer Folk*," a friend here tells me. "It's the best thing written about white South Africa today." When I read this play about turn-of-the-century Russian gentry, I see what he means. Maxim Gorky's characters are families on vacation in the country. They read poetry aloud, play the piano, and prepare endlessly for some amateur theatricals which never come off. The characters talk of flamelike love and prisonlike marriage; everyone is having an affair with someone else's mate. From time to time they argue about the country's dreadful poverty, which they vaguely know exists somewhere off in the distance; then they go back to their piano playing and love affairs. All the while, watchmen patrol the woods around the summer houses, cleaning up picnic debris, chasing away beggars, blowing their whistles to scare off thieves. We rarely see the watchmen, but the sound of their whistles recurs; it is the last sound in the play.

I'm reminded of these summer folk when I look at the South African newspapers. By now I would have expected, no matter how much distortion or censorship, that their pages would be dominated by the ongoing violence and political upheaval: the country has been in non-stop turmoil for the better part of a decade, after all, and thousands of army conscripts have been patrolling the black townships during most of that time. But most newspapers are filled with the same kind of stories that I remember from being here many years ago, stories that evoke that nation of dreams that most white South Africans imagine they live in. It is the country the tourist brochures call Sunny South Africa.

Sunny South Africa's inhabitants, judging by the newspaper photos, are almost all white, although a sprinkling of them are unthreatening blacks—Zulu dancers, cute children, an Indian cricket champion, an African businessman in a three-piece suit gratefully receiving an award. In clothing advertisements, only one model in three or four is black, a proportion doubtless calculated to catch the eye of black buyers without scaring off white ones.

Above all, the Sunny South Africa of the newspapers is relentlessly *normal*. There are ads for computer matchmaking, advice-to-the-lovelorn columns, articles about beauty tips, lost cats, high school reunions, tennis matches, and even one piece on an all-white bank robbery, long and lavishly illustrated, as if the editors were relieved at finding some violence that was not racial. A personals column: "White male professional, 35; likes wine, sports; seeks female companionship." "Selective top quality Jewish only introductions. Miriam, 783-5892." Human interest features: a water-skiing dog; a story, WOMAN MARRIES HER FATHER; and another, URBAN MAN IN A CAGE: "With grunting rhinos and roaring lions for neighbors, Bernard Rich quietly goes about his business of living in a cage in the Johannesburg Zoo. The 27-year-old salesman is being exhibited as Homo Sapiens Urbanus. . . . 'The hardest part will be having to ignore the public,' says Bernard."

Why has the Sunny South Africa of the newspapers always so fascinated me? As a cocky nineteen-year-old, I think, it was because I, with my superior knowledge, knew this country was about to have a violent revolution, and the insensitive, carefree whites who lived here didn't. Reading their newspapers was like having a window onto the last days of Louis XVI. Now, of course, the revolution hasn't happened, but few whites are unaware that big changes are inevitable. So the fascination lies in something else: in how they choose to push aside that awareness. And in how the whole society is arranged to make that an easy thing to do.

For white South Africans, as for Gorky's summer folk, the simmering violence is out of sight. Of the more than five thousand people who have died in the upheavals since 1984, less than half a dozen have been white. Only now and then can Sunny South Africa hear the watchmen's whistles. In the post office, for example, a poster shows a picture of a limpet mine and warns in the two official languages, Afrikaans and English: SO LYK DIE DOOD!/THE LOOK OF DEATH! But the actual warfare is almost entirely confined to the black townships. And to the summer folk, the townships are almost invisible.

Indeed, many whites go through the average day encountering no blacks at all—except those who are maids, waiters, or the nannies that I can see accompanying almost every white child on the grass of those downtown parks. There is a moving song about the nannies, by Thembi Mtshali and Barney Simon:

> My sister breast-fed my baby
> While I took care of you
> We met when you were three months old
> and I a woman of forty-two. . . .
> Your first word was my name
> Your first song was in Zulu. . . .
>
> My children watched Soweto burn
> while I took care of you
> My children breathed tear-gas smoke
> while I took care of you
>
> Your eyes are bright and clever now
> Your legs are straight and strong. . . .
> my children sing at funerals
> while I take care of you . . .
> child of my flesh
> May God protect my children from you.

One morning I leave the land of the summer folk and visit the African squatter settlement of Crossroads. It is surprising how swift is the passage from one South Africa to another. Twenty minutes' drive from downtown Cape Town, with its elegant seafood restaurants and well-stocked delicatessens displaying half a dozen varieties of ham, are the sand streets of Crossroads, where women are going door to door selling sheep's and pigs' heads, the very cheapest type of meat. At an intersection on the edge of Crossroads, several dozen men are sitting on rocks, waiting, in the hope that pickup trucks will come by and collect crews for temporary labor, paying 10 or 12 rand (less than $5) for a day's work.

The African huts I walk past here are made of corrugated zinc, tarpaulins, plastic sheeting, or pieces of the walls of demolished buildings, with painted advertisements still on them. Cocks are crowing. The sand streets and shack floors are dry today, but in the rainy season they will be mud.

In one two-room hut I visit, the ceiling is black from the smoke of a tiny kerosene stove and the room smells of its fumes. There is no room for a closet: clothes, in plastic bags, are hung high up near the ceiling. Twelve adults and children share four beds in these two rooms. But what strikes me most is the walls. They are wallpapered with the shiny paper from Sunday newspaper ad supplements. And so lining this pair of cramped rooms are hundreds upon hundreds of color photos of dishwashers, remodeled kitchens, dining table-and-chairs sets, sofas, stereos, deck chairs, and Jacuzzi tubs.

On the street outside this house, I see a giant Casspir armored car following a small white truck. "That's the post office truck," explains a woman who lives in these rooms. "Without the Casspir the comrades would burn it." The war is still on.

These days, however, the "comrades"—the young militants—are in retreat here; in most of the Cape Town African townships a conservative black vigilante group is in control, backed up by the armored cars of the army and the police. That police force itself is now more than half black. An unemployment rate of more than 50 percent in places like Crossroads means the police have little trouble recruiting. But at the height of the current wave of violence a number of black policemen were "necklaced" by angry crowds; nationwide, more than nine hundred others had their homes burned. In some parts of the country, black police and their families had to be evacuated from townships in the middle of the night and moved to special tent villages behind barbed wire, next to police stations.

As they now take revenge for homes destroyed and companions burned alive, they become as feared as the white police.

Standing outside a clinic in Crossroads, I see some of that history in the grim face of a black policeman, as he looks down from an open-topped armored car that suddenly roars into view along a winding sand path—in search of someone? Or just on patrol? His eyes are narrowed; he is holding a submachine gun. Children shrink away from the vehicle's path.

Inside the clinic this morning, a white pediatrician is seeing patients. She is instructing some medical students as she does so. She explains to them that the swollen cheeks on some of these children are not due to infection, as medical textbooks might have them believe, but to kwashiorkor, a disease of malnutrition. Bottle-baby syndrome is a major problem here, the doctor tells me: this is the tragic near-starvation that occurs when a mother does not breast-feed, then can't afford enough baby formula or the fuel to boil water for it. "Mothers have so little confidence they can't believe that something they produce *themselves* is what's best for their baby." The doctor examines each child carefully, hands out packets of protein powder, explains the importance of vegetables, then fishes into a big box of old clothing and gives each mother a wool blanket or sweater. Incongruously, a shelf behind the packed benches of waiting mothers and babies holds some children's books donated from some household in Sunny South Africa: *Walt Disney's Wonderful World of Knowledge*, *Black Beauty*, and *The Young Ballet Dancer*.

Back in Sunny South Africa myself one afternoon, I am jogging through the beautiful pine and eucalyptus forest on the slopes of Table Mountain. I round a bend and come upon some stone ruins. A plaque explains that this was the house of a local dignitary, built in 1797. Everywhere around Cape Town I constantly stumble onto vine-covered houses, museums, three-hundred-year-old farms, all with brass plaques celebrating the longevity of white settlement in this corner of the country. Hundreds of monuments and oil portraits show the early Dutch *burgers* of this city, stern-looking men with ruffled lace collars and a somber, righteous gaze. Scores of history books record the conflicts between the English and the Dutch and the activities of the Dutch East India Company, to whom the colony for its first 150 years actually belonged. But, until recently, nobody paid much attention to the fact that this was a society built not only on conquest but on slavery. When I was here in 1962, I lived in a rented room off cobblestoned Greenmarket Square, unaware that it had once been the city's slave market.

The threat of punishment kept the slaves in line, and those who revolted or escaped were dealt with harshly. A major instrument of control, then as it is now, was Robben Island, one of the oldest penal colonies on earth. You can see it from the hill above Cape Town harbor, a low smudge on the horizon. Even before Dutch settlers arrived at the Cape, both British and Dutch ships left mutinous sailors on Robben Island to die. The Dutch later used the island as a prison for rebellious slaves, and for members of the Cape's native population who resisted Dutch rule. Two prisoners stole a leaky boat and escaped to shore in 1659.

No prisoner has successfully escaped since. For a time the island was put to other uses—a lunatic asylum, a leper colony, a military base. But when South African jails began filling with long-term political prisoners in the early 1960s, Robben Island, a blacks-only prison, was where most of them went.

One evening, I talk to one of them, Neville Alexander. He spent ten years on Robben Island. For four years after that he was under house arrest. His large, alert eyes are touched with humor and intelligence as they take in everything around him; his brown face is gentle, scholarly, easily forming into a quizzical smile. Classified as "Coloured," or of mixed race, he works today as an author and teacher. With the cachet of being a veteran of "the Island," he is an influential strategist of the resistance movement in the Cape Town region. When a wave of preventive detentions began a few years ago, the police came looking for him and he lived in other people's houses for some months. But for the moment things seem to have cooled off, and, wearing sandals and a tan windbreaker, he is willing to spend a few hours at a friend's house talking. After a decade of confinement in a notoriously harsh prison, I would have expected an angry or bitter man. But instead, Alexander talks of the experience almost as a privilege, and one that he was able to learn much from:

"Of course that time on the Island was a bit long. But it was never boring, never uninteresting. To come to one's maturity under those circumstances was an important experience. I found myself among older people who had thought deeply." Though Alexander has degrees from universities in both South Africa and Germany, he says, "Robben Island was certainly the best university I could have gone to."

Alexander describes the psychological effect of prison as a closed space: things you say rebound back to you; you cannot run away from anyone or from any opinion you've voiced. "The impetuosity of a young person runs up against those you are in close contact with. You realize the seriousness of words. For instance, if out of a sense of pride, vanity, immaturity, you push a particular polemic too far, it leads to strained relations. That affects the unity of the whole group. And you are responsible to the whole group; you have to stand together against the authorities.

"Through exchanging hints and opinions we were able to teach one another how to learn, the best way of making notes, the best way of writing an essay, and so on. We were able to have seminars and tutorials even while we were working. Although most talk has to take place while you are working in the lime quarry. People would make sure that they worked together. Everyone was picking and shoveling, but we'd use lunchtimes or weekends to do diagrams and things like that.

"The other thing about maturing was to be with people like Mandela, Sisulu, and Mbeki, who have had decades of experience. Amidst the petty quarrels you find in all prisons, they were people who ennobled their environment. Mandela even the warders treated with great deference.

"In prison you have a lot of time. I had a two-year discussion with Mandela about what a 'nation' means in South Africa—is there an African 'nation'? A Coloured 'nation'? And so on. He is a man with a judicial temperament and an abiding interest in people. Even when you disagree with him, you never feel offended. I learned a hell of a lot from him, even though I disagree with some ANC policies. I admired particularly his lack of sectarianism. You can always reopen a question. It is an event in one's life to meet someone like that.

"On an emotional level, I discovered things about myself. I think the thing I missed most was children, not women. I remember the first time all of us heard children's voices in the quarry. They were from the warders' village there; they're normally kept well out of sight of prisoners. It was as though we'd been struck by lightning. All of us. We all stood dead still. The warder quickly went and made sure we didn't actually see the kids. But that reminded me, those lone voices, that that was the one occasion in ten years when I actually heard the voice of a child."

In downtown Cape Town, however, the fog rolls off Table Mountain like a silent waterfall, and Crossroads and Robben Island are out of sight. The newspaper announces public events: Captain Steven Banks, chairman of the SA Antique Collectors' Society, will speak on miniature paintings. The Kennel Association will hold its all-breed championship dog show at the Cape Hunt and Polo Grounds. Swami Yatiiṣhvarananda will lecture on meditation and self-realization. Charlie Parker's Fully Licensed Restaurant and Disco will present the Miss SA Wet T-Shirt Contest. In the center of the city, a few blocks from Parliament, inside a gate guarded by plaster lions, white schoolboys are playing cricket: red knee socks, white shorts, and a satisfying *thock* as bat hits ball. For the moment, the watchmen's whistles are still in the distance, and the summer folk are still at play.

MICHAEL PALIN

Pretoria, Johannesburg, Soweto, a gold mine, and the Blue Train to Cape Town: 1991

"THE MAGNIFICENT LANDSCAPES OF AFRICA BUILD TO A TREMENDOUS
CLIMAX. TOWERING HAZE-BLUE MOUNTAIN RANGES—THE MATROOSBERG,
THE SWARZBERGEN AND THE HEX—PART LIKE STAGE CURTAINS TO REVEAL
THE FINAL EPIC IMAGE OF TABLE MOUNTAIN AND THE WIDE ATLANTIC."

*Actor, writer, and television presenter Michael Palin first made the world
laugh in* Monty Python's Flying Circus. *Since then, he has appeared in
other films, including* The Missionary *and* A Fish Called Wanda, *and
written* Ripping Yarns *with Terry Jones and several books—God help us!—
for children. He's also been around the world a couple of times.*

The first time was when he incautiously agreed to go Around the
World in 80 Days *for the BBC, eschewing aircraft and following, sort of,
the route taken by Jules Verne's Phileas Fogg and also, not long before
Palin, by British writer Nicholas Coleridge. The result was a book and a
multipart television series.*

*Barely recovered from that jaunt, and with taxi drivers still saying
things to him like, "You should try going round this lot in 80 days!,"
Palin, as game as he is incautious, agreed to do it again for another BBC
book and television series. The difference this time was that the trip would
be* Pole to Pole, *north to south, following the thirty degrees east line of
longitude, chosen because it offers the largest amount of solid ground.*

*Still game, Palin undertook yet another, even more ambitious, jour-
ney for a series called* Full Circle. *This one took him all the way around
the Pacific Rim. The series aired in 1997.*

For Pole to Pole, *Palin and a film crew traveled, between July and*

Christmas of 1991, through seventeen countries, using "ships, trains, trucks, rafts, Ski-Doos, buses, barges, bicycles, balloons, 4-litre Land-cruisers, and horse-drawn carts."

"1991 was an exceptional year," Palin writes in the introduction to the book. "A quarter of the countries we visited had undergone, or were undergoing, momentous changes. Communism disappeared in the USSR and apartheid in South Africa. We arrived in Ethiopia 4 months after the conclusion of a civil war that had occupied parts of the country for 30 years and in Zambia on the day Kenneth Kaunda's 28-year reign ended."

By the time Palin boards a bus in Bulawayo, Zimbabwe, heading for the border crossing into South Africa at Beitbridge on the Limpopo River, he is nursing a cracked rib and worried that the Agulhas, the ship that is to carry him and his crew to Antarctica, will not be able to accommodate them.

His journey on the Blue Train from Johannesburg to Cape Town can be compared with Michael Wood's journey in the opposite direction in 1979.

For Palin, a self-confessed trainspotter from his childhood and a participant in the Great Railway Journeys of the World project, the Blue Train was a special pleasure.

DAY 122 · BULAWAYO TO THE SOUTPANSBERG MOUNTAINS

UP AT 6 O'CLOCK TO PACK AND LEAVE BULAWAYO FOR our last African country. The next cities of any size on the line south will be Pretoria and Johannesburg in South Africa.

It all seems to be happening fast now. We can travel long distances on these straight, tarmacked roads and there are few diversions on the way. Today we are aiming to move another 400 miles closer to the Pole.

7.15: Bulawayo bus station. For a republic founded and led by an avowed Marxist, Robert Mugabe's Zimbabwe displays a healthy respect for private enterprise. Among the innumerable bus companies are Sun-Shine Coaches, Hit-Man Buses, the Hwange Special Express and the magnificently titled Dubies Megedleni Omnibus Service. The buses are circled by salesmen with travel-aids of every description from Afro-combs to balls of string with which to tie up baggage.

Lunchtime: After a long and uneventful morning's drive by bus and minibus across monotonous miles of dry bush, we have reached Beit-bridge, a nondescript frontier town whose most recent claim to fame was an appearance in the film *Cry Freedom*, for it was the crossing point where Donald Woods escaped South Africa dressed as a priest. (In Bible-booming Southern Africa I can see that this was the perfect disguise to choose.)

After a mixed grill at the Beitbridge Inn, on the Zimbabwean side, we drive across the Limpopo and into South Africa.

I wish I didn't have to dismiss the crossing of the Limpopo so lightly, for like the Ngorongoro Crater, Lake Tanganyika and the Zambesi, the Limpopo is one of those most mysterious and evocative of all African names. I wish I could say I bathed in it (as I did in Lake Tanganyika and the Zambesi) or at least paddled in it, or at least got a little closer to the hippos that wallow in its red and muddy water. But it has suffered the fate of all rivers that become national boundaries—it is a security risk. Nowhere more so than on this border between the white-run economic giant of the south and black Africa to the north. Although apartheid is being rapidly dismantled, the thousands of yards of coiled razor wire, the two ten-foot-high steel mesh fences, the guard-posts and the searchlight towers at 20-yard intervals remain to guard the Republic of South Africa against the world, and the Limpopo from its fans.

The South African immigration office has a quarry-tiled floor, modern, efficient air-conditioning, computers and tinted glass. There are posters on the wall but they aren't displaying the beauties of the country. Instead, under the heading "Look and Save a Life," they show you how to recognize an SBM limpet mine, a PMN (TMM) anti-personnel mine, a TM 57 land mine and grenades M75, F1 and RGD5.

Outside, the first white soldiers we've seen in Africa check the vehicles that go through. They seem an ill-disciplined, loutish lot, unhealth-ily red-faced and red-eyed. They deal mainly with commercial vehicles here, there are few private cars going through. Some African women are thumbing lifts on the big trucks belonging to Wheels of Africa or Truck Africa, as they grind through the checkpoint bringing cobalt and copper from Zambia and Zaire.

Clem has rented for me not only a BMW but a white BMW. Hardly the discreet way to enter the country, but when you've been on the road for four months and fourteen countries you seize whatever bonuses come your way. I check the map, slip Bob Seger's *The Fire Inside*—noisiest and liveliest of my tapes—into the cassette player, and flicking on the engine ease southwards into the Transvaal. The economic transformation from the wild, unruly and unavailable to the comfortable, expendable and the infinitely possible, which began at Victoria Falls and continued in Zimbabwe, is complete.

DAY 123 • THE SOUTPANSBERG MOUNTAINS TO JOHANNESBURG

AFTER A HOT NIGHT AT A MOTEL IN THE SOUTPANS-berg (Salt Pan Mountains), with my cracked rib giving me no relief unless I sleep sitting up, we are on the move, passing along a series of tunnels through the folded, faulted range that is part of the Drakensburg Mountains. If I'm not much mistaken the Verwoerd Tunnels (after Dr Hendrik Verwoerd, Prime Minister and staunch advocate of apartheid, assassinated in 1966) are the first tunnels we have been through in nearly 12,000 miles of travel. Forty miles further on I'm surprised to be reminded that part of South Africa is in the tropics, as we pass a tall, modern, chrome-tipped monument marking the Tropic of Capricorn.

How different my circumstances were when we crossed into the tropics nine weeks ago. From the Wadi Halfa ferry to a BMW.

We reach Pietersburg, to the passing eye clean, well-kept and affluent, and on through towns whose lumpy names, like Potgietersrus and Naboomspruit, declare their origin in the years following the Great Trek of 1837 when 10,000 Boer settlers, unable to coexist with the British, left the Cape and moved north. Now they're proud communities announcing themselves with weighty concrete signs. Hotels and shopping malls are going up behind false brick façades and the car parks are full of BMW's like mine. Sanctions don't appear to have caused much pain up here.

We run on toward Pretoria, across another immense and spectacular African plain. This is the High Veld. The four-lane highways are in good condition and not busy. Puffy altocumulus clouds are stacking up in a wide blue sky.

We arrive at Pretoria, over 200 miles from last night's stop-over, in good time for the afternoon's big football match. Christopher, the black driver of the minibus into which we have transferred, is becoming increasingly agitated the nearer we get to the Atteridgeville Super Stadium. Atteridge is a black area, he says, and will not be safe for us. Looking around at the township, set on a hill, with a church and a lot of brick houses with pitched corrugated iron roofs, I can't see quite what he's worried about. The streets are unswept and there has been no attempt to plant a public tree or two, but no one is shaking their fist at us. The traffic begins to build up as we near the stadium and Christopher falls apart completely. This is not a safe place, they are all black people here, and do we not know what they do to white people in a place like this? They kill them.

Then suddenly his fear subsides. He has spotted several white faces queuing up for tickets for the game. All of them are alive and well.

We follow an expensive red car into the ground. "Soweto BMW" says the rear window sticker. Admission is five rand—about a pound, which is not bad value considering this is a cup semi-final between the local team, Sundowns, and the holders, Jomo Cosmos from Johannesburg.

The status of football being relatively humble here, Sundowns arrive squeezed into a minibus, bearing their motto which, with an unfortunate letter missing, comes out as—"Sundowns. The Sky is the Limi."

The Jomo Cosmos team is as far as I can tell the personal property of Jomo Sono, a Pele and a Charlton of South African football. It has been managed for the past nine years by a Scot from Arbroath called Ray Matthews. I am privileged to hear his warm-up chat in the dressing room. He exhorts his players in a broad Scots accent that gives no hint of 20 years spent in South Africa:

"Mothale, you feed Minkhalebe . . . Masinga overlap Singiapi . . ."

The players all nod as if they understand. I ask him how much difference he thinks his chat makes. He shrugs and shrinks even lower into his shoulders.

"It's like talking to children. You just don't know how they'll play on the big occasion."

His team, nine blacks and two whites, run out onto a pitch respectably green considering the shortage of water. A concrete ramp surrounds the pitch. On it graffiti slogans like "Viva Joe Slovo," "ANC Lives," "ANC Leads," "Smash Capitalists," co-exist with ads for Caltex, Shell and Philips. Under "Socialism Never," someone has added "failed."

The first half is a bit of a plod. Half-time comes as a relief, in more ways than one. The top row of the cantilevered terracing becomes an impromptu urinal from which a gentle curtain of golden rain descends 40 feet to the ground.

There are few police in evidence and despite losing to a soft goal from Ray Matthews' team, the local crowd-behaviour is good. Everyone, including the players, seems quite free of the surly posturing that was once so common in English football.

Thirty-five miles away down swift, modern highways is Johannesburg—capital city of the Transvaal with 1.6 million souls. Tall, unblinking tower blocks of glass and steel climb up into the sky. As we wait in the Muzak-sodden lobby of the Johannesburg Sun Hotel, Nigel looks helplessly round at the chrome and the preserved plants and the water-effects and asks:

"What happened to Africa?"

DAY 125 • JOHANNESBURG

"... SUMMER'S HERE! MAKE IT A GOOD ONE WITH THE Trimrite Trimmer. Only 179 Rand! ... This is High Veld Stereo on 94.95 *Eff*-Em. ... 22 to 23 degrees out there ... real swimming-pool weather!"

A November Monday morning in Johannesburg. The silent skyscrapers are coming to life after the weekend and the traffic jams are growing on the freeways, like in any big city in the world. We are heading southwest, out of town, to visit somewhere quite unlike any other city in the world.

Soweto, 12 miles south-west of Johannesburg, comprises 33 townships with a population of 3.5 million people. The first buildings went up in 1933 and a competition was held to decide on a name. Verwoerdville was one of the unlikely contenders but Soweto—South Western Township—was chosen. It's a cold and functional name for a cold and functional purpose—to house a cheap disenfranchised work-force with which to exploit the mineral wealth of the area. That wealth, needless to say, went back into Johannesburg and not Soweto, which is why, nearly 60 years on, the contrast between the two is such a shock. The skyline of Soweto is unbroken by cover of any kind. Row upon row of basic single-storey houses sprawl across bare, unlandscaped hillsides. The streets are full of uncollected rubbish, some of which has just been set on fire where it lies. The rest blows and swirls in the wind. The stations from which hundreds of thousands of workers leave for the city each morning are currently patrolled by guards with Armalite rifles, following a spate of violent attacks on passengers. As many people as can afford it have taken to using the ubiquitous minibuses, privately owned, which cover the city. The stories of Inkatha violence are sickening. They have added to the fear in the city. As someone told me, "When Mandela was released everyone was wearing ANC T-shirts, now you don't see any."

This is the grim first impression of Soweto, but as soon as you look beyond the physical differences, beyond the outrageous disparity between the quality of surroundings in two cities so close to each other, and so dependent on each other, there are plenty of signs of life and hope. I am here to visit a family from Soweto who were once our neighbours in London, and who have recently been allowed back into their own country. We are accompanied by a Sowetan called Jimmy, who has made a good living from guided tours of the area. Jimmy, full of wisecracks—he tells me in Soweto BMW means "Break My Windows"—is by turns charming, congenial, garrulous, curt and businesslike. He is a professional and a survivor. He offers breakfast at his house, which is a long way from the traditional image of the tin-roof shack.

It is approached through wrought-iron gates and past newly-planted jacaranda trees. Inside is a fitted kitchen with all mod cons hung with pictures and paintings. He is particularly proud of a personally signed copy of a Robert Carrier cook book.

Whilst we eat breakfast he is constantly on the phone doing deals of some kind. He breaks off just long enough to give a public wigging to Roy, the gardener, who has arrived half-an-hour late this morning.

"Blue Monday," nods Jimmy, as Roy retires chastened, "the people here they just drink all weekend long."

I ask him if there are any whites in Soweto.

"Oh sure . . . 20 percent of the taxi businesses here are white-owned . . . there's a lot of whites work at the power station . . . there's an area there called Power Park which has a lot of white residents . . ."

As we leave Jimmy's house, Roy is scooping dog-shit off the lawns.

In Jimmy's neighbourhood—the Diep Kloof extension, or Prestige Park as it is known—there are streets full of architect-designed, venetian-blinded villas with double-garages, clipped lawns and herbaceous borders. Mercedes back lazily out of radio-controlled garages and one mansion boasts the ultimate in Soweto chic—a white security guard. These houses went up in the last five years and were bought by businessmen, doctors and lawyers. One was for a man who makes a 150,000 rand a year profit from the butchery business, another cost the Reverend Chikane 800,000 rand (£150,000).

"Money makers in the name of the Lord," muses Jimmy as we drive by.

At our insistence and with, I detect, a slight weariness, he shows us another side of Soweto, a shanty town known as Mandela Village. Looming in the distance, beyond the tin roofs and the undrained streets, are the long straight lines of the gold mine dumps.

A baby is born in Soweto every five minutes, says Jimmy. 50 per cent of the population is under 16. Many thousands of them live in conditions like these, makeshift cabins which can be put up overnight, made of anything their occupants can lay their hands on. There are frequent fires and no sanitation other than a few plastic lavatories provided by the council. The shacks consist usually of one room, with maybe the added luxury of a scavenged gas-ring or an old car-seat. Very often the inside walls are papered with pages from sales catalogues or fashion magazines. Three-piece suites, televisions, showers, refrigerators and all the other things the occupants can't afford form a constant backdrop to their lives.

The "Blue Monday" effect can be seen in a number of sad characters who lurch along the dirt track between the huts, but the children are wide-eyed and curious, quick to smile, easy to make laugh. It is fairly unbearable to dwell on their prospects in life—taken away from the simple, hard but traditional way of life in a mud hut in the bush to a life equally hard, but suddenly not as simple.

Having seen the unreal best and the depressing worst of Soweto I'm ready for a little normality—a dose of straightforward friendship uncluttered by projections and statistics. I repair to the Orlando district to see the Gwangwas. Outlawed from South Africa for belonging to the ANC, Jonas, a musician and co-composer of the music for *Cry Freedom*, his wife Violet and their two children took refuge in many cities including London. I never imagined I would ever see them in their own home, and the pleasure of the reunion is tremendous. Violet welcomes me with such a hug that I fear another rib will crack, and on the yard of their house is what I am assured is a traditional African greeting—"Welcome Michael, To Gwangwa Family"—marked out in dried cow-dung.

Violet apologizes for Jonas' absence. "He's at a meeting with Nelson Mandela." Now there's an excuse.

We go to lunch at a shebeen, originally the name for an illicit liquor shop, but now applied to a rather decorous front room in a nearby street where, over a licit can of Castle lager, Violet talks about being back home.

After eight years away she finds the surroundings worse—"seventy-five per cent of people can't afford the new houses they're building"—a growing middle class and a growing violence and uncertainty, but she recognizes the danger of the returned exile coming back to tell those who live here how to run their lives. Her travels round the world echo my own feelings:

"Most countries you go to, you find that people want to be hospitable, they're proud of their country, you know, whatever, whether they're rich or poor, they want to make you feel welcome and they want to sort of show you how they live, and I think that's the same here too."

Later I meet Jonas—another short, sharp shock for the rib-cage—back from his meeting. I ask how Mandela was.

Jonas smiles, "He still has a powerful handshake."

Jonas has been away for 30 years and is still dazed by the reaction, "people I haven't seen since the sixties coming up and shaking my hand."

When I ask him if he detects a difference in the people he nods very firmly.

"They're broad-shouldered now, you know . . . before they walk looking down, they were cowed so easily."

On which optimistic note we leave Soweto.

The last thing I hear from High Veld Stereo, "94.95 *Eff*-Em," is that Terry Waite has been released.

DAY 126 • JOHANNESBURG

FIRST GOOD NIGHT'S SLEEP—FIVE UNBROKEN HOURS— since my dip in the Zambesi. Probably just as well for today promises no respite for the body. We are to go down one of the gold mines on which the wealth of Johannesburg and indeed the whole of South Africa is based. One third of the country's export earnings come from gold, and the proceeds from coal, platinum, uranium and other minerals found in these rich seams raise this to almost two thirds. A new mine can cost 20 billion rand (£3.8 billion) to develop. It isn't surprising therefore that mining is a tight, white-run operation.

The Western Deep Mines, developed by Anglo-American, one of the six private companies that control 95 per cent of gold production, is kept almost pathologically clean and tidy. Despite the water-shortage, sprinklers gently douse the lawns on the approach to the offices, and men with pointed sticks are at work removing curbside litter.

We are briskly and efficiently processed, like patients at an expensive private hospital, into a reception-room where coffee and pastries are served under the clean-cut, clear-eyed gaze of the directors of Anglo-American whose framed photos are the only decoration. Then we are shown into a changing-room where every single item of our clothing has to be exchanged for a company outfit, and minutes later, we re-emerge, in white boiler suits, safety helmets and rubber boots, as Western Deep Visitors.

Martin de Beers, solidly-built, moustachioed in the style of a Southern Hemisphere cricketer, begins a long and doubtless ritualized public relations spiel as we are fitted out with headlamps and batteries.

Western Deep Mine is in *The Guinness Book of Records* for the deepest penetration of man into the Earth's crust—3773 metres, that's nearly two and a half miles. Within the next year that will be surpassed by a new shaft which will be sunk beyond the 4000-metre mark. It has been honoured on a 30-cent postage stamp as one of the three best achievers in technology in South Africa since 1961, along with Christiaan Barnard's heart transplants and a machine for harnessing wave power. At any one time there are 7000 men working beneath the surface, and it takes four hours to get them all down. The work-force is 72 per cent migratory labour, the majority coming from the Siskei and Transkei (two "homelands" set up in the spirit of apartheid, to encourage Bantus to develop separately), but also from Mozambique—"very placid, they are the only people who mix freely with all the other tribes." Martin prefers to talk rather than be asked questions. I sense that there is anger in there, probably a lot nearer the surface than anything else at Western Deep.

Have seen no black faces yet, apart from the gardeners. I presume they're all underground. We pile into a lift to join them. It rattles and clangs towards the earth's core at 70 metres a second. Another form of transport to add to the list. Two kilometres down we are released into a world almost as spotless as the one we've just left. It smells of fresh cement—like a newly constructed underground car park.

I ask Martin if this is a model mine, the showpiece of the company.

"This is Anglo-American standard, the model mine's the South Mine. They all drive around in Land Rovers down there."

Temperatures at this depth are around 50 Centigrade, and so Anglo-American have had to air-condition the earth's crust to a maximum of 28.5 degrees . . . "the limit set by the human sciences laboratory."

So far the experience has been curiously undramatic, the surroundings clean and spacious. Then quite suddenly there comes a point where underground car-parking becomes pot-holing and all of Anglo-American's environmental cosmetics cannot disguise the realities of mining.

The shaft narrows to a slippery rock passage, full of water. The only light is from my helmet, and footholds are not easy to find. A scramble up spilled rock-fall leads through to a narrower chamber. The noise of the drills makes it difficult to hear instructions and it is no longer possible to stand upright. Away from the air-conditioning the heat quickly rises and the sweat begins to run. We edge carefully through into a man-made cave with little more than three foot clearance where crouching miners are at work on the rock-face. There is great heat and terrific noise when the drills are in action.

Three-men gangs work at the face in temperatures approaching 90 Fahrenheit for 6 hours per shift. One operates the drill, another checks the equipment and a third directs water into the hole keeping the dust down. A fourth man, and the only white in the team, is the mining engineer who has to check the face and mark in red paint the bands to be drilled. I am close enough now to the gold seam to reach out and touch it. It doesn't glitter. The gold here is in carbon form, in fact the gold-bearing strip only inches wide, studded with white quartzite pebbles against a dark background of limestone and lava, looks more like black pudding.

Before we leave Western Deep we're allowed limited access to the Holy of Holies—Number 2 Gold Plant—where at temperatures of 1600 Centigrade one of history's most ancient, magical and mysterious processes comes to its conclusion as black pudding is turned into gold. Security is tight, a steel mesh doorway is locked behind us. Every camera angle is checked by armed security men, and Nigel is given strict instructions:

"You must shoot nothing west or your camera will be confiscated."

Tension builds as the crucible is slowly upturned and the molten material begins to flow.

"Is that gold? . . . Is that gold?" we first-timers keep asking, but the experts peering through the green visors that enable them to look at the quality of the smelt shake their heads. For the first minute only slag appears. I should have remembered from the rivers of Lapland that gold is always at the bottom. Then a lighter, whiter stream comes through and every one breathes a sigh of relief as each ingot tray is filled with gold worth £150,000.

I'm told that if I can lift an ingot I can have it. But they've only ever lost one like this.

On the way back from Western Deep through a landscape scarred by flat grey spoil heaps 50 feet high and yellow and white plateaux of rubble hundreds of yards long I keep trying to find the answer as to why gold should still be so sought-after, so valued as to create monster technological feats like Western Deep Mines. No one seems to have a satisfactory answer.

Back at the hotel I ring my son whose 21st birthday it is today and realize after I put the phone down that I'm a very long way away from home, and still have a lot further to go.

Our future progress is still uncertain. The *Agulhas* remains adamant that there are no places, and the only alternative would be to approach Antarctica from a quite different direction, such as Australia, New Zealand or the tip of South America. But we are booked on the Blue Train to Cape Town, and as reservations on this exclusive express are almost as valuable as the ingots I tried to lift earlier, there seems no point in not completing our crossing of Africa, even if we don't know what on earth it's leading to.

DAY 127 · JOHANNESBURG TO CAPE TOWN

DISCOMFORT IN MY BACK AT NIGHT IS STILL ACUTE. Time will heal, people keep reassuring me, but I wouldn't mind a bit of help. A cheerful and obliging Johannesburg chemist recommends arnica, a homoeopathic remedy, and bonemeal tablets. They join the growing stash of pain-relieving drugs which have just about made up in weight for the bag lost in Lusaka.

Johannesburg station is deserted at 10.15 a.m. apart from a straggle of passengers and their porters booking in beside the sign "Bloutrein

Hoflikheids Diens." The Blue Train porters must be the smartest in the world, in their blue blazers, grey trousers with knife-edge creases and leather shoes polished to a mirror-like sheen. Sadly, they wear rather sour expressions as if they all might have toothache, but as our man leads us into a lift he makes it pretty clear what he's surly about.

"Sorry about the smell," he turns to pull the gate across, "it's the coons. They piss all over the place."

A group of fellow-travellers is squashed onto a piece of carpet at a specially erected check-in area, in the middle of an otherwise long and empty platform. They look a little nervous and exposed, as if the ability to take the Blue Train marks you out as one of the world's most muggable prospects. Some are scanning the information board which gives details of unashamed luxuries that await us.

"Dress is smart casual for lunch and elegant for dinner."

Rack my brains to think of anything in my depleted wardrobe that could by any stretch of the imagination be described as elegant. Fail.

Two azure-blue diesel locomotives, bringing the 17 coaches of colour co-ordinated stock down from Pretoria, ease into the curve of the platform and quietly glide to a halt, whereupon stewards move smartly forward to lay out matching carpets, monogrammed with the letter "B," before each door.

And so it goes on. My compartment has a wall of a window—big and double glazed—air-conditioning, carpet, individual radio and temperature controls, half a bottle of champagne, a newspaper and an electronically operated Venetian blind.

Just before 11.30 a husky female voice breathes over the intercom, "The Blue Train is ready to depart," and barely noticeably, we begin to pull out of Johannesburg, due to cover the 900 miles to Cape Town in 22 hours. For the first time since Tromso we are moving *west* of our 30 degree meridian and may not meet it again until, God willing, I reach the South Pole.

A travel-worn maroon and white local from Soweto passes us, heading into the city. We gather speed through grubby stations like Braamfontein and Mayfair, whose platforms are crowded with blacks in headscarves and sweaters, accelerating into the smarter suburbs with names like Unified and Florida. It is the most comfortable train ride I've ever experienced, and combined with the air-con and the thick glazing and the wall to wall carpets it is like being in an hermetically sealed capsule, enabling the passenger to observe the outside world whilst remaining completely detached from it—an unconscious paradigm, perhaps, of the apartheid system, officially abolished only five months ago.

There are 92 people in 17 coaches—as opposed to 4000 in 18 on the Nile Valley Express. No one is allowed to travel on the roof. On Zambian Railways the restaurant car was out of food altogether, on the Blue Train I count 13 pieces of cutlery in front of me at lunchtime. Terrine of king clip (a local fish) and Cape salmon are served as we move across the wide, flat expanse of the High Veldt. Grain and gold country. Far in the distance the mountains are temporarily obscured by a thunderstorm.

The *Johannesburg Star* carries more evidence of the rapid emergence of the country from the years of isolation. South Africa is to be allowed to take part in the Olympics for the first time in 30 years. There is an advert for the resumption of South African Airways services to New York and a report that Richard Branson hopes to bring Virgin Airlines into Johannesburg by 1993. Meanwhile uniformed attendants move discreetly along the carpeted corridors collecting clothes to be pressed. Muzak lightly dusts the tranquil atmosphere, occasionally interrupted by train announcements:

"You can look out for some rhinos now on the compartment side."

We search unsuccessfully for rhinos. All I can see is telegraph poles.

"Well, we don't seem to be in luck today." Fade up Strauss waltzes. But they don't give up easily. Fade down the Strauss waltzes.

"Ladies and gentlemen, you can now look out for flamingoes on the corridor side."

Have a shower before dinner, and taking my all-purpose tie out to add that indefinable touch of elegance, saunter down to the bar. The windows are of such a size, with minimum partitions giving maximum view, that one has this strange sensation of floating, unsupported, over the countryside. Fraser says he saw a car coming towards him on a road running alongside and instinctively moved to one side. Poor old sod.

The barman Matt is put to work by Basil to make the perfect martini, but after three attempts Basil drinks it anyway. Matt comes up with the surprising information that the noisiest tourists he deals with are the Swiss.

"Swiss people are noisy?"

He relents a little: ". . . Well, not noisy, but they're happy drinkers."

A glorious sunset over the town of Kimberley which boasts of being the home of the World's Largest Man-Made Hole. At one time there were 30,000 frantic diamond prospectors digging in the hole at once. When it was closed in August 1914 it was three and a half thousand feet deep with a perimeter of a mile.

Meet one or two of my fellow-travellers. A couple from Yorkshire whose daughter manages a vineyard on the Cape, a Swiss tour-guide (Swiss and Germans are the most numerous tourists), a lady from the Irish Tourist Board who thinks that they have similar problems to South Africa in attracting visitors—beautiful countries but political problems— and an exotic couple, she Colombian, he German, who are working in Gabon. We get back to the hoary old subject of malaria. Their view is that the pills are as bad for you as the disease, quite seriously affecting digestion and eyesight.

Fortunately my digestion is, for once, settled, as I move through to the restaurant and the mountain of cut-glass that awaits me.

DAY 128 · JOHANNESBURG TO CAPE TOWN

5.30: WOKEN WITH PIPING-HOT TEA IN A WHITE CHINA pot. For the first time since Victoria Falls I was able to sleep without a pain-killer, and for the first time in Africa I was able to sleep well on a train. I now regret that I gave such enthusiatic instructions to be woken at sunrise.

We are travelling across the Karoo, a wide landscape of bare mountains and scrubby plain, deriving its name from the Hottentot word meaning "thirstland." Stimulated by this information I make my way down to the restaurant car, past train staff already polishing the door handles.

We are close now to the end of Africa. Beyond a succession of tightly folded mountain ranges lies Cape Town, the richest corner of a rich province. God's Own Country. Sit and watch the sun warming the mountains and allow myself a nostalgic drift back to a sunrise in August as we drew in from the Mediterranean and saw the lights of Africa for the first time. It's now late November and high summer has turned to early spring. I don't exactly know what lies ahead but I have a sudden surge of optimism that everything is going to turn out right. We have been tried and tested by Africa in every possible way and, bruised and battered maybe, we have survived. My children call these moments of mine "Dad's happy attacks," and, as we glide out of an 11-mile tunnel into a dramatic, sweeping bowl of land filled with vineyards I know that this one may last some time.

The magnificent landscapes of Africa build to a tremendous climax. Towering haze-blue mountain ranges—the Matroosberg, the Swarzbergen and the Hex—part like stage curtains to reveal the final epic image of Table Mountain and the wide Atlantic. It is a breathtaking display of natural beauty and one which raises all our tired spirits.

DAY 130 • CAPE TOWN

YESTERDAY I STOOD ON THE CAPE OF GOOD HOPE, A low stack of rocks pounded by the ocean and strewn with giant seaweed, and this morning I sit on top of Table Mountain, a sheer cliff rising 3500 feet above the city of Cape Town. It's a warm spring morning and the rock hyraxes start mating wherever we point the camera and the magnificent view extends towards Cape Point where the warm waters of the Indian Ocean meet the cold waters of the Atlantic. Everything about this coastline is on the grand scale. The rolling breakers steaming in from thousands of miles of open sea, the long white beaches and the tall craggy walls of exposed rock that circle the city to the east—Signal Hill, the Lion's Head, the Twelve Apostles and Table Mountain itself. A brisk wind blows in off the sea, combining with the sun and the scenery to cleanse and reinvigorate and over-travelled system.

Looking down at the massive natural harbour it is ironic to think that this most prosperous corner of Africa was dealt a serious blow by one of the poorest when de Lesseps chose to build a canal through the Egyptian desert 130 years ago. All at once the trading ships from India and the East had a shorter, more convenient and more sheltered route to Europe and Cape Town's 200-year monopoly as a supply and maintenance base for East–West shipping came to an end. There isn't much activity in port today, with the poignant exception of a sturdy red-hulled survey vessel making final preparations for an eight-day journey to the Antarctic. With a pair of strong binoculars I can just about make out the name on the hull—MV *S. A. Agulhas*.

Though there could be worse places to be marooned than Cape Town the good news is that after some feverish international telephonic activity we have secured an alternative passage to the Antarctic via the town of Punta Arenas in Southern Chile. The bad news is that we must abandon any hope of clinging to the 30 degree meridian and any further surface travel. We have only two options left open to us, to fly into the Antarctic or to fail altogether.

EDDY L. HARRIS

A black American watches apartheid fall: ca. 1990

"I WENT TO SOWETO. IT IS INDEED A GHETTO, BUT NOT THE HORROR I HAD
IMAGINED. I'VE SEEN WORSE NEIGHBORHOODS IN CHICAGO."

Eddy L. Harris first won attention with Mississippi Solo, *his book about
a black man's travels in the modern American South. After that, he lived
out the dream of many black Americans and went to Africa to travel
around and meet Africans. And he finally came to a difficult conclusion.
"We are not Africans," he writes. "We are something else entirely."*

*His African travels ended in South Africa and he was surprised by
what he found.*

I WENT TO SOUTH AFRICA EXPECTING TROUBLE, EVEN
looking for it, hoping for it. I wanted desperately to hate the place,
wanted to be told I couldn't stay in a very nice hotel, wanted to be
restricted to black parts of town, wanted to ride the fabled Blue Train to
Cape Town and be forced to get off in the middle of nowhere. It supposedly is a train reserved for whites only, but when I arrived at a ticket
agent's to book passage, there was no fuss, merely a call to see if there
was space available.

On the Wednesday after I arrived in Johannesburg, apartheid in city
recreation areas was officially abolished. It was a small, small step, but

in the right direction. As Johannesburg goes, so goes the rest of South Africa. Bus integration was coming a few days later. The Group Areas Act was doomed.

In fact the Group Areas Act, though officially on the books, was not entirely enforced. The act limits according to the color of his skin where a person can live. Hillbrow district in Johannesburg is supposedly all white. In practice it is anything but. Progress is being made, however slowly.

I went to Soweto. It is indeed a ghetto, but not the horror I had imagined. I've seen worse neighborhoods in Chicago. And compared to other blacks in Africa, these blacks are doing very well.

But I guess that's not the point. They eat. They work. They drive expensive German cars. Many live in fairly nice homes. But they cannot vote.

I guess I'm not the best judge.

I don't want to be an apologist for apartheid and a racist regime. Certainly my eyes have been clouded by this long voyage. Certainly my vision has been affected by what Africa lacks, by the poverty, by the oppression of blacks by blacks, and by what I as an American have grown used to. Joburg is a modern city. There are steaks to eat, vegetables, milk shakes and cole slaw and ice cream. There are fast-food joints, and the fast food tastes exactly as it tastes at home.

My skin is black. My culture is not. After almost a year in Africa, I have no answers. Only this one question remains: *Who am I?* I have more in common, it sometimes seems, with the Dutch Afrikaner, the Boer.

The British South African has an emotional and even a political attachment to Britain. When the volcano finally erupts, he will have a place to go. He can easily obtain a British passport. Not so the Boer. This is his home, his only home. He is an African and he will vehemently tell you so. He has no place else to go. He will live and fight and die here, make his stand here, make it work or lose it all here. He, ironically, is the example Blackamericans should follow. Africa is not our home. Should the volcano erupt, we will have no place but the United States. If it isn't going to work there, if we can't make it work there, it isn't going to work. As I said during my captivity in Liberia, I could no more return to Africa to live than I could live on the moon. And if someone put a gun to my head and said I must, the only places possible would be Zimbabwe and South Africa.

If you cannot know yourself, how can you expect to know a place like Africa? You can't. You cannot know this place in such a short time, such a short passing through—or should I say, these *places*. Africa is a myriad of people and ways. And Africa is more than that. Africa is change. Africa is contradiction. And Africa brings out the contradictions in the traveler.

There are so many Africas that, like a river, you cannot step into the same Africa twice. There is Africa the cliché, Africa the postcard view. Africa is a Biafran baby with its belly distended from starvation. Africa is flies and illness everywhere, AIDS and malaria and green monkey disease. Africa is a tired old woman selling mangoes by the side of the road, a woman with a baby strapped to her back, a woman walking home with a basket on her head, her feet covered with dust, her back noble and strong but stooped a little from fatigue and from the years of carrying. Africa is music and song and endless patience. Africa is traditions that will not allow it to move forward. Africa is a tired old man waiting for the dirt walls of his ancient house to collapse. Africa is a six-thousand-year-old baby trying to find his legs. Africa is pain. Africa is joy in spite of the pain. Africa is enduring. Africa is the essence of mankind's ability to hunger for something better and the patience to wait for it. The traditions make movement slow, but they make the waiting easier. Africa is incredible generosity, Africa is selfish opportunism, Africa is contradiction. Africa is. . . .

Africa is the birth of mankind. Africa is the land of my ancestors. But Africa is not home. I hardly know this place at all.

But I have drawn my finger in a great S-curve across the icing of the cake that is Africa and I have tasted it, the bitter, chalky-sweet taste and texture of chocolate. The sweetness lingers, leaving me with a desire to return here, to taste still more.

Toward the end of his life, Auguste Renoir was nearly blind from seeing so much, but still he worked, still he painted. By then his colors were muted, his edges soft and gentle, his scenes warm and wonderful, like a grandmother's memories. You cannot get that soft imagery and vision when you're too close and your eyesight is clear and sharp. You have to step back to see what you've got, to see how the colors and shapes blend and blur to create the impressions.

There is also a tendency in man to recollect with kindness, to soften the edges of even the harshest memories, to remember fondly. Otherwise, you get too close and you remember too much, and those memories are full of dullness and pain. So you color them, and you soften them. I hope that with time I do not glorify the horrors and hardships of this place; I hope I do not forget them. When asked how it was, I will say interesting and agony. When asked if it was fun, I will say no.

I do not feel a part of this place, it's true, nor a part of these people simply because of an accident of birth. I am not one of them. I do not like their endless patience and their endless waiting, always waiting—for someone else to do, for the will of God to happen. And I do not appreciate how they treat one another, the powerful over the weak, nor this blind respect for authority. Some of this lunacy is tribal and traditional and reaches up out of dark mysteries where I understand nothing. Much is a product of colonial servitude—to the Arab empires and their god Allah, to the Europeans and their gods Jesus and money. The Baptist missionaries and the Arabs teach the same music: Wait for God's time; He'll make everything all right. Just trust.

As much as I would like to trust in God myself, I know that sometimes God is too busy elsewhere and you just have to do things for yourself.

I will go home to my world. I will eat steaks and drink milk shakes and put on the weight I have lost. I will shower when I want and have at the turn of a tap all the clean water I can handle. I will drive the road as far as my eye can see and beyond. There will be no roadblocks to stop me. No one will ask me for my identity papers. And the roads will be good.

When I'm tired of driving, an airplane will be waiting to fly me somewhere else. I am lucky to live where I do.

It is easy to have all the solutions, to say that Africa must reject postcolonial colonialism, that Africa must end its dependence on America and on Europe, on the Peace Corps and Christian churches and missionaries, that we in the West need to stop treating these people as babies and—worse—as statistics, and start treating them as human beings, that we should stop stealing from them and that we should stop throwing money to plug gaps that wouldn't be so big if the interference ended. Perhaps we should let them sink for a while, let them figure out their own way. We did, in our own way and in our own time. But that is very easy—too easy—to say from the comfort of a full belly.

I will eat my steaks and fill my belly the same as always, but now when I do these things there will be second thoughts—I hope—for although I am not one of them, I really am one of them, the Arab and the Berber, the Bassar and the Bantu, and the Boer. There is a connection now, a real one—a racial one, to be sure, but more important, a human one.

Love and hate do not come from the color of your skin, but from what you carry inside.

I went to Cape Town to fish for trout in the nearby mountains. A white farmer invited me onto his land and pointed me toward the stream. It ran through a broad meadow. The hills behind were green. Clouds descended and all the colors changed. A rainbow trout splashed.

It is a beautiful country. It's easy to see why the white South Africans want to keep it for themselves. It is man's nature.

But it could be such a beautiful world, if we could defy the darker sides of our nature.

On the edge of a hill overlooking Victoria Falls, I looked down through the mist of the falls, the smoke that thunders, the roar of the Zambezi plunging into the canyon below. I felt I was sitting on top of the world. My journey came to me all at once in a torrent of sunsets and rivers, people I had met, the ones who had angered me and the ones who had made me laugh. As I watched another African evening come on, the serenity of Eden at twilight fell over me. Evening really does become this place. I felt what God must have felt. Amazement and sadness. But also a touch of hope.

A year from now the roads between Mauritania and Senegal will be closed. There will be tensions along the border between Senegal and Guinea-Bissau. A coup will have taken place in Liberia—the coup they no doubt were expecting when I stumbled across the border. Samuel Doe will suffer a fate similar to the one he dealt to his predecessor: he will be shot and left to die of wounds untreated.

There will be demonstrations in the streets of Abidjan. Presidential elections will be held for the first time in memory.

There will be turmoil too in Zaire. The country's economy will be in shambles and the people finally will begin to clamor for democracy and a voice. And Mobutu will yield—just a little.

In South Africa the Zulus will turn their violence against the Xhosas.

Hundreds and hundreds will be killed at the hands of their brothers. But apartheid will be coming apart. Nelson Mandela will have been released from twenty-seven years of imprisonment. Apartheid's end will be a little light at the end of a long, dark tunnel, a tiny light barely visible in the distance—but visible. There is always hope.

On the corner of Mookistraat and the Soweto Highway in Johannesburg, near the Chicken Licken shop, there is a sign: TO SEEK PEACE IS OUR RESPONSIBILITY.

Farther down on the opposite side of the street, another sign: TO-GETHER WE WILL BUILD THE FUTURE.

And the evening and the morn were the seventh day. He looked up to the virgin sky, purest azure and brilliant by day, licorice black and velvet soft by night and sprinkled with those stars that sparkle like bubbles in a glass of champagne, and the sun was a flat orange disk setting rayless in the dimming light of the western sky. Here then was Eden at twilight. There were baby elephants learning to galumph and lion cubs hiding in the tall grass. There were mountains and hills, and there were rivers and streams, slow moving or swift, muddy or crystal clear, but always clean. And over it all he put men and women together in dominion. And he saw that his creation was very good. So he stopped right there. His work was done.

Africa's work remains. And ours too.

LAURA RESNICK

Cape Town townships: 1995

"ONE MERCHANT WELCOMES ME TO SOUTH AFRICA BY GIVING ME A BAG OF
FREE PRODUCE, SAYING, WHEN I TRY TO PAY FOR IT, THAT IF HE GIVES TO
OTHERS, THEN GOD WILL GIVE TO HIM."

*Laura Resnick's dozen novels have won her a following among fantasy
fans.* A Blonde in Africa, *an account of her travels, was published in
1997.*

*One observation she makes in the following essay seems particularly
worthy of note. "Throughout the years of apartheid," she writes, "the
townships and homelands were all I knew of South Africa, for they
appeared weekly—even daily—in the international media. They are at
least as much a part of South Africa as the fabulous coastline, the
well-administered game parks, and the comfortable white communities
which are all far more accessible to the average visitor."*

*There is no denying South Africa's history, no forgetting it, and the
townships have been as vital and characteristic a part of the nation's history as the downtown skyscrapers, the prison cells of Robben Island, and
the cozy seaside bed-and-breakfasts.*

IT IS LATE JANUARY IN 1995, A BEAUTIFUL SUMMER'S
day in Cape Town. Pale bodies slowly turn bronze along the coastal
beaches. More energetic visitors travel an hour inland to visit the Cape's

famous vineyards and sample fabulous wines that, until recently, were unavailable in most countries. Businessmen meet for lunch in the cosmopolitan city center, housewives inspect produce at their local supermarkets, and scented blossoms line the tidy lanes of the white suburbs.

In the black township of Langa, a woman bends over an open fire to brush the charcoal off the mutton feet she is roasting. Children play in the sandy, unpaved lane behind her. Another woman with a baby strapped to her back returns my greeting as I descend from the car to enter the dilapidated, two-story hostel built by the white South African government to house men who, until abolishment of the pass laws, couldn't bring their families with them when they came to Cape Town to seek work.

I enter a second-floor apartment that has sixteen beds allocated to six bedrooms. A bed previously rented by an individual male may now be rented by an entire family. The cost, according to my guide, is R6.70 (just under two U.S. dollars) per bed, per month. The inhabitants of these sixteen beds share a communal kitchen with a single, bare light bulb— no oven and no outlets for electrical appliances. A man inside the kitchen nods to me before returning his attention to the meal he is cooking on the ancient, single-burner camp stove. On the other side of the communal room that serves as both sitting room and dining room, there is a tiny bathroom with a toilet and shower.

The hostel is relatively quiet, perhaps because most of the inhabitants are out at the moment. It is tidy for such a densely inhabited place; but then, there are too few personal possessions here to create clutter. There is a strong odor inside the hostel, not of filth, but of a place inhabited by too many people for too many years. Another odor is even stronger in here: the smell of despair. This is the other side of Cape Town's sunny summer.

I am visiting Langa under the auspices of One City Tours, a small Cape Town tour company run by four black men and founded less than two years ago. My guides, Cinga (pronounced with a characteristic Xhosa clicking noise which I cannot begin to imitate) and Sizwe, are taking four of us—all white and all foreign—on their Township Educa-Tour. The people in the townships, Cinga explains to me, have long been excluded from tourism and its economic benefits. He sees his guided visits as a way of bringing township dwellers, foreigners, and tourist dollars together for the first time, as well as a way of educating people about the townships and the legacy of South Africa's former apartheid government.

Bringing visitors into the townships is a very unusual venture in South Africa. My inquiries have discovered only one Johannesburg operator offering educational day trips into Soweto (an acronym for SOuth WEstern TOwnships), the city's biggest and most notorious township area. One City Tours is one of only two small companies teaching visitors about the other side of South African life down on the Cape.

The other Cape Town guide taking visitors into the townships is Aly Khan of Otherside Tours, who has been doing it for over seven years. An interesting and enterprising individual, Khan initially launched Otherside Tours as a marketing program designed to promote business interest in the Cape Flats, the geographic location of Cape Town's major townships. Determined to promote development and interracial cooperation, Khan continued running his guided visits into the Cape Flats even after the apartheid government ordered him to stop and launched an investigation into his activities. It is fortunate that Khan persevered. His tours introduced a number of Cape Town's white business executives and industrialists to their counterparts on the Flats for the first time ever. And it is estimated that his efforts alone generated more than seven million rand (two million U.S. dollars) worth of new business. In recognition of his efforts, Khan received the Mayor's Award for Service Excellence in tourism, and, in 1991, the Institute of Marketing Management named him Emergent Entrepreneur of the Year.

Otherside Tours and One City Tours (whose motto is "One City For All") both begin their tours at the site of what was once known as District Six, a notorious area in Cape Town. It lies just beyond the Grand Parade, formerly a busy market area, but now little more than a vast parking lot where the masses gathered to cheer Nelson Mandela as he appeared on the balcony of the old Town Hall after being released from prison.

District Six was a "colored" community, an overcrowded, lively neighborhood which, under the terms of the Group Areas Act, was reclassified as a "white area" because of its convenient proximity to downtown Cape Town. The people who had lived there for five generations were ordered to leave in 1966, and their houses and shops were then razed to the ground by bulldozers.

Once home to as many as sixty thousand people, District Six is now just a barren field of broken bricks, weeds, and rubble; only a few buildings—mostly churches and mosques—were left standing. However, the controversy surrounding the eviction and destruction of this community ensured that no one else ever had the temerity to build on this site—except, of course, the government, which erected the Cape Technical College here. (Happily, however, it is estimated that more than half of the college's students are now "people of color.")

From District Six, where a beautiful mural on the wall of a convent is all that remains to remind visitors of the lives that were once lived in this tumbled wasteland, both tours proceed to the townships, which lie well away from the rest of Cape Town. Under apartheid, non-whites were legally bound to live in townships or homelands unless they received special dispensation to live elsewhere—which usually meant living on their employers' property as domestic servants or farm workers. Consequently, the townships have been home not only to South Africa's poorest citizens, but also to the (admittedly small) non-white middle classes.

Operated by blacks who themselves have grown up in the townships, One City Tours focuses the visitor's attention on the black townships, only driving through a colored township to expose the contrast in the way the former government administered different communities. While the living conditions in any of these areas are an almost unfathomable contrast to the white suburbs in which I awoke this morning, the colored township through which we drive has demonstrably better roads, better housing, and more electricity than the black townships.

With a bland irony that seems to have gone unnoticed, the road to Guguletu—the township where the American girl Amy Biehl was killed during a riot in 1993—is called "Valhalla." Cinga points out where Amy died and recalls her family's pilgrimage to this very spot. Today it is so quiet that the imagination cannot conjure up the horror of that day. Nonetheless, I am well aware of how appalled many people would be that I have come to the Cape Flats today. Yet, given the opportunity, how could I not? Throughout the years of apartheid, the townships and homelands were all I knew of South Africa, for they appeared weekly—even daily—in the international media. They are at least as much a part of South Africa as the fabulous coastline, the well-administered game parks, and the comfortable white communities which are all far more accessible to the average visitor.

Even the most avowedly liberal whites here have warned me (rather intensely) not to go to a township alone. Considering the parts of many

American cities where I would tell a visitor (rather intensely) not to go alone, I am glad to have discovered One City and Otherside, which are not the most widely publicized operators in Cape Town's growing tourism industry, despite the fact that both companies publish excellent brochures.

Now that I am here, I realize how much I need my guides. There are very few street signs, and these neighborhoods aren't detailed on any map that I've ever seen. Indeed, many regional maps don't even identify the general location of the townships. Without someone who knows these areas, I doubt I could find my way around or out. Not that I feel an overwhelming urge to leave. The people here are extraordinarily friendly to white visitors. Children all over the world are, of course, fascinated by strangers, especially if their clothing and speech and skin are different. But even the adults, despite the long walk to freedom, now welcome me to their communities. Perhaps they are pleased to see a few whites swimming against the daily stream of non-whites who must travel away from their homes and communities here to work in white homes and business districts.

But there are, so far, only a few white visitors. And, with rare exceptions, all of One City's clients are foreigners. Because of Aly Khan's focus on bringing business people together, he has had more white South African clients than One City; but I am one of only two clients the morning he takes me to Athlone, and the other woman is Canadian.

A colored community and busy business area, Athlone reminds me somehow of Fourteenth Street in New York City. An eclectic assortment of shops brim with low-cost household supplies and practical necessities. On the street, market stalls overflow with fruit and vegetables. One merchant welcomes me to South Africa by giving me a bag of free produce, saying, when I try to pay for it, that if he gives to others, then God will give to him. Aly also introduces us to Ameer Mohamed, who is busy thanking good customers by giving away some of his stock. He is well-read (able to reel off quotes from memory of the first author whose works I mention) and an avid theatre-goer. He is also active in anti-drug counseling.

Aly Khan encourages us to roam the small business district and talk with as many people as possible, taking our time—not only here, but also in an "informal business district" in the black township of Khayelitsha. Originally founded to solve the problem of quickly multiplying squatter camps in nearby Crossroads, Khayelitsha has since become one of the biggest squatter settlements in the world. Without a proper census, no one is sure how many people live in Khayelitsha, but half a million is the lowest estimate I have heard. One of the guides with One City Tours says that an estimated three hundred new shacks per day are going up in Khayelitsha, as people continue migrating to the city to find work.

There is no electricity in the unpaved market street we visit in Khayelitsha. A local barber uses a generator to power his electric shaver. Someone roasts sheeps' heads over a tin drum. People bargain for live chickens nearby. The clothing and dry goods shops are all inside shacks which characterize this vast township, where the government gave up building "core housing" early on.

Core houses were the two-room rental structures with running water that non-white families were moved into as new townships were established during the forced removals resulting from the Group Areas Act. I visit one such house with One City Tours, a shebeen in Guguletu run by a woman named Carol. Electricity was installed here nine months ago, ten years after she and her husband moved in. The house is tiny and simple, well-tended but badly built. When a family starts outgrowing a house this size, they often add on a third room or construct a shack on their small lot.

After the government gave up building core houses, they established "serviced sites," tiny plots of land families rent along with a cement toilet block and one tap of running water. The next step down the socioeconomic ladder are the many communities here whose inhabitants jointly share a single water tap.

The employed inhabitants of the townships are now allowed to purchase their own land and homes, and the results are easily identifiable: well-tended yards, well-built homes, permanent addresses, one- and two-car garages. These homes are icons of self-worth, motivation, ambition, and upward mobility—a proud response to the malignancy of apartheid.

One City Tours and Aly Khan's Otherside Tours not only educate visitors about the history that has created the diverse communities in South African townships, but also correct the image created by the international media that these are relentlessly violent, hostile environments which no white dares enter. No one would try to deny that there is often trouble in the townships, as there is in impoverished communities everywhere, but the guides point out that knowing when and where to go is the essential thing (a comment which could also include my own—or almost anyone's—native city).

At Aly Khan's suggestion, we end our day on the Cape Flats by taking the fruit given to us by his friend and giving it away to some kids in Khayelitsha. Though children keep appearing out of nowhere to join the fast-growing crowd around me, there is no shoving or grabbing. Each child only comes forward when I make eye contact and specifically offer a purple-skinned plum. They all approach me with solemn eyes, shy smiles, and a breathless whisper of *"nkosi"*—the equivalent of "God bless you" in Xhosa. Any child who forgets to thank me is sharply elbowed and reminded to do so by the older kids.

I don't know what kind of future these children face, growing up in the grinding poverty of the townships. Fortunately, though, with the death of apartheid, their lives at least shine bright with possibilities denied to the generations that inhabited the barren, windblown Cape Flats before them. And their faces, like everyone else's today, shine bright with warmth and welcome as they offer blessings to a white woman who has travelled against the flow of traffic, centuries long, to visit them.

J. MARK MOBIUS

Looking at the future from 1997

"THE KEY QUESTIONS FOR US AS INVESTORS ARE: IS IT SAFE TO INVEST IN
SOUTH AFRICA, AND DOES SOUTH AFRICA HAVE A LONG-TERM FUTURE? WE
THINK THE ANSWER IS, 'YES.'"

*In the world of investments and mutual funds, J. Mark Mobius is among
the most respected authorities on emerging markets—and the most successful. An American based in Asia since 1970, Mobius is portfolio manager of
the Templeton Emerging Markets Fund, a closed-end fund, and the Templeton Developing Markets Trust, the largest open-end emerging markets
fund in the United States. Mobius and his team are responsible for more
than $12 billion in emerging markets investments for Franklin Templeton.*

*Mobius may hold the record for worldwide travel in our time. His
style is bottom-up and value-oriented and his method is hands-on; he believes in going personally to look over a company's office, walk the aisles
in the factory, and inspect the trucks outside. Barron's has said of him:
"Shunning the top-down approach some rival managers employ, Mobius
insists on going out to kick the tires, no matter how inconveniently located
those tires might be."*

*Mobius on Emerging Markets, a revised edition of his book that is
probably the most important one to read on the subject, was published in
1996.*

*After a visit to South Africa with his team of hard-jawed young ana-
lysts early in 1997, Mobius wrote the following report for the* Franklin
Templeton Developing Markets Quarterly.

WE ARRIVED IN JOHANNESBURG, SOUTH AFRICA, AFTER a short plane ride from Gaborone, Botswana's capital city. The primary purpose of our visit was to evaluate the prospects of adding new companies to our South African portfolio and to help us gauge the extent of the country's political and economic change.

As we sped along the highway toward the airport in Cape Town, I took time to admire the view. On the surface, everything seemed peaceful and orderly in this country of 45 million people, but there exists a strong undercurrent of tension. The ruling African National Congress party, headed by Nelson Mandela, has not fulfilled all of its promises. Mandela told people to be patient, but in a country where the majority of people have waited so long for basic resources, let alone prosperity, many are naturally impatient. Mandela has limited resources to spread around, and where he puts them is crucial for South Africa's economic prospects. In my view, inadequate education is of paramount concern because there is a shortage of skilled workers; therefore, government resources diverted into the education sector may produce the highest returns. Language barriers are also a major problem, undermining the mobility of labor and the ability to secure productive work.

Despite language difficulties, Johannesburg is a magnet for people from throughout the country seeking economic betterment. It is South Africa's largest city, which a population of nearly two million—and rising—and is situated at the heart of the gold mining district. However, many migrants' feelings of dislocation after leaving tribal lands and their inability to secure work have led to discontentment, and crime rates in Johannesburg have risen sharply. The government has designed a reconstruction development program to help alleviate the problems of housing, education, electrification, and fresh water. As we drive past the slums on the outskirts of Cape Town, we could see this will be a monumental task. Despite these problems, the basic infrastructure in South Africa appears to be excellent compared with other parts of Africa and many other parts of the world. The beautifully built, four-lane highway we drove along was evidence of this.

The process of adjusting to a more equitable society has been difficult for South Africa—its people, the economy, and many companies—yet it has been a boon for some exporters. The abolishment of apartheid has opened up many new markets to South African goods, and companies are beginning to explore opportunities abroad.

The key questions for us as investors are: Is it safe to invest in South Africa, and does South Africa have a long-term future? We think the answer is, "Yes." I believe the South African economy and its diverse people have a bright future. It could become one of the major emerging markets, as well as the driving force for strong economic growth in sub-Saharan Africa.

PERMISSIONS ACKNOWLEDGMENTS

FRANK G. CARPENTER From *Carpenter's World Travels* by Frank G. Carpenter. Originally published by Doubleday, Page & Company, 1924. Reprinted by permission of Joanna H. Noel.

ILKA CHASE From *Second Spring and Two Potatoes* by Ilka Chase. Copyright © 1965 by Ilka Chase Brown. Used by permission of Doubleday, a division of Bantam Doubleday Dell Publishing Group, Inc.

NEGLEY FARSON From *Behind God's Back* by Negley Farson. Copyright © 1941 by Negley Farson. Originally published by Harcourt, Brace and Company, 1941. Reprinted by permission of the Estate of the late Daniel Farson and A. M. Heath & Company Limited.

MARTIN FLAVIN From *Black and White: From the Cape to the Congo* by Martin Flavin. Copyright 1949, 1950 by Martin Flavin. Copyright renewed © 1978 by Sean Flavin, Martin Flavin, Jr., Flavia Flavin Edgren. Reprinted by permission of HarperCollins Publishers, Inc.

EDDY HARRIS From *Native Stranger: A Black American's Journey into the Heart of Africa* by Eddy L. Harris. Copyright © 1992 by Eddy L. Harris. Reprinted with the permission of Simon & Schuster.

ADAM HOCHSCHILD "Summer Folk" from *The Mirror at Midnight* by Adam Hochschild. Copyright © 1990 by Adam Hochschild. Used by permission of Viking Penguin, a division of Penguin Putnam Inc.

J. RAMSAY MACDONALD From *Wanderings and Excursions* by J. Ramsay MacDonald. Originally published by Jonathan Cape & Harrison Smith, 1925. Reprinted by permission of Ishbel Lochhead.

G. H. MASON From *Life with the Zulus of Natal, South Africa* by G. H. Mason. Originally published by Longman, Brown, Green, & Longmans, 1855.

J. MARK MOBIUS "Future Looks Bright for South Africa" from *Franklin Templeton Developing Markets Quarterly*, Second Quarter, 1997, published by Franklin Templeton Distributors, Inc. All further republication rights and all other rights strictly reserved by Franklin Templeton Distributors, Inc. Reprinted by permission.

ALAN MOOREHEAD From *No Room in the Ark* by Alan Moorehead. Copyright © 1957, 1958, 1959 by Alan Moorehead. Originally published by Harper & Brothers Publishers, 1959. Reprinted by permission of Laurence Pollinger Limited and the Estate of Alan Moorehead.

JAN MORRIS From *South African Winter* by James Morris. Copyright © 1958 by James Humphry Morris. Originally published by Pantheon, 1958. Reprinted by permission of the author and IMG Literary.

H. V. MORTON From *In Search of South Africa* by H. V. Morton. Originally published by Methuen & Co. Ltd., London, 1948. Reprinted by permission of Random House UK Limited.

P. J. O'ROURKE "In Whitest Africa" from *Holidays in Hell* by P. J. O'Rourke. Copyright © 1988 by P. J. O'Rourke. Reprinted by permission of Grove/Atlantic, Inc.

MICHAEL PALIN From *Pole to Pole* by Michael Palin. Copyright © 1992 by Michael Palin. Originally published by BBC Books, 1992. Reprinted with the permission of BBC Worldwide Limited.

E. ALEXANDER POWELL From *Yonder Lies Adventure!* by E. Alexander Powell. Originally published by the Macmillan Company, 1932.

LAURA RESNICK "The Other Side of the Sun" by Laura Resnick. Copyright © 1997 by Laura Resnick. Originally published in *The Journal of African Travel-Writing*, Number Two, 1997. Reprinted by permission of the author.

MARK TWAIN From *Following the Equator: A Journey Around the World* by Mark Twain. Originally published by Harper & Brothers Publishers, 1897.

A. W. WELLS From *South Africa: A Planned Tour of the Country To-day* by A. W. Wells. Originally published by David McKay Company/J. M. Dent & Sons Ltd., 1939. Reprinted by permission of the Orion Publishing Group Ltd.

MICHAEL WOOD "Zambezi Express" by Michael Wood from *Great Railway Journeys of the World*. Copyright © 1981 by Michael Wood. Reprinted with the permission of BBC Worldwide Limited.